Debating Reform

Debating Reform

CONFLICTING PERSPECTIVES ON HOW TO FIX
THE AMERICAN POLITICAL SYSTEM

EDITED BY

RICHARD J. ELLIS
Willamette University

AND

MICHAEL NELSON
Rhodes College

CQ PRESS

A Division of SAGE
Washington, D.C.

CQ Press
2300 N Street, NW, Suite 800
Washington, DC 20037

Phone: 202-729-1900; toll-free, 1-866-4CQ-PRESS (1-866-427-7737)
Web: www.cqpress.com

Cover design: Matthew Simmons, www.Myselfincluded.com
Cover photo: Istockphoto.com
Composition: C&M Digitals (P) Ltd.

⊗ The paper used in this publication exceeds the requirements of the American National Standard for Information Sciences—Permanence of Paper for Printed Library Materials, ANSI Z39.48-1992.

Printed and bound in the United States of America

14   13   12   11   10   1   2   3   4   5

Library of Congress Cataloging-in-Publication Data

Debating reform : conflicting perspectives on how to fix the American political system / edited by Richard J. Ellis and Michael Nelson.
    p. cm. — (The debating politics series from CQ Press)
  Includes bibliographical references and index.
  ISBN 978-1-60426-552-1 (pbk. : alk. paper)
  1. United States—Politics and government. 2. Political participation—United States. 3. United States—Social conditions. 4. United States—Economic conditions. I. Ellis, Richard (Richard J.) II. Nelson, Michael. III. Title. IV. Series.

JK274.D398 2010
320.60973—dc22

                                                                    2009051863

*In memory of Nelson W. Polsby,
who loved few things
more than a vigorous debate*

CONTENTS

PREFACE

The best American government texts do a superb job of conveying how the American political system works: what citizens know, who votes and who doesn't, how campaigns are financed, how the electoral college operates, how members of Congress make decisions, how lobbyists behave, how judges are appointed, how presidents manage the executive branch, and how public policy is made. The best texts also document how American politics has changed over time: the development of mass media, trends in voting behavior, the changing relationship between the president and the parties, the expansion of the federal government, and the evolution of civil liberties and civil rights. These texts provide, in short, the political knowledge that is an essential part of good citizenship.

We accept that teaching the introductory course effectively requires communicating to students how American government works and how its institutions got to be the way they are. Imparting this knowledge is a necessary but not, we believe, a sufficient condition for a successful American politics class. The most successful classes are not those in which instructors treat students as passive receptacles to be filled with the knowledge that political scientists possess. Instead, the most memorable classes are those that invite active student engagement through discussion, debate, and argument. We want to foster the development of citizens who are not only well informed but also politically involved. We also want our students both to know the answers to test questions and to believe that the answers and the questions are worth thinking and arguing about, even after the class bell has rung.

There are, of course, many ways to promote student engagement in the classroom. We do not pretend to have discovered the one true way. But we do believe, based on many years of undergraduate teaching, that inviting students to debate concrete proposals to reform the political system they are studying is an excellent vehicle for promoting active learning.

Why a debate format? And why reform? A standard textbook, no matter how well it is written or how carefully it is put together, can be very intimidating. This has less to do with the complexity or quantity of material that students are asked to absorb than with the authoritative tone of most texts. Scrupulous evenhandedness is a virtue in a textbook, but it can leave students feeling that there is almost nothing for them to contribute, no room for them to argue back. In a standard American government text, the loose ends seem neatly tied up and the gaps in knowledge are papered over. The accent is on what political scientists agree upon, not the many things they disagree about.

Our text reverses that pattern. By inviting scholars to debate resolutions, we highlight argument and disagreement. Summarizing existing knowledge through evidence can make for a good lecture, but vigorous classroom discussions and engaged student writing, we believe, are best spurred by contests between competing perspectives. Students listening to a lecture or reading a textbook chapter expect the author to sift through the evidence and lead them to a more balanced understanding. The debate format, in contrast, places the onus on students to sift through competing claims and evidence. It invites them to take sides, to challenge what they are being told, to enter into the discussion.

Why make institutional reform the focus of these debates? For several good reasons. First, reform proposals are explicitly normative: they are about what *should* be done. Many debates in political science are empirical; that is, they are mainly descriptive, explanatory, or predictive. Scholars debate the best way to measure voter turnout, the best model for predicting the winner in a presidential election, or whether Congress has become more polarized or voters more ideological. Each of these empirical debates is important and should be taught to undergraduates. Yet when the question is empirical, classroom debates are understandably circumscribed and sporadic. Discussion will generally be oriented around the teacher trying to help students understand an argument rather than the students staking out and defending a position. Normative arguments invite students to offer their own opinions and build confidence that they can contribute productively to the conversation. They can make and defend claims of their own rather than just ask questions of the teacher.

A second reason we have chosen to focus on institutional reforms is that we wanted to minimize ideological arguments about liberal or conservative public policies. Although it's not difficult to have passionate classroom debates about abortion, same-sex marriage, or welfare, these arguments tend to run in well-worn grooves and students tend to line up on the same side in debate after debate. The debate may be vociferous but it is unlikely to lead to a re-examination of one's views.

Because institutional reforms generally do not strike familiar ideological chords, students are more willing to change their minds based on evidence and arguments and are less prone to array themselves in predictable patterns of support or opposition.

Policy debates in the introductory course are also unsatisfying because often they seem divorced from the institutional core of the course; more like an entertaining sideshow than an integral part of learning to think more deeply about American politics and government. Debating reforms, in contrast, connects the classroom conversation directly to American political institutions.

A third and final reason we focus on institutional reform is that we want students not only to understand how American government functions but also to think about how it can be made to work better. Too often we take our institutions for granted, assuming that what has been must always be and that it is for the best. Many of the reforms debated in this book—such as limiting the terms of Supreme Court justices, abolishing the electoral college, establishing a national initiative and referendum process, and making it easier to amend the Constitution—would require a constitutional amendment. Others—for instance, scaling back the outsourcing of government tasks, gutting the filibuster, or increasing the size of the House of Representatives—could be achieved through statutory changes. At least a few of the proposed reforms debated in this book stand no chance of being adopted, most notably, changing the two-senators-per-state rule. Yet even reforms that are unlikely to be enacted make for valuable debates because they require us to think carefully about the principles that underlie our constitutional system and to evaluate how well our political institutions help us to realize our deepest values and beliefs.

The introduction to American government course is not and should not be a gateway to graduate school. Only a minority of students in the course will even become political science majors. For many students this will be their only politics course. As political scientists we naturally want to teach students how to think like political scientists, but even more important in the introductory course is that we help students to think like democratic citizens—citizens who understand how and how well their political institutions are functioning. Inviting students to debate fundamental political reforms helps to model active and engaged citizenship.

Our focus on reform does not mean that we think our political system requires fundamental change. This book is not an argument for reform, fundamental or otherwise. We favor some of the reforms debated in this book, think that others are worse than the ills they aim to cure, and are agnostic about the rest. We want to start an argument, not advance a particular political agenda. Some readers may come away from these debates with a renewed appreciation for American political institutions; others may find that these debates open their eyes to problems of which they had been blissfully unaware. We want students to enter the debate about American politics; we do not care which side they come out on.

It bears repeating that this book is not designed to replace a standard text but to supplement it. That is why we have organized the debates around the chapter topics that generally structure American government texts: the Constitution, federalism, public opinion, the media, interest groups, Congress, the presidency, bureaucracy, the judiciary, civil liberties, civil rights, foreign policy, and so on.

One final word of explanation is owed the reader. Unlike other debate-style readers, our text includes only original essays that we commissioned specifically for this volume—no reprinted selections here. We chose to solicit original essays because we wanted authors to directly address a specific, concrete debate resolution. Nothing is more frustrating than a debate in which the participants don't actually address the same question, as often happens in books that try to fit a debate topic around a set of existing essays. We invited each of our contributors to choose a side and defend it as vigorously as he or she could; the charge was not to judiciously weigh the evidence on all sides but rather to present the most persuasive case they could for the position they had taken.

Many of our contributors told us that they found this assignment much tougher than they had originally expected it would be. What made this format difficult or at least unfamiliar was that it asked scholars to abandon their usual stance of objectivity and balance, leaving the familiar task of weighing arguments and evidence to the reader. Yet our contributors also described the experience of writing the essays as "exhilarating," or at least "quite fun." We hope that teachers and students will have as much fun reading these debates as our contributors had writing them.

Our task as editors was made much easier and more enjoyable not only by our talented and conscientious contributors but also by the skilled and experienced crew at CQ Press. We are especially grateful to editorial director Charisse Kiino, for her characteristically wise guidance and valuable encouragement throughout the development of this project. Our thanks, too, go to editorial assistants Jason McMann and Christina Mueller, copy editor Talia Greenberg, and production editor Belinda Josey. There can be no debating the debt we owe to each of them for helping us bring this work to fruition.

CONTRIBUTORS

Bruce Ackerman is Sterling Professor of Law and Political Science at Yale University and the author of fifteen books that have had a broad influence in political philosophy, constitutional law, and public policy. His major works include *Social Justice in the Liberal State* and his multivolume constitutional history *We the People*. He has also served, pro bono, as a lawyer on matters of public importance. He was a lead witness for President Bill Clinton before the House Judiciary Committee's Impeachment Hearings and a principal spokesperson for Al Gore before the Florida legislature during the election crisis of 2000. Ackerman is a member of the American Law Institute and the American Academy of Arts and Sciences.

Douglas J. Amy is professor of politics at Mount Holyoke College. His research has focused primarily on electoral reform and alternative election systems, and he has written extensively about these issues. His books include *Behind the Ballot Box: A Citizen's Guide to Voting Systems* (2000) and *Real Choices/New Voices: How Proportional Representation Elections Could Revitalize American Democracy* (2002). His latest work is a Web site entitled "Government Is Good."

Lawrence G. Baxter began his academic career at the University of Natal in South Africa. He joined Duke University School of Law in 1986. In 1995 Baxter joined Wachovia Bank in Charlotte, N.C., serving first as special counsel for strategic development and later as corporate executive vice president. He was Wachovia Corporation's chief e-commerce officer from 2001 to 2006. Baxter rejoined Duke Law in 2009 as a visiting professor of the practice of law. He is teaching and researching in the field of financial services regulation and is the author of scholarly and industry works on regulation, financial services, and technology.

Nicholas J. Bell is an undergraduate at the College of William & Mary, majoring in international relations. His research interests include legislative behavior, comparative politics, and constitutional law.

Justin Buchler received his doctorate from the University of California, Berkeley, in 2004. He is currently assistant professor of political science at Case Western Reserve University. He is the author of several articles on competitive elections, including "The Social Sub-optimality of Competitive Elections," in

Public Choice, which received the Gordon Tullock Award for 2007. His book, *Hiring and Firing Public Officials*, is under contract and forthcoming from Oxford University Press.

Steven G. Calabresi is George C. Dix Professor of Constitutional Law at Northwestern University. He cofounded The Federalist Society and serves as chair of its board of directors. He also served in the Reagan and first Bush administrations from 1985 to 1990. He is the coauthor (with Christopher Yoo) of *The Unitary Executive: Presidential Power from Washington to Bush* (2008).

Todd Donovan is professor of political science at Western Washington University in Bellingham, Wash. He has published scores of articles in scholarly journals and has coauthored or coedited several books. His most recent coauthored book are *State and Local Politics: Institutions and Reform* (2nd ed., 2010) and *Why Iowa? Caucuses, Sequential Elections and Reform of Presidential Nominations* (forthcoming).

George C. Edwards III is Distinguished Professor of Political Science at Texas A&M University and Jordan Chair in Presidential Studies. He has written or edited twenty-three books on American politics and is also editor of *Presidential Studies Quarterly* and general editor of the Oxford Handbook of American Politics series. His most recent book, *The Strategic President* (2009), offers a new formulation for understanding presidential leadership. Edwards has served as president of the Presidency Research Section of the American Political Science Association, which has named its annual dissertation prize in his honor and awarded him its Career Service Award.

Richard J. Ellis is Mark O. Hatfield Professor of Politics at Willamette University. His recent books include *Presidential Travel: The Journey from George Washington to George W. Bush* (2008), *Judging Executive Power: Sixteen Supreme Court Cases That Have Shaped the American Presidency* (2009), and *Debating the Presidency: Conflicting Perspectives on the American Executive* (with Michael Nelson, 2nd ed., 2010). In 2008 he was named Carnegie Foundation for Advancement of Teaching Oregon Professor of the Year.

C. Lawrence Evans is Newton Family Professor of Government at the College of William & Mary. He has published two books and numerous articles about congressional politics, and from 2003 to 2007 he was coeditor of the *Legislative Studies Quarterly*, the leading scholarly journal specializing in legislatures.

Ward Farnsworth is Nancy Barton Scholar and Professor of Law at the Boston University School of Law. He has written many articles on the Supreme Court, including *The Legal Analyst: A Toolkit for Thinking about the Law*—a guide to analytical methods for lawyers and law students.

James C. Fell is senior program director with the Pacific Institute for Research and Evaluation in Calverton, Md. He recently completed research on grants from the National Institute on Alcohol Abuse and Alcoholism and the Robert Wood Johnson Foundation that assessed the status and enforcement of the various components of the Minimum Legal Drinking Age 21 (MLDA 21) laws in the states and determined the relationship of those laws to teenage traffic deaths. Fell formerly worked at the National Highway Traffic Safety Administration from 1969 to 1999 and has forty-two years of traffic safety and alcohol research experience. He has both bachelor's and master's degrees in human factors engineering from the State University of New York at Buffalo.

Brian Frederick is assistant professor of political science at Bridgewater State College (BSC) in Massachusetts, where he specializes in American politics. His research focuses on the U.S. Congress, women and politics, and judicial elections. He is the author of *Congressional Representation and Constituents: The Case for Increasing the House of Representatives* (2010). His research has appeared in a number of journals, including *Political Research Quarterly*, *Public Opinion Quarterly*, *American Politics Research*, *Social Science Quarterly*, and *State Politics and Policy Quarterly*, as well as numerous edited volumes. Frederick also serves as a research fellow with the BSC Center for Legislative Studies.

Charles T. Goodsell is Emeritus Professor of Public Administration at Virginia Tech in Blacksburg. He was educated at Kalamazoo College and Harvard University and previously taught at the University of Puerto Rico and Southern Illinois University. He is the author of several books, including *Administration of a Revolution* (1965), *American Corporations and Peruvian Politics* (1974), *The Social Meaning of Civic Space* (1988), *The American Statehouse* (2001), and *The Case for Bureaucracy* (4th ed., 2004). He is currently completing *Mission Mystique: Belief Systems in Public Agencies*, under contract to CQ Press.

Patrick O. Gudridge is associate dean and professor of law at the University of Miami. His writing on constitutional law since the 1990s has frequently addressed the form constitutional law takes in emergency circumstances, such as the Japanese American internment in World War II, cold war internal security law, the watershed Birmingham civil rights demonstrations, and recent debates about military commissions and other antiterror measures.

Ron Hayduk is associate professor of political science at the Borough of Manhattan Community College of the City University of New York. He has written about American politics in the areas of voting rights, social movements, immigration, and race. His books include *Gatekeepers to the Franchise: Shaping Election Administration in New York* (2005) and *Democracy for All: Restoring Immigrant Voting Rights in the United States* (2006), and he is coeditor and contributing author of two edited books and a dozen journal articles and book chapters. Formerly a social worker, Hayduk was director of the New York City Voter Assistance Commission from 1993 to 1996 and has been a consultant to public policy organizations. He is also a founding member of the Coalition to Expand Voting Rights.

William G. Howell is Sydney Stein Professor in American Politics at the University of Chicago. He has written widely on separation-of-powers issues and American political institutions, especially the presidency. His current research examines the impact of war on presidential power. His recent edited and authored books include *Power without Persuasion: The Politics of Direct Presidential Action* (2003), *While Dangers Gather: Congressional Checks on Presidential War Powers* (2007), and *The Handbook on the American Presidency* (2009). His research also has appeared in numerous professional journals and edited volumes.

Terence M. Hynes practices law with Sidley Austin LLP. He represents transportation industry clients in connection with mergers and acquisitions, commercial litigation, regulatory proceedings, and homeland security and safety issues. He is a member of the Association of Transportation Law, Logistics, and Policy and of the American Bar Association's Section of Antitrust and Public Utility, Communications, and Transportation Law. He has written articles on transportation-related topics and teaches a course on transactional skills at Duke University School of Law.

Nancy Kassop is professor and chair of the department of political science and international relations at the State University of New York at New Paltz. She writes on issues of the presidency and law. Her articles include "The White House Counsel's Office" (coauthored with Karen Hult and Mary Anne Borrelli), in *The White House World: Transitions, Organization, and Office Operations* (edited by Martha J. Kumar and Terry Sullivan, 2003), and "A

Political Question by Any Other Name: Government Litigation Strategy in the Enemy Combatant Cases of *Hamdi* and *Padilla*," in *The Political Question Doctrine and the Supreme Court of the United States* (edited by Nada Mourtada-Sabbah and Bruce E. Cain, 2007). She is past president of the Presidency Research Group of the American Political Science Association, and is currently a book review editor for *Presidential Studies Quarterly*.

David E. Kyvig is Distinguished Research Professor in the department of history at Northern Illinois University and has held fellowships from the American Council of Learned Societies, the National Endowment for the Humanities, and the Woodrow Wilson International Center for Scholars. He won the 1997 Bancroft and Henry Adams Prizes for his book *Explicit and Authentic Acts: Amending the U.S. Constitution, 1776–1995* (1996). Most recently, his book *The Age of Impeachment: American Constitutional Culture since 1960* was a *Choice* Outstanding Academic Title for 2008.

Sanford Levinson holds a chair at the University of Texas Law School and is also a professor in the government department of the University of Texas, Austin. He is the author of many books and articles on the Constitution, including, most recently, *Our Undemocratic Constitution: Where the Constitution Goes Wrong (and How We the People Can Correct It)* (2006). He was elected to the American Academy of Arts and Sciences in 2001.

Tod Lindberg is a research fellow at the Hoover Institution, Stanford University. He is editor of *Policy Review,* Hoover's Washington, D.C.–based journal. He is the author of *The Political Teachings of Jesus* (2007), a philosophical analysis of Jesus's teaching about worldly affairs. He is coauthor (with Lee Feinstein) of *Means to an End: The U.S. Interest in the International Criminal Court* (2009). He is a contributing editor to the *Weekly Standard* and is frequently heard as an analyst on National Public Radio.

James Lindgren is professor of law at Northwestern University. He is a cofounder of the Association of American Law Schools (AALS) Section on Scholarship and a former chair of the AALS Section on Social Science. His wide-ranging publications have appeared in many of the nation's leading law reviews, including the *Yale Law Journal,* the *William and Mary Law Review,* and the *University of Chicago Law Review.*

Robert E. Litan is Vice President for Research and Policy at the Kauffman Foundation in Kansas City and a senior fellow in economic studies at the

Brookings Institution. He has published extensively on entrepreneurial approaches to boosting economic growth, government policies affecting financial institutions, regulatory and legal issues, and international trade. His most recent book coauthored with William Baumol and Carl Schramm is *Good Capitalism, Bad Capitalism, and the Economics of Growth and Prosperity* (2007). Litan has previously served in several capacities in the U.S. government as associate director for the office of management and budget (1995–1996), deputy assistant attorney general, antitrust division, Department of Justice (1993–1995), and regulatory staff economist, president's council of economic advisers (1977–1979).

Burdett Loomis has been a political science professor at the University of Kansas since 1979. He has published more than twenty-five books in various editions, including *The New American Politician* (1989); *Time, Politics, and Policy: A Legislative Year* (1994); *The Sound of Money* (1999); and seven co edited editions of *Interest Group Politics*. Loomis has served as a Fulbright Senior Scholar in Argentina and has lectured on American politics for the State Department in Brazil, Mexico, Malaysia, Singapore, China, Iraq, Taiwan, Nepal, and Bangladesh. He is currently working on a major study of political change from the late 1950s through the mid-1970s, as well as a large-scale edited work on American interest groups and lobbying.

Daniel H. Lowenstein is Emeritus Professor of Law at the University of California, Los Angeles, and director of the UCLA Center for the Liberal Arts and Free Institutions. He served as the first chair of the California Fair Political Practices Commission from 1975 to 1979 and joined the UCLA faculty in 1979. His publications touch on all major aspects of election law. His textbook, *Election Law*, now in its fourth edition, was first published in 1995 and was the first twentieth-century American textbook on the subject.

John McCardell is Vice Chancellor and President of Sewanee: The University of the South and was President Emeritus and professor of history at Middlebury College, where he has been a faculty member since 1976 and served as president from 1991 to 2004. He received his bachelor's degree from Washington and Lee University and his doctorate from Harvard University. In 2006 he founded Choose Responsibility, an organization whose mission is to engage the public in informed and dispassionate discussion about the place of alcohol in the lives of young adults. A scholar of nineteenth-century America, he has written and spoken extensively on the effects of alcohol policies, especially the National Minimum Drinking Age Act of 1984.

Michael P. McDonald is associate professor of government and politics at George Mason University and a nonresident senior fellow at the Brookings Institution. He received his doctorate in political science from University of California, San Diego, and his bachelor's degree in economics from the California Institute of Technology. He held a post-doctorate fellowship at Harvard University and has previously taught at Vanderbilt University and the University of Illinois, Springfield. He has published numerous articles and reports on the U.S. electoral system. With regards to redistricting, he has served as a consultant or expert witness in Alaska, Arizona, California, Michigan, and New York.

Michael Nelson is Fulmer Professor of Political Science at Rhodes College. He also is a senior fellow of the Miller Center of Public Affairs at the University of Virginia and a former editor of the *Washington Monthly*. His recent books include *The American Presidency: Origins and Development, 1776–2007* (with Sidney M. Milkis, 5th ed., 2008); *How the South Joined the Gambling Nation: The Politics of State Policy Innovation* (with John Mason, 2008), which won the Southern Political Science Association's V. O. Key Award for outstanding book on southern politics; *The Elections of 2008* (2010); and *The Presidency and the Political System* (9th ed., 2010). More than fifty of his articles have been reprinted in anthologies of political science, history, music, sports, and English composition.

Anthony J. Nownes is professor of political science at the University of Tennessee, Knoxville, where he has taught since 1994. He received his bachelor's degree from the University of California, Berkeley, in 1986, and his doctorate from the University of Kansas in 1993. He teaches courses on interest groups, political behavior, and political parties. He has published more than two dozen scholarly articles and two books. His latest book, *Total Lobbying: What Lobbyists Want (and How They Try to Get It)*, was published by Cambridge University Press in 2006.

Bruce I. Oppenheimer is professor of political science at Vanderbilt University. He earned his bachelor's degree from Tufts University and his master's degree and doctorate from the University of Wisconsin. He specializes in research on Congress, congressional elections, and American political institutions. With Frances Lee, he is coauthor of *Sizing up the Senate: The Unequal Consequences of Equal Representation* (1999). In addition, Oppenheimer is coeditor of *Congress Reconsidered*, the ninth edition of which was published by CQ Press in 2009.

Norman J. Ornstein is resident scholar at the American Enterprise Institute for Public Policy Research. He also serves as an election analyst for CBS News and writes a weekly column called "Congress Inside Out" for *Roll Call.* He has written for the *New York Times, Washington Post, Wall Street Journal, Foreign Affairs,* and other major publications and regularly appears on such television programs as *The NewsHour with Jim Lehrer, Nightline,* and *Charlie Rose.* At the thirtieth anniversary party for *The NewsHour,* he was recognized as the most frequent guest over the thirty years. His many books include *The Broken Branch: How Congress is Failing America and How to Get it Back on Track* (with Thomas E. Mann).

John J. Pitney Jr. is Roy P. Crocker Professor of American Politics at Claremont McKenna College. He received his bachelor's degree from Union College and his doctorate from Yale University. He has been a New York State Senate Legislative Fellow and a Congressional Fellow of the American Political Science Association. He has written articles for *National Review Online,* the *Los Angeles Times,* and *Politico,* among others. His most recent books are *Epic Journey: The 2008 Elections and American Politics* (with James W. Ceaser and Andrew E. Busch, 2009) and *American Government and Politics: Deliberation, Democracy and Citizenship* (with Joseph M. Bessette, 2010).

David P. Redlawsk is professor of political science and director of the Center for Public Interest Polling at Rutgers University. He received his bachelor's degree from Duke University, master's degree from Vanderbilt University, and doctorate from Rutgers University. His forthcoming book, *Why Iowa? Caucuses, Sequential Elections and Reform of Presidential Nominations* (with Caroline J. Tolbert and Todd Donovan) examines the role the Iowa caucuses and other early nominating contests play in the modern presidential nominating system. Other books include *How Voters Decide: Information Processing during Election Campaigns* (with Richard Lau, 2006) and *Feeling Politics: Emotion in Political Information Processing* (2006).

Stanley A. Renshon is professor of political science at the City University of New York and a certified psychoanalyst. He has published more than ninety articles and fifteen books in the fields of presidential leadership, American national security, and the psychology of immigration and American national identity, including *One America? Political Leadership, National Identity, and the Dilemmas of Diversity* (2001); *America's Second Civil War: Dispatches from the Political Center* (2002); *The 50% American: Immigration and National Identity in an Age of Terrorism* (2005); and, most recently, *Noncitizen Voting and American Democracy* (2009).

Mark E. Rush is Robert G. Brown Professor of Politics and Law and head of the department of politics at Washington and Lee University. He has written extensively on voting rights and constitutional law in the United States and abroad. His most recent book *Judging Democracy* (with Christopher Manfredi), was published by the University of Toronto Press in 2008. A lifelong, diehard fan of the Boston Red Sox, he lives in Lexington, Va., with his wife, Florinda, and sons Alex and William (Boston College, '12).

E. S. Savas is Presidential Professor in the School of Public Affairs at Baruch College, City University of New York. He is the author or editor of fifteen books, which have been published in twenty-three foreign editions. A privatization pioneer, his first article on the subject was published in 1971. He served as assistant secretary of the U.S. Department of Housing and Urban Development under President Ronald Reagan and as first deputy city administrator of New York.

Wendy J. Schiller is associate professor of political science and public policy at Brown University and a six-time winner of the Undergraduate Research and Teaching Award. She served as a legislative staff aide to Sen. Daniel P. Moynihan and a federal lobbyist in the office of Gov. Mario M. Cuomo. She has held fellowships at Princeton University and the Brookings Institution. She is the author of *Partners and Rivals: Representation in U.S. Senate Delegations* (2000) and the coauthor, with Burdett Loomis, of *The Contemporary Congress* (2005). She is currently working on a National Science Foundation grant project on the election of U.S. senators in state legislators in the nineteenth and twentieth centuries and writing an introductory American politics textbook *Gateways to Democracy.* Schiller is a frequent political commentator for local and national news outlets.

Steven S. Smith is Kate M. Gregg Distinguished Professor of Social Sciences, professor of political science, and director of the Murray Weidenbaum Center on the Economy, Government, and Public Policy at Washington University. He has taught at George Washington University, Northwestern University, and the University of Minnesota, where he was the Distinguished McKnight University Professor of Political Science and Law. He has authored or coauthored several books on congressional politics, including the textbook *The American Congress* (2009). He has worked on Capitol Hill in several capacities, served as a Congressional Fellow of the American Political Science Association, and was a senior fellow at the Brookings Institution. He served as chair of the Legislative Studies Section of the American Political Science Association, served on the Executive Committee of the Research Committee of Legislative Scholars of the

International Political Science Association, and served as a member of the board of directors of the Dirksen Congress Center. He served as an editor of *Legislative Studies Quarterly* and on the editorial boards of the *American Journal of Political Science*, *Journal of Politics*, and *Congress and the Presidency*.

Robert J. Spitzer is Distinguished Service Professor of Political Science at SUNY Cortland. He is the author of thirteen books, including *The Presidential Veto* (1988), *President and Congress* (1993), *The Politics of Gun Control*, 4th ed., (1998), *The Presidency and the Constitution* (2005), and *Saving the Constitution from Lawyers* (2008). He has also written more than 400 articles, papers, and essays. He formerly served as president of the Presidency Research Group of the American Political Science Association and is a recipient of the SUNY Chancellor's Award for Excellence in Scholarship. He is series editor for the American Constitutionalism series for SUNY Press.

Adam D. Thierer is president of the Progress and Freedom Foundation (PFF) and the director of PFF's Center for Digital Media Freedom. Prior to joining PFF, he was director of telecommunications studies at the Cato Institute and a fellow in economic policy at the Heritage Foundation. He is the author or editor of seven books on media regulation, Internet governance, intellectual property, regulation of network industries, and the role of federalism within high-technology markets. He earned his bachelor's degree in journalism and political science at Indiana University, and his master's degree in international business management and trade theory at the University of Maryland.

Caroline J. Tolbert is professor of political science at the University of Iowa and the author of six books and more than thirty articles in scholarly journals. She is a coauthor of *Digital Citizenship: The Internet Society and Participation* (2008) and *Virtual Inequality: Beyond the Digital Divide* (2003). *Digital Citizenship* was ranked one of twenty best-selling titles in the social sciences by the American Library Association for 2008. She is also a coauthor of *Educated by Initiative: The Effects of Direct Democracy on Citizens and Political Organizations in the American States* (2004) and coeditor of *Democracy in the States: Experiments in Election Reform* (2008) and *Citizens as Legislators: Direct Democracy in the United States* (1998). Her latest coauthored book, *Why Iowa? Caucuses, Sequential Elections and Reform of Presidential Nominations* (forthcoming), examines how presidents are nominated in the United States and ways to reform the process. She is editor of a recent *PS: Political Science and Politics* symposium entitled "Reforming the Presidential Nomination Process."

RESOLVED, Article V should be revised to make it easier to amend the Constitution and to call a constitutional convention

PRO: Sanford Levinson

CON: David E. Kyvig

The final article in the Articles of Confederation declared that no "alteration at any time hereafter [shall] be made" to any of the articles unless "agreed to in a Congress of the United States, and be afterwards confirmed by the legislatures of every State." Unanimous consent meant, in practice, that institutional deficiencies could not be corrected. Unable to amend the Articles of Confederation, those who were dissatisfied were forced to overthrow them instead. And that is precisely what happened in Philadelphia in 1787, when those whom we now call "framers" ripped up the existing constitution and wrote a new one.

The starting point for the convention's business was not the Articles of Confederation but the "Virginia Plan," authored principally by James Madison and presented to the delegates at the outset of the convention by Virginia governor Edmund Randolph. Its thirteenth resolution stated "that provision ought to be made for the amendment of the Articles of Union whensoever it shall seem necessary, and that the assent of the National Legislature ought not to be required thereto." Madison and his Virginia colleagues were determined to avoid a situation in which a single recalcitrant state, no matter how small or unreasonable, could prevent the rest of the nation from amending its constitutional charter.

When the convention took up the Virginia Plan's thirteenth resolution on June 5, only two delegates spoke, one against and one in favor. South Carolina's Charles Pinckney "doubted the propriety" of excluding the national legislature from the amendment process. Massachusetts governor Elbridge Gerry offered his support, arguing that the "novelty and difficulty of the experiment" his colleagues were embarking upon suggested the wisdom of allowing for "periodical revision." They were unlikely to get everything right and so would need an amendment process to fix their missteps and miscalculations. The delegates were in no mood, however, to contemplate how to change a constitution they had not yet created, and so they voted to put off consideration of the resolution.

A week later the thirteenth resolution was back before the convention. This time, several members raised doubts about it. Virginia's George Mason defended it, insisting, as Gerry had, that amendments would be necessary to remedy the defects in their handiwork and that it was "better to provide for them, in an easy, regular and Constitutional way than to trust to chance and violence." Mason also defended the proposal to enable constitutional reform to go forward without the consent of the national legislature. The delegates endorsed Mason's position that some provision ought to be made for amendments. They remained undecided, however, about the wisdom of allowing the constitution to be amended without the consent of the national legislature, and again voted to postpone the question.

The delegates did not return to the amendment process that month or the next, and so the task of devising an amendment procedure fell to the five-man Committee of Detail, which worked for ten days from the end of July to the beginning of August to compose a rough draft of the Constitution. On August 6 the committee presented its handiwork to the convention, including Article XIX, which read: "On the application of the Legislatures of two thirds of the States in the Union, for an amendment of this Constitution, the Legislature of the United States shall call a Convention for that purpose." On August 30, the delegates unanimously approved Article XIX.

The question of how the new constitution should be amended was reopened on September 10, only a week before the delegates would affix their signatures to the final document. New York's Alexander Hamilton asked the delegates to make it easier to remedy "the defects which will probably appear in the new System." In Hamilton's view, those defects were most likely to be spotted by the national legislature, so he proposed that the article be modified to allow the national legislature, contingent on a two-thirds vote in each house, to call a constitutional convention. Madison also urged the delegates to take a second look at the article. He was particularly bothered by the "vagueness of the terms." How would the convention be formed, he asked, and what rules would govern its decisions?

Doubts about the article were sufficiently widespread that nine of the eleven states voted to reconsider. Connecticut's Roger Sherman seized the opportunity to amend the article to allow the national legislature to propose amendments but to require that any such change be "consented to by the several States." Pennsylvania's James Wilson was quick to modify the proposal so that a constitutional amendment would require the approval of only two-thirds of the states. The proposal narrowly lost, but a compromise proposal of three-fourths of the states was agreed to without a dissenting vote. Madison then proposed wording that incorporated both Hamilton's earlier proposal and the three-fourths approval mechanism. The delegates overwhelmingly approved it, though only after adding a provision, at the insistence of South Carolina's John Rutledge, that forbade any amendment relating to the slave trade for the next two decades.

The Committee of Style was charged with polishing the final draft of the Constitution, and on September 15 the committee presented to the delegates the wording of what had now become Article V. Several delegates remained dissatisfied, however. Sherman wanted a guarantee that no change could be made to the Constitution that deprived states of "equality in the Senate." Initially the convention rejected the change, prompting an angry Sherman to propose that Article V be struck altogether. "Circulating murmurs" of discontent moved Gouverneur Morris to play peacemaker; he proposed that Article V be amended so that "no State, without its consent shall be deprived of its equal suffrage in the Senate." Eager to bring their proceedings to a close and to avoid jeopardizing the carefully crafted compromises between large and small states, the delegates quickly agreed to Morris's proposal.

One further change was made to the work of the Committee on Style. The committee's Article V included no method for calling a constitutional convention, and Morris and Gerry proposed to remedy this by requiring a constitutional convention on application of two-thirds of the states. Their proposal was endorsed unanimously, and the opening sentence of Article V was revised into its final form. Two days later the delegates—though not Gerry, Mason, and Randolph—signed the Constitution. Their work was done, but the debate over the wisdom of Article V had just begun.

Sanford Levinson and David E. Kyvig renew this centuries-old argument. Levinson seconds the complaint that was first voiced by Patrick Henry at the Virginia Ratifying Convention in 1788: "The way to amendment," Henry thundered, had been "shut"; Levinson agrees that Article V is "an iron cage" and fundamentally undemocratic. Kyvig, in contrast, thinks that Article V gets it just about right, endorsing Madison's judgment in *Federalist* No. 43: "It guards equally against the extreme facility which would render the Constitution too mutable; and that extreme difficulty which might perpetuate its discovered faults." Twenty-seven amendments later, we are still debating the question of whether the framers got it just right or made constitutional reform too difficult.

PRO: Sanford Levinson

The United States has the hardest-to-amend Constitution in the world, at least among democratic nations.[1] Indeed, even illiberal constitutions, like that of Saudi Arabia, may be easier to amend because the ruler often has the unilateral power to change it. It is not merely that the U.S. Constitution stands out among world constitutions; most American states also have considerably easier amendment procedures than does the federal government. Whatever else one may say about Article V, it does not bespeak any general "American consensus" that foundational documents should be extremely difficult to change. There is no such consensus; at best, Americans are split on the issue, though one might argue from observing what John J. Dinan has aptly called America's "state constitutional tradition" that the consensus, if such there be, is in favor of easier forms of constitutional change.[2]

Article V sets out two paths toward amendment, one going through Congress (and requiring the assent of two-thirds of both the House and Senate), the other going through a convention that must be called by Congress upon a petition of two-thirds of the states. The text also establishes two paths for ratification: approval by three-fourths of the state legislatures or by three-fourths of specially convened state conventions. Which "mode of ratification" shall be used is left up to Congress to decide, and Congress has almost always opted for approval by state legislatures. Since each state legislature, save for Nebraska's, is bicameral, any amendment needs to be approved by a minimum of seventy-five legislative houses in thirty-eight states, whereas any proposed amendment can be defeated by the negative vote of only thirteen legislative houses in separate states.

Congress is far too busy to spend its time reflecting on the inadequacy of our eighteenth-century Constitution to our twenty-first-century reality. Even if one sets aside the obscene amount of time that legislators must spend raising money for their next elections, Congress has too much on its plate as it seeks to address pressing issues such as national security, the environment, and the economy. Congress's incapacity to devote adequate time to thinking about possible changes in our basic political structures is why I strongly support a new constitutional convention. I also hope that any such convention will modify Article V and make its own handiwork easier to amend than is currently the case.

America is stuck with Article V not because of a deep national commitment to the idea of a close-to-unchangeable constitution, but rather because of decisions made in the waning days of the Philadelphia convention of 1787.

The convention was a ringing repudiation of Article XIII of the Articles of Confederation, which required the unanimous assent of the state legislatures in order to amend the Articles. No one at the convention defended this change-prohibiting system. So a key question is: Did those who wrote the Constitution decide, after significant debate, that two-thirds of each house plus ratification by three-quarters of the states was the right decision rule, the Goldilocks-style "just right" between a method of change that would be either "too hot" (by being too flexible) or "too cold" (by emulating the Articles)? The answer is no. Almost all of the debate in Philadelphia and thereafter about Article V concerned the roles of states and Congress in the amendment process. Wariness about entrusting the process exclusively to Congress is what accounts for the now-ignored ability of the states to trigger a new constitutional convention should two-thirds of them petition Congress to do so. Most of the framers of the Constitution would likely be surprised that this part of Article V has become, practically speaking, moribund and that constitutional change now, realistically, must go through Congress. In any event, no one actually addressed why two-thirds and then three-quarters were just right for the new United States.

The first discussion in the Philadelphia convention of the numbers required for amendment took place on September 10, a mere week before the delegates signed the final document. Elbridge Gerry of Massachusetts was among those who pointed out that one of the major defects of the Articles of Confederation was the unanimity requirement of Article XIII. "It was," said Gerry, "desirable now that an easy mode should be established for [correcting] defects which will probably appear in the new System." Article V reflected the delegates' view that the new constitution needed to be more flexible than the one it was replacing.

At least one leading critic of the Constitution condemned it for making change still too difficult. At the Virginia ratifying convention, Patrick Henry warned his fellow citizens that only one-tenth of the American people might be able to block necessary changes. "It will be easily contrived," he suggested, "to procure the opposition of one tenth of the people to any alteration, however judicious." Interestingly, James Madison, who was the Constitution's primary defender at the Virginia ratifying convention, chose not to confront Henry directly on this point. One searches in vain for any ringing endorsement of Article V. All that its defenders were willing to say in its behalf was that it was better than the disastrous Article XIII.

It is worth noting, incidentally, Henry's reference to "the ten percent" who might be able to block needed change. His calculation was based on the fact that the total population (including slaves) of the four smallest states at the time (Delaware, New Hampshire, Rhode Island, and Georgia, with approximately 325,000 people) could block an amendment supported by the nation's other 3.6 million people. Consider the contemporary reality. The thirteen smallest states in 2008 have approximately 14.3 million people out of the national population of around 305 million. So less than 5 percent would be sufficient to veto an amendment desired by states with 95 percent of the American population. Anyone who defends the present Article V should note that there is no correlation between the percentage of states required to ratify an amendment and the percentage of the nation's population. No system that pretends to be based on the principle of one person/one vote should take any pride in Article V, which in almost every respect resembles the justly despised Article XIII of the Articles of Confederation.

Perhaps one should place Article V alongside other unfortunate compromises made in Philadelphia, such as reinforcing the power of slave states and acquiescing to Delaware's demand for equal representation in the Senate, which were the price of gaining the Constitution in the first place. This may explain the decision reached in 1787, but it would be as crazy to embrace Article V because that's what the framers decided as it would be to embrace the sanctity of recognizing property rights in other human beings, as was done by the notorious Three-Fifths Compromise and the Fugitive Slave Clause.

For those who think it's important to remain faithful to the wisdom of the founders, consider the closing lines of James Madison's *Federalist* No. 14:

> Is it not the glory of the people of America, that, whilst they have paid a decent regard to the opinions of former times and other nations, they have not suffered a blind veneration for antiquity, for custom, or for names, to overrule the suggestions of their own good sense, the knowledge of their own situation, and the lessons of their own experience? . . . They formed the design of a great Confederacy, which it is incumbent on their successors to improve and perpetuate.

We should, then, turn to the lessons of our own experience in deciding whether or not "improvement" of the "great Confederacy" designed in 1787 requires radical surgery on what is, in significant respects, its most important Article, Article V.

Any discussion of the present adequacy of Article V requires that we answer two quite different questions: First, how does one evaluate the possible gains attached to risking changes in the status quo against the fear that such changes will generate negative costs? It is obvious that Article V has a tremendous bias toward the status quo and places an extremely high burden on anyone who believes that change is desirable. Second, can we develop some way of measuring, over our 220-year history, whether we have procured enough gains from this bias that any costs attached to the near-impossibility of amending the Constitution are worth it?

I will return to those questions. But there is a third question that needs to be considered first: How important are constitutional amendments? A number of distinguished law professors, including Bruce A. Ackerman, Stephen M. Griffin, and David Strauss have argued that most important changes in the American constitutional order have taken place outside of Article V.[3] If they are right, then this debate is much ado about relatively little. Although I believe that much important constitutional change has occurred outside of Article V, I also believe that many needed changes have not. Much of the Constitution is "hard-wired" against interpretive cleverness.

Perhaps the easiest, and least controversial, example has to do with when we inaugurate new presidents. A recurrent feature of the American political system is the election of a new president who has run on a platform repudiating key policies of the incumbent. A hiatus of about eleven weeks ensues between the repudiation of the sitting president and the inauguration of his successor on January 20. The United States pays a real cost in having a legal president who has been repudiated by the electorate and a politically legitimate president without any legal authority to act. This is surely not the most serious defect in our Constitution, but it is perhaps the clearest example of a hard-wired feature that cannot be "worked around." This example should prove chastening to those who proclaim the irrelevance of formal amendment.

So let me return to the first two questions, which are more central to the debate. In his defense of Article V, David E. Kyvig remarks that the rigors of Article V have "contributed to a stable but not cripplingly inflexible government for more than two centuries." The appropriate response to this is: "Says who?" What, precisely, are the proper tests of flexibility and, for that matter, of stability? Indeed, whatever the test, could any reasonable person believe that we really have had two centuries of stability? What about the Civil War, a conflagration that to a significant degree was generated by the Constitution of 1787, which William Lloyd Garrison described as a "covenant with Death and agreement with Hell" because of the support it gave to slavery? The Three-Fifths Compromise, for example, gave slave states enhanced representation in the House of Representation and directly contributed, through the electoral college, to the election of American presidents who either owned slaves or were part of national political coalitions dedicated to protecting the interests of slaveowners.

As for the Fourteenth Amendment, which became part of the Constitution after the war, Bruce A. Ackerman has demonstrated that it is almost impossible to shoehorn it into a plausible Article V framework.[4] Proposal of the amendment by Congress was made possible by the refusal of the Republican Congress in December 1865 to seat most southern representatives and senators. Had they been seated, it would have been impossible to procure the needed two-thirds majorities in each house. As for ratification, military reconstruction was established in order to engage in the kind of "regime change" that would generate approval by the South. Moreover, the defeated states were told that their representatives and senators would not be seated unless they had ratified the amendment.

No historian should pretend that the Fourteenth Amendment is evidence of the flexible operation of Article V. Constitutional reform literally grew out of the barrel of a gun. One must, therefore, reject Kyvig's notion that the Fourteenth Amendment reflects in any unproblematic sense "the high threshold of consensus required for amendment." Indeed, it and the other so-called "Reconstruction Amendments" went into hibernation, so far as racial justice was concerned, for at least three-quarters of a century following the "Compromise of 1877" that returned control of the South to the white ruling class.

What is the situation today, with regard to needed constitutional changes, and is Article V more likely to prove efficacious than it was during this earlier era? I have written an entire book, *Our Undemocratic Constitution: Where the Constitution Goes Wrong (and How We the People Can Correct It)* outlining the negative features of the Constitution, and I won't repeat all of them now. I have already mentioned one, the hiatus between election and inauguration generated by the Inauguration Day Clause of the Twentieth Amendment, only because it is both crystal-clear in its operation and in its indefensibility in the twenty-first century. Here's another: Why should the newly inaugurated president be guaranteed a full four-year term even if he or she proves incompetent or otherwise loses the confidence of the public? There are worse things than being a criminal, but the Impeachment Clause means that noncriminal presidents, however inept and even dangerous, have an almost feudal tenure in the Oval Office, with all of the formidable legal powers of the presidency. Among these legal powers is the ability to negate the will of hefty (but not quite two-thirds) majorities in each house of Congress through use of the presidential veto. At worst, this gives the president powers that the British monarch has long since lost. At best, if one wishes to distinguish the president from the Queen because the former is elected (which is no small point), then we should acknowledge that this effectively establishes a "tricameral" rather than a bicameral legislature.

At this point, invariably, defenders of Article V will play the "risk-aversion" card, by suggesting that the wonderful thing about a functionally unamendable

Constitution is that it prevents bad amendments. That it certainly does. An anti–flag burning amendment, for example, would have been a terrible addition to the Constitution. The possibility of such an amendment being enacted would certainly count as a cost of a more flexible system of amendment. What those who endorse such arguments never do, though, is to ask about the potential risks (and costs) of our *not* being able to make desirable changes. Are we better off, for example, not having an Equal Rights Amendment in the Constitution, even though it received the support of both the House and Senate and two-thirds of the states, with well over a majority of the national population? Nor do proponents of Article V address the cost of having a political system in which there is no serious discussion of our hard-wired structures because of an altogether rational belief that it is basically impossible to change them in our era. Kyvig proffers the Seventeenth (direct election of senators), Twentieth (moving up the inauguration date), and Twenty-second (two-term limit) Amendments as examples of change, and they are. Is it not of some relevance, though, that they were added, respectively, ninety-five, seventy-six, and fifty-eight years ago?

Although we were close to third party–induced electoral train wrecks in 1948 and 1968, and many people believe that such a train wreck occurred in 2000, there has been no serious attempt to amend the electoral college because at least one-fourth-plus-one of the states would view any change as negatively affecting their parochial interests. It is even more utopian to suggest changing the indefensible allocation of power in the Senate, by which Wyoming gets the same voting power as California—which has seventy times the population—because Article V at that point becomes like the Articles of Confederation, requiring unanimity for amendment.

One of the worst features of Article V is that it infantilizes our entire political dialogue. We are totally unlike the founders in our systematic refusal to discuss the adequacy of our institutions and to think of needed improvements, in part because they imprisoned us in an iron cage that makes change nearly impossible. And the success of Article V is in part the refusal to perceive ourselves as trapped in such a cage! Proponents of Article V basically argue that "Article V isn't broken and therefore doesn't need fixing." I am far more pessimistic. I think it *is* one of the most important parts of a broken Constitution. And what is worse, precisely because most of us believe—perhaps rationally—that Article V works to stave off any realistic possibility of fixing what is wrong, we adopt the classic mechanism of denial: "If it can't be fixed, then it really isn't broken to begin with." We are, as a citizenry, much like a battered spouse who perceives no real possibility of exit and therefore is inclined to put the best spin on what might well be described, by an objective outsider, as a situation that merits escape.

Thus I enthusiastically support a new constitutional convention that would, as one of its most important actions, significantly modify Article V. It is possible that most Americans, even in a world that made constitutional change easier, would disagree with me and come to the conclusion that things are basically fine as they are. That would disappoint me, but at least one might say, "Well, at least We the People have really thought about our polity, and one can respect the process by which we came to our conclusion even if one disagrees with the ultimate decision." In our present reality, there is only a deafening silence with regard to the adequacy of our political institutions, even as we are engaged in a vigorous national debate about fundamental reform of our economy and our health care system. Those debates are taking place because of a perception that change is possible, making it worthwhile to organize and participate as democratic citizens in political struggles. Because Article V generates, in the minds of most rational people, the perception of impossibility of change, there is no serious debate at all. Some people may be cheered by this. I obviously am not. I see it as cause for alarm, and perhaps even despair, if the policy changes we need (and desire) are thwarted by an outdated and undemocratic Constitution that is kept that way by the barriers to institutional change created by Article V.

CON: David E. Kyvig

When the men who would frame the U.S. Constitution first met in Philadelphia in May 1787 a fundamental question faced them: How should they design a government to strike an effective balance among competing desires for popular sovereignty, functional effectiveness, stability, and adaptability to changing circumstances? The framers were committed to establishing a government that would ultimately reflect the will of the people while at the same time not be so sensitive to momentary public enthusiasms that it would constantly change its character or direction, and thus be considered unsteady. The solution that they devised for balancing the competing pressures of democratic responsiveness and government stability, the mechanism of constitutional amendment embodied in Article V of the Constitution, was a vast improvement over previous constitutional arrangements and has since proven its worth over the course of more than two centuries.

The question at hand is whether Article V still serves America's best interests or whether its rules for constitutional reform should be relaxed. No doubt,

Article V is a daunting obstacle to those eager for change. Taken as a whole, however, the history of efforts to use Article V suggests that its high standards have not been an insurmountable barrier to needed reform. At the same time, Article V has saved the United States from adopting some momentarily popular but fundamentally imprudent measures. The dramatic change in approval of the conduct of the presidency registered in public opinion polls between the middle of 2008 and the middle of 2009 should serve as a reminder that temporary unhappiness or enthusiasm with those leading government should not be confused with endorsement or dissatisfaction with the design of government itself. The functional utility and simplicity of a structure has more lasting importance than the conduct for good or ill of its temporary occupants.

The idea of constitutions—legal instruments defining the responsibilities, powers, and limitations of governments—originated with the English Magna Carta in 1215, a negotiated agreement between King John and the principal peers of the realm regarding the limits of royal authority. In a series of further agreements over the next five hundred years, British monarchs and Parliaments refined their definition of governmental structures and powers in a series of acts collectively, if not entirely accurately, referred to as an unwritten constitution. The distinguishing feature of Great Britain's master plan of government was less its haphazard manner of construction in several parts and more the fact that it could be and several times was radically altered by a simple parliamentary majority. Allowing a bare majority to define the law and thus the rules of government proved to be a prescription for sudden, dramatic shifts in government.

Britain's North American colonies developed on the basis of less flexible, more precisely defined instruments; for the most part, corporate or royal charters set forth the terms by which the colonies would operate. The colonies grew more comfortable with such specific written instruments of government as they observed the erratic evolution of British government through the English Civil War, the Restoration of the monarchy, and the Glorious Revolution of 1689. By the time of the 1776 Declaration of Independence, the newly independent American states all opted for written constitutions, either modeled on earlier instruments or created anew. The idea of a charter delegating the authority of the sovereign people to a government functioning under agreed-upon rules was widely embraced not only at the state level but also in the creation of a confederation of the states. A written constitution that could be read and comprehended by all seemed necessary and valuable for maintaining a well-defined and limited government under democratic control. Yet written constitutions carried with them the question as to how they should be altered if experience proved they needed reform.

The Articles of Confederation required the unanimous agreement of all thirteen states to be changed. This system of amendment quickly proved unworkable, since it allowed a single state to thwart any constitutional reform, something that happened repeatedly and quickly rendered the Articles unpopular. Dissatisfaction with a rigid and unsatisfactory government of too few powers led to the call for states to send delegations to a constitutional convention in Philadelphia in the summer of 1787. Once the delegates gathered, every aspect of the Articles of Confederation was regarded as eligible for reform.

High on the agenda of the Philadelphia convention—along with the creation of a more effective national government with a balance of structures to carry out necessary legislative, executive, and judicial tasks without any one of them being able to exercise unlimited power—was the objective of devising a workable amending mechanism. The founders repeatedly demonstrated a concern for protecting minority interests while still respecting majority preferences. The Constitution won approval from every sector of the new nation by reassuring each of them that its interests would not be abused. Important decisions, those with long-lasting consequences, would require the greatest degree of consensus to take effect. To ratify an international treaty, one with the highest legal status, or to remove from office a properly chosen but subsequently impeached president or judge required a two-thirds vote by the Senate. Adoption of laws that Congress had passed but the president had vetoed required a two-thirds vote in each house of Congress. The most significant change, an alteration of the powers or procedures of government, required the highest degree of consensus, the founders believed. Thus they agreed that an amendment should be approved by two-thirds of Congress or by a constitutional convention called by two-thirds of the states. But to make such a basic change in the rules of government, the amendment would also have to be ratified or approved by legislatures or democratically elected conventions of three-fourths of the states. The founders did not insist on unanimity for constitutional change, but they clearly feared that too easily altered fundamental rules of government could lead to changes being made without sufficient thought or agreement. Were they too cautious? More than two hundred years of experience offer evidence that they were not.

Article V, the amending provision, proved one of the Constitution's great selling points. As the original states considered whether to ratify the Philadelphia convention's proposal, many had doubts about one aspect or another. A common complaint was the absence of a bill of rights providing specific protections for individuals against overweening governmental power. The ratifying convention in Massachusetts was the first to call for the immediate addition of a bill of rights, and it showed its confidence in the functionality of the new amending process by proceeding to approve the Constitution on the assumption that it would be promptly amended. Several other states did likewise, affirming their faith that the amending system would work by accompanying their ratification with a call for a bill of rights. The two late ratifications critical to putting the Constitution into effect, those of Virginia and New York, were both obtained on the basis of pairing ratification with a call for amendment. Without the presence of a method of amendment that the founding generation regarded as workable, it is unlikely that the Constitution would have won approval.

James Madison, one of the Constitution's principal architects elected to the first Congress, perceived that the new framework of government would not be fully accepted until its amending system could assuage the concerns of various ratifying conventions. He devoted himself to drafting a set of amendments that would constitute a bill of rights on the basis of the host of proposals emanating from state ratifying conventions. Madison's amendments were approved by the House, modified by the Senate, and emerged from the first session of the first Congress. Ten of Madison's package of twelve amendments gained ratification within two-and-a-half years. The incorporation of the Bill of Rights into the Constitution brought about the full acceptance of the new charter of government, an affirmation made possible only by the successful functioning of Article V.

The early discovery of oversights and flaws in the original Constitution led to two more amendments in short order, a further indication that the amending process could function when needed. Otherwise, the Constitution remained unaltered until the end of the Civil War. It is hardly surprising that this would be the case, since the matter most likely to provoke amendment—slavery—was what most deeply and evenly divided the country. A consensus on fundamental changes in the nature of government was hardly possible until one side or the other in the slavery debate gained a controlling upper hand, as only occurred with the Southern surrender in 1865. The amendments that ended slavery, guaranteed equal treatment and due process of law regardless of race, and secured black suffrage reversed the terms of the racial settlement in the original Constitution and demonstrated the unlimited power of Article V to transform the entire government and society. Such authority, as the framers had foreseen, was not to be used lightly. The high threshold of consensus required for amendment anchored the fundamental reorientation of the United States from a confederation of powerful states to a centralized national government, not a transformation to be taken lightly.

Following the Civil War amendments, no more constitutional reform occurred until the early twentieth century, and the belief grew that the requirements for amendment might be insurmountable. But then the image of amendment as difficult under the terms of Article V was repeatedly refuted. Progressive reformers, unhappy with a Supreme Court ruling that a federal income tax was unconstitutional and disenchanted with the process for selecting U.S. senators, found constitutional amendments effective and achievable remedies. Indeed, as a growing number of states demanded a constitutional convention to draft a direct senatorial election amendment, and as Congress began to contemplate that such a convention would be as unrestrained as its 1787 predecessor in proposing changes to the basic terms of government, the House and Senate moved quickly to adopt a direct election amendment and send it to the states for ratification. As soon as the income tax and direct election of senators amendments were ratified early in 1913, advocates of women's suffrage and national prohibition of alcoholic beverages launched amendment campaigns. By the end of the decade, organized political crusades for each of these reforms achieved success. Once the belief that amendment was impossible was overcome, these fundamental changes in income distribution, democratic participation, and social practice were rapidly achieved by means of Article V. Two more amendments followed in little more than a decade—one an important speeding up of the presidential and congressional transition after a national election, and the other a reversal of the national alcohol ban.

The national prohibition amendment delivered multiple lessons about the nature of constitutional amendment. First, the antiliquor amendment demonstrated that the threshold for adoption of even a radical constitutional reform was not beyond reach. The required two-thirds of each house of Congress and majorities in three-fourths of state legislatures for amendment approval were not merely assembled but exceeded in support of prohibition. At the same time, the next decade would demonstrate that the adoption of an amendment did not guarantee that it would be universally embraced; widespread violation of the liquor ban suggested that there were limits to public respect for the Constitution. The greatest lesson may have been provided by the repeal of the Eighteenth Amendment only fourteen years after its adoption. Passage of the Twenty-first Amendment showed that the high standards of Article V were not an insurmountable obstacle to the construction of a public consensus overwhelming enough to reverse a previous constitutional agreement, even one of fairly recent standing. The Twenty-first Amendment, the one constitutional reform that directly reversed another, was a measure whose ratification Congress removed from the hands of state legislatures and gave to popularly elected state conventions. The use of bodies of delegates chosen solely on the basis of their position on this one issue underscored the democratic intentions of the Constitution. Prohibition and its repeal also made clear the liabilities of dramatic shifts in fundamental government practice, a cost that would increase if standards for achieving amendment were relaxed. At the same time, the episode demonstrated the capacity of a democratic polity operating under the terms of Article V to repair a constitutional error.

The prohibition episode is not the only evidence of the possibility of adopting questionable amendments, despite the elevated standards of Article V. The Twenty-second Amendment, limiting a president to two terms, was speedily approved by a conservative coalition of Republicans and southern Democrats following the death of Franklin Roosevelt, who had been elected four times to the presidency. The anti-Roosevelt sentiment that spawned the amendment produced a situation that thereafter politically hobbled every second-term president, ironically many of them conservatives, by barring them from running again. As a result, Presidents Dwight Eisenhower, Richard Nixon, Ronald Reagan, Bill Clinton, and George W. Bush all found themselves politically weaker in their second terms. The Twenty-second Amendment stands as a reminder that constitutional change can restrict democratic choice. Such reform ought to be approached cautiously and only adopted if a substantial national consensus is supportive.

Four amendments during the 1960s demonstrated once again that the Article V process could work effectively. As attention became focused on various issues, the necessary degree of consensus was attained for measures broadly perceived as worthwhile: racially progressive steps to prohibit poll taxes and grant electoral votes to the District of Columbia, a complex measure to replace departed or disabled presidents, and a grant of voting rights for eighteen- to twenty-year-old citizens. At the same time, certain measures that divided the society were unable to attain the political support necessary to move forward. Reaction against various Supreme Court decisions also led in the 1960s to proposals for amendments that would strengthen the authority of states while restricting that of the federal government, overturn the requirement of equal representation of citizens in state legislatures, and authorize state-sponsored school prayer composed by a local majority. Adoption of these amendments, each of which enjoyed support—in the latter two cases substantial—would have had significant, arguably antidemocratic and liberty-restricting consequences. Advocates of anti–equal representation and prayer amendments once again proposed a constitutional convention and stirred concern that such a convention could produce radical change. As a result, interest in such measures rapidly declined. A lower threshold for amendment approval could have conceivably facilitated the adoption of such measures.

The battle for women's rights showed both sides of the Article V question. The Equal Rights Amendment (ERA), first proposed to Congress in 1923, did not achieve two-thirds support in both houses until 1972. It was ratified by thirty-five states, 70 percent of the necessary total but not the required three-quarters. The failure of the ratification effort did not prevent the Supreme Court from repeatedly during the 1970s and 1980s deciding to extend women's rights to due process and equal protection of the law. At the same time, widespread opposition to the Court's *Roe v. Wade* decision acknowledging a woman's right to choose to have an abortion spurred calls for an amendment to invalidate the ruling. In this case, the same high Article V standard that frustrated ERA supporters prevented abortion foes from achieving an anti-abortion amendment even though they had the support of President Reagan. The framers' notion that a high degree of consensus should be required for constitutional empowerment kept either side in an ongoing social debate from imposing its will on a still fundamentally divided society.

A lower threshold for adoption of constitutional amendment combined with the momentary enthusiasm displayed in the 1980s for proposed amendments to ban flag burning and require balanced annual federal budgets might well have facilitated adoption of imprudent amendments. The anti–flag burning amendment would have overturned a Supreme Court ruling that such acts represented symbolic free speech, and would have constituted the first significant constriction of the free speech guarantees of the First Amendment. Such an outcome might have encouraged attempts to restrict through amendment other provisions of the Bill of Rights ranging from gun possession to criminal justice protections. The so-called Balanced Budget Amendment would have posed difficulties for the federal government in responding to an economic or military emergency with large-scale economic stimulus or defense spending. While the flag burning and balanced budget amendments enjoyed wide support at the moment they were first introduced, enthusiasm gradually faded as their consequences became evident. Had the Article V threshold for adoption of such amendments been lower, they might well have been installed in the Constitution to the detriment of effective government.

The original constitutional principle that the fundamental rules governing the conduct of government should be based on a widespread public consensus is a concept that has served the United States well for more than two centuries. Each adoption of a constitutional amendment, the most recent in 1992, has represented a reaffirmation of the consensus that in other respects the terms of the existing Constitution remain acceptable. The repeated unwillingness to embrace a new constitutional convention offers additional evidence that easier amendment is not widely sought. Even the high standards of Article V have allowed such amendments as national prohibition and presidential term limits to win approval. Easier requirements for constitutional change might well allow other ill-considered measures to be installed in the basic framework of government and then be difficult to remove. While it is certainly possible to think of possible attractive changes to the Constitution—from electoral college reform to broader protection of individual human rights to clearer articulation of federal government responsibilities—it is hard to imagine continued confidence in the Constitution and the steady functioning of the federal government in the absence of a high degree of consensus on the terms of constitutional design. Article V, with its requirements of two-thirds congressional agreement and three-quarters state approval for constitutional change, has contributed to a stable but not cripplingly inflexible government for more than two centuries. Article V has served the nation well and deserves to be retained.

RESOLVED, Congress should restore each state's freedom to set its drinking age

PRO: John McCardell

CON: James C. Fell

Important debates about public policy often encompass both an obvious and a less obvious dispute. The obvious dispute is about what the policy should be. Should casino gambling be legalized? Should tougher controls on air pollution be enacted? Should bike riders be forced to wear helmets?

The less obvious dispute is about who should decide what the policy will be. Sometimes this involves a family feud within the national government. Should Congress or the president decide when to pull American troops out of Afghanistan? Should the elected branches or the Supreme Court set public policy concerning affirmative action? At other times the dispute is about which level of government in the federal system—the national government (usually called, a bit confusingly, the federal government), state governments, or local governments—should make public policy on welfare, education, law enforcement, and a wide range of other issues. Or, in the case of this debate, should Congress restore each state's freedom to set its drinking age?

Arguments about the powers of the federal government and the state governments run through much of American history. Could the federal government establish a national bank and exempt it from state taxes? A Supreme Court decision, *McCulloch v. Maryland* (1819), was needed to resolve that question. Could a state refuse to be bound by a federal tariff law that it considered oppressive? In 1832 President Andrew Jackson said no, Vice President John C. Calhoun of South Carolina resigned from office to say yes, and the great Nullification Crisis was born. Could states decide to secede from the Union? It took four years of civil war, from 1861 to 1865, to settle that one. For several decades beginning in the late nineteenth century, additional battles were fought about the state governments' authority to regulate business and about the federal government's authority to enforce civil rights for African Americans and other racial and ethnic minorities.

In the twentieth century, the federal government's efforts to expand its policy-making domain at the expense of the state governments took a new form. Instead of fighting legal battles about Washington's constitutional authority over the states, the federal government increasingly used its power of the purse to, in effect, buy the states' cooperation. Through grant-in-aid programs, Washington gave the states money to spend and clear instructions about how to spend it. The number of grant programs grew from just a few as recently as the early 1930s to several hundred today. The interstate highway system, for example, took shape when the federal government passed a law in 1956 that offered the states ninety cents of every dollar used to build highways according to Washington's specifications.

A grant program is a gift that comes with strings attached. In 1984, at a time when each state still set its own drinking age without federal interference and most states had recently decided to reduce the age to under twenty-one, Congress passed the National Minimum Drinking Age Act. The act did not order the states to do anything; nor could it have done so without provoking a fierce constitutional challenge in the Supreme Court. Instead, the act stipulated that any state with a drinking age below twenty-one would lose 10 percent of its annual federal highway grants. Within a few years, every state decided to bring its legal drinking age into conformity with the new federal standard.

Laws are not passed in a political vacuum. In the Vietnam War era, many states had lowered their drinking age because eighteen, nineteen, and twenty-year-olds argued persuasively that if they were old enough to fight, they were old enough to drink. A steep increase in alcohol-related traffic fatalities among younger drivers changed the political climate by spurring the formation of a new and politically savvy grassroots organization called Mothers Against Drunk Driving (MADD) in 1980. MADD lobbied vigorously for legislation to raise the drinking age to twenty-one.

In theory, disputes about who should make public policy on a particular issue are different from disputes about what the policy should be. In reality, these disputes seldom remain separate. John McCardell and James C. Fell are on opposite sides of the resolution that Congress should restore each state's freedom to set its drinking age: McCardell is for it and Fell is against it. What both know, however, is that in the foreseeable future Congress is highly unlikely to reduce the drinking age to eighteen but that if each state were free to reduce it, some of them probably would. McCardell wants to see that change occur, and so he wants to move the decision from the federal government to the state governments. Fell supports the current drinking age, and so he wants to leave the decision right where it is, in Washington.

PRO: John McCardell

"Some may feel that my decision is at odds with my philosophical viewpoint that state problems should involve state solutions," said President Ronald Reagan in July 1984; however, he continued, "in a case like this, where the problem is so clear-cut, then I have no misgivings about a judicious use of federal inducements to encourage the states to get moving."[1]

The "problem" that, in this case, trumped philosophy involved drunken driving fatalities. The solution seemed as clear-cut: raise the drinking age to twenty-one. With the stroke of a pen, the president signed into law the National Minimum Drinking Age Act, in effect wresting away, seemingly for good, what had explicitly and unequivocally been a state prerogative since 1789. The bill did not, because it could not, mandate a national drinking age. But it did create a powerful "incentive." States would remain free to set the age, but any state setting the age lower than twenty-one would forfeit 10 percent of its federal highway funds each year.

If the president's decision ran counter to his own pro-state government political instincts, it also renewed an historic debate over the limits of federalism and situated that debate in the highly charged arena of alcohol policy. Led by South Dakota, twelve states (the others were Colorado, Hawaii, Kansas, Louisiana, Montana, New Mexico, Ohio, South Carolina, Tennessee, Vermont, and Wyoming) challenged the constitutionality of the act. Eventually the case reached the Supreme Court, which in 1987, by a vote of 7–2, upheld the law. Writing for the majority, Chief Justice William H. Rehnquist noted, "we need not decide in this case whether [the Twenty-first] Amendment would prohibit an attempt by Congress to legislate directly a national minimum drinking age. Here, Congress has acted indirectly under its spending power to encourage uniformity in the States' drinking ages. . . . [W]e find this legislative effort within constitutional bounds even if Congress may not regulate drinking ages directly."[2] And with those words, public debate on the issue ceased.

Thus, since 1984, there has been a *de facto* national drinking age. The results have been sufficiently mixed to warrant a reopening of what for too long was viewed as a settled question. Yet the forces, and the "incentives" militating against any change in the status quo, have for a quarter of a century successfully stifled serious discussion and debate over the consequences—intended and unintended—of this legislation. It is time for that debate to resume. It is time to change the law.

To understand the urgency for change, as well as to grasp the irony of the present condition, one needs to recognize that in many ways history is repeating itself. America has always had an uneasy relationship with alcohol, swinging wildly over the years from periods of remarkable laxity and permissiveness to periods of prohibition. Unlike most other countries, where alcohol has generally been viewed as a food rather than an intoxicant and as an enhancement to social and family relationships rather than an irresponsible escape from reality, the American experience reflects an uncertain, and always unsettled, cultural attitude toward alcohol.

Federalism did little to resolve the uncertainty and contributed much to the unsettling, because the authority to set alcohol policy resides, under the Constitution, exclusively with the states. Moreover, many states carried the federal principle still farther, allowing individual counties, under the rubric of "local option," to make laws reflecting the prevailing attitudes within particular localities. As a result, laws governing the production, purchase, possession, and consumption of alcoholic beverages resembled a crazy quilt of the permissible and the impermissible.

To minds more comfortable with tidiness and consistency, such an approach always seemed undesirable. To attitudes shaped by a particular set of understandings—often but not always grounded in religious beliefs—that sought to differentiate moral from immoral behavior, such an approach seemed unacceptable, a secular impediment placed in the way of realizing God's design in a fallen world.

From time to time, a prohibitionist impulse has amassed sufficient muscle to neaten the untidiness and clean up the moral squalor. During the first half of the nineteenth century, a "temperance" movement began. By 1836 the American Temperance Society claimed more than eight thousand local chapters and over 1.5 million members. But because merely encouraging temperance did not mean outright prohibition, it failed to satisfy those who, moved by religious revivals to eradicate sin wherever it could be found, turned to the government for assistance.

As early as 1830 most states had some form of licensing law meant to limit the right to sell alcohol to responsible retailers. Over the next twenty years, temperance advocates pushed to strengthen these regulations by limiting the quantities that might be sold to a particular individual and by allowing a local option on whether intoxicants could be sold at all. New York enacted local option legislation in 1845 and, following the lead of Maine, which passed the first statewide prohibition law in 1846, Vermont, Rhode Island, and Minnesota Territory embraced prohibition in 1852, as did Michigan in 1853; Connecticut and New York in 1854; and New Hampshire, Tennessee, Delaware, Illinois, Indiana, Iowa, and Wisconsin in 1855.

Themes that would become familiar and recurrent continued to surface. Enforcement of prohibition proved almost impossible. Per capita consumption of alcohol increased dramatically. Public opposition to prohibition grew, especially in the rapidly growing cities. Many of the laws, having been hastily drafted and passed, proved susceptible to legal challenge. Finally, as civil war loomed, ending slavery took priority over other reform efforts.

Thus the pattern was set: elision of temperance into prohibition; the graphic depiction of the evils of strong drink; the increasingly extreme certitude of temperance advocates; the belief that only legislation could solve the problem; acquiescence to the argument that governmental intrusion may be necessary for the public good; difficulties of law enforcement; an increase rather than a decrease in drinking; and finally, gradually, a dawning awareness that legislative intervention in private life may have more unintended than intended consequences

In the late nineteenth century, under the leadership of the Women's Christian Temperance Union, one of the first organizations to keep a professional lobbyist in Washington, the reform impulse revived. The movement was strongest in rural, small-town, Protestant America. Unlike the 1850s, when prohibitionists sought legislation (and discovered that what a legislature could do it could just as easily undo), in the 1880s they sought reform via state constitutional amendments. Five states—Kansas, Maine, Rhode Island, North Dakota, and South Dakota—adopted constitutional prohibition while New Hampshire and Vermont continued prohibition by statute. In 1893 the newly formed Anti-Saloon League joined the prohibition effort but elevated the movement's sights from the state to the national level.

There was no disputing that alcohol regulation remained entirely a state matter. But, thought Wayne Wheeler, president of the Anti-Saloon League, what if the U.S. Constitution itself could be amended? What better way to "hurl a missile at the giant wrong?"[3] The United States' entry into the Great War in 1917, coupled with the Progressive era belief that government regulation could, by adjusting unwholesome environments, bring about social change, provided the opportunity. Joining the fervor for supporting American troops in the field, prohibitionists insisted that not a single grain of wheat or barley or a single kernel of corn should be diverted to produce alcoholic beverages. No effort should be spared to defeat the Hun (whose name was often associated with beer).

Thus in 1917 Congress adopted, and forty-four states by 1919 ratified, the Eighteenth Amendment to the Constitution, embedding prohibition in the fundamental law of the land. A joyful leader of the Anti-Saloon League believed that "there is as much chance of repealing the Eighteenth Amendment as there is for a humming-bird to fly to the planet Mars with the Washington Monument tied to its tail."[4]

The Eighteenth Amendment's attempt to ban "the manufacture, sale, or transportation" of alcohol soon came face to face with a more potent law, the law of unintended consequences. By 1929, per capita consumption of alcohol was higher than it had been in 1918, a year before Prohibition became law. Criminal behavior—moonshining, bootlegging—became rampant. Enforcement of prohibition proved almost impossible. "Prohibition has driven the saloon off the sidewalk," wrote one observer, "but has put it in the cellar, where it is out of sight."[5]

Within little more than a decade, by December 1933 the unthinkable and the impossible happened. For the first and only time in American history, two-thirds of the House and Senate, and three-fourths of the state legislatures, voted to repeal a constitutional amendment. With the repeal of Prohibition, the making of alcohol policy reverted to the individual states, and the untidiness and inconsistency returned as well.

Almost forty years would pass before the question of the drinking age reappeared. The catalyst was not concern over alcohol and its effects but rather an unpopular war in Vietnam—one fought mostly by draftees deemed capable of defending their country but incapable of exercising any of the other responsibilities of adulthood. The inconsistency received its most forceful and articulate expression in a simple slogan: "Old enough to fight—old enough to vote." Persuaded by the justice as well as the logic of the argument, Congress passed and the states ratified the Twenty-sixth Amendment, which stated that "the right of a citizen age 18 to vote shall not be abridged on account of age."

The Twenty-sixth Amendment prompted a serious reconsideration of twenty-one as the age of majority. Indeed, if eighteen-year-olds were capable of voting intelligently and placing their lives on the line for their country, by what right, or logic, ought they to be denied other privileges and responsibilities of adulthood? As a result, by the end of the 1970s most states had redefined the age of majority as age eighteen and the rest as age nineteen. At the same time, between 1970 and 1979, twenty-nine states lowered their drinking ages.

Once again, the law of unintended consequences held sway. In the states choosing to lower the drinking age, no provision was made to prepare those on whom a new privilege had been conferred to exercise responsibility. It was as if the privilege to drive a car were granted without any driver training or any probationary period during which new drivers could gain experience and confidence. Not surprisingly, alcohol-related traffic fatalities rapidly increased in the eighteen-to-twenty age group. The problem of drunken driving was both genuine and serious. In 1980 the mother of a thirteen-year-old girl who had been killed by a forty-seven-year-old, repeat-offender drunken driver founded Mothers Against Drunk Driving (MADD), and the drinking age debate began in earnest.

As fatalities quickly reached unacceptable levels MADD led a public call for action. In 1982 President Reagan appointed a special Commission on Drunk Driving, which brought forward, unanimously, thirty-nine recommendations. Of these, the most prominent was that "States should immediately adopt 21 years as the minimum legal purchasing and public possession age for all alcoholic beverages." In addition, recognizing the potential constitutional conundrum, the commission added: "Legislation at the Federal level should be enacted providing that each State enact and/or maintain a law requiring 21 years as the minimum legal age for purchasing and possessing alcoholic beverages. Such legislation should provide that the Secretary of the United States Department of Transportation disapprove any project under Section 106 of the Federal Highway Act . . . for any State not having and enforcing such a law."[6]

The need for uniformity, in the view of Sen. Frank Lautenberg of New Jersey, a principal sponsor of the legislation, arose from the problem posed by so-called "blood borders": boundaries that separated a state with a higher age from a state with a lower age. Too many young people, the senator argued, were driving across these borders, in his case from New Jersey into New York, where the age was lower, and then driving home, sometimes with fatal consequences. A uniform drinking age, he argued, would end this fatal practice.

By a bipartisan vote of 81–16, the measure passed, and on July 17, 1984, President Reagan signed the National Minimum Drinking Age Act, effectively creating a national drinking age of twenty-one.

In the years since this law was enacted, there have been occasional efforts in the states to reopen the question of the drinking age. For example, at various times the legislatures of Wisconsin, Kentucky, New Hampshire, and South Carolina have considered exempting active-duty military personnel from the twenty-one-age requirement. Vermont considered a bill to educate and license eighteen-year-olds as a way of lowering the age. Missouri voters attempted a ballot initiative to lower the age. In every case, however, these efforts failed because the prospect of losing 10 percent of federal highway money loomed. If the purpose of attaching a highway fund "incentive" to the drinking age law was to end serious debate over the matter, then the measure must be adjudged a success.

Therein, however, lies a deeper problem. No public policy, however effective or worthy its supporters may deem it, should be placed, for all time, effectively outside the arena of political debate and rendered virtually impossible to change. A growing body of evidence suggests that the National Minimum Drinking Age Act has not been an unmitigated blessing. Some of that evidence serves as a reminder of the country's experience under Prohibition. The vast majority of young people between the ages of eighteen and twenty routinely disobey it.[7] The proliferation of fake IDs reflects a determination to flout the law and risks breeding disrespect for law in general. As a result, the law has proven virtually impossible to enforce: it is estimated that of every one thousand violations only two result in arrest or citation.[8]

Not only is the law regularly violated, the violations occur behind closed doors, in the latter-day equivalent of the "speak-easy" of the 1920s. There, out of public view and easy detection, young adults are consuming alcohol in quantities that are life- and health-threatening. The law has not eliminated drinking; it has simply displaced it from visible, public venues into clandestine locations. Assaults, date rapes, property damage, and emergency room calls attest to a persistent, intractable problem of "binge" drinking that all too often proves toxic.

It also proves unnatural, in that the drinking age has served to split the previously concentric worlds of alcohol consumption and social intercourse into separate spheres. Young people "do shots" or "pre-load" before going to a social event, where they know alcohol will not be available. This behavior is very different from that observed in most of the rest of the world, where a lower drinking age and a more open cultural attitude toward alcohol has created a very different—and healthier—environment for young people.

The law unquestionably represents an abridgment of the age of majority, which young adults considered capable of voting, signing contracts, serving on juries, and fighting in the military have difficulty comprehending. In addition, the role of parents in teaching their children has been unintentionally marginalized by a law that places alcohol off-limits until one turns twenty-one.

Finally, though drunken driving fatalities have in fact been reduced, the reduction has occurred in all age groups, and has been paralleled in Canada, where the drinking age has remained either eighteen or nineteen.[9] Safer automobiles, mandatory seat belts, and the "designated driver" have had far more to do with the downward trend than the higher drinking age.

Moreover, over the past quarter-century, we have wrought a fundamental shift in Americans' attitudes toward drinking and driving. As a senior official at the National Highway Traffic and Safety Administration put it, "If you look back, it's no longer acceptable to drive drunk. It's socially reprehensible, in fact, to drive drunk."

The problem of drunken driving has not been eliminated, but it has been addressed and reduced, and technology now exists, in the form of ignition interlocks, to take drunks of all ages off the highways. The need to reduce drunken driving by adjusting the drinking age has been superseded by more effective and targeted possibilities.

It has also been supplanted by a very different sort of problem, which has at least in part been caused by the higher drinking age. Reasonable people may disagree about how closely related the drinking age and the problem of clan-destine binge drinking may be, but the relationship cannot be denied. The looming public health crisis of the twenty-first century, occasioned by toxic and secretive alcohol consumption, may require a different set of solutions from those used to solve a very different problem in the last century.

There is only one place where, constitutionally, the whole matter may be examined and public policy adjusted to meet a new reality, and that place is the state capitals. But the drinking age, as a part of any possible solution to the problem of binge drinking, remains off limits, so long as the federal highway fund "incentive" remains on the books.

If that "incentive" were removed or, alternatively, if states were to be granted waivers for a period of time in order to try new approaches, fresh, creative ideas would surely emerge. This is the genius of federalism. Allowing states to try something different, something appropriate for its own population, can lead to better practices, better policy, and safer environments.

This is not an unreasonable prediction. In the twentieth century, states were viewed as "laboratories of progressivism." Many things we now take for granted nationally—regulation of corporations, the secret ballot, women's suffrage—were all innovations, thought by some to be too radical to be acceptable, that were first tried on the state level. It is hard to imagine that a state might have had its highway funding reduced for allowing women to vote. But had a similar "incentive" existed one hundred years ago, would any state have had the cour-age to put such funding at risk?

What works in one state may not work as well in another state. The federal government should not tell New Jersey what its drinking age should be; neither should New Jersey dictate to South Carolina, Vermont, or Montana. And before the concern over "blood-borders" is allowed to thwart debate, it should be remembered that states bordering Canada or Mexico already have "blood-borders." Even more to the point, unless legislatures enact uniform closing hours for bars, there will be "blood-borders" within every community where some bars close at 1 a.m., others at 2 a.m., and still others at 3 a.m. State boundaries are only one form of "blood-border."

There is likely never to be a genuine national consensus over what the drink-ing age should be. Rather than continuing to coerce such a consensus and sustain the illusion that the question of the drinking age is settled—and that all the evi-dence lies on one side of the debate—let Congress restore to the states the right to do what, under the Constitution, only the states may do. Let Congress allow the states, unimpeded by federal "incentives," to make public policy that reflects the particular reality that exists within each state. Let federalism work its genius without interference. Return the right to set the drinking age to the states.

CON: James C. Fell

Perhaps no alcohol safety measure or policy has attracted more research and public attention or shown more consistent evidence for its effectiveness than the minimum legal drinking age (MLDA) in the United States. MLDA laws were established in the states after the repeal of Prohibition in 1933. At that time, control of alcohol was left to the states, most of which set the MLDA at twenty-one. By 1969, thirty-five states still had MLDA laws set at age twenty-one (see Map 2-1). However, when the Twenty-sixth Amendment lowered the voting age from twenty-one to eighteen in 1971, many states lowered their drinking age to eighteen or nineteen. Consequently, by the end of 1975 only twelve states had MLDA laws set at age twenty-one (see Map 2-2).

Map 2-1

U.S. Minimum Legal Drinking Ages as of December 31, 1969

Source: Insurance Institute for Highway Safety.

Studies in the 1970s and 1980s showed significant increases in alcohol-related crashes involving youths aged eighteen to twenty in states that lowered their drinking age. There was also anecdotal evidence that many youths under age twenty-one who resided in a state with an MLDA-21 law were driving long distances to a neighboring state with an MLDA of eighteen or nineteen so they could legally drink at bars. Some of these youths were involved in crashes when they were driving back to their state in a highly intoxicated condition. Concern over these developments and other drunk-driving issues led to the establishment of Mothers Against Drunk Driving (MADD) in 1980 and the President's Commission on Drunk Driving in 1982. Both of these organizations advocated a uniform drinking age of twenty-one in all states in order to eliminate the "blood borders" and reduce drinking and driving by youth.

Map 2-2

U.S. Minimum Legal Drinking Ages as of December 31, 1975

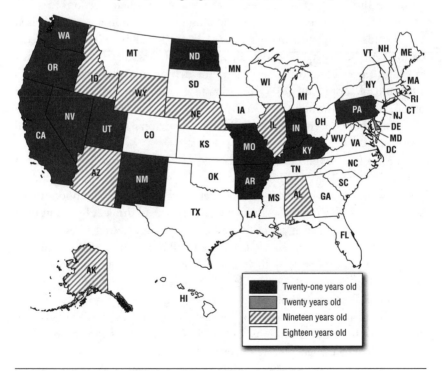

Source: Insurance Institute for Highway Safety.

In 1984 Congress adopted the National Minimum Drinking Age Act, which provided a substantial incentive for states to set their MLDA at twenty-one. If they did not do so by 1988, they faced losing 10 percent of federal highway construction funding. By 1988, all fifty states and the District of Columbia had set the MLDA at age twenty-one.

Between 1982 and 1998, the population-adjusted involvement rate of drinking drivers aged twenty and younger in fatal traffic crashes decreased 59 percent.[1] MLDA-21 laws have been shown to be associated with this decline. The National Highway Traffic Safety Administration (NHTSA) has estimated that MLDA laws save approximately eight hundred to nine hundred lives a year in traffic fatalities alone.[2] However, despite the strong evidence of the effectiveness of MLDA-21, there are movements in some states to lower it, and there is at least one organization that is working to repeal the national uniform drinking age act.

Technically, each state still has the freedom to set its drinking age. That right was never taken away by the federal government. So far, however, no state has chosen to forgo the millions of dollars in federal highway construction funding that would result from exercising their freedom to lower the drinking age. This incentive, or sanction, is a common mechanism used by the federal government to persuade states to adopt policies when the nation's public safety is at stake. This mechanism was also used to persuade all states to adopt zero tolerance laws for drivers under age twenty-one in 1995 and to adopt 0.08 g/dl (g/dl refers to grams of alcohol per deciliter of blood, which is the standard way to report alcohol concentrations) as the blood alcohol concentration (BAC) limit for drivers aged twenty-one and over in 2000.

The National Minimum Drinking Age Act only required states to adopt statutes that made it illegal for persons younger than twenty-one to publicly possess alcohol or to purchase alcohol. It allowed states many exceptions to the law, including allowing those under age twenty-one to drink at home, in their parents' presence, or in any private residence. This was allowed, in part, so that parents who choose to do so can teach their children responsible alcohol consumption in the privacy of their home. The act said nothing about states adopting laws making it illegal to provide or sell alcohol to those under age twenty-one, hosting alcohol parties for those under twenty-one, or even using a fake ID to purchase alcohol. So the states had considerable flexibility and could allow for many exceptions. In addition to the possession and purchase laws required by the federal act, fourteen additional laws have been adopted by some states. These include laws making it illegal to consume alcohol unless you are twenty-one, using a fake ID to purchase alcohol, or furnishing alcohol to those under twenty-one; and establishing minimum ages of twenty-one for selling and serving alcohol.[3]

Critics of the National Minimum Drinking Age Act advance many different arguments for its repeal. Here I focus on four: (1) Europeans let their kids drink from an early age, yet they do not have any more alcohol-related problems than we do; (2) anyone old enough to be drafted into the military is old enough to drink; (3) young people are drinking anyway, so we should teach them to drink responsibly; and (4) the drinking age should be regulated by the states, not the federal government. Each of these arguments is fundamentally flawed.

THE DRINKING AGE IN EUROPEAN COUNTRIES

The drinking age of twenty-one in the United States is one of the highest in the world. In Europe, for example, the MLDAs range from fourteen in Switzerland to sixteen in France and Italy to eighteen in Ireland. European countries are often held up as examples of where liberal drinking age laws and attitudes foster responsible styles of drinking by young people. It is often asserted that alcohol is more integrated into European culture and that young people in these countries learn to drink at earlier ages within the context of the family. As a result, it is said that young Europeans learn to drink more responsibly than do young Americans. The evidence suggests that this is not the case.

Intoxication is a strong measure of problematic drinking, and is associated with a wide variety of personal and social problems. If socialization into drinking was related to more responsible drinking, young Europeans would presumably have lower rates of intoxication. Figure 2-1 displays the thirty-day prevalence rates for self-reported intoxication for European and American adolescents aged fifteen to sixteen. In the 2003 Monitoring the Future (MTF) survey, U.S. adolescents show a moderate rate of intoxication (18 percent) compared with their European peers, and one that is substantially lower than in most other countries. According to the European School Survey Project on Alcohol and Other Drugs (ESPAD), only in Turkey and Cyprus are the intoxication rates of fifteen- to sixteen-year-olds substantially lower than in the United States.

Concern with these high rates of adolescent intoxication has prompted European nations to initiate a debate about the most appropriate age for legal access and to look to the United States' MLDA of twenty-one as a possible model. What Europeans and others find when they examine MLDA-21 laws is that they help to keep hazardous consumption of alcohol down, save lives, reduce injuries of all types, and decrease other alcohol-related problems.

Figure 2-1

Prevalence of Intoxication in the Past Thirty Days, United States and Europe

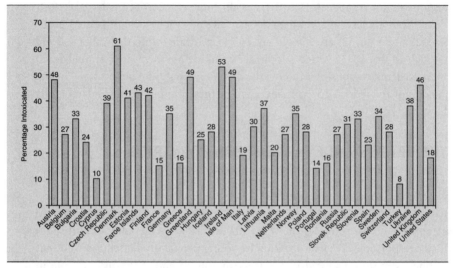

Sources: 2003 European School Survey Project on Alcohol and Other Drugs (ESPAD) survey and 2003 Monitoring the Future survey.

AGES OF INITIATION

"If I'm old enough to go to war, I should be old enough to drink," is another oft-heard argument for lowering the drinking age. In truth, however, many rights have different ages of initiation. In most states, a person can obtain a hunting license at age twelve and drive at age sixteen. Other rights we regulate by age include the sale and use of tobacco, the right to gamble in casinos and buy lottery tickets, and legal consent for sexual intercourse and marriage. Vendors, such as car rental facilities and hotels, also have set a minimum age for a person to use their services—twenty-five years old to rent a car and twenty-one years old to rent a hotel room. The minimum age for initiation is based on the specific behaviors involved and takes into account the dangers and benefits of that behavior at a given age. The military recruits eighteen-year-olds fresh out of high school because they are physically fit and highly trainable. This does not mean they are ready to drink.

Alcohol affects young people differently than adults. A teenager may look like an adult and even be more physically fit, but the teenager's body is still developing. According to the American Medical Association it actually takes less alcohol for a teenager to get drunk than it does for an adult in his or her twenties. A normal adult's liver can safely process an estimated one ounce of 80 proof alcohol per hour, but a teenager's liver can only process half that amount—about one-fourth of a "light" beer.

The MLDA-21 law takes into account that underage drinking is related to numerous health problems, including injuries and death resulting from alcohol poisoning, car crashes, suicide, homicide, assaults, drowning, and recreational mishaps. In fact, the leading cause of death among teens is car crashes, and alcohol is involved in close to one-third of these fatalities. In 2006, 31 percent of drivers between the ages of fifteen and twenty who were killed in motor vehicle crashes had been drinking. Twenty-five percent had a BAC of 0.08 g/dl or higher and another 6 percent had a BAC of 0.01 to 0.07 g/dl. These percentages, however, were much higher during the 1970s and 1980s, when many states had lower drinking ages.

There is mounting evidence that repeated exposure to alcohol during adolescence leads to long-lasting deficits in cognitive abilities, including learning and memory in humans. Susan Tapert and Sandra Brown, alcohol researchers at the University of California, San Diego, have conducted a series of studies examining the effects of alcohol use on neuropsychological functioning in adolescents and young adults. In one study of subjects aged thirteen to nineteen recruited from treatment programs, it was observed that a return to drinking after the program ended led to further decline in cognitive abilities—particularly in tests of attention—over the next four years. Early onset of drinking by youth has also been shown to significantly increase the risk of future alcohol-related problems, such as addiction, getting into fights, and automobile crashes.

TEACHING RESPONSIBLE DRINKING

Some argue that the MLDA-21 law is obsolete and is actually exacerbating high-risk, hazardous drinking in clandestine locations. They say that if the drinking age was lowered, youths would learn to drink responsibly because they will get an idea of their tolerance by learning to drink under supervision at bars or on campus, rather than at uncontrolled private parties away from school.

The problem with this argument is that no evidence exists to indicate that young people learn to drink responsibly when they are able to consume alcohol legally at a younger age. Countries with lower drinking ages suffer from alcohol-related problems as great or greater than those in the United States. Responsible consumption comes with maturity, and maturity largely comes only as certain protective mechanisms, such as age, marriage, and employment, begin to take hold.

Supervision does not necessarily lead to responsibility. Many bars encourage irresponsible drinking by deeply discounting drinks and by heavily promoting specials, such as happy hours, two-for-ones, and bar crawls. Many bars also serve obviously intoxicated patrons. On college campuses, fraternity and sorority members drink more frequently than their peers and are more likely to accept high levels of alcohol consumption as normal.

Some have suggested issuing special licenses to eighteen- to twenty-year-olds that allow them to drink alcohol if they complete an alcohol education course. This sounds like a good idea. However, there is no evidence that lowering the drinking age to eighteen for those who complete an education program will reduce the problem. In fact, there is strong evidence to the contrary. Take driver's education programs in the high schools as an example. They were designed to teach young drivers about the dangers of driving and give them the skills and knowledge to drive responsibly. Yet a recent study finds "little support for the hypothesis that formal driver education is an effective safety measure." Although "driver education does teach safety skills students are not motivated to use them"; in addition, "driver education fosters overconfidence."[4] Studies sponsored by NHTSA have shown that the crash rates of young drivers who completed driver education courses were no different from crash rates of young drivers who did not. Based on this experience, it does not seem likely that a forty-hour alcohol education program would work to reduce underage drinking problems.

THE FEDERALISM ARGUMENT

A final argument advanced by critics of the National Minimum Drinking Age Act is that the drinking age is a matter best left to the states. The trouble with this argument is that providing for the public safety is a primary responsibility of government at all levels, including the federal government. Moreover, surveys show that 80 percent of the public supports setting the drinking age of twenty-one and that there is little or no variation by state in these public attitudes.

Despite the strong public support for MLDA-21, it is likely that if Congress had not adopted twenty-one as the national drinking age MLDAs would still vary considerably from state to state.

If the federal law is repealed, there will again be state variability in the drinking age. Highways cross state borders and most are built with federal funds, so it is very much the federal government's business to ensure that we do not return to the "blood borders" for young people that were created by different drinking ages in different states.

The federal government has a special obligation to protect young people. If the minimum drinking age is lowered to eighteen, the result will be greater availability of alcohol not only to eighteen- to twenty-year-olds but also to those younger than eighteen. Studies have shown that lowering the drinking age to eighteen also increases alcohol-related crashes for fifteen- to seventeen-year-olds. The earlier young people start to drink, the greater the odds that they will be injured while under the influence, have a motor vehicle crash after drinking, or get into a fight. Youths who start drinking at age eighteen are twice as likely to get drunk as those who start at age twenty-one. Youths who start drinking at age eighteen also have a greater chance of becoming alcohol dependent.

The federal government should act when it can appreciably improve the health and safety of its citizens. By creating an incentive for states to adopt MLDA-21 laws, the federal government has clearly done that. MLDA-21 laws save approximately nine hundred lives each year in reductions in traffic fatalities involving young drivers. Medical research shows that excessive drinking by youths aged twenty and younger may cause brain damage as well as reduce brain function. Early onset of drinking before age twenty-one increases the risk for future alcohol abuse, automobile crashes, and assaults, among other alcohol-related problems.

Congress enacted the National Minimum Drinking Age Act to protect the health and safety of the public. The experiences of other countries that have tried lowering the drinking age show that the federal government's decision was a wise one. In 1999 New Zealand lowered its drinking age from twenty to eighteen. The result, according to a recent study, was a dramatic increase in automobile crashes. The rate of traffic crashes and injuries to eighteen- and nineteen-year-old males increased 12 percent and increased 14 percent for males aged fifteen to seventeen. For females, the effect was even greater—rates increased 51 percent for eighteen- to nineteen-year-olds and 24 percent for fifteen- to seventeen-year-olds.[5]

When the lives and well-being of so many young people are at stake it is appropriate for the federal government to step in and protect the public. States, it is worth underscoring one final time, are still free to set their drinking age lower than age twenty-one so long as they are willing to accept the increase in youthful deaths and give up federal highway monies. The federal government is not directly coercing any state to adopt twenty-one as the drinking age. The National Minimum Drinking Age Act has been a balanced, effective, and popular tool in helping to combat the many problems associated with youthful drinking. Repealing it would be a grave mistake.

RESOLVED, the United States should adopt a national initiative and referendum

PRO: Todd Donovan

CON: Richard J. Ellis

The question of which Americans are allowed to vote is an important one. So is the question of what Americans get to decide with their votes. The answer to both questions has changed a great deal over time, and almost always in the direction of greater democracy.

The Constitution originally left it entirely to the states to decide matters of voter eligibility. Their typical decision during the founding period was to confine the franchise—that is, the right to vote—to white male property owners who were at least twenty-one years old. During the 1820s and 1830s—often called the era of Jacksonian democracy—states dropped the property qualification, thereby bringing white working men into the electorate. In 1870, right after the Civil War, the Fifteenth Amendment forbade states from denying African Americans the right to vote, although many southern states found ways to keep blacks from exercising this right until a very tough enforcement bill, the Voting Rights Act, was enacted nearly a century later, in 1965. The Nineteenth Amendment extended voting rights to women in 1920, and the Twenty-sixth Amendment did the same for eighteen-year-olds in 1971. Many states still bar mentally ill people and felons from voting, but apart from these significant exceptions, the franchise belongs to every American citizen eighteen years and older.

The historic spread of the franchise across boundaries of class, race, gender, and age is one measure of how America has grown more democratic over the years. Another is the steadily lengthening list of the matters that Americans can decide with their votes. From the beginning, voters elected the House of Representatives, but not until the Seventeenth Amendment was added to the Constitution in 1913 were they empowered to elect senators. (Until then, senators were elected by the state legislatures.) The president is still chosen by the electoral college, and occasionally a candidate with fewer popular votes than his opponent wins a majority of electoral votes and becomes president, as George W. Bush did in 2000. The Constitution even leaves it to each state to decide whether its voters get to choose the state's electors, although no state since South Carolina in 1860 has done things differently. Starting in the early twentieth century—the Progressive era—voters not only have been able to elect officials in general elections but also, increasingly, to choose most of the candidates for those elections in party primaries.

In addition to creating primary elections, another reform of the Progressive era was to allow a state's voters to vote on proposed laws or constitutional amendments through initiatives and referendums. Here's the difference between the two: an initiative is placed on the ballot by citizen petition, and a referendum is placed on the ballot by the state legislature. What initiatives and referendums have in common is that once they are on the ballot, the voters decide whether or not they become law.

Referendums are much more common than initiatives, both around the world and in the United States. Several democratic nations employ national referenda, but only Switzerland allows national initiatives—and even there the Swiss legislature can weigh in before an initiative actually goes on the ballot. All fifty American states allow the legislature to place a referendum on the ballot, and forty-nine of them (all but Delaware) require that amendments to the state constitution be approved by referendum. Only twenty-four states, however—the vast majority of them west of the Mississippi River—allow initiatives. In some of these states, notably California (where initiatives are called "propositions") and Oregon, the rules for qualifying an initiative on the ballot are lenient, and so these states vote on lots of initiatives. In other states the rules are so restrictive that initiatives hardly ever make the ballot.

At the national level, the United States allows neither referendums nor initiatives. Should it? The resolution that forms the basis of this debate proposes that it should. American national democracy properly values both majority rule and minority rights, argues Todd Donovan in support of the resolution, but in practice minorities—especially those representing wealthy economic interests—have too many advantages. Reforming the system to allow national initiatives and referenda would allow the majority to rebalance the scales. Richard J. Ellis, writing in opposition, sees things differently. In states where initiatives are used frequently, he argues, the record shows that wealthy economic interests are among those best positioned to finance expensive initiative campaigns in their own behalf. Another issue on which Donovan and Ellis disagree is the effect that allowing national referendums and initiatives would have on Congress. Would Congress be hamstrung by the legislative end runs that ballot measures represent, or would it clean up its act so that ballot measures would become less necessary?

PRO: Todd Donovan

A representative legislature is the core of a democratic system, and the initiative and referendum are tools that make a legislature both more responsive and more responsible. The initiative process allows citizens to draft laws and petition to have the public vote on the proposed law. The referendum process allows voters to decide with their ballots the fate of laws proposed by a government. Many modern democracies use referendums to resolve major political disputes, and initiatives are common in Switzerland and several American states.[1]

At times, governments find themselves in positions where the decisions they face are of such consequence that relying on regular representative institutions may be inadequate. Consider these questions: Should Ireland, a nation dominated by a Roman Catholic Church steadfastly opposed to divorce, eliminate its constitutional ban on divorce? Should Canada extend special constitutional status to the French-speaking Province of Quebec? Should Denmark approve a European constitution that many Danes view as a threat to their national sovereignty? Should the U.S. Constitution be amended to provide equal rights for women? In all but the last case, these questions were answered by a direct public vote.

Representative institutions are not always in a position to resolve such controversies. A government may hold a solid majority in parliament, or in the case of the United States, one party might control the White House and Congress. Majority control may give a government the ability to implement major political changes. That is different, however, from having the ability to accomplish change that has widespread legitimacy.

Consider again the European Union (EU). Like the Danish government, the French government put the European constitution to a popular vote in May 2005. President Jacques Chirac could have had the French parliament ratify the constitution. That is what governments in Italy, Germany, and many other EU nations did. Chirac, however, had promised a referendum. Accepting the EU constitution would mean greater primacy of EU law over French law in areas such as labor and human rights. French voters rejected the proposed change, slowing the long process of ratification. If Chirac and the French parliament simply adopted the change without popular support, they may have strengthened the hand of EU skeptics by appearing to ignore the public mood.

Public votes on such matters need not be vetoes. Seventy-six percent of Spanish voters said "yes" to the EU in an advisory vote in February 2005. This set the stage for broad-based consensus when Spanish legislators met two months later to approve the constitution. Irish voters approved lifting their country's ban on divorce in 1995. The vote was close, but contrary to opponents' predictions, the floodgates to divorce did not open, and the once-controversial matter seems to have been resolved.[2]

THE WEAK ROLE OF POPULAR MAJORITIES IN THE UNITED STATES

Democracies require a means for giving voice to popular majorities, while protecting minority rights. The United States places a much greater emphasis on the latter than the former. Once every four years, the nation elects a president. Other than that, there are no other opportunities for the nation to express its collective opinion.

In contrast, the U.S. Constitution has many mechanisms to ensure that the interests of well-funded political minorities are protected, including federalism, separation of powers, a bicameral legislature, the electoral college, checks and balances, an appointed Supreme Court, and staggered elections. Senate tradition also includes the filibuster and other tools that give political minorities tremendous power to block policy change that might have majority support. By design, the system is rife with veto points. The argument for a national initiative and referendum is ultimately an argument for countering some of the power of these veto wielders by increasing the influence of popular majorities.

NEED FOR A NATIONAL INITIATIVE AND REFERENDUM PROCESS

The United States lacks any mechanism for the expression of public sentiment on matters of policy. Even presidential elections have only indirect effects on public policy.[3] As a result, controversial questions about civil rights for racial minorities, equal rights for women, and abortion policy lingered unresolved for decades. Policy changes that had support of a national majority were blocked for many years by a political system that granted a veto power to conservative southern states, most notably in the case of civil rights for African Americans. National support for civil rights legislation increased after World War II, in part due to President Harry Truman's postwar desegregation of the U.S. Army, and in 1954, 58 percent of Americans (80 percent outside the South) approved of the Supreme Court's school desegregation decision in *Brown v. Board of Education*.[4] Yet most civil rights legislation was blocked in

Congress until 1964 by racist southern Democrats who chaired key Senate committees.[5] A national referendum could have served as an end-run around these powerful committee chairmen.

The constitutional amendment process also inflated the influence of southern opposition to equal rights for women. The Equal Rights Amendment was approved by huge majorities in Congress in the 1970s: 354–24 in the House and 81–7 in the Senate. Thirty-five state legislatures (of the thirty-eight required for ratification) approved the amendment, but North Carolina's Democratic senator, Sam Ervin, attached a requirement that the ratification process conclude in seven years. No southern states ratified, and the proposal died. Had the ERA been put to a national public vote, it almost certainly would have been approved.

To this day, political controversy about abortion continues to affect American politics, just as divorce did in Ireland prior to 1995. Yet in the United States, the courts, rather than the people, have been forced to deal with abortion policy.[6] Decades of legal wrangling have failed to resolve the controversy. This is not for the lack of a public consensus, a consensus that had begun to take shape even before the Court's 1973 *Roe v. Wade* decision created a constitutional right to abortion. Since 1973 Court majorities have pulled back from the *Roe* decision,[7] but a majority of Americans continue to support access to abortion in the first trimester of a pregnancy.[8] Opponents of legal abortion have been able to keep the controversy alive by attacking the "judicial activism" of the Court. A national referendum on abortion would disarm the extremists and provide the nation a policy with broad public support and legitimacy.

WHO INFLUENCES CONGRESS: VOTERS OR WEALTHY INTERESTS?

Decision making in Congress is decentralized among committees and subcommittees that focus on narrow, specialized areas of policy. Corporations, unions, and interest groups influence legislation by lobbying and by financing the re-election campaigns of members of Congress who have jurisdiction over the issues that the groups are concerned about. Businesses and interest groups employed over 15,000 lobbyists and spent $3.2 billion lobbying the federal government in 2008. They spent another $400 million to influence congressional elections.[9] Most of these groups represent businesses and professions trying to increase their profits.[10] Some members of Congress are explicit about expecting contributions from business interests who are seeking earmarks and other favors.[11] Given the power that a single subcommittee—or even a single senator—may have over policy, these expenditures are often a wise investment.

The product of these arrangements are issue networks, or "iron triangles," consisting of interest groups, congressional committees, and regulatory agencies that amplify the influence of wealth in Washington while diluting the influence of the general public. Representation would be improved by a process that grants groups outside of these iron triangles the ability to affect congressional agendas. In many states, and in Switzerland, the initiative process allows citizens to propose a public vote on a statute if they collect enough signatures to qualify.

PROTECTING MINORITIES?

One valid critique of the initiative process is that it threatens minority interests. There are numerous examples of state initiatives targeting racial, ethnic, and sexual orientation minorities.[12] But any measure approved by voters would be subject to review by an independent, unelected judiciary. At the state level, courts have been aggressive in rejecting voter-approved initiatives that violate civil rights and liberties.[13]

With this safeguard already in place, the role of minorities in politics can be considered from a different perspective. As noted earlier, the American political system grants substantial power to influential minorities by giving well-funded interest groups the ability to block popular policies and to advance unpopular policies. In Congress, the interests of only a few people often prevail. An influential theory of politics, the logic of collective action, predicts that small, well-funded economic interests are much more likely to have full-time lobbyists than groups representing the general public.[14] Banks, telecommunications companies, pharmaceutical firms, dairy farmers, defense contractors, and many other businesses make billions of dollars by lobbying for tax breaks, subsidies, earmarks,[15] protections against risk, and bailouts. Taxpayers and consumers pick up the tab in the form of higher taxes, higher prices for cell phone service, higher credit card fees, higher prices for dairy products, and so on.

These facts are relevant to another critique of the initiative process—that it will be dominated by wealthy interests at the expense of the "grass roots."[16] But consider money and Congress. Interest groups give money to members of Congress to encourage them to do things that serve a group's narrow self-interest. This leads to perceptions of congressional corruption, if not actual corruption, that the U.S. Supreme Court says justifies regulating contributions to members of Congress. Spending on initiative campaigns, in contrast, involves attempts to win the support of a majority of voters[17]—and money spent advancing initiatives is no sure key to victory for wealthy interests.[18]

As examples, in 1988 Californians rejected well-funded industry proposals for regulating car insurance but supported a rival proposal written by consumer activists,[19] and in 2006 Arizonans approved a minimum wage increase opposed by wealthy interests while rejecting a well-funded tobacco industry proposal to open restaurants to smoking.

In contrast, consider the relationship between money and policy in Congress. Wealthy interests have been successful spending heavily on lobbying to secure approval of unpopular bankruptcy laws, "free" trade laws, and deregulations of media ownership. It is difficult to imagine a scenario where they could have spent money to convince voters to adopt such laws. Moreover, a single U.S. senator has power to advance laws that could never secure a majority vote by attaching a "rider" to bills that assist their campaign donors; riders are attached to important bills that the senators know a president will have to sign. For instance, Republican senators used riders to advance a host of anti-environmental measures after accepting over $800,000 in contributions from companies that would benefit from the riders.[20] The House Appropriations Committee is known as the "favor factory" because it allows members a lucrative method of raising campaign money and setting policy by earmarking millions of dollars to favored constituents and supporters. Many relatives of members of Congress earn large salaries lobbying them for earmarks.[21]

An initiative process would give voters the opportunity to promote laws that nullify such expenditures. It would also give people who oppose such behavior the tools to promote congressional reforms by targeting lobbying and earmarks. This, in turn, could help restore public confidence in Congress.

STRENGTHENING CONGRESS WITH DIRECT DEMOCRACY

Another concern about direct democracy is that it may undermine the role of representative institutions.[22] It is difficult to imagine what is left to undermine about Congress, but it is conceivable that the initiative and referendum would actually improve how Congress functions as a representative body.

Congress has lost the ability to effectively check the president.[23] It has delegated much authority over policy to executive agencies staffed by personnel who worked (or will work) in the industries they regulate.[24] It has delegated much of its budgeting and war-making authority to the president.[25] The modern Congress is regularly rocked by scandals, routinely characterized by gridlock, and often seen as irrelevant. These factors undermine its standing with the public. Large majorities of Americans believe that government is run for "a few big interests," rather than for the benefit of "all the people."[26] Most

Americans disapprove of how Congress does its job, regardless of which party is in power. These opinions highlight an enduring crisis of our representative government.

The modern Congress, with its maze of iron triangles, allows incumbents to do a masterful job serving constituents but a poor job of acting collectively in ways that would serve the country. Incumbents in safe seats raise huge sums of money and scare off potential election challengers.[27] These incumbent advantages diminish the responsiveness of Congress to voter preferences.[28] In addition, congressional elections rarely produce representation for moderates. For these reasons, Congress may not be the optimal institution for reflecting the preferences of the mass public.[29] Nor is it well suited for advancing innovative policies, particularly if Congress and the White House are controlled by different political parties.

As Progressive-era advocates of direct democracy argued a century ago, the initiative and referendum should make representatives both more responsive and more responsible. Initiatives send representatives signals about the scope and intensity of public concerns. Regardless of whether measures qualify or pass, the process may push legislators to adopt policies that are closer to what the public wants.[30] It serves as a sort of "gun behind the door" that organized groups can use to prompt Congress into responding to national concerns. If designed like the Swiss indirect initiative system, the process might reinvigorate Congress by encouraging the representatives to craft responses to issues that the public is concerned about. Under the Swiss model, initiative proposals that qualify for a public vote are first considered by the legislature. The legislature may adopt the proposal, modify the proposal in consultation with proponents, or suggest an alternative proposal and let voters decide between their idea and the original proposal. Absent such pressure, legislators from safe, one-party districts may have little pressure to heed national opinion.

Legislators also have incentives to avoid controversial decisions. For example, while popular opinion has shifted away from the 1980s "war on drugs," many in Congress and the state legislatures have not. Initiative proposals on questions such as drug policy and medical use of marijuana, not legislatures, have spurred policy innovation in this area. Voters in several states have approved measures to allow the medical use of marijuana, and (in Utah) to ease rules that allow government to seize any property associated with drug crimes. By forcing the legislature to deal with issues that the people care about instead of those that wealthy campaign contributors care about, a national initiative process could push the legislature to do a better job of representing the interests of the people rather than just those of a favored few.

STRENGTHENING POLITICAL PARTIES WITH DIRECT DEMOCRACY

A national initiative process would likely be difficult to use. Even a relatively modest signature standard for qualifying a statutory initiative could require that a proponent collect over six million signatures.[31] A rule that required a distribution of signatures across a certain number of states would make the task of qualifying even more daunting. Well-heeled economic interests that have success lobbying Congress may find it much more difficult to convince six million Americans to put their schemes on the ballot. Think of it this way: the mining industry might be able to convince a couple of senators who need campaign funds that open-pit cyanide gold mines are a great idea. The industry would have a much tougher time convincing voters to sign a petition to put such a question on the ballot.

Certain broad-based organizations might have the resources to qualify a national initiative. These include mass-membership interest groups such as AARP, NRA, NOW, and the Sierra Club, as well as unions and political parties. Political parties are perhaps in the best position to take advantage of a national initiative process. Petitioning would require organized efforts in dozens of states. Unlike narrow interest groups, parties have grassroots organizations in every state, and are one of the only vehicles that exist for mobilizing campaign workers.

In many states, partisan elected officials currently work with initiative proponents to advance new policies.[32] Divided partisan control of government, and veto players in the legislature, often prevent the adoption of popular policies. The initiative process has allowed partisan elected officials who supported popular policies to avoid legislative roadblocks and work outside of the system. In various states, parties have worked with unions and used the initiative process to advance several measures that had been held back by legislative logjams, including teacher pay raises, K–12 class size reduction, and minimum wage increases.

CONCLUSION

Initiatives would prompt Congress to be more responsive to the public rather than to narrow economic interests. If used to promote reforms of lobbying and earmarks, initiatives could also cause Congress to be more responsible. An indirect initiative process would mean congressional majorities would always have some say about proposals that go before voters. As for national referendums, in order to increase the influence of the legislative branch of government, the decision to have a referendum should rest with a majority in Congress, not the president. Majorities in each chamber should be required to authorize a statutory referendum, and supermajorities of each house should be required to propose any constitutional referendum. Empowering Congress with the initiative and referendum would give it an additional tool for making policy, and restore some balance to relations between the two branches. With these new tools, Congress could also resume its place as the primary institution in American politics.

CON: Richard J. Ellis

If democracy is good, then surely more democracy is better. And if government for the people is our aim, then surely it makes sense to establish or at least experiment with government that is truly of the people and by the people. Why should we settle for representative democracy if we can have direct democracy, real democracy, pure democracy? Sure, the framers of the U.S. Constitution, most of whom were wealthy and well-educated elitists, feared the people, but why should we allow their fears to dictate our politics? The framers wanted the Constitution to erect a barrier against the envious and short-sighted passions of the poor, the debtors, and the dispossessed. But after 220-plus years of experience with democracy, isn't it time we recognize how misplaced their fears were? The masses, after all, clamor for tax cuts more than they do soaking the rich. And the elites who run the national government seem to be notable less for their wisdom and foresight than for their hyper-responsiveness to special interests and campaign contributors. So why not give the initiative and referendum process a try at the national level? What do we have to lose?

The answer is plenty, though much depends on the precise form that the process takes, particularly the requirements proponents must satisfy in order to qualify a measure for the ballot. Twenty-four states have an initiative process, but usage of that process varies dramatically. Voters in Oregon and California, where qualifying an initiative for the ballot is relatively easy,[1] routinely see between five and ten initiatives on each ballot, and occasionally more; in 2000, for instance, eighteen initiatives qualified for the ballot in Oregon. However, voters in initiatives states where qualification is more burdensome rarely see more than one or two initiatives in an election, and many see none at all.

Consider the case of Mississippi, the last state to add an initiative process. The Magnolia State does not permit statutory initiatives or popular referenda. So although voters can change the constitution through the initiative process, they cannot use it to make laws, nor can they repeal laws passed by the state legislature. Mississippi's signature threshold is very high—the state requires initiative petitioners to gather signatures equaling 12 percent of the number of votes in the last gubernatorial election—but even more restrictive is the requirement that one-fifth of the signatures must come from each of the state's five congressional districts. In addition, Mississippi permits the legislature to place an alternative measure on the same ballot, thereby giving the voters a choice between two amendments. Moreover, every initiative that has revenue implications must identify the amount and source of revenue required to implement it, and if the initiative reduces revenues or reallocates funding, it must specify which programs will be affected. Finally, Mississippi prohibits initiatives that would modify the initiative process or that would alter either the state's bill of rights or its constitutional right-to-work guarantee. Since adopting the initiative process in 1992, the citizens of Mississippi have voted on only two initiatives—both of them term limit measures that failed.

The consequences of a national initiative process, in short, depend crucially on the details. If the signature requirement is high and there is a geographic distribution requirement that requires a certain percentage of the signatures to be collected from a large number of states, then the effect on the nation's politics is likely to be minimal. Conversely, if the signature requirements are low and there is no geographic distribution requirement, then the effects could be revolutionary. When proponents of a national initiative and referendum go beyond ringing declarations about the value of "real democracy" or stinging indictments of the corruptions of "repocracy" (rule by representatives) and finally get down to filling in the crucial details, they usually come down on the side of low signature thresholds. A well-publicized constitutional amendment introduced in 1977 by Sens. James Abourezk and Mark Hatfield, for instance, required the signatures of only 3 percent of voters gathered from at least ten states. A signature threshold that low virtually guarantees a very large number of initiatives on the ballot.

Proponents of a national initiative often try to blunt criticisms by pointing to the Swiss experience with direct democracy. In a 1981 book, for instance, Jack Kemp, then a New York congressman and later a presidential candidate, cabinet secretary, and vice-presidential nominee, lauded Switzerland as the only country in the world "that has more democracy than the United States." In Kemp's view, the existence of a national initiative and referendum process explained why Switzerland was also the one nation that was "more peaceful and prosperous than the United States."[2]

Yet few of the people who tout the virtues of direct democracy in Switzerland seem to know much about how the Swiss system actually works. Nor do they recognize how radically different it is from the system that advocates of a national initiative process typically have in mind. To begin with, at the federal level the Swiss initiative power—as in Mississippi—is limited to constitutional amendments; no statutory changes can be made by initiative. Moreover, initiatives at both the federal and cantonal level in Switzerland are indirect—that is, they must first be presented to the legislative assembly. Although the federal assembly cannot stop an initiative from reaching the ballot, the legislature is allowed four years to deliberate upon the measure before sending it to the people. If the federal assembly approves an initiative it is presented to the voters with the legislature's stamp of approval, but this rarely happens. Between 1891 and 1991 only three of the approximately one hundred initiatives that reached the voters carried the legislature's official blessing. The Swiss assembly is not required to take a position on an initiative measure, but it almost invariably does. There were only two initiatives during this hundred-year period on which the assembly failed to take an official position. When sending an initiative to the voters, the Swiss assembly will typically include an explanation of why it believes the initiative should be rejected. The legislature also has the option of placing its own counterproposal on the ballot along with the citizen initiative (in which case the legislature is allowed five rather than four years to take action). The Swiss assembly has offered the voters a counterproposal about one-quarter of the time, and voters have adopted the counterproposal more often than not. In only two cases did voters approve the citizen initiative and reject the legislative counterproposal.[3]

When the Swiss electorate is offered a legislative counterproposal together with a citizen initiative, they are asked to indicate which they prefer if both measures gain a majority of votes. As a result, a citizen initiative can receive a majority, even a large majority, and still not be enacted if more citizens indicate a preference for the legislative alternative. A more blatant constraint on majority rule is the Swiss requirement that a federal initiative (or the legislative counterproposal) must be approved not only by a majority of those voting but also by a majority of cantons. Since the population of Swiss cantons varies enormously (five of the twenty-six cantons contain well over half of Switzerland's population, and the largest canton, Zurich, has more than twice as many people as the ten least-populous cantons combined) an initiative can readily achieve a majority of the votes and yet fall short of a majority of the cantons. Not surprisingly, the percentage of federal initiatives that are successful is exceedingly small. Of the approximately one hundred citizen initiatives voted on by the Swiss people between 1891 and 1991, only ten were successful.

The success rate is even lower when one considers the large number of initiatives in Switzerland that are submitted to the federal assembly with the required number of signatures but then are withdrawn by the sponsors before the legislature submits the initiative to the people. In fact, almost as many qualified initiatives are withdrawn as reach the ballot. Reasons for withdrawing a measure are various, but probably the most common is that the assembly has promised or taken legislative action that satisfies the initiative's sponsors. In many of these instances the objective of the sponsors in presenting the initiative is more to prompt a legislative deal than it is to take the issue to the voters. The initiative in Switzerland is thus an integral part of the legislative process, and is often used as a spur to get a majority in the legislature to heed the concerns of minority groups that have previously been thwarted in the assembly. Unlike in the United States where the initiative process is typically a confrontational, zero-sum game, in Switzerland it is often employed to arrive at a consensus by facilitating legislative deliberative and compromise. In short, the Swiss initiative system, particularly at the federal level, is radically unlike the initiative system envisioned by advocates of a national initiative and referendum process. Instead, they have in mind the wide-open direct initiative process characteristic of high-use states like California, Oregon, and Colorado.

So what is wrong with bringing California's style of initiative politics to the national stage? Aren't initiative skeptics really, at heart, antidemocrats, fearful of the people? Only if one holds to a crude conception of democracy. The democratic ideal is not just to mirror public preferences, but to engage in reasoned debate about the public interest. The point of having selected individuals study, discuss, and debate public policy in a face-to-face forum is that they might reach a judgment that is different from the opinions or prejudices with which they began. Expert testimony might lead them to revise their beliefs, or the intense pleas of affected groups might unsettle their convictions. The rival interests of other constituencies need to be heard and considered, and compromises may need to be reached. Individual preferences are to be negotiated and not just aggregated. Grover Norquist, the longtime president of Americans for Tax Reform, says that the "one big difference between initiatives and elected representatives is that initiatives do not change their minds once you vote them in."[4] Maybe so, but why should we make inflexibility and imperviousness to reason a hallmark of democracy?

Of course, critics are right that the legislative process is often excruciatingly slow. Washington State's premier initiative activist, Tim Eyman, defends the initiative process as "a laxative to a constipated political process."[5] And, in small doses, perhaps there is something to this. But why should we equate more legislation with more democracy? The framers of the Constitution assumed that the political process worked best when decisions were made slowly, deliberately, and with great care. In emergencies rapid action would be necessary, but in the normal way of things speed would only empower the passions of the moment and lead to ill-considered plans. Haste was the enemy of rational dialogue and effective public policy. Enduring policies were to be built through the long, laborious process of building consensus among diverse groups of people. Legislative inaction, from this perspective, is not necessarily a sign of failure. Instead, the legislature's reluctance or inability to act may be a wise and necessary response to the clash of profoundly different interests and values. That is, governmental inaction often reflects the fact that the people are deeply divided about what they want.

Democracy, for proponents of a national initiative and referendum, is largely about counting votes. It is a very simple idea: whoever has the most votes wins, so long as the policy is not an unconstitutional infringement on the minority. No allowance is made for intensity of preference. Imagine three friends, two of whom wish to eat at McDonald's but don't feel strongly about where they eat, and one who wishes to go to Burger King because McDonald's makes him sick. Under the initiative process or most versions of electronic direct democracy, every preference is weighed equally. The majority rules, and so the three friends go to McDonald's, forcing the one friend either to go hungry or become physically ill. In the legislative process, however, intensity of preference matters. The two friends may possibly try to coerce the third into eating at McDonald's, but more likely they will come up with a compromise. Not feeling strongly about the matter, the two friends may defer to the third and eat at Burger King. Or they may decide to eat at Burger King one time, and McDonald's the next. Or they may look for a third option, perhaps Wendy's. Although Wendy's may be nobody's first choice, it has the advantage of not making the third friend ill, and the other two friends prefer it to Burger King. By accommodating intensity of preference rather than only counting votes, democratic deliberation can produce policies that are acceptable to minorities as well as majorities. In contrast, initiative elections promote policies that pay scant attention to the consent of the minority and thus encourage losers to take their grievances to the least democratically accountable branch of government, the courts.

Of course, legislatures do not always or even mostly operate in fact as they are supposed to in theory. Weighing intensity of preference may be the ideal, but the mobilization of resources often owes more to organization and money than it does to the intensity with which values and beliefs are held. The polarized partisanship among political elites often seems disconnected from the apolitical middle ground occupied by many American citizens. Amendments tacked onto legislation in the closing days of the legislative session receive nothing like the critical scrutiny envisioned by the framers of the Constitution. Disinterested policy expertise is often in short supply—particularly in states like Oregon, in which professional staff are at a minimum and the legislature meets only once every two years.

But legislatures, for all their failings, have the singular virtue of being capable of identifying, correcting, and learning from errors. Citizens are accustomed to viewing legislatures as fallible, imperfect instruments, and so neither citizens nor legislatures see anything wrong or unusual in changing and improving current laws. There is nothing sacred about the status quo. Competitive elections between political parties are expected to result in changes of public policy. A government policy enacted by the legislature is treated as the law of the land, not as the Godlike voice of the people.

The real problem with initiatives is not that they are more likely to produce poor public policy than are legislatures, though they may be, but rather that mistakes made by initiative are generally more difficult to correct. A successful initiative, unlike a legislative action, is widely assumed to be the authentic expression of the "voice of the people." Legislators or interest groups who dare to suggest amending or jettisoning a law enacted by initiative are vilified for violating the popular will, as if they were trying to alter one of the commandments brought down from the mountain by Moses rather than an imperfect government policy written by special interests. Even the modest attempt to have voters reconsider their decision brings howls of populist outrage.

Yet initiatives typically reveal more about the ideology and preoccupations of those who supply the initiatives than they do about the priorities and values of voters. Initiative sponsors, not voters, decide whether an issue will be a constitutional amendment or a statutory change. And it is the initiative sponsors who frame the issue and the choices in ways that importantly shape the answer. Voters may prefer a particular initiative to the status quo—yet, given a wider range of options, they may rank that initiative near the bottom. Take tax-cutting initiatives. In Oregon in 1996, voters were asked to vote upon Measure 47, which dramatically rolled back property taxes. Voters were offered the choice between a large rollback in taxes and no change in their taxes. They were not allowed to choose between a large and a more moderate rollback, or between the proposed measure and a system of rebates for low-income or fixed-income property owners. Nor was the alternative of differential tax rates for business and homeowners put to the voters. So while the vote on Measure 47 reflected a slim majority's preference for lower property taxes (52 percent supported the measure), the precise policies (the extent of the reduction and the restrictions on future increases, the limits on new bonds and replacement fees, and the requirement that property tax levies achieve a 50 percent turnout rate) that were enacted did not reflect the will of the voters so much as the will of the measure's author, Bill Sizemore.

The vote on an initiative, moreover, is often powerfully swayed by the wording of the ballot title and summary. As anyone familiar with polling knows, public opinion on many issues is extraordinarily sensitive to how questions are worded. Ask people whether they support spending for the "poor" and their responses are far more favorable than if they are asked about spending on "welfare." Question wording was central to the battle over Proposition 209, a 1996 initiative that banned state affirmative action programs in California. The sponsors were careful not to mention affirmative action; instead the initiative prohibited the state from "discriminating against, or granting preferential treatment to, any individual or group" on the basis of race or gender. Polls showed that overwhelming majorities supported this language, but support plummeted when respondents were asked about outlawing state affirmative action programs for women and minorities. Conscious of the vital difference that wording makes, Republican attorney general Dan Lungren, a strong critic of affirmative action programs, avoided any mention of affirmative action in the hundred-word title and summary of the initiative that appeared on the ballot. Opponents of Proposition 209 took the attorney general to court, and a superior court judge directed Lungren to rewrite the summary because omitting the words *affirmative action* misled voters. Upon appeal, a district court rejected the lower court's judgment. The title and summary, the court concluded, conveyed to the public "the general purpose" of the proposition. "We cannot fault the Attorney General," the court concluded, "for refraining from the use of such an amorphous, value-laden term" as affirmative action. The decision not to include the words *affirmative action* was a critical ingredient in the passage of Proposition 209.[6]

Moreover, passage of a measure reveals little or nothing about an issue's salience to voters. In 1996 affirmative action actually ranked near the bottom of the list of issues that most concerned Californians. Citizens expressed far greater concern about jobs, education, the environment, and taxes. In 2000 antitax initiatives dominated state ballots—appearing in Alaska, California, Colorado, Massachusetts, Oregon, South Dakota, and Washington—even though polls consistently showed that voters were far less concerned about reducing taxes than with improving the quality of government services. Candidates for office tend to be much more responsive to the issues that matter most to voters than are initiative advocates, for whom there is little or no incentive to select issues that are salient to voters. Candidates, unlike initiative activists, must seek out issues that are not only popular but that matter to ordinary voters.

When activists proclaim that the initiative process "belongs to the people," they obscure political reality behind a fog of populist platitudes. The initiative literally belongs to the few who write the measures, not to the many who vote. A national initiative would do little or nothing to empower the people; instead, it would simply provide political activists, politicians, and special interests another way to get what they want.

RESOLVED, broadcasters should be charged a spectrum fee to finance programming in the public interest

PRO: Norman J. Ornstein

CON: Adam D. Thierer

Many millions of trees have been felled, and untold billions of pixels mobilized, to convey to readers all the books and articles that have recently been written about politics and the mass media. The vast majority of commentary has been devoted to exploring (and as a rule deploring) the effects of television and, more recently, of the Internet and other contemporary forms of information-sharing technology on election campaigns, presidential leadership, public policy debates, and other subjects.

Students of political history know, however, that as important as television is, radio was the truly revolutionary technology. Until radio entered American homes in the 1920s and 1930s, political leaders and candidates could only be heard by audiences that were physically present. Even with microphones, that meant audiences of at most thousands at a time, all gathered in the same place. Radio allowed political figures to be heard by millions of people, not massed together inside an arena or outside in a field or plaza, but gathered in groups of three or four listening in their homes. Franklin D. Roosevelt pioneered the "fireside chat," artfully creating the illusion that the president had just dropped in from Washington to tell average American families what he was working on.

The rapid growth of radio created unprecedented challenges for the federal government. New stations clogged the airwaves, often operating so close to each other on the broadcast spectrum that none of them could be clearly heard. After making a first stab at federal regulation in 1927, Congress passed the Communications Act of 1934 and created the Federal Communications Commission (FCC). The FCC's job was to award spots on the dial to a limited number of stations. In return, the stations would have to "serve the public interest, convenience and necessity" by, for example, granting equal access to competing political candidates (the equal time rule) and providing balanced coverage of controversial public issues (the fairness doctrine).

Television developed just as rapidly and spread just as widely in the 1950s and 1960s as radio had in the previous generation. It also brought political leaders into American homes in the same way radio did, only on television they could be seen as well as heard. And, as with radio, the FCC assigned television stations places on the dial and, in return for this lucrative privilege, insisted that they "serve the public interest, convenience and necessity" by devoting some of their programming to public affairs in a politically balanced way.

The FCC has never abandoned the equal time rule, but in 1987 it repealed the fairness doctrine, arguing that the recent proliferation of FM radio stations and cable television channels meant that multiple perspectives would be aired without the federal government requiring it. In 1996 Congress passed the Telecommunications Act, which granted the television industry a host of additional privileges associated with converting from analog to digital broadcasting by 2009. But the 1934 law's "public interest, convenience and necessity" requirement remained on the books, and in 1997 President Bill Clinton appointed an advisory committee to explore ways to breathe new life into the standard.

The advisory committee, on which Norman J. Ornstein served as cochair, ended up making toothless recommendations in the hope of achieving unanimity. Now freed of that goal, Ornstein argues in this essay that Congress should drop the public interest requirement and instead charge each broadcaster an annual fee in the form of rent on its place on the spectrum. He proposes that the money from these fees be spent to help the Public Broadcasting System (PBS) fund a new "Public Square" channel devoted to public affairs, to provide matching funds to political candidates so they can purchase commercial time on radio and television stations, and to award grants to fund documentaries and children's programming. Adam D. Thierer opposes the imposition of such a fee. Television broadcasters are already beleaguered by stiff "competition for eyeballs" from cable, DVDs, on-line sites, and video games. Radio stations face similar "competition for our ears" from satellite and online radio and iPods. Besides, Thierer argues, cable news stations and Internet news sites are already meeting the demand for public square–style programming.

PRO: Norman J. Ornstein

The airwaves may be invisible but, like the vast expanse of land that made up the American frontier, they were public assets available for those who could occupy them when radio emerged as a new technological force about a century ago. But just as there were conflicts over who owned that frontier land, leading to a public lands policy, there were conflicts that developed early over the occupants of the public airwaves. Before 1927, the Commerce Department had authority over radio broadcasting, but it had little or no authority to block anybody from setting up a radio station and broadcasting on a particular place in the spectrum. That led to chaos, with overlapping channels and crossed signals. Radio broadcasters demanded some way of regulating and limiting access to each spot on the airwaves, both to eliminate interference and to permit the commercial expansion of broadcasting.

That led in turn to the Radio Act of 1927, which created the first serious regulatory regime for the airwaves in the United States. The 1927 act, viewing radio broadcasting as interstate commerce, created a regulatory regime under a commission, the five-member Federal Radio Commission, and gave it the authority to grant or deny licenses, assign frequencies, and oversee station operations. The commission was authorized to act in the "public convenience, interest or necessity."

The commission soon made it clear that broadcasters had to meet public interest standards if they were going to exploit the publicly owned airwaves. A set of guidelines issued in 1929 laid out the standards: a station was supposed to meet the "tastes, needs and desires of all substantial groups among the listening public . . . in some fair proportion, by a well-rounded program, in which entertainment, consisting of music of both classical and lighter grades, religion, education and instruction, important public events, discussions of public questions, weather, market reports, and news, and matters of interest to all members of the family, find a place."

Broadcasters wanted protection by the government—but, not surprisingly, did not want strings attached. They wanted no regulation of what they could air or who was allowed to buy airtime. Other groups, such as educators, religious groups, and labor, wanted to ensure public access to the publicly owned airwaves.

The debate over this set of tensions was not resolved by the 1927 act. Seven years later, Congress decided to step in again and both refine and expand the regulatory role. The Communications Act of 1934 replaced the Federal Radio Commission with a more robust Federal Communications Commission

(FCC). In a nod to broadcasters, the 1934 act banned "common carrier" regulation, which would have required broadcasters to allow anyone to buy airtime. It also required that broadcast licensees operate in "the public interest, convenience and necessity."

By this set of laws, broadcasters were placed in a different category than other media, such as newspapers or magazines. All had First Amendment rights, but broadcasters, unlike newspaper publishers, were granted scarce and valuable public resources by virtue of the limited number of broadcast licenses available. In return, the broadcast license holders had to act in the public's interest.

In the 1934 act, Congress did not define what it meant to act in the public interest beyond the vague phrase "public convenience, interest or necessity." The expectation was that the definition would evolve as stations went through the license renewal process every three years; at that time, alternate visions of how to operate a station in the public interest could compete for the license. But in practical terms, licenses rarely if ever were taken away from those who held them, and broadcasters even succeeded in increasing the license terms from three years to eight years. Thus, in the early years of the FCC, little was done to define public interest obligations or the content of broadcasting. In 1943 the Supreme Court gave the commission an impetus to do more; in *National Broadcasting Co. v. United States,* the Court underscored the broad regulatory powers of the FCC and held "that the public interest standard is the touchstone of FCC authority; . . . and that FCC license revocations and non-renewals do not violate the First Amendment rights of broadcasters."

Following this ruling, the FCC began to define what public interest obligations entailed. In 1946 the commission issued a policy statement known as "The Blue Book," which said that these obligations had four basic components: live local programs, public affairs programming, limits on excessive advertising, and "sustaining" programs (that is, high-quality network shows without sponsors), many designed for smaller audiences.

The Blue Book was widely lauded, but the FCC never ratified it. Nonetheless, the payola and quiz show scandals of the 1950s spurred the FCC into another attempt to issue more robust public interest standards. In 1960 the commission identified fourteen major elements that make up a public interest approach, including educational programs, public affairs programs, editorials by licensees, political broadcasts, news programs, weather, sports, service to minority groups, and entertainment programming. No rigid formulas or requirements were laid out in the report, only guidelines.

In the Reagan era, a new approach to public interest obligations by broadcasters turned to the marketplace and away from any significant government role. License renewals, presumably the major weapon in the FCC's arsenal to induce broadcasters to participate in public interest–oriented activities, became almost automatic. The fairness doctrine, long used by the FCC to ensure vigorous and lively debate on politics and public affairs, was abolished. At the same time, the National Association of Broadcaster's (NAB) voluntary code of conduct, which at least set out specific parameters for stations to meet public interest standards and had been updated as recently as 1977, was abolished in 1981 because of antitrust concerns over advertising collusion.

In 1996 Congress passed a sweeping and important law, the Telecommunications Act, which furthered deregulation of broadcasting and laid the groundwork for a transition from analog broadcasting to digital. At the behest of broadcasters, who engaged in an overwhelming lobbying campaign, Congress allowed television stations to use a huge swath of prime airwaves—what many observers called "beachfront quality spectrum"—for better than a decade at no cost, even as the stations kept their analog spectrum, to make that transition.

Digital television meant profound changes for television broadcasters and viewers alike. The quality of digital signals was dramatically better than the old analog ones. Digital broadcasting also meant that stations could compress signals and send out as many as six streams simultaneously in the same spectrum space as their single analog channel—meaning the possibility of six simultaneous programs on parallel channels, or data streaming at the same time as programs were airing.

In 1997 President Bill Clinton signed an executive order to create a presidential advisory committee on the public interest obligations of digital television broadcasters, to study the issues and report to Vice President Al Gore. There were several reasons to create such a panel, which came to be known as the Gore Commission. One was that the changes to be wrought by the digital revolution left many unanswered questions about public interest obligations. If a station went digital and decided to run six separate programs at a time, would only one stream be subject to public interest obligations, or all of them? If the total audience for the six channels was the same as it had been for one analog channel, would this be too onerous, increasing the burden on broadcasters six-fold? But if there were no obligations applied to any channels beyond the one digital equivalent of the single analog channel, would that mean that broadcasters had a loophole to get away with sharply reduced public interest activities, with five extra channels getting away with no public obligation even as the public was "lending" billions of dollars worth of public airspace to the broadcasters?

The issues were tricky, since no one had a clear sense of where technology was going, how fast it would get there, and when consumers would jump on the fast-moving vehicles. But there was also a broader reason for the Gore Commission. Public interest obligations had been enshrined in the law going back to the early stages of radio, but had never been enshrined in the reality of broadcasting. Whether it was quality local news and local programming or quality reporting on politics, elections, and public affairs, only a handful of broadcast stations and groups had really tried, much less succeeded, in meeting those standards. Even the peer pressure that came from a voluntary code of conduct had disappeared, and the threat of punishment for bad or mediocre behavior had disappeared along with it, with the virtual demise of the only real weapon in the federal regulatory arsenal, the forfeiture of the broadcast license.

By appointing seven prominent local and national broadcasters to the twenty-two-person Gore Commission, the administration made clear that it hoped to find some kind of consensus, one in which broadcasters and public interest advocates could agree on a new way to revitalize public interest standards. Clinton also communicated directly to the two cochairs (of whom I was one) that he wanted a new and better role for broadcasters in campaign discourse—a new standard of public interest obligations for politics and public affairs.

During the early stages of our deliberations, which went on for almost eighteen months and included a series of public hearings, we enjoyed a clear, cooperative spirit. Broadcasters were perhaps a bit cowed by the strong interest shown in the issue by the president—and by their fear that Congress would reconsider the 1996 act that had generously given them such a huge swath of valuable public airwaves.

The broadcasters' attitude changed markedly early in 1998 after FCC chair William Kennard speculated publicly that the FCC had the power, under the public interest standard, to require broadcasters to provide free time to political candidates. The comments provoked a negative reaction on Capitol Hill, with a wide range of lawmakers, some of them protecting congressional prerogatives, some protecting incumbency, and some protecting their broadcasting patrons, threatening serious retribution for Kennard's apostasy. From that point on, the fear that broadcasters had of political retribution for recalcitrance dissipated.

Most of the broadcasters on the commission continued to profess publicly a desire to cooperate with the rest of the panel. But the NAB showed no willingness to compromise. When the commission's broadcasters lamented the demise of the NAB's code of conduct, saying that it had worked well and obviated the need for heavy-handed government regulation, the commission got a legal opinion from the Justice Department that the antitrust concerns were not relevant if we redrafted the code without any elements on advertising.

Commission member Cass Sunstein, a nationally renowned legal scholar, volunteered to redraft the old code and make it relevant for digital broadcasting, something he did with enormous care and competence without changing the substance or intent of the code.

The NAB board then made clear that whatever the commission's broadcaster members had said, they had no interest in adopting a new code. Several of the broadcasters on the commission were embarrassed by the NAB board's action, but it did not leave the rest of us with much confidence that there would be any deep or broad effort to find solid common ground.

Nonetheless, we continued to work to reach some consensus. That meant diluting our recommendations to gain support from broadcasters without losing the support of most of our other members; specifically, it meant moving more toward voluntary commitments than iron-clad requirements. We did have broadcasters, notably James F. Goodmon of Capitol Broadcasting in North Carolina, who believed that there was a sacred obligation for broadcasters to act in the public interest, and who advocated a concrete list of minimum public interest requirements, which became one of the commission's recommendations. But many of the other recommendations were framed as calls for voluntary action.

And nearly all resulted in disappointment. The best example, other than the code of conduct, concerned political discourse. When it came to free TV time to expand political discourse, what we got from our broadcasters was, "We'll do our part if Congress will first do its part. If Congress will do something about the financing of campaigns then we will respond." Their point was reasonable; the first responsibility to make the campaign system work better was with Congress, not with broadcasters. But when Congress did its part by passing the Bipartisan Campaign Reform Act of 2002, the broadcasters responded with nothing.

The Gore Commission asked broadcasters for a couple of specific things. The most significant was remarkably modest. The commission proposed that broadcasters voluntarily devote five minutes to political discourse each evening, sometime between 5:30 p.m. and 11:30 p.m., in the thirty days before the election. In a nod to editorial independence, we said that each station should choose the races most relevant to their viewers. The five minutes could be done in one block or five one-minute segments spread out over the broadcast evening—that would be up to the individual broadcasters. The broadcasters got to decide whether they would have a minidebate between the candidates or give each of them a minute of time to talk to viewers.

As an experiment in the seriousness of broadcasters to act in the public interest without being coerced to do so, our proposal was an abject failure. Less than 1 percent of broadcasters around the country said they would take that modest step. And in practice, most of them fell significantly short of even that very modest standard.

Most members of the Gore Commission, particularly those from the non-broadcast side, accepted and embraced a consensus model, basically believing that by getting a consensus and buy-in from broadcasters, we could get productive, incremental change that would actually work. What we did not want was another report that was the equivalent of pounding the table and screaming that would make a lot of people feel good and get a lot of wonderful editorials from the *New York Times* and *Washington Post* but then would sit on a shelf.

It was a good idea that proved basically not to work, even though the commission report did achieve a consensus. Only one member at the end, A. H. Belo broadcasting executive Robert Decker, refused to sign the commission's modest recommendations.

In the aftermath of my experience with the Gore Commission, I have developed a different perspective on the best approach to making sure that the public airwaves satisfy public needs, through a different "bargain" with the broadcasters who benefit from the grant of this valuable public space. Of course, my perspective is shaped in part by the disappointing reaction of broadcasters to the Gore Commission's report and its recommendations—especially by their nearly universal failure to do even the smallest things voluntarily to meet their commitments and obligations. My perspective also reflects a belief that virtually all the public interest activities broadcasters now do comes not because of their belief that they are trustees of the airwaves, or because they fear regulatory repercussions if they fail to act, but because those activities fit their business models. Here is an example: When the Washington, D.C., NBC affiliate Channel 4 does Race for the Cure, a major effort to fund research into breast cancer, and does all kinds of ads in the public interest to promote its sponsorship of the event, does anybody believe that that they are doing so because they have a public interest obligation? Channel 4 promotes Race for the Cure because it is great advertising for Channel 4, and brand reputation-building in the community.

I have come to believe that there is no way to enforce any set of reasonable and workable standards on broadcasters to meet the test of the eighty-year-old public trustee model. It is time to move to a completely different model, one articulated some years ago by Henry Geller, a longtime communications lawyer and former top FCC executive. Geller described his model as follows:

> It makes no sense to try to impose effective, behavioral regulation . . . when conventional television faces such fierce and increasing competition, and viewership is declining rather than growing. It would be much sounder to

truly deregulate broadcasting by eliminating the public trustee requirement and in its place substituting a reasonable spectrum fee imposed on
existing stations (and an auction for all new frequency assignments), with
the sums so obtained dedicated to public telecommunications. . . . For the
first time, we would have a structure that works to accomplish explicit
policy goals. The commercial system would continue to do what it already
does: deliver a great variety of entertainment and news-type programs.
The noncommercial system would have the funds to accomplish its goals
to supply needed public service such as educational programming for
children, cultural fare, minority presentations, and in-depth informational
programs.

For years, the NAB has put out a glossy publication touting the public interest and community-driven activities of its stations; these efforts, according to
the NAB, were valued at over $10 billion last year. One way to change the policy
would be to craft a simple bargain: relieve broadcasters of all their public interest obligations in return for annual rental fees totaling one-fifth of what they
are currently spending for them, or $2 billion. Another way, proposed by
Geller, would be to charge a flat percentage of 5 percent of advertising revenues, a figure comparable to what cable operators are typically charged as an
access fee for their use of public streets.

Of course, not all the activities broadcasters perform in the public interest
would continue if they were relieved of any legal obligations. Commercial
children's television programming would likely decline. So might coverage of
political campaigns, local coverage and programming, and other concerns.

The best way to deal with these issues would be to use the revenues from
spectrum rental fees to create mechanisms to enhance the public interest
objectives of fostering local programming, taking care of the needs of children,
enhancing public discourse, education, public safety, and so on.

One option would be to create a foundation into which the spectrum rental
fees would be deposited. The foundation could give grants to public broadcasting to support its stated goal of creating a dedicated digital channel called the
"Public Square" to focus on local and national politics, policy issues, debates,
campaigns, and other vital issues. The Public Square could use both national
and local programming to achieve these ends.

Of course, the fact is that commercial broadcasters are still the medium of
choice for political candidates to advertise and get messages across. Reaching
broad audiences remains a goal of candidates and of a vital democracy. So
some portion of the revenues could also be used to finance matching funds for
small contributions to political candidates, who in turn could use those funds
for advertising on broadcast stations.

Another portion of the spectrum rental revenues could be used to give grants to producers, including stations, to come up with high-quality children's programming, or public affairs shows, or documentaries—and perhaps even to buy commercial time to air those programs. Additional funds could go to public broadcasting for its consistently excellent children's programming

Technological change continues apace; the availability of spectrum, including so-called "white spaces"—unused fragments of airtime, or those used intermittently—is expanding rapidly. The notion of spectrum scarcity, which drove the public trustee model, is no longer as relevant as it was even a decade ago. But over the long run, broadcasting will still be a medium of choice. There will always be a need in the society to have a public square. It is worrisome that we are moving toward more and more fragmented audiences that are becoming the communications vehicles of choice for people who can cocoon themselves in and narrowly get a reinforced message over and over again.

Surveys suggest that we no longer have a common basis of shared knowledge and facts to debate. I'd like to think of ways to encourage broader audiences for some things other than just the *American Idol*–type debates that we get periodically for presidential and vice-presidential candidates. But the fact is we have to accommodate ourselves to the reality of a world where there are going to be dizzying numbers of channels of communication.

It may well be that the best thing to do is to find a way to unleash the creativity of the public and to create more avenues and opportunities to do so. The best option would be a model that leases public airwaves to broadcasters in the same way that we have farmers in the West leasing grazing lands, or oil companies leasing off-shore spaces or even on-shore drilling areas. Then we will have a more complete opportunity to use the public resource of the airwaves for the public interest.

CON: Adam D. Thierer

There's always been a bit of mythology surrounding so-called "public interest" regulation of broadcasting in America.[1] Those who advocate expansive regulatory obligations for licensed radio and television operators typically express the belief that they are directing the content or character of broadcasting toward a nobler end—a sort of noblesse oblige for the information age. At times, their rhetoric takes on a fairy-tale quality as lawmakers and regulatory advocates speak of the *public interest* in reverential and fantastic terms, all the while deftly evading any attempt to define the term.

For example, while testifying before the Senate Commerce Committee in 2003, Federal Communications Commission (FCC) commissioner Michael Copps paid homage to the public interest standard as follows:

> At all times, I strive to maintain my commitment to the public interest. As public servants, we must put the public interest front and center. It is at the core of my own philosophy of government. . . . The public interest is the prism through which we should always look as we make our decisions. My question to visitors to my office who are advocating for specific policy changes is always: how does what you want the Commission to do serve the public interest? It is my lodestar.[2]

That is nice rhetoric, but Commissioner Copps's public interest "lodestar" ultimately provides little practical guidance. Nonetheless, many public interest proponents assume that their values or objectives—which they believe are consistent with the needs and desires of the public—should ultimately triumph within the public policy arena. As a result, volumes of government rules and speeches have been laced with the term. Yet, even though "the public interest" has served as the rhetorical cornerstone of communications and media policy since the 1930s, the term has never been defined in a clear fashion.[3]

Since the term *public interest* has no fixed meaning, the public interest standard is not really a "standard" at all;[4] instead, the standard has shifted with the political winds to suit the whims of those in power.[5]

How the term has been interpreted and applied by the FCC has often depended on the ideological disposition of whatever party is in charge at the time. As Ford Rowan, author of *Broadcast Fairness,* once noted: "Many liberals want regulation to make broadcasting do wonderful things; many conservatives want regulation to restrain broadcasting from doing terrible things."[6] Consequently, during periods of liberal rule, the "public interest" has been seen as a method of politically engineering more "educational" and "community-based" programming. By contrast, in the hands of conservative appointees, the public interest has been seen as an instrument to curb "indecent" speech.

Practically speaking, however, public interest regulatory efforts haven't succeeding in changing the character of modern broadcasting much one way or the other. What five FCC commissioners think is in the public's best interest, and what the public actually demands, are often at odds. There's been no way to force the audience to pay attention to what some in Washington want them to see or hear—especially in an age of abundant media content and device choices. "Today, the scarce resource is attention, not programming," notes Ellen P. Goodman of the Rutgers-Camden School of Law. "Given the proliferation of consumer filtering and choice, these kinds of interventions are of questionable efficacy. Consumers equipped with digital selection and filtering tools are likely to avoid content they do not demand no matter what the regulatory efforts to force exposure."[7]

Moreover, the formidable broadcast lobby in Washington has successfully evaded many of the most onerous forms of public interest obligations through the years.[8] Indeed, broadcasters have occasionally benefited from the aura surrounding such obligations since they have been able to obtain special favors (or "rents" in economic parlance) from policy makers. Lawrence J. White of New York University's Stern School of Business has noted, "Under the 'public interest' banner the Congress and the FCC have established far too many protectionist, anticompetitive, anti-innovative, inflexible, output-limiting regulatory regimes and unnecessarily infringed on the First Amendment rights of broadcasters."[9]

As White suggests, constitutional questions have also haunted FCC efforts to read the public interest more expansively. Until roughly the 1980s, the courts granted the agency fairly generous leeway to interpret the term as they wished. In recent decades, however, court scrutiny—especially on First Amendment grounds—has been increasing, especially in light of marketplace changes that have not escaped the attention of judges reviewing FCC and congressional efforts to expand public interest obligations.[10]

SHIFTING MARKETPLACE REALITIES AND NEW REGULATORY PRIORITIES

Regardless of the rationale used to advance public interest regulation—public spectrum ownership, licensing, scarcity, pervasiveness, or public enlightenment—it is hard to explain why we have singled out broadcasters for unique regulatory obligations while operators of other media platforms have been given a free pass. Such regulatory asymmetry is more difficult to justify today in light of rising competition from many new platforms and players.

The combination of these factors has forced many traditional public interest regulatory advocates to reconsider the wisdom, or at least the practicality, of the old regime. One alternative that has received increasing attention in recent years would see broadcasters largely relieved of their public interest obligations and charged instead an annual fee for their use of the airwaves. The proceeds would then be dedicated to more public broadcasting initiatives,[11] a "Public Square" channel,[12] greater election coverage or political advertising,[13] or some combination of all of the above.

We might think of this proposal as a sort of reparations policy for the regulatory sins of the past. That is, broadcast spectrum fees are typically pitched as a way to "repay the public" for use of the spectrum that broadcasters obtained originally at no charge. But this, too, is an idea whose time has passed. Broadcast spectrum fees make little sense today, even if the notion might have made some sense two or three decades ago.[14]

First, using spectrum fees as a reparations policy today fails to "punish" those who originally got all that spectrum free of charge. The vast majority of broadcast spectrum licenses have traded hands in the secondary market for lucrative sums. In many cases, those television and radio properties have traded hands numerous times.

Second, there is no need for a reparations policy because, ultimately, broadcasting is a medium of rapidly diminishing relevance. Norman Ornstein himself has noted that "Over-the-air broadcasting is a dinosaur. It's not going to last very long."[15] Indeed, whatever weight the broadcast medium might have had in the past, that is now ancient history. For most of the past century, broadcasting was a fairly stable industry that did not witness business model–shattering types of changes. As its very name implies, broadcasting attracted broad audiences. Consequently, returns were stable, even substantial at times.

Today, however, stability has given way to volatility. This entire media marketplace is in a state of seemingly constant upheaval. Long-standing industry players are shedding assets or even disappearing as underdogs rapidly enter the sector and become big dogs overnight. It has become a textbook example of Schumpeterian "creative destruction" in action.[16]

Consider what this has meant for broadcasters in terms of audience share and advertising revenues. Begin with broadcast television. The television audience has grown increasingly fragmented since the 1950s. The top shows on TV during that era (e.g., *I Love Lucy*) garnered 40 percent to 50 percent of the viewing audience. By the 1970s, the top broadcast TV shows (e.g., *All in the Family*) were pulling in roughly 30 percent of the audience. Today, however, with so many other media options vying for our increasingly scarce attention, the top shows on television (e.g., *American Idol*) are lucky to break 15 percent, and most shows rarely break single digits.

The "problem" is competition for eyeballs. Broadcasters face a growing array of rivals: cable and satellite multichannel distributors, DVDs and Netflix, VOD and online video, video game platforms, and much more. According to Nielsen Media Research, the "Big Three" networks of the past (ABC, CBS, and NBC), which held a 90 share of the primetime market in 1980, control only a 30 share today. In terms of total "day shares," cable blew past broadcast television at the turn of the century and never looked back. The advertising situation is equally bleak for television broadcasters. According to McCann Erickson Worldwide, broadcast television's overall share of media advertising revenues dipped below 20 percent back in 1990 and continues to fall steadily, standing at approximately 15 percent today.

Unsurprisingly, some major network television executives are now thinking about doing what was unthinkable just a decade ago: casting off their local broadcast affiliates and repurposing their content on alternative media platforms. For example, in early 2009, CBS Corp. president and CEO Les Moonves told an investor conference that moving all the CBS network programming to cable and satellite platforms would be "a very interesting proposition."[17] One wonders how local broadcast affiliates will pay for a new federal spectrum fee once their content providers start following their audience in the continuing mass exodus to alternative distribution platforms.

The situation for broadcast radio operators is even grimmer. The competition for our ears has never been more intense, with satellite radio, noncommercial radio, iPods and Mp3 players, online radio, downloadable music, and much more competing with terrestrial broadcasters for audience share. As a result, radio operators have seen their audiences dwindle and their revenues nosedive. According to Arbitron, time spent listening to radio has dropped for every age demographic they have measured for the past decade. And BIA Financial Network notes that while radio revenue growth rate ran between 7 percent and 14 percent during the late 1990s, the industry hasn't seen growth above 3 percent since 2002, and in recent years growth has rarely broken 1 percent. Again, can struggling radio broadcasters absorb the added burden of a new national spectrum tax in the midst of such upheaval?

WHERE WOULD THE MONEY GO?

Questions also surround the pool of funds that would be amassed through the creation of a broadcast spectrum fee. Given the declining fortunes of the broadcast industry, it seems unlikely the fee would generate as much revenue as some proponents might imagine. Let's assume, however, that the spectrum levy netted respectable sums. How would those funds be used?

Our recent experience with spectrum auction proceeds suggests that Congress would first look to use a spectrum fee to offset federal spending priorities or past budget deficits instead of channeling those funds to new "public square" initiatives. But, for the sake of argument, let's assume Congress honored a pledge to use the broadcast fee for its intended purpose. What exactly counts as a "public square" initiative, and who would be in charge of it?

Some proponents of a spectrum fee seem to long for a world in which everything looks or sounds like a combination of National Public Radio (NPR), the Public Broadcasting Service (PBS), and cable "public access" channels. But regardless of the quality of such networks or the programming on them, the viewing and listening public has shown a clear desire for programming of a very different nature. While critics might lament what they regard as the "low-brow" entertainment or supposedly lower-quality news seen or heard on some commercial networks or stations, there is no denying that citizens tune into commercial programs in very large numbers. Whether regulatory advocates care to admit it, supply and demand are at work in America's media marketplace, and citizens vote with their eyes and ears all the time. Ben Compaine, coauthor of *Who Owns the Media?*, focuses on the real issue here, choice:

> If large segments of the public choose to watch, read, or listen to content from a relatively small number of media companies, that should not distract policy makers from the key word there: choose. . . . It may indeed be that at any given moment 80 percent of the audience is viewing or reading or listening to something from the 10 largest media players. But that does not mean it is the same 80 percent all the time, or that it is cause for concern.[18]

Commenting on efforts to make the modern media landscape look more like PBS or NPR, Compaine notes: "Content might well be different. But it wouldn't necessarily be better. . . . This might work only in a . . . world of enforced equality, where no democracy of content was allowed, where the voice of the audience was not heard."[19] He notes that PBS is instructive in this regard since, even in the days when it only had three primary rivals, it could rarely get the attention of more than 2 percent of the total TV audience. And as television journalist Jeff Greenfield has noted, "[W]hen you no longer need the skills of a safecracker to find PBS in most markets, you have to realize that the reason people aren't watching is that they don't want to."[20]

Again, in a world of unlimited options and freedom of media choice, there's just no way to force the audience to tune in.

OUR MANY PUBLIC SQUARES

More importantly, there seems to be little need for a new spectrum fee for a "public square" channel in light of the explosion of civic-oriented and culturally enriching programming on both traditional and new media platforms. In essence, we now have many "public square" channels.

For example, the growth of news channels and programs (CNN, Fox News, MSNBC, Current TV, many financial news networks, and more) and international news outlets (BBC America, CNN International, etc.) has been well documented. Most notable in this regard is the stunning success of the cable industry's C-Span network and its sister properties. But these cable news programs are also a growing force online. "Like their television programs, the major cable news channels' websites attracted record viewership in 2008, driven in a large part by the political and economic news of the year," reports the Pew Project for Excellence in Journalism.[21] Moreover, these cable news sites "have also evolved into true multimedia destinations. All now feature video archives, RSS feeds and features for accessing the sites on mobile devices. They all offer live streaming content."[22]

Americans have many other ways of finding important news and civic information online. The 2008 presidential election serves as a dramatic illustration of how voters have become better informed and how candidates have exciting new ways to connect with them. The Pew Internet and American Life Project has found that "some 74 percent of Internet users—representing 55 percent of the entire adult population—went online in 2008 to get involved in the political process or to get news and information about the election."[23] And Barack Obama's unprecedented use of new media tools during 2008 is often credited with helping to propel him into the White House. Millions of Americans made their views known about various issues on sites such as Obama's Change.gov Web site. *Wired* reported that "Obama's online success dwarfed [Sen. John McCain's], and proved key to his winning the presidency."[24]

Volunteers used Obama's Web site to organize a thousand phone-banking events in the last week of the race—and 150,000 other campaign-related events over the course of the campaign. Supporters created more than 35,000 groups clumped by affinities like geographical proximity and shared pop-cultural interests. By the end of the campaign, My.BarackObama.com chalked up some 1.5 million accounts. And Obama raised a record-breaking $600 million in contributions from more than three million people, many of whom donated through the Web.[25]

Four years earlier, Joe Trippi, former campaign manager of Howard Dean's 2004 presidential campaign run and the author of *The Revolution Will Not Be Televised: Democracy, the Internet, and the Overthrow of Everything*, had noted that the Dean campaign's heavy use of new, interactive media and communications technologies was "a sneak preview of coming attractions—the interplay between new technologies and old institutions. The end result will be massive communities completely redefining our politics, our commerce, our government, and the entire public fabric our culture."[26] He concluded: "[W]hat we are seeing—at its core—is a political phenomenon, a democratic movement that proceeds from our civic lives and naturally spills over in the music we hear, the clothes we buy, the causes we support."[27] President Obama's campaign certainly seems to have been proof of that.

Of course, all this comes in addition to the stunning proliferation of user-generation media sources such as blogs, discussion boards, listservs, and social networking sites. Dan Gillmor, author of *We the Media: Grassroots Journalism by the People, for the People,* notes just how profound the impact of new media and citizen journalism will be:

> Tomorrow's news reporting and production will be more of a conversation, or a seminar. The lines will blur between producers and consumers, changing the role of both in ways we're only beginning to grasp now. The communications network itself will be a medium for everyone's voice, not just the few who can afford to buy multimillion-dollar printing presses, launch satellites, or win the government's permission to squat on the public's airwaves.[28]

CONCLUSION

In light of these developments, it is hard to take seriously the charge that "deliberative democracy" is somehow on the decline in America and that the imposition of a new spectrum fee to create a new, government-controlled "public square" channel would actually change the constitution of news, culture, or civic engagement in any significant way. And even if such a channel was filled with civically and culturally enriching programming, there's no way to force people to tune into it.

Finally, regardless of how spectrum fee proceeds might be spent, the proposal raises additional fairness issues for broadcasters. Indeed, it is doubly insulting for them. Not only has public broadcasting and noncommercial media been siphoning off more and more market share in recent years, but this proposal would impose a new tax on private broadcasters to fund those competitors (or some other media outlets) at a time when broadcasters are struggling for their very existence. In essence, if Congress imposed a spectrum fee on broadcasters, it would be tantamount to signing a death warrant for the medium. It's hard to see how that is in "the public interest."

RESOLVED, political parties should nominate candidates for president in a national primary

PRO: Caroline J. Tolbert

CON: David P. Redlawsk

From the beginning, the Constitution offered a clear answer to the question of who should elect the president: the electoral college. Or did it? Virginia delegate George Mason thought that after everyone's choice to become the first president, George Washington, left the scene, the electoral college would seldom produce a winner. In such a far-flung and diverse country, Mason (and many others) reasoned, hardly any candidate would be able to secure the required 50 percent plus one of electoral votes. Mason forecast a failure rate of "nineteen times in twenty"—that is, of 95 percent. What would happen, he thought, was that the electoral college would end up nominating the candidates and the House of Representatives would actually select the president from among the top electoral vote recipients.

Mason was wrong: in the fifty-four presidential elections held through 2008, the electoral college has chosen the president fifty-two times, a *success* rate of 97 percent. Not since 1824 has the House chosen the president. As for nominating the candidates, that has been done not by the electoral college, but by political parties.

The framers of the Constitution dreaded the prospect of parties. Based on their reading of ancient and European history, they equated political parties with conspiratorial factions. But a two-party system nonetheless began to emerge while Washington was still president and, from the start, it has functioned much better in practice than the framers feared. Indeed, it's hard to imagine how the Constitution could work without parties to choose candidates, aggregate voters' preferences, and help bridge the gap between the legislative and executive branches of the national government as well as between the layers of the federal system.

Over the years, the parties have experimented with different methods for nominating presidential candidates. The resolution proposed in this debate raises the possibility of trying yet another method: a national primary.

A national primary, if one was adopted, would be the fifth method of presidential nomination that the parties have used. The first was the congressional caucus, in which each party's members of Congress met in private to choose their candidate for president. The problem with "King Caucus," as critics called it, was that it denied a voice in the decision to every party member, activist, and leader who did not happen to be in Congress. To meet this objection, the congressional caucus was gradually replaced during the 1830s by a second method of nomination: the national convention, consisting of delegates chosen by all of the state parties and conducting most of its business in public instead of behind closed doors.

Conventions are still around; what has changed over the years is the way the delegates to these conventions are chosen. Originally, they were picked by the leaders of each state party. During the early twentieth century, some states continued to do things this way, but others began requiring that convention delegates be chosen through state primaries in which rank-and-file voters could participate. This third method—often called the "mixed system"—lasted through 1968, a year dominated by controversy over the war in Vietnam. Many voters were so frustrated that no major-party nominee, neither Democrat Hubert H. Humphrey nor Republican Richard Nixon, opposed the war that they demanded the parties create a fourth method of nomination in which every state party was required to choose its delegates in either a primary or an open caucus.

The fourth nomination method—the one still in use—resembles each of its predecessors by involving more people and thus further democratizing the process. Like its predecessors, too, the state primary and caucus method has come under criticism. Some complain that the process takes too long and costs too much. Others argue that it gives the small states that hold their caucuses and primaries first—namely, Iowa and New Hampshire—much too important a say about which candidates have any realistic chance to win. To some, like Caroline J. Tolbert, the logical next step is to replace the fifty state primaries and caucuses with a single national primary in which the entire country would cast its ballots on the same day and every vote would count equally. Others, such as David P. Redlawsk, find more advantages than disadvantages in the current nominating method and, in any event, are convinced that a national primary would make things worse rather than better.

PRO: Caroline J. Tolbert

The way we nominate our presidential candidates today is clearly unfair. The citizens in states that hold their nominating contests early in the process get smothered with attention from candidates and media, while citizens in states that vote later in the process barely get noticed. Frequently the contest is over almost before it starts, leaving many citizens (sometimes the majority of Americans) with no role in selecting their party's nominee. Turnout in these later states naturally plummets. In 2008 the Republican nomination was decided soon after Super Tuesday, leaving Republicans voting in later states with no meaningful choice, while Democrats were limited to either Barack Obama or Hillary Clinton. The selection of presidential candidates, one of the most important decisions that American voters make, should not be determined by a haphazard sequencing of state nominating contests. It is time for a national primary in which the citizens of all fifty states would go to the polls on the same day.

A national primary solves three problems that plague the current system: the chaotic and self-defeating race to be among the first states to hold a nominating contest, abysmally low voter turnout, and the unjustifiable privileged position of Iowa and New Hampshire. A national primary would boost citizen participation while also restoring order and fairness to the way we select our presidential nominees.

SOLVING THE CHAOTIC RACE TO THE FRONT

Everybody knows that the current system is broken. As Rob Richie, executive director of FairVote, expresses it: "The entire political universe, from the heights of the Washington establishment to the depths of the grassroots, agrees that our presidential nominating process needs to be reformed."[1] Every four years the parties try to fix the problems in ways that often only make things worse. Of particular concern to the parties is the phenomenon known as "front-loading"[2]—that is, the process by which states schedule their primaries and caucuses near the beginning of the delegate selection calendar in order to have a greater voice in the process. As part of their ongoing efforts to address the front-loading problem, both the Democratic National Committee (DNC) and Republican National Committee (RNC) revised the schedules and rules for 2008. The Democrats allowed two states (Nevada and South Carolina) to join Iowa and New Hampshire in violating the official February 5 start date. (Nevada and South Carolina were selected because of their racial diversity—Hispanic in the former case, African American in the latter case—in order to compensate for the demographically unrepresentative character of Iowa and New Hampshire, a problem we return to later.) Any state that moved its nominating contest before February 5 would lose all of its delegates at the party's national convention. The Republicans adopted less draconian rules—violators of the start date would lose only half of their delegates. Yet these changes did little to lessen front-loading; 70 percent of all delegates were chosen by the beginning of March. Two large states (Michigan and Florida) defied both national parties and held their nominating contests before February 5. There is little chance that the parties will be able to arrest the rush of states wanting to push their nominating contests earlier and earlier, particularly after Democrats capitulated and seated the Michigan and Florida delegations in the name of party unity.

The front-loading problem is exacerbated by what is known as the "invisible primary"—that is, the period before the first nominating event during which candidates engage in extensive fund raising.[3] As candidates increasingly opt out of public financing (as both Obama and McCain did in 2008), early money matters even more than in the past. The concern with a highly front-loaded nomination schedule is that candidates with the most money, name recognition, and media attention early on will win their party's nomination. As Todd Donovan and Shaun Bowler have pointed out, between 1980 and 2004 all but one candidate who raised the most money the year before the first primary won their party's nomination.[4] Front-loading means that strong candidates who lack financial resources may never have a chance to compete.

The sequential nomination process was originally designed so that a wide field of candidates could compete in early nominating events, followed by a winnowing process. Those candidates who exceeded expectations in early contests were able to raise campaign dollars to compete in later contests. Those who did worse than expected dropped out of the race.[5] However, events over the last decade have undermined the logic of the sequential nomination process. Early money in the invisible primary continues to increase in importance, regardless of the ever-changing schedule of state nominating contests. Conventional wisdom holds that retail or face-to-face politics in Iowa and New Hampshire were supposed to level the playing field among candidates, but new research finds that only candidates with sufficient financial resources are competitive, even in early nominating events such as the Iowa caucuses, which require extensive and expensive grassroots campaigning.[6]

Critics of the national primary suggest that it offers an extreme form of front-loading. If front-loading and the invisible primary are a problem, these critics reason, then the national primary will only make things worse. They argue that a national primary would restrict the presidential nomination to candidates who were already well known or well financed and could increase the influence of money, which is needed to purchase television ads.

This may have been a valid criticism of the national primary in the 1980s and 1990s, but the rise of the new media means that candidates no longer need huge financial resources or elite endorsements to compete effectively in a national primary. New information technologies level the playing field. Dark-horse candidates can reach voters by using new online media, such as e-mail, listservs, candidate Web sites, YouTube videos, blogs, Facebook, and even Twitter. The diversity of online media makes candidate campaigns more cost-effective and able to reach wider audiences because of the relatively low cost and twenty-four-hour availability of the Internet.[7] Online fund raising has become increasingly important, as Howard Dean first showed in 2004. Obama's victory in 2008 was made possible by raising huge amounts of money online: $750 million accrued from 3 million contributors.

One thing is certain: the current system cannot be fixed by patching it. State legislatures, secretaries of state, and state party leaders have a vested interest in holding their state's nominating event early in the process to receive attention from the candidates and mass media and to boost their state economies. Michigan and Florida acted rationally by breaking party rules in 2008. Left to their own self-interest, states will continue to move their primaries and cau-cuses closer to the beginning, exacerbating the front-loading problem. What is individually rational for each state, however, is bad for American democracy. Instead of ineffective party rules that try to penalize states for pursuing their self-interest, we should adopt a national primary that takes away the incentive that states currently have to circumvent the rules and leapfrog other states. By requiring all states to hold their nominating contest on the same day, a national primary solves the problem of individually rational states producing a collec-tive outcome that is preferred by nobody.

SOLVING THE TURNOUT PROBLEM

Observers often bemoan the low turnout of American elections. But turnout in the general election is positively robust compared to the turnout in primary elections, let alone caucuses. In 2000, for instance, turnout of the voter-age population was only 14 percent in the Democratic primaries and 17 percent in the Republicans primaries. In other words, less than one-third of age-eligible Americans participated in a presidential primary. In contrast, more than half of the voting age population voted in the general election. In 2004, when President George W. Bush was unopposed for the Republican nomination, primary turn-out plummeted even lower, down to 24 percent. Meanwhile, 55 percent of age-eligible voters voted in the general election contest between Bush and Democrat John Kerry. The 2008 presidential nomination saw the largest primary turnout in history (estimates put the number at 55 million people, more than double the number who voted in the 2004 primaries), but even this was far less than the roughly 130 million people who voted in the general election. Primary turnout in 2008, moreover, sunk precipitously on the Republican side after Super Tuesday, when John McCain effectively wrapped up the nomination.[8]

A national primary would do more than any other reform to increase participation in the nominating process. Holding an election on the same day across the entire country will create intense media interest and focus voters' attention on the election. With many viable candidates contesting the election, candidates will have an incentive to mobilize potential voters in all fifty states. As Lonna Atkeson and Cherie Maestas argue: "A national primary would focus broad voter attention on the race as candidates compete nationally instead of locally. Because everyone's primary would be 'coming up,' all interested voters would tune in to candidate debates to assist them in making their choice."[9]

Recent experience with the current nominating process confirms what common sense tells us: creating a competitive election on a single day will increase turnout. Over the past decade, an increasing number of states have held their primary on Super Tuesday, inching us ever closer toward a de facto national primary. In 2008, twenty-three states held their primaries or caucuses on Super Tuesday, and these states experienced significantly higher turnout in primaries and caucuses.[10]

SOLVING THE IOWA PROBLEM

The "Iowa problem" refers to the fact that since 1972 this small Midwest state has always gone first, followed by another small state, New Hampshire. What rational reason is there for Iowa and New Hampshire to receive this special status? The electorates of both states are highly unrepresentative of the nation. Iowa is 96 percent white, largely rural, and has an economy that is mainly agricultural.[11]

Adding to the Iowa problem is the fact that turnout in the state's caucuses is extremely low. Caucuses are time-consuming party business meetings and present substantial barriers to participation. Only 6 percent of the voting eligible population caucused in Iowa in 2004 and 7 percent in 2000. Competitive contests on the Democratic and Republican side in 2008 boosted turnout to 16 percent, but even this higher turnout rate is much lower than turnout in the early 2008 primaries. In New Hampshire, for instance, over half of the eligible population voted, and in South Carolina, 30 percent turned out to vote. Some research suggests participation in the relatively high-turnout 2008 Iowa caucuses may not have been as biased in terms of partisanship and socioeconomic factors as is usually the case, but even high-turnout caucuses are less representative than low-turnout primaries.[12]

Low turnout means that Iowa caucus goers are highly unrepresentative of Iowa's rank-and-file party members. Caucus participants are better educated, older, and have higher incomes.[13] They are also more committed to and active in their party than the average citizen. Low turnout in the caucuses also makes it costly for candidates to campaign in Iowa; contacting caucus goers has been compared to finding "a needle in a haystack."

Even if Iowa were not unrepresentative of the nation, and Iowa's caucus goers were not unrepresentative of Iowa's citizens, its disproportionate impact on the primary process would still be a problem. Analysis of the 2004 election found that early voters have up to twenty times the influence of late voters in the selection of presidential candidates, and that preferences of Iowa voters were six times as influential as Super Tuesday voters.[14] Why should voters in these two tiny states be given wildly disproportionate influence in choosing who our presidential nominees will be?

Defenders of the Iowa caucuses and New Hampshire primary highlight the grassroots or face-to-face politics that are made possible by the small populations of these two states.[15] As we have argued above, however, the Internet allows grassroots politics without Iowa and New Hampshire always voting first. Even if we concede that a national primary would involve making some sacrifices in face-to-face politics, those sacrifices are well worth making to achieve a fairer process that gives all citizens, not just a few favored ones, an equal say in which candidate will represent their party in the contest for the nation's highest and most powerful office.

THE PEOPLE SUPPORT A NATIONAL PRIMARY

The American people understand that the current system is unfair and dysfunctional. Two separate surveys conducted in 2008 found that the people's preferred reform is the national primary. In both surveys, about seven in ten Americans said they favored a national primary.[16] These numbers are consistent with earlier surveys.[17]

Even when proposals for a national primary are framed in terms of the costs (for example, when respondents are prompted that if a national primary is adopted small-population states may lose influence), a clear majority of Americans still support a national primary.

Support for a national primary varies some by state size. In a 2008 Cooperative Campaign Analysis Panel (CCAP) survey, those from states with small populations are somewhat more likely (73 percent) to support a national primary than those from the largest-population states (63 percent). The result is perhaps surprising since critics of a national primary often argue that a national primary would disadvantage small states that would rarely get campaign visits. It suggests, however, that those who reside in small states (apart from those living in Iowa and New Hampshire) are the ones who harbor the greatest frustrations with the current process.

The 2008 CCAP survey also asked respondents about an alternative reform that would rotate the order so that "a different state goes first each time." This idea attracted much lower levels of support. Only a bare majority (51 percent) reported that they favored it. Rotation, Americans understand, is fairer than what we have now, but not nearly as fair as having everybody vote at the same time. The only citizens who seemed satisfied with the way things are now are the people of Iowa. A 2008 telephone survey found only 26 percent of Iowans favored a reform to rotate the order of state primaries.[18]

HOW A NATIONAL PRIMARY WOULD WORK

One way of implementing a national primary is to declare the person with the most votes the winner. However, there are four other methods of implementing a national primary that I believe are preferable to this plurality system.

First, a national primary could be followed several weeks later by a runoff election, in which the two candidates with the most votes would compete head-to-head. This would be similar to the French presidential election system. The advantage of a runoff election is that the parties would be assured that the candidate with the support of a majority within the party would win the nomination. A runoff election would prevent a candidate from winning with only a plurality of the votes of rank-and-file party members. The disadvantages are a costly additional election and potentially lower turnout in the runoff election.

Second, the parties could use a more complex preference ballot, called instant runoff voting (IRV), which allows voters to rank-order their candidate preferences. IRV simulates a runoff election without the need for a costly second election. Here is how it works. Voters rank candidates in order of preference (first, second, third, fourth, etc.). They can rank as many or as few candidates as they want. First choices are then tabulated, and if a candidate receives a majority of first choices, he or she is elected. If no candidate has a majority of votes on the first count, a series of runoffs are simulated, using each voter's preferences indicated on the ballot. The candidate who received the fewest first-place choices is eliminated first. All ballots are then recounted. Voters who chose the now-eliminated candidate will have their ballots counted for their second-ranked candidate, but all other voters continue supporting their top candidate. Candidates continue to be eliminated and voters' ballots redistributed until a candidate gains a majority of votes.

IRV has been recently adopted in a number of American cities, including San Francisco, Minnesota, San Jose, and Aspen (see www.fairvote.org). It is cost-effective, requires only one election, and allows voters to choose their favorite candidate without having to fear that their vote (say for a Ralph Nader) will elect their least-favorite candidate (what is called the "spoiler effect"). Most important, like an actual runoff election, it ensures that the winner enjoys true support from a majority of party voters.

Third, one could design a national primary that required the winning candidate to gain a majority of the delegates but without IRV and without a runoff election. A virtue of this approach is that it could make party conventions meaningful again. In a crowded field of candidates, no candidate would be likely to gain a majority of delegates, and therefore the nomination would have to be settled at the convention. Making party conventions meaningful again could help to strengthen political parties and party leaders.

Finally, one could design a compromise system that retained state-by-state primaries and caucuses (perhaps in small-population states only) but culminated in a National Primary Day. As the candidates compete they would accumulate delegates as usual, narrowing the field as candidates doing poorly gradually drop out. In the first week in June or thereabouts, the remaining candidates would go head-to-head in a national primary open to party voters across the entire country. Combing a national primary with sequential state elections retains the best of both worlds. A National Primary Day would ensure that all voters across the country would have a chance to play a decisive role in the selection of their party's nominee, while the sequential state contests would allow sufficient time for examination of the candidates' character and skill. The political parties could limit the number of candidates in the final primary to the top two, or they could allow more candidates to participate using IRV.

CONCLUSION

The American people are ready for a fundamental change in the way we choose our presidential nominees. Their clear preference is for a national primary, which treats all citizens alike and makes each vote count the same. A national primary will give every state a meaningful, competitive contest, increase turnout and participation, and eliminate the ever-changing, crazy-quilt system of primaries and caucuses. A national primary, in short, will give the nation, at long last, a nomination process that promotes popular participation and is both simple and fair.

CON: David P. Redlawsk

> It has been said that democracy is the worst form of government except
> all the others that have been tried.
>
> —Sir Winston Churchill, *House of Commons*, November 11, 1947

Let's start with a proposition. Like democracy itself, the sequential arrangement of state caucuses and primaries that makes up our presidential nominating system is about the worst system imaginable. Yet, that is only until we consider the alternatives. Given our federal system, no other approach has been found to be any better, at least not by those who would have to adopt it. And a national primary? While nearly three-quarters of the American public say they want one, a national primary is the last thing on the agenda of those who actually have to live with the system: candidates and parties.[1] *The Hill* newspaper, covering inside-the-beltway Washington, recently reported that "a national primary is something everyone hopes to avoid."[2] According to the article, Bob Bennett, former Ohio Republican Party chair, said: "If you go back and you talk to any of the presidential candidates [from 2008], they will tell you they do not want to go through what they went through last year." If nothing changes, he added, "We'll have a de facto national primary in '12, and I think that nobody is in favor of that."

Why this disconnect between the public's desire for something called a "national primary" and party leaders' preference for anything but? The reason is simple. As much as candidates, pundits, and the public like to complain about the current system, at the least it allows candidates to build their campaigns over time, to develop and hone their strategies, and to potentially build momentum as they move through the events that define the modern presidential nomination system. Our system begins slowly—with the small states of Iowa and New Hampshire—and then builds through a few more states (in 2008, Nevada and South Carolina) before exploding onto the scene with "super," "tsunami," or perhaps "overwhelming" Tuesday, when dozens of states hold their contests. By starting in a few places rather than nationally, candidates can nurture the hope that they might break through and become the one.

We only need to consider the scorn heaped on Super Tuesday by academics and candidates to wonder how a national primary could be better than what we have now. Super Tuesday is a consequence of "front-loading," and it seems to get earlier every cycle. Front-loading means that rather than pacing the caucuses and primaries out over some period of time (say thirteen weeks or so), states rush to go as early as possible, in order to be "relevant" and to reap whatever benefits attention might give them. The lesson of Iowa and New Hampshire is not lost; in 2004 by one measure Iowa received 243 times the media coverage of any other state, while an analysis of candidate momentum in 2004 found the preferences of Iowa voters were six times as influential as Super Tuesday voters.[3] With twenty-three states voting on Super Tuesday in 2008, a de facto national primary has developed through front-loading.

Why is front-loading a problem? William Mayer writes that "[f]rontloading increases the amount of early fundraising required and thereby limits the number of candidates who are able to mount a credible, competitive campaign."[4] Moreover, Mayer argues, front-loading gives voters little time to learn about the candidates and forces candidates to be less substantive as they rely heavily on paid media rather than personal contact. One can only imagine the results if all fifty states (and the District of Columbia and territories) held their nominating events on the same day. Candidates would be unable to focus in any one place; media would be stretched thin trying to cover all of the states; and voters would likely end up seeing a superficial media campaign, focusing on six-second television news sound bites or perhaps thirty-second YouTube videos.

Neither candidates nor the parties want to see a national primary of any type. If anything, their desire is to design a rational system retaining the sequential nature of the process but spreading it out over time. The public, on the other hand, seems solidly in favor of a national primary. This might be compelling, except that the public is also in favor of rotating state primaries (about 63 percent, according to a February 2008 poll). This suggests that while the public as a whole may say they prefer something other than the current system, it is not clear that there is a clamor for a national primary as such. Instead, it is more likely that respondents are simply parroting a media-driven sense that something must be wrong with the current system since pundits routinely tell us that it is flawed. In fact, in the same survey, voters were just as likely (about 72 percent) to support a rotating system that guaranteed Iowa and New Hampshire's preeminence as a national primary.

From the voters' perspective the question of a national primary would seem to be relatively unimportant. Most never vote in primaries, anyway. And for those who do, the campaign does not start months before, as it does for those in Iowa and New Hampshire, but instead really gets going only a few weeks ahead of the vote. Voters in each state do not have time to become fatigued by the election. But who does become fatigued? It's the media, who begin following the candidates long before the Iowa caucuses and find themselves listening to the same stump speech over and over, attending too many county fairs, riding on busses across the country, and otherwise becoming exhausted by the process. Their exhaustion then plays out in their commentary. For example, in

2008 the timing was such that six weeks passed between the March 11 Mississippi primary and the next one in Pennsylvania in late April. This allowed intense focus on Pennsylvania by both candidates and media. But the media treated the campaign as if it had already happened and that Pennsylvanians should already have been aware of all the issues and candidates. This became clear in the debate between Hillary Clinton and Barack Obama in which the debate moderators, Charles Gibson and George Stephanopoulos, seemed focused on trivia, failing to ask good questions on important issues.[5] No doubt part of the reason is that while the campaign was new to Pennsylvania voters, who were likely paying close attention for the first time, it was very old to the media, who assumed everyone else had also heard it all before.

Although the exhaustion of a cynical media would not be a problem with a national primary, whether the media are tired of the process is not the point. A national primary might make things easier in some ways for the media—at least make the campaign coverage period shorter—but numerous other negative consequences suggest that it would bring more harm than good. Before addressing these negative consequences, let's consider what a desirable system would look like. We should evaluate reform on its ability to promote four goals: candidate quality, voter information, voter participation, and state equality. A presidential nomination system should choose *quality candidates*, not simply those who are the most well known or the best financed. The system should allow voters to *learn*, to provide them with appropriate information. Moreover, a nomination system should encourage voter *participation*, so that voters become interested and involved. Finally, it should strive for *equality* among the states in terms of allowing all Americans to cast a meaningful vote.

A true national primary—a system where all primaries are held on one day—is likely to fail these tests. We can already see this in what happens during the general election. Candidates focus on a few "swing" states, pouring resources into them while ignoring most states as uncompetitive. Candidates spend much of their money on thirty-second television ads, which seem designed to confuse rather than to explain. And few voters ever actually see a candidate in person, unless it is for fifteen minutes on an airport tarmac as the candidate flies in, gives a canned stump speech, and flies out to the next stop. This country is simply too large to campaign effectively across all states if the election in each state is held on the same day.

It is difficult to define just what makes a "quality" presidential candidate. Political scientists consider a quality congressional candidate to be one who has held previous elected office and who can raise enough money to contest the election.[6] But most presidential candidates have held public office, and at least at the beginning it is difficult to tell who will be most effective at raising campaign funds. It is clear, however, that a national primary would advantage certain types of candidates at the expense of others. Those with ready access to very large sums of money very early—certainly at least in the year before the primary—would be able to buy the media needed to contest the whole country at the same time, while others who might also be good candidates but cannot initially raise large sums would be locked out. The simple math of a national primary is that money would speak loudly. And it would speak through massive media campaigns, rather than personalized grassroots campaigns. Instead of building the campaign over time, most potential candidates would have to opt out. It is already quite difficult for underdogs to come out on top, but at least they have a fighting chance. In 2008, had a national primary been in place, it is likely that the largest money raisers of 2007 would have been the leading candidates—Mitt Romney and Hillary Clinton. Barack Obama and John McCain might have remained afterthoughts.

Moreover, and much more important, the sequential nature of the current system tests candidate campaigns in complex ways that would not happen otherwise. Caucuses, for example, require extensive organization. It is harder for candidates to reach caucus participants because there are fewer of them. Lower turnout in caucuses means that grassroots mobilization ("retail politics") is critical, compared to the mass media campaigns that would prevail in a national primary. And grassroots campaigning tests a candidate's ability to build an organization, to create something that directly connects with voters. This ability to build, manage, and connect is an important skill for any would-be president, and one that would not be well tested in a national primary.

Candidates learn from a sequential process; they take lessons learned in one state and apply them to the campaign in the next. Few, if any, candidates really know how to run a national campaign before they start. Few, if any, have had experience that would qualify them to head a massive bureaucracy and to lead the nation. Building what amounts to a half-billion-dollar business from the ground up is not easy, and our current system allows candidates to learn how to do this over time. This means the quality of candidates can be improved by the nature of the sequential campaign season.

Just as candidates can learn from campaigning from one state to the next, so too do voters learn over time. One major advantage and unique feature of sequential voting is that voters later in the process have more information about candidates, including election outcomes, delegate totals, candidate traits, ideology, and policy information.[7] This may give later voters the opportunity to make more informed decisions than they would otherwise, while earlier voters may actually be slightly disadvantaged. But early states make up for this by the greater amounts of attention they get from the candidates and the media, enhancing their voters' political interest and knowledge. Examination of the 2008 campaign finds exactly that. Early nominating events shaped perceptions of whether candidates could win the nomination and presidency (viability and electability) and in turn shaped candidate choice in later primaries and caucuses. Early voters were mobilized and later voters became more aware and involved as long as the campaign remained competitive.[8]

As voters learn from a sequential system they are also encouraged to participate, especially with candidates on the ground holding events that are open and accessible. Granted, this is much more likely in smaller early states than in larger later states, but the counter-example of Pennsylvania in 2008 is instructive. Because there was a period before Pennsylvania where no other primaries were scheduled, candidates had time to hold events, build the grass roots, and encourage participation. And Pennsylvania voters responded. While the same cannot be said of most of the states on Super Tuesday, this is a problem of front-loading rather than of a sequential system. A properly spaced sequential process enhances voter participation in ways a national primary cannot. Voters are encouraged to participate when candidates can build an organization, and are discouraged when candidates primarily rely on media campaigns. Political operative Dan Leistikow, who worked for both John Edwards and Obama, made this point in talking about Iowa:

> In Iowa, regular people can look candidates in the eyes, size them up, and ask tough questions. Changing the schedule to favor larger states where TV commercials matter more than face to face contact with voters might be good for the frontrunner, but it isn't good for our democracy.[9]

Finally, the fact that some states seem less important and others more important in a sequential system is hard to overlook. Obviously, some state must go first. And because we generally know the dates of our elections in advance, both candidates and the media will flock to the earliest states as early as they can. This is unavoidable in a sequential system and certainly one area where a national primary might fix a perceived problem. But why should we expect that candidates will treat all states equally in a national primary? Treatment of states in a national primary will depend heavily on how the votes are aggregated. If the system proposes simply counting votes nationally and awarding the nomination to the candidate with the most voters, then candidates will focus on the largest vote-rich states, to the detriment of the majority of states. Perversely, moreover, Democrats will focus on the most Democratic states and Republicans will focus on the most Republican states. Thus not only will some states be ignored, but the process is likely to reinforce the current dichotomy between red states and blue states. Perhaps, instead, the national primary should award delegates state by state, as is now the case. But this would do nothing to solve the problem for Republicans, since the largest states get the most delegates and in many of these states delegates are awarded on a winner-take-all basis. If anything, this would cause Republican candidates to focus even more intently on the largest, most Republican states. Democrats, because they do not use winner-take-all for delegate selection, would focus on a mix of the largest Democratic states and ones in which a given candidate might think he or she has a particular advantage. So while Iowa and New Hampshire would clearly lose their privileged place in a national primary, it does not follow that voters in all states would become equal in their influence on the nomination.

These points lead to an interesting problem with the national primary idea: Who gets to decide how the individual states run their contests? Most national primary proposals envision a single set of rules—using a primary election—that would apply to all states. While in theory this sounds reasonable, in practice our federal system leaves wide latitude to states to run their own elections. It is not even clear who could impose a national primary in the first place. Even the parties themselves do not have complete control over the timing or nature of their contests, since many states pay for the elections and legislate their dates and forms. In addition, those states that prefer caucuses would be overridden by a national primary.

A proposal that mandates that all contests be held on the same day but leaves the mechanism to the states is problematic as well. Problems arise even with as simple an issue as aggregating the votes nationally. Democratic state caucuses, for example, generally report delegate counts, not actual votes. Any system that imagines tallying up the vote across all states would run into problems unless the form of voting was mandated and regularized across all states. A lack of consistency would doom any attempt at a national primary. And then there is the problem of determining who wins. Both parties currently require an outright majority of delegates to the national convention to win the nomination. Would this translate into requiring a majority of votes? Would that then mean a runoff if no one gets a majority, as is likely? Alternatively, one could imagine a voting mechanism that would allow voters to specify first and second choices (generally known as instant runoff voting), but this then moves us back into the challenge of setting the same rules nationwide. Probably the biggest single problem with a national primary is that no one quite knows what is meant by it and what its unintended consequences might be.

In defending the current system, I should make one thing clear: it has its problems. The incentive structure for the states causes them to rush to the earliest possible date, hoping to get the attention of both candidates and media. The campaign starts earlier and earlier every four years. The parties could solve this problem, however, by establishing rules and sticking to them. Some attempt was made to do so in 2008, but in the end, after threatening Florida and Michigan with loss of their delegates for violating the rules, both parties gave in and seated both states. Thus the lesson is that the rules can be violated with relative impunity.

Beyond this front-loading problem, the other problem that gets the most complaints is that nominees are usually decided well before the end of the primary season, resulting in some (maybe many) states becoming irrelevant. Obviously, this was not a problem for the Democrats in 2008, where the contest went down to the very last primary. But John McCain effectively wrapped up the Republican nomination on February 5, while about two-fifths of the states had not yet voted. This happened because, while Democrats allocate their delegates proportionally, Republicans mostly use winner-take-all primaries. So, for instance, McCain could get nearly all the delegates in South Carolina despite winning only 33 percent of the vote. This makes it more likely that a Republican will clinch early and that most states will not get much of a say in deciding the Republican nominee. Since 1972, only two Democratic candidates clinched earlier than June—Al Gore in 2000 and John Kerry in 2004. In contrast, only the 1976 Republican contest went beyond June, and four of the remaining six were wrapped up in April or earlier. The claim is that a national primary would solve this, making every state count. But the experience of the Democrats suggests that it could also be solved by proportional allocation of delegates.

The early twentieth-century development of the primary election system was part of a series of reforms championed by the progressives of the era, designed for the most part to take power from political bosses and machines and to place it in the hands of the rank and file. Primaries were seen as a way to break the control of bosses in the smoke-filled rooms, allowing voters a direct say in who would be their party's nominee. As primaries developed at the state level, interest began growing for a national presidential primary. Theodore Roosevelt offered to use a national primary in the 1912 Republican nomination, but incumbent president William Howard Taft declined.[10] Numerous national primary bills have been introduced in Congress since that time, but none has come even close to passing. Putting aside the question of whether Congress actually has the constitutional power to mandate a national primary, it is interesting that, despite a long list of complaints about the current system, a national primary has not come to pass.[11] And, in fact, it never should. While the current system may not be perfect—few if any human institutions are—the law of unintended consequences should be carefully noted. A national primary of any type—forcing all states to hold nominating events on the same day—simply does not offer significant improvement over the sequential nomination process we have today and which has served us reasonably well despite the complaints that have been lodged against it.

RESOLVED, the electoral college should be abolished

PRO: George C. Edwards III

CON: Daniel H. Lowenstein

When James Madison crafted the Virginia Plan as a rough draft of a new plan of government on the eve of the Constitutional Convention, he proposed that the "National Executive" be elected by the "National Legislature" but said nothing about whether the executive would be an individual or a committee. When the delegates to the convention began debating what the executive should look like, they were confident where Madison was uncertain and uncertain where he was confident. The convention quickly decided that the executive should be a person—the president of the United States. But they went around and around on the issue of how that person should be elected. In political scientist Robert A. Dahl's description, "The Convention twisted and turned like a man tormented in his sleep by a bad dream as it tried to decide."[1]

Madison's idea that the national legislature—that is, Congress—should choose the president had many champions. In fact, throughout most of the convention, which lasted nearly four months from May 25 to September 17, 1787, the delegates held to the idea that Congress would elect the president with a one-term limit. But two problems with this idea emerged from the debates. One was that many delegates wanted the president to be eligible for more than one term, but did not want Congress both to elect and reelect the president. The desire for reelection, they feared, would give the president every incentive to bribe members of Congress to support him for a second— and perhaps a third, fourth, and fifth—term. The other problem was more practical: How would Congress actually elect the president? Delegates from the larger, more populous states wanted to see members of the House of Representatives and Senate vote for president as one body, which by definition would be dominated by large-state representatives. Delegates from the small states wanted the House and Senate to vote separately until they agreed on the same candidate, who at a minimum would have to be acceptable to the small states.

Not surprisingly, other ideas for presidential selection also were advanced. One proposed that the governors of the states, as fellow chief executives, should choose the president. Another was that each state should put forward its best citizen and Congress should elect one of them. Still another proposal was to entrust the choice to a small group of legislators chosen by lot. Another was to let the voters choose the president in a direct national election. That one was dismissed with particular contempt by Virginia delegate George Mason, who said, "It would be as unnatural to refer the choice of a proper character for chief Magistrate to the people, as it would to refer a trial of colours to a blind man."[2]

In early September, just days before the convention ended, a committee proposed a solution that was nobody's first choice but that most delegates decided they could live with: the electoral college. Every four years, each state would choose presidential electors equal in number to its delegation of representatives and senators in Congress. If a candidate received support from a majority of electors, he would become president. If no candidate received majority support, then the House would choose the president from the ranks of the top electoral vote recipients, with each state delegation in the House casting one vote.

Over the years few provisions of the Constitution have proven more controversial than the electoral college. More constitutional amendments have been proposed in Congress to replace it than on any other subject. In the 1950s, the leading alternative was a proportional plan, under which each state's electoral votes would be cast in proportion to the candidates' shares of the state's popular vote. A more recent idea has been to bypass the Constitution entirely and get each state to agree to cast its electoral votes for whichever candidate receives the most popular votes across the country, regardless of how the voting goes in the state. Two states, Nebraska and Maine, exercise their constitutional option to assign their electoral votes so that the candidate who carries the state gets two (corresponding to the state's two senators) and the remaining votes are assigned according to who carried each House district—the so-called "district plan."

The reform proposal that has received the most support for the longest period of time has been the one that Mason dismissed at the 1787 convention: do away entirely with the electoral college and replace it with a direct presidential election by the people. George C. Edwards III defends this proposal in his essay, and Daniel H. Lowenstein opposes it, preferring to keep the electoral college in place. Although it is an old debate, Edwards and Lowenstein bring fresh vigor and new arguments to the table.

PRO: George C. Edwards III

Political equality lies at the core of democratic theory. It is difficult to imagine a definition of democracy that does not include equality in voting as a central standard. Because political equality is at the core of democratic government, we must evaluate any mechanism for selecting the president against it.

The percentage of electoral votes received by a candidate nationwide rarely coincides with the candidate's percentage of the national popular vote for several reasons, the most important of which is the winner-take-all (or unit-vote) system.[1] All states except Maine and Nebraska have a winner-take-all system in which they award *every* electoral vote to the candidate who receives the most popular votes in that state. In effect, the system assigns to the winner the votes of the people who voted *against* the winner.

The operation of the winner-take-all system effectively disenfranchises voters who support losing candidates in each state. In the 2000 presidential election, nearly three million people voted for Al Gore in Florida. Because George W. Bush won 537 more votes than Gore, however, he received *all* of Florida's electoral votes. A candidate can win some states by very narrow margins, lose others by large margins (as Bush did by more than one million votes in California and New York in 2000), and so win the electoral vote while losing the popular vote. Because there is no way to aggregate votes across states, the votes for candidates who do not finish first in a state play no role in the outcome of the election.

African Americans, who are the nation's most distinctive minority group, are concentrated in the Deep South. They rarely vote for the Republican candidates who win their states. Thus their votes are wasted because they are never added up across the country. It is not surprising that presidential candidates have generally ignored these voters in their campaigns.[2]

In a multicandidate contest such as the ones in 1992, 1996, and 2000, the winner-take-all system may suppress the votes of the majority as well as the minority. In 1996, for example, less than a majority of voters decided how the electoral votes of twenty-six states would be cast. In each case, less than half the voters determined how all of their state's electoral votes were cast.

The unit-vote system also allows even small third parties to siphon more votes from one major-party candidate than the other and thus determine the outcome in a state, as Ralph Nader did in both Florida and New Hampshire in 2000. Indeed, by taking more votes from Gore than from Bush, Nader determined the outcome of the entire election. The results distorted the preferences of the voters, because the preferred candidate in both Florida and New Hampshire in a two-person race was Al Gore, not George W. Bush, who ultimately won the states.

One result of these distorting factors is that there is typically a substantial disparity in almost all elections between the share of the national popular vote a candidate receives and that candidate's percentage of the electoral vote. In 1876, 1888, 2000, and, arguably, 1960,[3] the candidate who finished second in the popular vote won the election.

If no candidate wins a majority of the electoral votes, as happened in 1800 and 1824, the House of Representatives chooses the president. Here, each state delegation receives one vote, allowing the seven smallest states, with a population of about five million, to outvote the six largest states, with a population of about 123 million. It is virtually impossible to find any defenders of this constitutional provision, which is the most egregious violation of democratic principles in American government.

The electoral college violates political equality. It favors some citizens over others, depending solely upon the state in which they live, and at times denies the people their preferred choice for president. What good reason is there to continue such a system in a nation in which the ideal of popular choice is the most deeply ingrained principle of government?

CONSTITUTIONAL CONSISTENCY

Some defenders of the electoral college argue that its violations of majority rule are just an example of constitutional provisions that require supermajorities to take action. For example, it takes the votes of two-thirds of the senators present to ratify a treaty. The framers designed all such provisions, however, to allow minorities to prevent an action. The electoral college is different. It allows a minority to take an action—that is, to select the president. As such, it is the only device of its kind in the Constitution.

LEGITIMACY

Do the inflated numbers of the electoral college results provide a new president extra legitimacy? There is no evidence at all that winning a majority in the electoral college provides an additional element of legitimacy for new presidents who did more poorly in the popular vote. Even after two and a half years in office and the rally focused on the war on terrorism, 38 percent of the public, including a majority of Democrats and half the Independents, did not consider George W. Bush the legitimate winner of the 2000 presidential election.[4]

DEFENDING INTERESTS

Advocates of the electoral college often argue that allocating electoral votes by state, and states casting their votes as units, ensures that presidential candidates will be attentive to and protective of states' interests, especially the interests of states with small populations. They base their argument on the premises that (1) states have interests as states; (2) these interests require protection; (3) interests in states with smaller populations both require and deserve special protection from federal laws; and (4) candidates focus on state interests, especially those of smaller states.

STATE INTERESTS

States do not have coherent, unified interests. Even the smallest state has substantial diversity within it. That is why Alaska may have a Republican governor and one or more Democratic senators, and why "conservative" states like Montana and North and South Dakota vote Republican for president but sometimes send liberal Democrats to the U.S. Senate. As historian Jack Rakove argues, "States have no interest, as states, in the election of the president; only citizens do."[5]

NEED FOR PROTECTION

The Constitution places many constraints on the actions a simple majority can take. Minorities have fundamental rights to organize, communicate, and participate in the political process. The Senate greatly overrepresents small states and, within that chamber, the filibuster is a powerful extraconstitutional tool for thwarting majorities. Moreover, more than a simple majority is required to overcome minority opposition by changing the Constitution.

With these powerful checks on simple majorities already in place, do some minority rights or interests require additional protection from national majorities? If so, are these minorities concentrated in certain geographic areas? (Because it allocates electoral votes on the basis of geography, the electoral college protects only geographically concentrated interests.) Does anything justify awarding interests in certain geographic locations—namely, small states—additional protections in the form of extra representation in the electoral system that citizens in other states do not enjoy?[6]

Two of the most important authors of the Constitution, James Wilson and James Madison, saw little need to confer additional power to small states through the electoral college. "Can we forget for whom we are forming a government?" Wilson asked. "Is it for *men*, or for the imaginary beings called

States?"[7] Madison declared that experience had shown no danger of state interests being harmed by a national majority[8] and that "the President is to act for the *people* not for *States*."[9]

Congress, whose members are elected by districts and states, is designed to be responsive to constituency interests. The president, as Madison pointed out, is supposed to take a broader view. When advocates of the electoral college express concern that direct election of the president would suppress local interests in favor of the national interest, they are in effect endorsing a presidency that is responsive to parochial interests in a system that already offers minority interests extraordinary access to policy makers and opportunities to thwart policies they oppose.

Interestingly, supporters of the electoral college almost never specify what geographically concentrated rights or interests need special protection through the electoral college. They certainly have not developed a general principle to justify additional protections for some interests rather than others.

INTERESTS OF SMALL STATES

Do the states with small populations that receive special consideration in the electoral college have common interests to protect? The great political battles of American history—in Congress and in presidential elections—have been fought by opposing ideological and economic interests, not by small states and large states.

A brief look at the seventeen states with the fewest electoral votes (that is, three, four, or five) shows that they are quite diverse.[10] Maine, Vermont, New Hampshire, and Rhode Island are in New England; Delaware and West Virginia are in the Middle Atlantic region; North and South Dakota, Montana, and Nebraska are in the Great Plains; New Mexico is in the Southwest; and Nevada, Wyoming, Utah, and Idaho are in the Rocky Mountain region. Alaska and Hawaii are regions unto themselves. It is not surprising that their representatives do not vote as a bloc in Congress and that their citizens do not vote as a bloc for president.

Even if small states share little in common, are there some interests that occur only in states with small populations? Most farmers live in states with large populations. The market value of the agricultural production of California, Texas, Florida, and Illinois alone substantially exceeds that of all seventeen of the smallest states combined.[11]

For that matter, agriculture does not lack for powerful champions, especially in Congress, which has taken the lead in providing benefits, principally in the form of subsidies, for agriculture. Rather than competing to give farmers more benefits, presidents of both parties have attempted to restrain congressional spending on agriculture. The electoral college has not turned presidents into champions of rural America.

It is difficult to identify interests that are centered in a few small states. Even if we could, however, the question remains whether these few interests out of the literally thousands of interests in the United States deserve special protection. What principle would support such a view? Why should those who produce wheat and hogs have more say in electing the president than those who produce vegetables, citrus, and beef? Is not the disproportionate Senate representation of states in which wheat and hogs are produced enough to protect these interests? There is simply no evidence that interests like these deserve or require additional protection from the electoral system.

ATTENTION TO STATE INTERESTS

Ultimately, the argument that the electoral college protects state interests rests on what candidates actually do. Do they pay particular attention to small states, and do they focus on state-based interests that would otherwise be neglected under direct election of the president?

The most direct means for candidates to appeal to voters is to visit their states and address them directly. We know that when candidates appear at campaign events, they do not focus their remarks on what we might view as state-based interests as opposed to issues of national concern.[12]

But where do they appear? The 2008 election followed a typical pattern.[13] Barack Obama campaigned in only fourteen states and John McCain in just nineteen states. Joseph Biden and Sarah Palin each campaigned in eighteen states. Each of the four candidates campaigned in the competitive small states of New Mexico, Nevada, and New Hampshire. Presidential candidates Obama and McCain went to *none* of the other fourteen small states. Palin added a single visit to Maine and her home state of Alaska, while Biden visited Montana, West Virginia, and his home state of Delaware. In addition, none of the candidates campaigned in the four large states of California, Texas, New York, and Illinois, except for a single McCain event in New York, where he had to be for other reasons.

In the course of overlooking most states, candidates also avoid entire regions of the country. Democrats have little incentive to campaign in the heavily Republican Great Plains and Deep South, and Republicans have little incentive to visit most of Democratic New England.

In sum, the electoral college provides no incentive for candidates to pay attention to small states and take their cases directly to their citizens. Indeed, it is difficult to imagine how presidential candidates could be *less* attentive to small states than they are. Candidates go where the electoral college makes them go, and it makes them go to competitive states, especially large competitive states. In addition, they do not compensate for their lack of visits to small or noncompetitive states by advertising there.[14]

In sum, the fundamental justification of the electoral college—that it forces candidates to be attentive to particular state interests, especially those concentrated in small states—is based on faulty premises. In reality, the electoral college discourages candidates from paying attention to small states and to much of the rest of the country as well.

PRESERVING FEDERALISM

Defenders of the electoral college sometimes assert that it is a key underpinning of federalism. Actually, it is unclear what federalism has to do with the presidency, the one elective part of the government that is designed to represent the nation as a whole rather than as an amalgam of states and districts.

The founders did not design the electoral college on the federal principle. Neither the existence nor the powers and responsibilities of state governments depend in any way on the existence of the electoral college. Moreover, the founders expected electors to exercise their individual discretion when casting their votes. They did not expect electors to vote as part of any state bloc. No delegate at the Constitutional Convention referred to the electoral college as an element of the federal system or even as important to the overall structure of the Constitution. Indeed, the electoral college was "an anti-states-rights device," designed to keep the election of the president away from state politicians.[15]

Federalism is deeply embodied in congressional elections, in which two senators represent each state just because it is a state and in which members of the House are elected from districts within states. Direct election of the president would not alter these federalism-sustaining aspects of the constitutional structure.

PROTECTING NON-STATE-BASED MINORITY INTERESTS

Some observers claim that the electoral college ensures a "proper distribution" of the vote, in which the winning candidate receives majority support across social strata, thus protecting minority interests. This claim is nonsense. In 2000 George W. Bush did not win a larger percentage than Al Gore of the votes of women, African Americans, Hispanics, and Asian Americans; voters aged eighteen to twenty-nine or those aged sixty or older; the poor; members of labor unions; those with less than $50,000 of household income; those with a high school education or less and those with postgraduate education; Catholics, Jews, and Muslims; liberals and moderates; urbanites; or those living in the East and West.[16]

It strains credulity to claim that Bush's vote represents concurrent majorities across the major strata of American society. What actually happened in 2000 was that the electoral college imposed a candidate supported by white male Protestants—the dominant social group in the country—over the objections not only of a plurality of all voters but also of most "minority" interests in the country. This antidemocratic outcome is precisely the opposite of what defenders of the electoral college claim for the system.

ADVANTAGE OF DIRECT ELECTION

Direct election of the president would provide the incentive for candidates to encourage all of their supporters, and not just those strategically located in swing states,[17] to go to the polls, because under direct election, every vote counts. Thus direct election would increase voter turnout and stimulate party-building efforts in the weaker party, especially in less competitive states.

Moreover, candidates would find it easy to spread their attention more evenly across the country. Because the cost of advertising is mainly a function of market size, it does not cost more to reach ten thousand voters in Wyoming than it does to reach ten thousand voters in a neighborhood in Queens or Los Angeles. Actually, it may cost less to reach voters in smaller communities because larger markets tend to run out of commercial time, increasing the price of advertising.[18] Unsurprisingly, candidates do not ignore smaller markets when they campaign within states.[19]

It is possible that some candidates would find it more cost-effective under direct election to mobilize votes in urban areas or to visit urban areas where they would receive free television coverage before large audiences. Such actions would do nothing to undermine the argument against the electoral college, however. Small states receive almost no attention now. Instead, direct election would provide increased incentives for candidates to campaign in most small states, as well as increased incentives to campaign in many large and medium-sized states. Direct election would disperse campaign efforts rather than deprive small states of them.

Some critics of direct election mistakenly claim that it would splinter the two-party system. Their criticism is based on the premise that direct election would require a runoff between the two leading candidates. But it would not. Under the electoral college, victorious presidential candidates—including, most recently, John F. Kennedy (1960), Richard Nixon (1968), Bill Clinton (1992 and 1996), and George W. Bush (2000)—have received less than a majority of the national popular vote about 40 percent of the time since 1824, and there is no relation between the vote they received and their later success in, say, dealing with Congress. Some of our strongest presidents, including James K. Polk, Abraham Lincoln, Grover Cleveland, Woodrow Wilson, Harry S. Truman, and Kennedy, received a plurality, but not a majority, of the popular vote.

Nor is the electoral college the basis of the two-party system. Single-member districts and plurality election are, and the nation would be one electoral district under direct election. Thus direct election would not splinter the party system.

By contrast, direct election would protect the country from the mischief of third parties. The electoral college's unit rule encourages third parties, especially those with a regional base, because by winning a few states they may deny either major-party candidate a majority of the electoral vote. Such a result was certainly the goal of Strom Thurmond in 1948 and George Wallace in 1968. Imagine giving these racist candidates leverage to negotiate with the leading candidates before the electoral votes were officially cast. Moreover, even without winning any states, Nader inadvertently distorted the vote and determined the outcome of the 2000 election.

To put this analysis in another way, consider two candidates, one contemplating running as a third party candidate in a system of direct election, and the other running under the electoral college. A potential candidate in a system of direct election risks his or her political future by running against the official party candidate. And there is no compensation. Such a candidate can win nothing at all coming in third, even taking a significant portion of the vote. So there is little incentive to run. Under the electoral college, however, a candidate finishing, say, third, might win some electoral votes and have leverage in determining the winner of the election. There is much more incentive for third party candidates to run under the electoral college than under a system of direct election.

It is important that we not fall into a logical trap. It is circular reasoning to argue that direct election will produce a plethora of candidates, which in turn will force a runoff, which in turn will encourage candidates to run. In fact, direct election will not produce more general election candidates than the electoral college, and there is no need for a runoff.

CONCLUSION

There is no question that instituting direct election of the president will be difficult. Change will require amending the Constitution, a complex and time-consuming task. Although the public and many states and organizations support direct election, there are obstacles to change. Principal among them are officials who believe that their states or the members of their organizations benefit from the electoral college. We now know that these officials are wrong. They have reached their conclusions on the basis of faulty premises. Understanding the flawed foundations of the electoral college is the critical first step on the road to reforming the system of presidential selection. The culmination of this effort should be allowing the people to directly elect the presidents who serve them.

CON: Daniel H. Lowenstein[1]

Various arguments are made against the electoral college,[2] but the case against the constitutional method for selecting presidents depends overwhelmingly on a single impulse: the belief that the president ought to be the person who gets the majority of popular votes. It is a strong impulse for most Americans, seemingly grounded in common sense. Accordingly, the defender of the electoral college has a difficult task. But readers who are willing to question this impulse will find that the more attention they give to the electoral college, the better it looks.

The electoral college is pernicious, we are told, because it fails to guarantee that a candidate who wins a majority of the popular vote will be elected. Defenders dodge that thrust by pointing out, accurately, that few if any processes of American government are majoritarian in a thoroughgoing way. Whether and to what extent that defense is adequate is a complex question, but fortunately one that we can set aside as unnecessary. In fact, the electoral college is no less majoritarian than most of the proposals to replace it.[3]

The most prominent proposal is that the candidate who receives a *plurality* of the popular vote should be elected. Roughly a third of the time in American presidential elections, no candidate wins a majority of the popular vote. When that is the case, it is quite possible that a majority of voters would have preferred one of the other candidates over the plurality winner.

To avoid this problem, some have proposed permitting voters to cast an alternative vote. For example, if your first choice among three candidates, A, B, and C, is C, you'd be able to vote for C but also list B as your second choice. If C ran third, he would be dropped and your vote would be transferred to B. That may sound like an appealing idea, but the alternative vote would not solve the problem unless voters were required to rank all the candidates on the ballot. If there were more than a few candidates in the race, moreover, mandatory alternative voting would be burdensome for voters. In Florida in 2000, for instance, there were ten candidates on the ballot, a large but not extraordinary number. Making voters rank all ten would be unworkable.

Such logistical considerations aside, an alternative vote, whether voluntary or mandatory, would greatly change the nature of third-party and independent presidential candidacies. Currently, such candidacies derive their meaning from the fact that voting for a third-party or independent candidate is a "hard" vote. That is, if you vote for a liberal third party instead of the Democratic candidate or a conservative third party instead of the Republican, you are making a strong protest by depriving your usual major party of your vote. If the alternative vote permits (or requires) you to ultimately cast your vote for one major party over the other, then the strength of the protest is diminished. This change might be good or bad, depending on your view of third party politics in presidential elections. But if it is to be considered it should be considered on its own merits, not as a byproduct of trying to satisfy a dogmatic insistence on majoritarianism.

Opposition to the electoral college rests essentially on an abstraction; namely, that only the numbers generated by aggregating the national popular vote may be considered. But as the previous paragraph shows, the way those numbers are produced and aggregated can have consequences for the overall political system. Defenders of the electoral college believe that those consequences should be considered. As Bradley Smith has put it, opponents of the electoral college

> focus on inputs—the test of a proper democracy is who votes, and how these votes are weighted. . . . Supporters of the Electoral College talk of outputs—the test of a proper democracy is whether it produces good government and good presidents.[4]

We shall turn shortly to the consequences or, as Smith calls them, the outputs. But first we should note the strong performance of the electoral college over many years, even when measured by the opponents' own majoritarian criterion. First, on its face, the electoral college is no less majoritarian than proposals relying solely on the popular vote. Within a given state, the electoral vote goes to the plurality winner, just as the entire election would go to the national popular vote plurality winner under the most prominent proposal of the opponents. No candidate can be elected without winning a majority of the electoral vote. A majority winner in the electoral college is almost inevitable, given our present two-party system—the electoral college has produced a winner in every election since 1824.[5] However, if for any reason there were no majority in the electoral college, the selection would be made in the House of Representatives, where a majority of the states would be required to elect a president and where each state's vote would require a majority of the House delegation from that state.

The electoral college thus contains the same plurality possibility as its most prominent rival at the first stage and is purely majoritarian thereafter. It may be objected that majorities of electors or of House delegations from the states are irrelevant, because only majorities of voters should count. But that is simply to restate the opponents' dogma. Of course, a conclusion that is assumed will indeed follow. But the assumption is an unreasonable one, not consistent with the general workings of democratic politics. Laws, for example, are passed by majorities of legislators, not majorities of voters. In parliamentary countries like Britain and Canada, the prime minister is chosen through a process as indirect as the electoral college, but the fact that it is the majority in Parliament that selects the leader rather than a majority in the electorate has not prevented those countries from being regarded as democracies.

Even if we concede to the opponents that the popular vote should be decisive, the electoral college still holds up surprisingly well. Since 1840, by which time a strong two-party system had taken hold, there have been three elections in which the winner in the electoral college has failed to win the most popular votes. In each case a Republican defeated a Democrat: Rutherford Hayes over Samuel Tilden in 1876, Benjamin Harrison over Grover Cleveland in 1888, and George W. Bush over Al Gore in 2000. Each of those elections was quite close in the popular vote, as is almost certain any time the electoral college and the popular vote do not go the same way. However, as Smith has pointed out,[6] large numbers of blacks who would have voted solidly Republican were disfranchised in 1876 and even larger numbers in 1888. Had all persons entitled to vote under the Constitution been able to do so, Hayes and Harrison would have received the most popular votes. If the national popular vote is valued because it is assumed to be an indicator of the choice of the majority of eligible citizens who choose to vote, then in two out of the three elections in which the electoral college vote and the popular vote diverged, the electoral college outdid the popular vote in picking the rightful winner.

But in truth, the opponents' position depends on grossly exaggerating the reliability of the national popular vote as an indicator of voter choices. As John McGinnis has demonstrated, the popular vote only approximates popular sentiment.[7] Voter opinion shifts throughout the campaign, so that in a very close election the result could be different if the election were held a week earlier or a week later. Different weather in different parts of the country and other conditions can affect who votes. Even with improvements in election administration that have occurred since 2000, significant numbers of votes are either not properly cast or not accurately counted. None of this is intended to detract from the importance of the votes cast in an election. But when the popular vote is close enough to make a divergence from the electoral vote a practical possibility, it is also close enough to be determined by a variety of random circumstances.

Let us now summarize the argument to this point. I have conceded that the impulse underlying opposition to the electoral college—namely, that the person who receives a majority of popular votes should be elected—is one that appeals to most Americans. But I have attempted to show that proposals to replace the electoral college with a national popular vote either run afoul of the majority principle at least as much as the electoral college or raise serious practical problems. Opponents insist that the unit to be counted in presidential elections should be individual voters rather than presidential electors, even though aggregation of majorities is common elsewhere in our political system, such as the requirement that a majority of legislators rather than constituents are needed to enact a law. Even when attention is given only to popular votes, the electoral college only rarely diverges from the popular vote. In two of the three instances when it did, the electoral college assessed the popular choice more accurately than the popular vote. Furthermore, whenever the popular vote is close enough to permit a divergent outcome from the electoral vote, random factors ensure that the popular vote result will fall within the margin of error.

Under these circumstances, the decision whether to jettison the electoral college should not be made on the basis of dogmas and abstractions, but rather on its practical effects. Yet the few practical arguments that electoral college opponents have put forth lack substance. One of these is that the electoral college unfairly discriminates between large and small states. Unfortunately, opponents have not been able to agree on whether the discrimination favors large or small states.[8] When those who complain about discrimination cannot agree on who benefits and who is harmed, the discrimination cannot be very flagrant.

Opponents also complain that in close presidential elections the campaigns focus their attention on "battleground" states that could go either way in the election. Campaigning is highly concentrated in those states, but it is not at all clear why that is a problem. A slightly more plausible version of this argument claims that presidential candidates make policy commitments that favor the battleground states' parochial interests at the expense of the national interest. The effect of such commitments on national policy is probably small compared to many other factors, such as similar commitments made by presidential candidates in the primaries and the advantages that some states have because their representatives in Congress hold leadership positions or important committee chairs. Furthermore, whatever small harm occurs to the national interest from this phenomenon is offset by the electoral college's removal of the temptation to make such commitments in states that are not battleground states.

We now turn to the practical advantages of the electoral college. I shall offer five. Though they are hardly overwhelming, they easily outweigh the theoretical and practical arguments against the electoral college, which have been shown to be without substance.

1. Although the candidate who receives a plurality or majority of the national popular vote usually also wins a majority of the electoral vote, the electoral vote margin is almost always substantially larger than the popular vote margin. In 2008, for example, Barack Obama received 53 percent of the popular vote but 68 percent of the electoral vote. The result is to promote confidence in the decisiveness of the election and therefore to enhance the new president's ability to lead.

   Sanford Levinson, an opponent of the electoral college, belittles this phenomenon as a "conjurer's trick" that works only because Americans do not understand how it is performed.[9] If it were a conjurer's trick it would be a bad one, because its workings are no mystery. Probably most Americans learn the basic idea of the electoral college in high school, and they are reminded of it by reporters and commentators each election year.

   But it is not a conjurer's trick. Opponents may think so because, as we have seen, they are dogmatically fixated on the popular vote. The national popular vote is a statistical artifact, though surely an interesting one. It has no bearing on the election of a president. Far from being an illusion, the electoral vote is the real way a president gets elected. The substantial majorities of electoral votes that most winners of a plurality or bare majority of the national popular vote have received were real majorities, not phony ones.

2. The electoral college causes presidential elections to be significantly oriented around states. There are many pressures for nationalization of our society, against which it is important to maintain the states as strong and vital elements of our system, both in practice and in popular understanding. Presidential elections draw far more popular attention than any other routine event in our politics. The fact that the electoral college orients those elections around states reinforces the popular sense that the states are the building blocks of the nation.

   To clarify, this is not an argument that the electoral college increases the relative power of the states compared to the federal government. To the contrary, in response to the argument of opponents that the electoral college enhances the power of battleground states to promote their parochial interests, I have argued that the effect in question is small enough to be disregarded. My argument is not one of relative power but that the electoral college enhances the actual and perceived importance of the states in the federal system.

3. The electoral college produces good presidents. Not in all cases, of course, but consider this list: Washington, Jefferson, Jackson, Lincoln, Cleveland, Theodore Roosevelt, Wilson, Franklin Roosevelt, Truman, Eisenhower, and Reagan. Probably no single person is a fan of all those presidents, but taken as a whole it is an impressive group of effective and distinguished leaders. With the possible exception of the United Kingdom, which also elects its chief executives indirectly, there is not a country in the world that has produced a comparable group.

    Perhaps a national popular vote system would have produced the same or a similar list. Perhaps. But "did" is better than "might have."

4. The fourth advantage of the electoral college was highlighted by the controversy following the 2000 election. The electoral college has the considerable advantage of confining such controversies to one state or, as in the somewhat comparable case of 1876, a handful of states. If we elect presidents on the basis of the national popular vote, then any time that vote is close enough to be within the "margin of litigation,"[10] the 2000 controversy will be magnified fifty-fold. The competing candidates and their legal teams will have as much reason to bring into question votes in states that were won handily by one of the candidates as in states that were close. In contrast, the electoral college places a firewall around the state or states in which the election was extremely close.

5. As we have been reminded in significant House and Senate races over the last several years, it is possible that a nominee shortly before an election or an elected person shortly after the election may die, become disabled, or for other reasons such as scandal become manifestly unsuitable for the office. This could be a serious problem for the country if it were to happen to a presidential nominee or a president-elect.

    It would be difficult to devise legislation to address such a problem directly. It would be necessary to define the circumstances in which the legislation would go into effect, create a process for applying the definition to actual circumstances, and decide how a replacement should be chosen. In a process established by law, neutral and objective standards would be necessary. Death would be easy to determine. Disability would be less so, but perhaps manageable. Manifest unsuitability would be almost impossible to define in a statute.

What is needed for such a situation is not a legal but a political solution. It so happens that the electoral college is ideally suited. The decision to depose the nominee or the president-elect would be made by people in each state selected for their loyalty to the individual in question. Abuse of the system to pull off a *coup d'état* would therefore be out of the question. But when death, disability, or manifest unsuitability plainly existed, the electors would be amenable to a party decision, which would be the best solution.

Admittedly, this problem is not particularly likely to arise, but it is hardly far-fetched. The electoral college shortens the period during which we would have no handy political means of dealing with the problem. Even that period could be eliminated if Congress were to pass a statute enabling a percentage of the electors who voted for the winner to petition to reconvene the electoral college any time up to the inauguration.

When I pointed out this important advantage of the electoral college on an earlier occasion, Professor Levinson objected that the choice of a replacement president or nominee would actually be made by the party's national committee, which would expect "thoughtless loyalty" from the electors.[11] That the choice would likely be a party choice seems to me a good thing, not bad. Although the national committee might "expect" loyalty from the electors, my guess is that to get it, they would have to act responsibly.

In sum, the electoral college enhances presidential majorities and thereby helps new presidents govern; it reminds us of the centrality of the states in the federal system; it has a track record of producing a generous supply of distinguished presidents; it protects us from having to fight 2000-type battles on a national stage; and it provides a flexible political solution in the event of death, disability, or manifest unsuitability of a presidential nominee or president-elect between the pre-election period and the time the electoral votes are cast (a period that could easily be extended to the time of the inauguration). The republic will survive if we abandon the electoral college and these benefits with it. But we will give up those benefits for theoretical and practical reasons that are without substance.

RESOLVED, proportional representation should be adopted for U.S. House elections

PRO: Douglas J. Amy

CON: Mark E. Rush

In the nineteenth century Americans typically looked upon European politics with a certain smug disdain. They regarded American political institutions as the greatest in the world, and certainly far superior to the corrupt and autocratic regimes of the "old world." In the twentieth century, however, educated Americans began to look upon Europe with a more envious eye. During the Progressive era, some American reformers viewed European nations as a model for more humane social welfare policies. During the 1950s a number of American political scientists looked admiringly to Great Britain and its "responsible party" model in which the Government governed, the Opposition opposed, and the voters knew which party to reward when things went well and which to blame when things went badly. Britain's parliamentary system seemed free of the divided government and diffused responsibility of America's system of checks and balances and separation of powers. Today, the responsible party model has fallen out of fashion and the European import that American students of politics seem most interested in is proportional representation.

Under a system of proportional representation, legislators are elected in multimember districts based on the percentage of vote their party receives. If, for instance, in a district with ten seats a party gets 40 percent of the vote, then it is allotted four seats. In a closed party list system, the voter casts a ballot for the party, and which of the party's representatives gets seated depends on the order in which the party slates its nominees. If a party wins four seats, then the first four candidates from the party list are elected. In an open list system, voters are able to indicate their candidate preferences as well as their party preference; the party vote determines the number of seats a party gets but the winners from each party are determined, at least in part, by the candidate preferences of that party's voters. The American system, in contrast, is a single-member plurality system in which one legislator is elected to represent each district and the winner is whoever gets the most votes.

Interest in proportional representation in the United States actually dates back to the Progressive era at the turn of the twentieth century. A Proportional Representation League was founded in the United States in 1893, which was modeled on the British Proportional Representation Society that had formed a decade earlier. Between 1915 and 1950, more than twenty cities in the United States adopted proportional representation, though none operated in partisan elections. Indeed, part of the appeal of proportional representation in America was that it would be a way to elect individuals who were independent of the party bosses. In every city but Cambridge, Massachusetts, proportional representation was soon repealed, and in all but a few cases the repeal was accomplished by a direct vote of the people. Ironically, one progressive reform—the popular referendum—was used to abolish another.

In 1908 the voters of Oregon approved an initiative that empowered the legislature to adopt proportional representation in multimember legislative districts. Its passage was fueled by popular outrage at the gross inequities that had been produced by single-member districts in state legislative races in the previous election. In 1906 fifty-nine Republicans and only one Democrat were elected to the Oregon House of Representatives, even though Republicans had gained only 57 percent of the statewide popular vote. The rest of the vote was split between the Democrats (32 percent), Socialists (7 percent), and Prohibitionists (5 percent). Since Republicans earned a plurality in every district but one, they won 98 percent of the House seats. The legislature, however, never used the power bestowed upon it by the 1908 initiative, and attempts to require the legislature to change to proportional representation failed three times at the ballot box and once in the legislature.

The revival of interest in proportional representation in contemporary politics owes much to frustrations people feel with the large number of uncompetitive and often uncontested legislative races as well as the blatant gerrymandering of districts to protect incumbents or to advance one party at the expense of another. Douglas J. Amy gives voice to those popular frustrations in advancing the case for proportional representation. Proportional representation, Amy argues, is more just and more democratic. Mark E. Rush, however, cautions us to beware of attractive-sounding foreign imports. There is nothing inherently wrong with proportional representation, Rush contends, but political systems are complex and interconnected, and changing one aspect may have unintended and deleterious consequences on other parts. A baboon's heart may work perfectly well in a baboon, but that does not mean that it will work in the body of a human being.

PRO: Douglas J. Amy

Proportional representation is the best political reform that most Americans have never heard of. If you ask most people if they think we should adopt proportional representation elections for the U.S. House of Representatives, you will probably be greeted with a blank stare. They have little idea what proportional representation (PR) is, or what the considerable advantages of this reform would be.

That's because most of us don't often think about electoral systems—the methods we use to cast votes and elect our leaders. We don't usually question the way we elect members of the House or consider whether there might be a better way. Our traditional system is what political scientists call a single-member plurality (SMP) system. House members are elected one at a time in single-member districts, with the winner being the candidate who gets the most votes—the plurality.

This is the usual way we elect the members of our legislative bodies in the United States, so most of us just take for granted that this is the only logical way to do so. But a large part of the rest of the world would disagree. Most Western industrialized democracies have long ago abandoned SMP elections in favor of proportional representation.

But why have they done that? Should we follow in their footsteps and adopt this reform? To understand the answers to these questions, we need first to understand what PR is, and then to understand how it solves many of the serious problems that afflict our current election system.

WHAT IS PROPORTIONAL REPRESENTATION?

Proportional representation comes in several varieties, but there are two basic ways that all PR systems differ from our current winner-take-all election system. First, all PR systems use multimember districts. Instead of electing one House member in each district, PR uses much larger districts in which several members are elected at once. The figures below illustrate districting maps for a hypothetical state that elects twenty members to the U.S. House. Figure 7-1 shows our current single-member district system, Figure 7-2 shows a PR system that uses four five-member districts, and Figure 7-3 shows a PR system with two ten-member districts. Each party nominates a slate of candidates equal to the number of seats at stake—five candidates in a five-member district. ·

The second way that PR differs from our current system is in the way that winners are chosen. Instead of a winner-take-all approach, winners of seats are determined by the proportion of the vote that a party receives. So if 40 percent

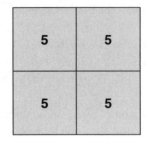

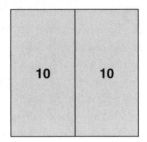

of the voters in a ten-member district cast their votes for Democratic candidates, that party would receive four of the ten seats, and those seats would go to the four Democratic candidates receiving the most votes. If candidates for a Green Party or a Libertarian Party win 10 percent of the vote, that party would receive one seat. (Those who want more details on the workings of specific PR systems—what the ballots look like, etc.—should consult the Proportional Representation Library at www.mtholyoke.edu/acad/polit/damy/prlib.htm.[1])

Since PR requires multimember districts with at least three or four seats to divide up among the parties, it would not be appropriate for some very small states that elect only one or two members to the U.S. House. However, PR would be perfectly feasible for larger states, and there is no constitutional barrier to its adoption. The Constitution allows states to choose the method of electing their representatives to the House.

Proportional representation was invented to correct what were seen as serious deficiencies in winner-take-all systems like single-member plurality and to produce election results that are fairer and more representative. So what exactly are the problems with our current system, and how does PR solve them?

UNREPRESENTATIVE ELECTIONS

The basic flaw with our single-member district voting system is that it does a terrible job representing the American public. All Americans should have a say in government, but this is impossible under our current system. It is intentionally designed to represent only one part of the public—those who vote for the winning candidate in a district. Everyone else—who may make up 30 percent, 40 percent, or more of the voters in a district—gets no representation. So if you are a Republican in a predominantly Democratic district (or vice versa), an African American in a white district, or a minor party supporter in any district, then you are usually shut out by our current election system. Your candidate is unlikely to win and you will have no one to represent you and speak for you in the legislature.

Typically, in U.S. House elections, about a third of all votes are wasted—cast for a candidate who loses. This means that over thirty million Americans usually come away from the voting booth with no one to represent them in the House. It's no wonder that many Americans feel little connection with their members of Congress—they are represented by someone they voted against.

Proportional representation eliminates this problem. Wasted votes are virtually eliminated and nearly all voters are able to elect someone to represent them. Even if you vote for a party that gets only 20 percent of the vote, you still win some representation. In PR elections, 90 percent to 95 percent of voters elect someone to represent them, in contrast to only 60 percent to 65 percent in current U.S. House elections. Instead of a winner-take-all system, PR is an all-are-winners system, which is one reason it is so popular in other democracies.

Wasted votes also tend to create unfair distortions in representation. Some political groups get more representation than they deserve and others get less. On the district level, for instance, the party with 51 percent of the vote gets 100 percent of the representation. On the legislative level, the result is that parties often receive many more or many less seats than they deserve based on their proportion of the vote. For example, in Massachusetts, all ten members of its U.S. House delegation are Democrats, even though upwards of one-third of Massachusetts voters cast their ballots for the Republican candidates. Sometimes the misrepresentation is so egregious that the party that comes in *second* in the popular vote is actually able to elect the *majority* of that state's representatives—which has happened in five out of the last nine House elections in Texas.

Such unfair and undemocratic outcomes would be eliminated by PR. For example, if Massachusetts adopted PR, Republican voters would be able to win three of that state's ten seats. The idea behind PR is that all parties should get the representation they deserve—no more and no less.

BREAKING THE TWO-PARTY MONOPOLY

Imagine that you log on to iTunes and discover that it now offers only the two most popular genres of music: pop and country. No alternative, no rap, no folk or electronic or world or classical. Just the big two. You would probably be outraged—along with millions of others. But Americans run into this very same situation every time they enter the voting both. The only real choice we have is between Republicans and Democrats, even if we think of ourselves as a Green, a Libertarian, a Progressive, or an independent. Only about 25 percent of Americans strongly identify with the Republican or Democratic Parties, and yet the House is made up of representatives from only those two parties. This is hardly democratic.

The main reason for this two-party monopoly is our single-member plurality system. In this system, only large parties that can receive a majority or plurality of the vote stand any chance for victory. A popular third party may pick up 20 percent or 30 percent of the vote but still fail to elect anyone. This discourages people from even voting for these candidates. Worse yet, if people do vote for a third party candidate, they may actually help elect the candidate they like the least! This is the classic "spoiler" problem. Voting for a Green candidate only takes away votes from the Democratic candidate and helps the Republican to win. In the 2000 election, votes for the Green Party candidate, Ralph Nader, allowed George W. Bush to win Florida—and the presidency. In short, our current electoral system discriminates against minor parties and often punishes people who dare to vote for them.

PR would break up this two-party monopoly and eliminate the spoiler problem. Under PR, all parties that get over the minimum required percentage of the vote—usually around 5 percent—are guaranteed their fair share of seats and representation. A minor party that receives 20 percent of the votes would receive 20 percent of the seats—one seat in a five-seat PR district. Voters could support the candidates and parties that they really believed in without fear of wasting their votes or aiding their opponents.

Americans want more choices at the polls. Two-thirds say they want to see other parties seriously challenge the Democrats and Republicans for office. But this is very unlikely to happen unless we get proportional representation. And only with PR would we be able to have a multiparty U.S. House that truly represented the diversity of political opinion in this country.

ELIMINATING GERRYMANDERING

Another problem that plagues American elections is gerrymandering. This is the manipulation of district lines to produce an unfair advantage for one party or another. The dominant party in a state often redraws districts lines to favor its own candidates. Republicans, for instance, might divide up a large mass of Democratic voters and incorporate them into two predominately Republican districts—thus ensuring that all the Democratic votes are wasted and only Republicans are elected.

Gerrymandering creates uncompetitive districts where only one candidate stands a real chance of being elected. If a district is drawn so that it is 70 percent Democratic, the Republican candidate has virtually no opportunity to win. So while voters think they are deciding who represents them when they go to the polls on election day, often that decision has already been made for them many years before by the politicians who drew their district's lines.

Thanks largely to gerrymandering, over 95 percent of House members now reside in uncompetitive districts and get reelected as a matter of routine. Real competition—and real voter choice—is largely absent from these elections. In a recent election in Florida, 43 percent of the U.S. House seats were not even contested by one of the major parties. And gerrymandering not only predetermines who wins a specific seat, but often who controls the House itself. That is why the parties fight so viciously over the redistricting process—they know that a favorable outcome can ensure a majority of the seats in the House even if that party doesn't get a majority of the votes. Gerrymandering helped Republicans to win a majority of the seats in the House between 1996 and 2004, even though they never received more than 50 percent of the nationwide vote.

Gerrymandering would be eliminated overnight in most states if we were to adopt PR for House elections. This is not simply because there would be fewer district lines to draw. Studies have shown that gerrymandering is virtually impossible in large multimember districts with at least five seats.[2] No matter how you draw the lines of these large PR districts, it has no effect on who gets elected. Every party—even the smaller ones in the district—is able to win its fair share of seats. And every district is competitive because all parties can win some seats. With PR, the voters decide who is elected, not line-drawing politicians.

BETTER REPRESENTATION OF WOMEN AND MINORITIES

Adopting PR would also greatly improve the representation of women and racial and ethnic minorities, and add important new voices and new perspectives to the House of Representatives. Right now, these groups are substantially underrepresented. For example, Hispanics make up 15 percent of the U.S. population but occupy only 6 percent of the seats in the House. And while women make up 51 percent of the population, they occupy only 17 percent of the House seats.

These groups tend to be much better represented in countries using proportional representation. For instance, most PR countries do better—often dramatically better—at ensuring fair gender representation. In Sweden, 47 percent of the lower house is made up of women. In Norway, it's 38 percent; the Netherlands, 37 percent; Germany, 32 percent.

What accounts for this? PR tends to increase the representation of women and minorities because more of them tend to be nominated under this system. The reason is that candidates are nominated in slates in PR elections. In a five-member district, each party puts up a slate of five candidates. With a slate system, parties can institute quotas, something that is not practical in an SMP system. Some European parties, for instance, require that at least 40 percent of the candidates on the slate be women. And because more women are nominated, more tend to get elected.

Some Americans would balk at such quotas. But even without quotas, adopting a PR system would still encourage the nomination and election of more women and minorities. In our current single-member district system, it does not seem odd if the sole party nominee is a white male. But with a slate of five candidates, it would seem decidedly odd if all the nominees were white males. This creates pressure that encourages parties to voluntarily include some female and minority candidates on their slates.

So if we want the U.S. House to be more inclusive and democratic—to be a true mirror of the U.S. population—then we need PR to ensure that voices of women and minorities are heard and acted on in this important policy making body. Imagine how different the House would be with 30 percent to 40 percent female representatives.

CONCERNS ABOUT PROPORTIONAL REPRESENTATION

With all of these advantages of PR, it is easy to see why most other industrialized Western democracies have switched to this system. Nevertheless, some Americans worry about the potential disadvantages of PR. For example, one common fear is that a multiparty House of Representatives would be a recipe for chaos and gridlock. If it is difficult to get legislation passed in a two-party House, imagine how much harder it would be with three, four, or five parties! However, if we look at the multiparty legislatures in Europe, we find that this gridlock rarely occurs. If fact, most of them pass legislation much more efficiently than our Congress. How can this be? It is simple: each party does not go its own way. Parties typically join together in two large coalitions: a center-right coalition and center-left coalition. And one of these has the majority of votes needed to pass legislation.

Some Americans are also concerned that they would have to give up their small, single-member districts to adopt PR elections. They like having an elected official that represents the interests of their local geographical area. However, there is a form of PR that does not require voters to give up their small local districts. It is called "mixed-member PR," where half the legislature is elected from small, single-member districts and the other half by PR so that all parties are represented accurately. This system has proved very popular among recent adopters of PR, such as New Zealand and the new parliaments in Scotland and Wales. In the United States, states with large delegations of House members could easily adopt this form of PR and have the best of both worlds: small districts and fair representation.

Another common misconception about PR is that voters would only be able to vote for parties, not individual candidates. But this is true of only one form of PR—the closed party list system. Most PR systems allow voters to cast their votes for the individual candidates that they prefer. For example, in the open list system, voters cast a vote for an individual candidate on a party's list of candidates. That vote counts two ways. First, it helps determine the party's portion of the overall vote and the number of seats it wins. Second, it counts for the individual candidate. Those candidates with the most votes go to the top of the list and are the first ones chosen to occupy any seats that are won by the party.

Finally, some people doubt whether a voting system like PR that is currently used in countries with different political systems and political cultures can be transplanted successfully to the United States. But in fact, during the twentieth century, several American cities experimented with PR, and the record shows that this system fulfilled its promise of providing more diverse and representative government with no gridlock.[3] Today Cambridge, Massachusetts, still enjoys the benefits of PR elections for its city council and school board.[4]

PR: TOWARD A BETTER DEMOCRACY

Ask yourself these questions: Do you believe that all citizens should have a voice in government, that all parties should compete on an even playing field, that both minorities and majorities deserve representation, and that our legislatures should reflect the true diversity of political views among the public? If you answered "yes," then you should be in favor of proportional representation.

In the end, the choice between proportional representation and SMP is not simply about deciding between two different voting systems. It is about choosing between having more or less democracy in the United States. Changing to PR elections in this country would be a major step toward creating a fairer, more representative, more inclusive, and ultimately more democratic political system.

That is why proportional representation is a reform that deserves much greater attention in the United States. In the two other major Western democracies that still cling to the SMP system, Great Britain and Canada, large and active citizens' movements are promoting a change to PR. We need that same kind of movement in this country.[5]

CON: Mark E. Rush

The single-member plurality (SMP) system used in the United States has many detractors and supporters. The manner in which that system is currently administered in the United States is admittedly flawed and in need of reform. Nonetheless, I am skeptical that the conversion to a system of proportional representation (PR) will solve the problems that critics identify in the SMP system or bring about the benefits that they associate with PR.

PR works the way it does in other countries because other countries have different party systems and constitutional structures. Accordingly, a conversion to PR without significant changes to the electoral and constitutional systems will fail to achieve the goals of reform that its advocates desire and possibly worsen some of the problems PR advocates associate with the American political system. Conversion to PR would likely bring about some positive changes to the existing manner in which the SMP system is administered in the United States, but the systemic reform that PR advocates desire would require much more extensive, costly, and probably undesirable changes.

THE CASE FOR REFORM

In *Real Choices/New Voices,* Douglas J. Amy offers perhaps the most succinct summary of the case for converting to PR.[1] He argues that PR would:

- Solve the problems associated with and caused by the SMP system and redistricting.

- Improve election campaigns by offering voters more diverse choices among candidates and providing incentives for candidates to debate and discuss relevant political issues (instead of focusing on personality and other distractions).

- Foster a multiparty system.

- Enhance the representational opportunities for women and minorities.

- Encourage voter turnout.

There is no gainsaying that a switch to some form of PR would change the conduct of American politics and elections. The question remains whether a conversion to PR would *improve* politics.

WHAT'S WRONG WITH THE AMERICAN ELECTORAL SYSTEM

The manner in which American elections are currently administered is in dire need of reform. Incumbent legislators, either directly or indirectly, control the process by which they are reelected. On the one hand, such control (and the clear conflict of interest that comes with it) is inescapable: someone must write campaign spending laws and draw legislative district lines. On the other hand, it is difficult to find a serious justification for allowing incumbents to draw and gerrymander the districts from which they and members of Congress are reelected.[2] In some states, the lines are drawn by either nonpartisan or bipartisan commissions but the state legislators ultimately decide whether or not to accept such commission-drawn districting plans.

This situation presents a clear conflict of interest and is perhaps the most obvious target for advocates of PR. Incumbent legislators control the process by which they are individually returned to office and by which the legislature collectively is reconstituted. Although the federal and state courts have placed some restrictions on this process (for example, the one person–one vote requirement[3] and restrictions on the division of municipalities) and Congress has also constrained it via the Voting Rights Act, it is clear from the last half-century of controversies and case law surrounding redistricting that such restrictions have done as much to promote more creative ways to keep incumbents in office as they have to render the process fairer. Court cases are littered with florid descriptions of voting districts whose contorted boundaries demonstrate that they were drawn to ensure particular electoral outcomes and decrease electoral competition.

Defenders of the current process contend that it is the most democratic because it enables the people to challenge districting plans by contacting their elected representatives. Such justifications are disingenuous. Redistricting plans are like budgets, road bills, or any other large piece of legislation. They require the efforts and attention of an entire legislature, special committees, and support staff. It is unreasonable to expect a lone constituent (or anything less powerful than a strongly organized group of voters with a lot of resources at their disposal) to scrutinize a redistricting bill, study the minutiae associated with it, and then have the wherewithal to force a lone legislator to change the will of a majority of his or her colleagues.[4]

CAN PR DELIVER ON ITS PROMISES?

Although Amy and I agree that the American political system is flawed, I do not share his confidence that PR is the solution to the problems he identifies.

I grant that PR would significantly reduce incumbent control over the electoral process. Since PR would replace single-member electoral districts with multimember districts, there would be fewer districts to draw and correspondingly fewer district lines to gerrymander. However, it is less clear that PR would achieve Amy's other main objectives of increasing voter choice among candidates and securing a more representative and responsive government.

If we look to European electoral systems, it is evident that PR does result in a broader variety of parties contesting elections. Multimember PR districts offer voters more choices, but who controls those choices? The answer is the parties, not the voters. To achieve proportionality in the legislature, PR systems typically limit voters' choices to a list of candidates chosen by party elites. Depending on the type of PR system, voters may have no choice whatsoever among the candidates they elect. If the lists are "closed," voters choose only between the slates of candidates constructed by each party. If the lists are "open," voters have the opportunity to choose among the candidates on the lists. In contrast, the electoral system in the United States offers voters a wide range of choices in selecting a party's candidates.

Advocates of PR justify the restriction on voter choice by pointing to PR's tendency to produce more diverse legislatures. Legislatures elected by PR, it is argued, would contain a greater diversity of parties and political perspectives as well demographic characteristics such as race and gender. The ends, they argue, justify the means.

Diversity of representation is clearly vital to governmental legitimacy. James Madison called for it in his republican solution to the problem of faction. In *Federalist* No. 10, he called for an extended republic so that the diversity of voices in the legislature would be increased and, as a result, no one voice would dominate. In the nineteenth century, John Stuart Mill called for a conversion to PR in England for similar reasons. He argued that there was no reason to bias the electoral process in favor of interests that were of the right shape, size, or geographic dispersion to fit into a single-member district.[5]

The elimination of single-member districts would certainly create incentives for the formation of new political parties that are more narrowly focused than the Democrats and Republicans. Minority representation would also increase under PR. Currently, state legislatures are criticized for drawing contorted districts in order to create district-based electorates with enough minority voters to ensure that they have the chance to vote as a minority and elect a "representative of their choice." Under PR there would be no need to draw these contorted districts because minority voters from across a state could coalesce in support of their preferred candidates. Their representational opportunity would not depend on the density of their geographical dispersion.

A conversion to PR, however, would not automatically enhance the representational prospects for women. To gain representation in PR systems, women have often depended on the use of gender quotas in the assembly of party lists.[6]

If we believe that the legislature should more accurately reflect the demographic diversity of society, then it is important to take steps to ensure that women and minorities have a fair shot at attaining legislative representation. However, if elites must structure the rules of a PR electoral system to ensure or enhance the probability of particular proportional results, then PR offers only the chance to switch from one form of gerrymandering to another. In both cases, voters' election day choices—and the electoral outcomes—are conditioned and controlled by elites. The electoral marketplace is not really any freer under PR than under SMP.

Thus the price of ensuring representative diversity in PR systems comes in no small part at the expense of limiting popular inputs into the electoral process. In the United States, we take pride in using the direct primary system to ensure that the people determine the nature of their options on election day. Party lists and quotas that ensure the election of particular types of candidates take this power away from the people and place it in the hands of party elites. In the end, one might argue that this makes for better democratic outputs. But do they justify limiting the scope of democratic inputs?

ACCOUNTABILITY AND GOVERNANCE

The role of elites in PR systems also raises questions about political accountability. As Amy correctly notes, PR systems are no more prone to political gridlock than majoritarian systems. PR parliaments tend to divide into two big blocs—a governing majority and an opposition. Insofar as these two blocs are more likely to be coalitions, they are that much more likely to cater to and represent a broader array of interests than the governing party in a two-party system. But, insofar as advocates of PR promote its tendency to foster a multiparty political system, it is important to note the consequences that a multiparty system would have on the formation of governing majorities in the House.

In a two-party system, we know that either the Democrats or the Republicans will govern the House and Senate. In a multiparty system it may not be clear which parties will constitute the government (i.e., the majority coalition) even after the election is over. Unless one party secures a majority of the seats in the parliament, there will be no "government" until at least two parties form a coalition big enough to comprise a majority of the legislative seats.[7] In some cases, this may produce a governing majority that does not represent the people's preferences.[8] In and of itself, this is not enough to condemn PR. In 2000 the electoral college elected George W. Bush despite the fact that Al Gore received a majority of the popular vote.

But, while the 2000 election was controversial, it manifested the predictable workings of the U.S. constitutional system. I would argue that the propensity of multiparty systems to form governments after the election is over is more pernicious than the idiosyncrasies of the electoral college because it subordinates the popular vote to the self-interested bargaining among elite party leaders. The electoral college, at least, elects the president on the basis of a formula that is not subject to partisan wrangling. In a multiparty PR system, the rules of the political game can change after the election is over.

A second point concerns the role of representatives in parliamentary systems and their capacity to voice the concerns of their constituents. If a party or group is fortunate enough to be part of the governing coalition in a parliamentary system, it will have a very powerful voice. However, if it is part of the opposition or, simply, not part of the governing majority, its members will have very little power. In contrast, in the U.S. Congress there are fewer parties (only two) but individual members of Congress have a great deal of power. They can introduce bills, block legislation in committees, filibuster (in the Senate), and so forth.

In parliamentary systems, the cabinet sets the political agenda. Members of the opposition and backbench members of the government may be free to voice concerns about the government's program. But, in the end, members of the majority are expected essentially to serve as a rubber stamp for the government. As well, in contrast to their congressional counterparts, members of the government have precious few opportunities to introduce legislation on behalf of their constituents unless the cabinet grants them the chance to introduce a "Member's Bill." Members of the opposition have no power to introduce or block legislation.

Thus, while PR may enhance the diversity of the legislature's composition, it will not necessarily augment the power of political minorities or the opposition. A governing coalition may appear to be more diverse than its counterpart in a two-party system, but its members still have less power than their congressional counterparts.[9] In fact, it could be argued that backbenchers in a parliamentary government have even less power than members of the opposition in the U.S. Congress because the latter at least have the power to block legislation in committees.

A third important point is that the impact of PR on the governing process will be buffered by the structure of the American constitutional system. PR is principally associated with parliamentary systems of government. In such systems, the executive and legislative branches are fused and correspondingly more dependent on each other than are the president and legislature in a system of separated powers and checks and balances such as that in the United States. In addition, in most cases, parliamentary systems are, for all intents and purposes, unicameral.

Accordingly, using PR for House elections could exacerbate the American system of checks and balances and, perhaps, enhance the likelihood of gridlock because adopting PR for House elections would not necessarily result in a change in the Senate. The two houses function in markedly different ways—even when they are both controlled by the same party.[10] Were the Senate to remain essentially a two-party body and the House to become a multiparty one, this would add to the propensity of the U.S. government to suffer from gridlock and, I suspect, result in a shift of power to the executive.

In the American constitutional system, this enhanced conflict between the two houses of Congress would be disastrous. In parliamentary systems, mechanisms exist to dissolve the government and call for new elections when gridlock occurs or when the governing party is unable to pass legislation. No such mechanisms exist in the American constitutional system. House and Senate terms are fixed. Accordingly, it is possible for the government to remain gridlocked indefinitely.

Fortunately, in the American political system gridlock does not last very long because, with only two parties, the leaders in the House and Senate can resolve differences with relative ease. But were the House to be fragmented among multiple parties, negotiations between the House and the Senate would be that much more difficult. When dealing with the Senate or the president, the Speaker of the House will have a much harder time speaking for a multiparty coalition—especially if the parties could withdraw from the coalition. This weakening of the House would render Congress less capable of passing legislation. Under such circumstances, the president would have a much easier time setting the political agenda and dominating the divided legislature.

Since the legislative process requires the president and Congress to cooperate, and since legislation must originate in Congress, a House divided among several parties would hamstring the entire government. Ironically, then, a more diverse legislature could result in a diminution of the power of the Congress and the capacity of the government to act.

CONCLUSION

Changing the electoral system without also implementing wide-ranging changes to the manner in which the House (and the government as a whole) conducts business would be an incomplete call for reform. A shift to PR—or any electoral system change—embodies much more than a mere shift in the way we translate votes into legislative seats. It includes many choices about the way elections are conducted, what voters vote for, and how governments are formed.[11] Do we want to vote for parties or candidates? What powers do we want our individual members of Congress to have? Do we want to risk more gridlock in order to attain a more diverse House of Representatives? Do we want to shift power toward the executive? Do we want to give parties more control over the candidates and the manner in which they appear on the ballot?

My goal in this essay is to offer a strong note of caution about conversion to PR or some other alternative electoral system for the House of Representatives. PR, in and of itself, is not a bad thing. Democracy thrives in PR systems as much as it does in SMP systems. But we cannot assess the impact of a conversion to PR without taking into account the ripple effect it would have on the rest of the political system. Truth in advertizing requires PR advocates to acknowledge that the sort of parliamentary politics they desire would require much more than a change in vote-counting rules. To prevent the unintended, but unavoidable, consequences I've discussed, a conversion to PR would also require a wholesale restructuring of the American constitutional system. Simply grafting PR onto the American constitutional system would be a very bad idea.

8

RESOLVED, the "no cup of coffee" rule should be adopted in Washington

PRO: Burdett Loomis

CON: Anthony J. Nownes

The origins of nearly all leading interpretations of American politics and government date back to James Madison, and in particular to *Federalist* No. 10. The subject of Madison's essay was faction, which he defined as "a number of citizens, whether amounting to a majority or a minority of the whole, who are united and actuated by some common impulse of passion, or of interest." Madison regarded factions as a necessary evil in a free society. He thought they were necessary because their causes are sown in human nature, and thus the only realistic way to eliminate them would be by "destroying the liberty" that "is to faction what air is to fire." He regarded factions as evil because the impulses that motivate them invariably are "adverse to the rights of other citizens, or to the permanent and aggregate interests of the community." Factions want what they want when they want it, according to Madison, and don't care about anybody else.

Contemporary scholars and commentators share Madison's view that organized groups are a necessary part of the political system. Americans today, protected by their constitutionally guaranteed rights to organize and express their views freely, are if anything even more prone to form groups to advance their ideas and interests than in Madison's day. Columnist George F. Will once said that the best way to get a short course in modern American politics would be to open the Washington, D.C., phone directory and scan the long columns of entries under "American" (the American Bar Association, American Medical Association, Americans for Tax Reform, and so on) and "National" (the National Rifle Association, National Association of Manufacturers, National Organization for Women, etc.).

Organized groups continue to be regarded as necessary, but do we still think of them as evil? The answer to that question is less clear. Look at the terminology people use when talking about groups. Those who are upbeat about the power and pervasiveness of groups in our political system often call them "stakeholders." Those who are critical are more likely to refer to them as "special interests." Sometimes the terminology boils down to what one thinks of a particular group—seniors may regard AARP (long called the American Association of Retired Persons) as a stakeholder and young people may consider it a special interest. In an effort to maintain some measure of analytic objectivity, political scientists generally use the less-charged term "interest groups."

The broad range of modern opinions about interest groups manifests itself in lively debates about what kinds of activities are appropriate for these groups. As the long lists in the Washington phone book demonstrate, most groups that can afford to maintain an office in the nation's capital do so. (The same is true in the various state capitals.) The groups' representatives are usually called "lobbyists" because back in the day they would wait in the lobbies outside the Senate and House of Representatives in hopes of catching the ear of influential legislators as they came and went. The most important job of the lobbyist is to persuade these legislators to help the group he or she represents, either by enacting policies to help it or by defeating policies that would harm it.

Much of what lobbyists do is entirely above board, such as making legal campaign contributions to legislators and providing them with information and arguments they may find useful in doing their jobs. Friendships sometimes form between lobbyists and members of Congress—in fact, one of the best reasons for an interest group to hire a particular lobbyist is that he or she already knows lots of people on Capitol Hill. Unlike other national capitals such as London and Paris, Washington is in many ways a small town, where lobbyists and legislators may run into each other in church, at a Redskins football game, or at their kids' school.

A friendly or professional relationship is one thing, but what happens when a lobbyist crosses the legal or ethical line, using money, patronage, and other favors to improperly influence what members of Congress do? As a general rule, friends feel comfortable treating each other to meals and giving each other gifts. But what if the giver is a lobbyist and the recipient is a public official? Is a small gift—say, a book or a scarf—okay? How about picking up the check at a restaurant? Or, to make the subject of this debate tangible, should a lobbyist be allowed to buy a legislator a cup of coffee?

No, argues Burdett Loomis—instead, Congress should adopt a rule that bars gifts of any size "from lobbyists and others who come into contact with lawmakers." According to Loomis, a clear and strict "no cup of coffee" rule will both enhance the reputation of Congress and reduce suspicion of lobbyists. Opposing the resolution, Anthony J. Nownes maintains that such a rule is unnecessarily severe and would not get at the real problem of improper influence.

PRO: Burdett Loomis

If you can't drink a lobbyist's whiskey, take his money, sleep with his women and still vote against him in the morning, you don't belong in politics.

—Jesse "Big Daddy" Unruh, *Speaker of California Assembly*, 1961–1969

Ah, the good old days of legislative life, when a strong state house speaker like Jesse Unruh could dismiss criticisms leveled against the overwhelmingly male California legislature, whose members roamed the capitol's corridors during the day and its hotspots at night.[1] Fifty years after Big Daddy ruled the California Assembly, no legislative leader could get away with such a cavalier, misogynistic statement. Times have changed. Today women constitute about one-fifth of all legislators, and reporters who cover legislatures don't wink at peccadilloes or ignore apparent conflicts of interest. Yet even in the post-1970s era of ethics reform, legislators have proven fully capable of unethical, sometimes illegal, behavior that has derailed dozens of careers and inflicted serious damage to the always-fragile reputation of the legislative branch.

What can be done to protect legislators from their own worst instincts and thereby buttress public confidence in legislatures and their members? Part of the solution is for legislatures to adopt a "no cup of coffee" restriction on gifts from lobbyists and others who come into contact with lawmakers. Although this blanket prohibition on gifts will not, by itself, salvage Congress's dismal reputation, it would be an important first step in building public support for legislative actions on Capitol Hill.

LEGISLATURES AND LEGITIMACY

All governmental institutions, including legislatures, must enjoy a reasonable level of public support if citizens are to comply with decisions made by their officeholders. The legitimacy of decisions made by a legislature derives from citizens' assessments of the fairness of the legislative process and the motivations of individual lawmakers.

The public's regard for Congress, seldom a popular institution, has hovered around near-record lows over the past decade, with favorable ratings generally in the mid-twenties. Although there has been a modest post–Barack Obama bump, survey data dating back to the 1970s demonstrate how badly frayed are the threads that bind together members of the public and their lawmakers (see

Figure 8-1

Percentage of Americans Approving of the Way Congress Is Handling Its Job, 1975–2009

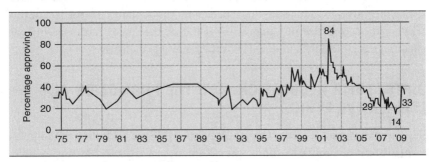

Source: Gallup 1975–2009. Reprinted with permission.

Figure 8-1).[2] Low levels of public approval remain the norm despite the adoption of myriad rules governing campaign funding, lobbying, and personal behavior.

Especially in recent years, the highly partisan nature of legislative politics has placed increasing strains on congressional approval and the legitimacy of the decisions reached by Congress. The declining presence of moderate lawmakers, moreover, makes compromises more difficult to reach, and partisan narratives often focus attention more on seeking political advantage in the next election than on productive deliberation over difficult issues. The harsh partisan environment in Washington makes it all the more important that lawmakers remain free from scandal; the combined weight of intense partisanship and personal corruption, real or perceived, would reduce Congress's legitimacy at the very time when it is addressing a host of major issues, such as health care and energy, where high-powered, expensive lobbying is the norm.

Congressional legitimacy and freedom from scandal are also significant goals for congressional parties, whose leaders desire to maintain the best "brand name" possible when their members run for reelection. Serious ethics laws may well protect legislative parties from the actions of those lawmakers who might act in illegal or unethical ways. Hence, protecting the overall legitimacy of Congress would be good politics, especially for the majority party, which hopes to remain in power. And the majority's control of the legislative process means that its members' ethical lapses will be more significant than those in the minority. Ethical questions surrounding Democratic Speaker Jim Wright in the late 1980s, along with the so-called House Banking scandal of the early 1990s, allowed Republicans to break forty years of Democratic control in the lower chamber in 1994.[3] Likewise, various illegalities surrounding Majority Leader Tom DeLay and lobbyist Jack Abramoff, among others, provided electoral fodder for the Democrats to win back control in 2006.[4] In the end, individual legislators, legislative parties, and the entire body of lawmakers all have strong incentives to reduce unethical behavior. Although in 2007 the House did create a modest Office of Congressional Ethics, the major responsibility for encouraging ethical behavior lies with the members themselves.

GIFTS, THEIR REGULATION, AND THE PROMOTION OF LEGISLATIVE ETHICS

Representatives and senators face a host of ethical issues, including the solicitation and use of campaign funds, the acceptance of trips to industry conferences, and possible financial conflicts of interest. Banning gifts to legislators will not address all of these concerns, nor will more comprehensive legislation. As legislative scholar Alan Rosenthal observes in his study of ethics in the state legislatures: "There is little indication that law, in and of itself, can address the ethical issues facing legislatures."[5] Such a conclusion does not mean, however, that regulation is a nonstarter. Gifts to public officials, whatever their form, create the clear possibility that the recipients will feel some obligation to reciprocate in the form of political or policy favors. As a National Conference of State Legislatures (NCSL) briefing paper puts it: "Lobbyists and lawmakers face the perception that having lobbyists provide travel, lodging, entertainment or food creates an expectation that the legislator will repay this 'gift' with favorable treatment."[6] Regulating or eliminating gifts offers both substantive and symbolic pay-offs. Substantively, enacting a low limit or a ban will reduce the possibility of a corrupt exchange; symbolically, the legislature can publicly advertise that it is not for sale.

REGULATING GIFTS: THE STATE EXPERIENCE

Although in the past fifteen years Congress has adopted meaningful rules on accepting and disclosing gifts, the most useful data on gift restrictions come from the fifty states. Forty-eight states place some kind of restriction on gifts, with only Indiana and South Dakota standing as exceptions, and several states have adopted complete or nearly complete bans on gifts. As NCSL staff member Peggy Kerns notes:

> The phrase, "no cup of coffee," implies that nothing can be given to a lawmaker from a lobbyist. Colorado, Florida, Kentucky, Massachusetts, Minnesota, North Carolina, Tennessee, and Wisconsin are in this category,

but none completely bans every gift. In Wisconsin, legislators can accept anything of value, if it also is available to the general public. Colorado allows gifts from the general public if they are under $50. Florida has a gift exception for floral arrangements or other celebratory items given to legislators and displayed in the chambers the opening day of the session. Except for its $3 per day limit for gifts and food and beverages, Iowa could be considered a zero tolerance state.[7]

The states have acted on gift regulations like the "laboratories of democracy" that they are reputed to be.[8] The mix of gift policies is wide ranging, and although there is no consensus on what is appropriate, some common themes emerge. These include: (1) the source of gifts, (2) the intent of the giver or the recipient, (3) limits on gifts, (4) exceptions to those limits, and (5) disclosure of gifts by either the giver or the recipient.

SOURCE OF GIFTS

Some states emphasize limiting gifts by lobbyists, while others cast their nets more widely, including principals (e.g., businesses or associations) as well as their agents (the lobbyists). With the growth of so-called "contract lobbyists," who represent multiple clients, states have focused much of their attention on such individuals, yet the wording of many statutes demonstrates the difficulty of addressing just lobbyists. For example, Illinois defines a "prohibited source" of gifts as "anyone who: is seeking official action, does business with the member, conducts activities regulated by the member, has interests that may be substantially affected by the performance or nonperformance of the member's duties, [or] is a lobbyist." Legislators' families receive special attention both as givers and potential recipients of gifts. Most states require the registration of lobbyists, along with some disclosure, so identifying them is straightforward. Increasingly, the NCSL notes, states differentiate between lobbyists and ordinary citizens. Alaska and Colorado, for example, set a "zero tolerance" level of $0 for gifts by lobbyists, while allowing $250 and $50, respectively, in gifts from ordinary citizens.

Motivations

In many states, legislators and lobbyists must become mind readers. Regulations often specify that neither lobbyists nor legislators should "knowingly" offer or receive a gift of more than a specified value. Likewise, some states assume that intent can be discerned. Alabama dictates: "No person shall offer or give to a public official or member of his household a thing of value *for the purpose of influencing official action.* No legislator or member of his household shall solicit or receive a thing of value for such purpose."[9] As various scandals have played out across the states, the question of determining the intent to influence has often stood at the center of legal actions against either recipients or providers of gifts.

Gift Limits

Every state but South Dakota and Indiana restricts the size of gifts to lawmakers. Beyond that blanket statement, nothing is simple. Limits are often conditional or partial, and are open to evasions in many circumstances. Still, an increasing number of states permit no gifts from either lobbyists or anyone else, subject to a handful of modest exceptions.[10] More common is what the NCSL labels a "Bright Line Test," which specifies a dollar limit on gifts to legislators, calculated by year, sometimes with monthly limitations as well. New Mexico sets its limit at the high end—a $1,000 annual total from a lobbyist, with a $250 single gift limit—while neighboring Arizona allows just $10 in gifts per year. Montana limits gifts to $50 a year, but Nebraska permits $50 per month. What is clear is that the states cannot agree at what level gifts may become a corrupting influence. Still, states work hard to specify the level at which corruption, or its appearance, will be discouraged. For example, Georgia has enacted a law that caps the speaking fee or honorarium that a public official can accept at $101. Apparently, $100 cannot corrupt, but $102 just might. On the whole, restrictions on gift levels appear arbitrary at best, often reflecting reactions to previous scandals, rather than well-considered policy choices.

Gift Limit Exceptions

Adding to the overall incoherence of gift limits are the numerous and detailed exceptions to these restrictions. Thus, while Alabama ostensibly bars all gifts "for the purpose of influencing official action," myriad exceptions render the policy—already suspect due to the need to establish intent—largely unworkable. Some particular exceptions include (1) "seasonal gifts" of under $250 total; (2) lodging and tickets to sporting events, "if the hospitality does not extend beyond three days;" as well as (3) transportation and lodging within the United States to educational or informational events, "up to $250 per day." Many states have enacted laws that exempt relatives from restrictions on gift giving. Hawaiian lawmakers cannot receive influence-oriented gifts, although this term is never defined, but exceptions to this policy include gifts from "a spouse, fiancé, fiancée, any relative within four degrees of consanguinity or the spouse, fiancé, or fiancée of such a relative."[11] In the close quarters of state legislative politics, lobbyists could easily be part of this extended family.

Some of the thorniest issues arise over gifts of modest value, such as promotional material and food and drink at receptions. The most frequent exception is "food and beverage for immediate consumption," although qualifications vary, often based on whether all legislators are invited or an event is open to the public. Still, the differences can be great, ranging from $3 worth of food and beverages in Iowa to $50 in Tennessee.

Disclosure

"Banning entertainment and gifts is easier said than done," states Rosenthal. "Indeed most states have not seriously considered an outright ban but instead have settled for disclosure."[12] Disclosure is an essential element in enforcing gift limits, and most states require the itemized listing of gifts over a certain amount; again, there is great variation on amounts and exceptions, and some states rely completely on banning or restricting all gifts or those from lobbyists. What is clear is that disclosure by itself has not proved adequate in stemming unethical behavior.

GIFT LIMITS IN CONGRESS

Congress came late to the question of regulating gifts. Until 1995, the rules governing lobbying and related activities flowed from the 1946 Federal Regulation of Lobbying Act, which the Supreme Court upheld in 1953, while severely limiting its scope. Only in 1995, with the passage of the Lobbying Disclosure Act, did Congress enact legislation that seriously addressed the relations between lobbyists and legislators, including the giving and receiving of gifts. Under this law, members and staff were prohibited from accepting a gift of more than $50 or any annual combination of gifts that exceeded $100. Lobbyists easily found ways to circumvent these seemingly straightforward limits, and the years between 1995 and 2006 proved highly lucrative for lobbyists.[13] Jack Abramoff and others skirted the gift regulations by having their clients, including corporations, foreign governments, and Indian tribes, pick up the tab for lavish meals, travel, and sporting events. The scandals surrounding Abramoff led Congress to consider more stringent reforms.

In the wake of Abramoff's 2006 conviction and the Democrats' capture of the House and Senate, Congress passed the Honest Leadership and Open Government Act of 2007, which bans members and staff from accepting gifts or privately funded travel from lobbyists and organizations that employ lobbyists, except as specified by each chamber's rules. This ban is coupled with stronger reporting rules and a requirement that legislators and staff receive *prior* Ethics Committee approval for travel paid from any outside sources.

In short, the 2007 legislation seriously tightened gift restrictions to members and staff; there remain a number of exceptions that mirror those most common in the states, such as the exchange of gifts with relatives, consuming food or drink of nominal value at a reception, and appearing at "widely attended" events, even when a meal is served.

THE CASE FOR THE NO CUP OF COFFEE RULE

So is the no cup of coffee rule worth adopting? Or is it just a stunt that will distract from the more systemic reforms that may be needed to clean up Congress and restore public confidence in the institution? Or, alternatively, might it prove counterproductive, obstructing essential communications between legislators and lobbyists?

Listen to the observations of Alan Rosenthal, the most distinguished state legislative scholar of the past fifty years. After viewing reams of evidence and observing hundreds of legislative sessions, Rosenthal has concluded that a no cup of coffee rule should be approved. He writes:

> A few years ago, when I chaired New Jersey's Commission on Legislative Ethics and Campaign Finance, I voted with the majority . . . to require lobbyists to report what they spent on individual legislators. We did not give too much thought to adopting the so-called no-cup-of-coffee rule. . . . More recently, I had occasion to testify on ethics legislation in New Mexico and then in Kentucky. In New Mexico I opposed the no-cup-of-coffee rule; in Kentucky I supported it. The switch was not because legislators in New Mexico are more trustworthy or more needy than legislators in Kentucky. It was just that in a period of less than a year I had changed my mind.[14]

Rosenthal sees legislators as "besieged" by the media and viewed suspiciously by the public, and under those circumstances, "it is prudent for legislators and legislatures to throw in the towel." Refusing all favors from lobbyists may well be overkill, as some legislators would contend, but Rosenthal concludes, "the elimination of such transactions rests on ethical, as well as prudential, grounds."

Legislators, as representatives of the electorate, are expected to hew to higher ethical standards than ordinary citizens, who do not exercise policy-making authority. Given their institution-based authority, lawmakers should adopt a no cup of coffee rule as a simple, easily understood way to demonstrate their embrace of strong, universal regulations to reduce corruption. In addition, as Rosenthal observes, this rule is "prudential," in that it protects legislatures and legislators from both the reality and appearance of corruption. Given the institutional need for legitimacy and the low levels of public support for Congress, legislators will profit from a clear demonstration of their willingness to abide by high ethical standards. If, simultaneously, adhering to a no cup of coffee rule helps insulate them from electoral defeat, then that too is a prudential action.

In arguing for a congressional no cup of coffee rule on gifts from the public, and specifically lobbyists, the irony is that Congress, for all intents and purposes, has already adopted such a rule in its 2007 reform legislation. Despite some minor exceptions, much like those found in state laws, Congress has essentially banned gifts from lobbyists. As the Senate Select Committee on Ethics observes, "As a general rule, Senators and staff can no longer accept gifts of *any* value from registered lobbyists, agents of foreign principals, or the private entities employing or retaining them."[15] Although the House and Senate have split on some exceptions, such as buying tickets for entire tables at charity dinners, such loose ends could easily be cleaned up. At present, representatives and senators have done most of the heavy lifting to eliminate gifts from lobbyists, but they have received little credit for their reforms.

Much as some state legislatures have done, and as Rosenthal advises, the House and Senate should adopt the no cup of coffee rule, and then widely publicize this action. Individual members would benefit, as would Congress, and public support might well grow in response. Since Congress is almost all the way there, why not go the final yard?

CON: Anthony J. Nownes

Most Americans think that lobbyists are corrupt, mendacious jerks. Indeed, in the wake of the Jack Abramoff lobbying scandal in 2006, a full 81 percent of respondents to a survey conducted by the Pew Research Center for the People and the Press said that it is "common behavior for lobbyists to bribe members of Congress." A similar 2006 CBS News/*New York Times* poll found that "77 percent of registered voters believe that lobbyists bribing members is just 'the way things work in Congress.'"[1] These results are not unusual. In my twenty years of studying lobbyists, I have seen polling results like these time and time again.

Why are lobbyists held in such contempt? There are several answers to this question. First, some lobbyists are bad apples. Occasionally lobbyists *do* cross the line, as periodic lobbying scandals illustrate. Second, the media tend to focus on the bad and the ugly of lobbying rather than the good. Honest, hardworking lobbyists who do a good job for their clients and charge reasonable fees do not make very good stories. Thus what most of us hear or read about are bad lobbyists. Third, most people do not trust government officials very much. In fact, polls show that most Americans think almost as poorly of government officials as they do of lobbyists. Thus it is no surprise that lobbyists, who make their living working closely with government officials, are held in low esteem. Finally, many lobbyists are prototypical "fat cats." Studies show that most professional lobbyists are well-educated and affluent. As such, they are obvious targets for spasms of populist rage.

In sum, there are several reasons for lobbyists' unpopularity. Unfortunately, by dint of their occasional misdeeds, lobbyists themselves are partially responsible for their tarnished image. No one who studies lobbyists, however, seriously believes that lobbyists are as bad as most people think they are. Indeed, virtually every major study of lobbyists indicates that most lobbyists are ethical, hard-working, honest people. Nonetheless, there are good reasons to regulate lobbyists and lobbying. Most important, we need to do everything possible to ensure the legitimacy of the political process. But is a draconian measure like the "no cup of coffee" rule a good idea? The short answer is "no."

I present two arguments against the no cup of coffee rule. The first comes from lobbyists themselves. Over the years I have interviewed or surveyed thousands of local, state, and federal lobbyists, and their opinions of strict regulations are nearly uniform. Most lobbyists believe that extremely strict regulations are simply unnecessary. They argue that neither lobbyists nor government officials are as corrupt as these types of regulations assume they are, and extremely stringent regulations are a waste of time and energy. The second argument is my own: strict rules such as the no cup of coffee rule are unnecessary palliatives that do not address the real problems associated with lobbying.

WHY NOT? THE LOBBYISTS' ANSWER

The view of the great majority of lobbyists that I have spoken with can be paraphrased as follows:

> We agree that lobbying should be regulated. But a prohibition on providing anything of value—even a cup of coffee—to a government decision maker is overkill. We agree that pricey gifts and lavish outings should be heavily regulated or banned. But cups of coffee, gifts of nominal value,

and food need not be regulated. We understand that some government officials are corrupt and open to undue influence from lobbyists. But most officials are not. Moreover, even the "bad apples" that are corruptible are not going to sell themselves for a cup of coffee; they will hold out for something of considerably more value. In short, regulating lobbyists makes sense. But banning gifts of nominal value and $2 cups of coffee is just silly.

Many lobbyists describe strict regulations in much stronger language, using words such as "ridiculous," "stupid," "insulting," and "absurd." Lobbyists argue that the no cup of coffee rule is based on the faulty premise that government decision makers are for sale to very, very low bidders. Their basic point is simple: legislators and other public servants are not the cheap whores regulators think they are.

People who lobby for a living acknowledge that they regularly meet face-to-face with legislators, legislative staffers, and executive branch personnel of various kinds. These meetings take place in government offices as well as in public places. Not surprisingly, food and beverages are sometimes involved. In other words, sometimes public policy is hammered out over Starbucks coffee and bagels. The idea behind the no cup of coffee rule is that a lobbyist's purchase of a $2 coffee is akin to a bribe—either a payment for government services rendered or an advanced payment on services to be delivered later. It is hard to believe, lobbyists say, that any government decision maker is for sale for the price of a cup of coffee.

One of the biggest problems that lobbyists have with stringent regulations such as the no cup of coffee rule is that they tend to stifle legitimate social interaction between lobbyists and government decision makers. Lobbyists point out that socializing with government decision makers is important, and in many cases useful. Politics, after all, is often about compromise. And compromise is easier when people work with people they know, trust, and respect. Lobbyists point out that the best way to get to know a person, and to learn whether or not you can trust that person, is to spend one-on-one time with him or her. Moreover, lobbyists point out that many policy problems facing our country are large, complicated, and confusing. Sometimes policy discussions between lobbyists and government decision makers last hours and hours. These policy discussions are likely to be more fruitful and informative if a lobbyist and a government decision maker are allowed to relax and get comfortable. In short, many lobbyists believe that socializing between lobbyists and government decision makers is actually good for the political process. And regulations that would lead to less socializing would actually make things worse in Washington rather than better.

WHY NOT? MY ANSWER

You can decide for yourself whether or not you agree with lobbyists that no government decision maker in Washington can be bought for a cup of coffee or a cheap gift. Whatever your answer, sadly, one thing is clear: some government officials can be bought if the price is right. Consider, for example, Randall "Duke" Cunningham, former Republican member of Congress from California, who is now in federal prison after admitting that he was essentially bought and paid for by some defense contractors. Consider also Bob Ney, former Republican member of Congress from Ohio, who in 2005 pleaded guilty to corruption charges. These cases and others like them invite the following question: Given that some government officials can be bought, what can they be bought for? To me, the answer is obvious—money. And this is why I have reservations about the no cup of coffee rule. The no cup of coffee rule is a palliative that does not address the real problem with lobbying, which is money.

The no cup of coffee rule assumes that unduly close relationships between lobbyists and government decision makers may lead the latter to do things that are not in the public interest—or worse, that are illegal or unethical. This may be the case, and it may not be. Most lobbyists think it is not the case, but let us assume for a moment that it is. In other words, let us assume that close relationships between lobbyists and government decision makers always lead to unethical behavior among government decision makers, always distort policy outcomes, and always undermine the public interest. This assumption invites the question: What can lobbyists do to foster close relationships with government decision makers? To people who push the no cup of coffee rule, the answer is, "they can buy government decision makers coffee and pastries." To me, the answer is, "they can give government decision makers money."

For proof that it is money rather than coffee and cheap gifts that allows lobbyists to forge close personal relationships with government decision makers—close personal relationships that have the potential to cause trouble—we need to look no further than the case of Jack Abramoff, the former Washington lobbyist who is now serving prison time for tax evasion, fraud, and corruption. Abramoff did not garner access to Republican power brokers by buying coffee or donuts for them (though he did do these things). Abramoff became Abramoff by raising and distributing money. In other words, he became part of the Republican "power elite" by providing money, not gifts or food. For example, between 2001 and 2004, Abramoff and his partner Michael Scanlon (who pleaded guilty to federal corruption charges in 2005) and his Indian tribal clients combined to contribute money to fully *one-third of all members of Congress*. In all, their contributions exceeded $1,000,000.[2]

The Center for Responsive Politics had this to say about Abramoff's monetary activities:

> [D]uring the time that Jack Abramoff was their lobbyist his clients contributed at least $5 million to members of Congress and their political action committees, to candidates for federal office and to political parties. More than 300 members of the 109th Congress received campaign contributions from a client of Jack Abramoff while he was their lobbyist—81 Senators and 227 members of the House of Representatives. . . . On average, each recipient got about $16,000.[3]

It is also worth mentioning that Abramoff was designated a "Bush pioneer" in 2004 for raising over $100,000 for the president's reelection campaign,[4] and that Abramoff and his clients contributed $68,300 to former Speaker of the House Dennis Hastert's campaign committee and leadership PAC (political action committee) between 1998 and 2004.[5]

Supporters of the no cup of coffee rule will undoubtedly point out that Abramoff provided loads of gifts and favors and trips to elected officials. And indeed, this is the case. But it was money that helped Abramoff forge his legendarily close ties to government officials, not coffee and donuts (or even the $74 steak at Abramoff's Washington eatery Signatures). Elected officials want and need money, and they go to great lengths to get it. Some even break the law to keep the money flowing. In sum, the case of Abramoff illustrates that it is money that allows lobbyists to forge close personal relationships with government officials, not coffee. A rule that outlaws cheap gifts and coffee but allows lobbyists to donate personal funds to—and raise money for—candidates, political action committees, and political parties is silly.

WHAT SHOULD WE DO?

How should we regulate lobbying, then? There are several steps we should take. First, we should bar registered lobbyists from contributing money to candidates' campaign committees or PACs, from soliciting campaign or PAC contributions from their clients, from serving as campaign treasurers for candidates, and from playing any role whatsoever in candidates' leadership PACs. Perhaps we should even consider a law that would bar registered lobbyists from playing any role whatsoever in federal election campaigns. If we are serious about regulating the gifts that lobbyists provide to government decision makers, we should regulate the most important gifts of all—the gifts of money and fund raising. Are such laws feasible? Yes. Many states already have provisions that limit lobbyists' roles in campaigns. Maryland, for example, bars lobbyists from soliciting contributions for candidates. Several other states have "pay-to play" laws that prohibit government contractors and their executives from making contributions to government officials who have a role in making state contract decisions.

Second, it is time to create an independent watchdog agency to implement and oversee federal lobbying laws. The lobbying laws that are now on the books are poorly enforced. Moreover, few resources are devoted to seeking out and punishing wrongdoers. Finally, even though federal law mandates that lobbyists disclose their activities, disclosure is often limited, and the records are difficult to access. I support the creation of a well-funded, independent, federal watchdog agency that vigorously enforces lobbying laws, rules, and regulations, and posts all lobbying disclosure reports in a way that is easy to access and understand.

There are other needed rules and regulations, including a ban on lobbyist-paid travel. However, the measures that make the most sense at this time are a ban on lobbyist contributions and fund raising and the creation of an independent lobbying watchdog agency. Adopting the no cup of coffee rule would do nothing to solve the real problem with Washington lobbying, the problem of money. Moreover, it would inevitably lead to more public cynicism as, over time, the public would see that despite extremely tight lobbying regulations, some lobbyists and government officials still break the rules.

CONCLUSION

Lobbying should be regulated. No one wants government decisions to be for sale. In this brief essay, I have raised two objections to the proposed no cup of coffee rule. The first objection comes from lobbyists. It says, essentially, that the no cup of coffee rule is silly, misguided, and insulting. Lobbyists maintain that socializing between lobbyists and government decision makers is not the evil that proponents of stricter regulations assert, but rather is a natural and indeed helpful part of the political process. The second objection is my own: money needs to be regulated, not coffee and other things of nominal value. If we are going to get serious about curbing the influence of lobbyists, we need to regulate the most precious lobbyist gift of all—the gift of money.

RESOLVED, the size of the House of Representatives should be increased to 675 seats

PRO: Brian Frederick

CON: C. Lawrence Evans and Nicholas J. Bell

"How many representatives are there in Congress?" is one of the standard questions on the civics test administered to immigrants applying to be American citizens. The answer, of course, is 435, not counting the nonvoting delegate from the District of Columbia. But the question was not always so easy. We take it for granted today that the number of representatives in the House is a fixed number. In the nineteenth century, however, the number of representatives was adjusted after each census to accommodate the growth in population. Only in the early twentieth century did the House of Representatives finally fix its size at 435 members.

Article I, Section 2 of the Constitution requires that "the number of representatives shall not exceed one for every thirty Thousand." The same section also specifies the initial allocation of representatives among the thirteen original states, ranging from ten representatives for Virginia and eight for Pennsylvania to one each for Delaware and Rhode Island—the total number equalled sixty-five members, or about one member for every sixty thousand people. In addition, Article I, Section 2 required that a count of the nation's population be taken within three years of the first Congress and every ten years thereafter so that the number of representatives each state received could be adjusted to reflect population changes.

The first census, which took place in 1790, counted a total population of 3.6 million (the true number was 3.93 million, of which nearly 700,000 were slaves, who counted as three-fifths of a person for the purposes of representation). If each district was to contain around 30,000 people, then the House of Representatives would need to grow to 120 members, almost twice the number that the Constitution had initially allocated. House members agreed that 30,000 should be the target for the ratio of representatives to population, but they argued fiercely over how to deal with the inevitable fractions. Connecticut's population was 236,841; should the House round up to eight? Treasury Secretary Alexander Hamilton thought so. Under his plan, the states with the highest fractional remainder would get an extra seat. Secretary of State Thomas Jefferson strongly disagreed, however, arguing that no state should be allotted more than one representative for every 30,000. Although Jefferson lost the argument in the House, which was dominated by Hamilton's Federalist Party, he managed to persuade George Washington to veto the bill—the first presidential veto in American history. Congress relented, adopting Jefferson's proposal to round down for each state, which reduced the size of the House to 105.

As the American population grew, so too did the size of the House. After the 1830 census the House, still using Jefferson's method of ignoring fractional remainders, reached 240 members, or roughly one representative for every 48,000 people. After the 1840 census, Congress opted for a new method, rounding up for those states that had a fraction of over one-half. The resulting House had 232 members, with each district representing about 70,000 people. For the rest of the nineteenth century Congress opted for a plan that was essentially the one Hamilton had proposed back in 1790: first decide the number of seats and then distribute those seats among the states based on their population, allocating leftover seats to the states with the largest fractions. By 1901 the House of Representatives was composed of 386 members, with each representing an average of just under 200,000 people.

The steady expansion in the size of the House over the course of the nineteenth century was motivated in part by members' desire to avoid taking representatives away from any state. With a rapidly increasing population, that goal could only be achieved by increasing the number of representatives. In 1910, for instance, the House fixed the number of seats at 433 (to be increased to 435 as soon as Arizona and New Mexico became states) because that was the smallest number that could still ensure that no state would have fewer representatives than it was allocated in 1900. In 1920, ensuring that no state lost representatives would have required 60 additional seats, a prospect that drew opposition among many who worried that the House was becoming too large to be an effective law-making body. So deep were the divisions that the House was unable to agree on a plan and failed for the first and only time in the nation's history to reapportion the number of representatives. Failure to act meant that for two decades the number remained fixed at 435.

In 1929 Congress finally acted, passing a bill that set the number of members in the House of Representatives permanently at 435. As a result, population change would now require that some states lose members when other states gained. Eager to insulate itself from the partisan and personal rancor that apportionment invited, the House also voted to delegate the unpleasant task of apportionment to the executive branch, specifically the secretary of commerce. Through the 1929 act, Congress largely washed its hands of the headaches that apportionment had brought for 140 years. Today, nearly a century after Congress set the number of House representatives at 435, each member of the House represents an average of about 700,000 members, about three times as many as in 1929. And even that average disguises significant variation, ranging from a low of about 530,000 for Wyoming's lone representative to almost 970,000 for Montana's one representative.

Is this a problem that we can or should do something about? Brian Frederick thinks we should expand the size of the House by about half, to 675 members, so as to make the institution more representative and more responsive. C. Lawrence Evans and Nicholas J. Bell disagree, arguing that a substantial increase in the size of the House would weaken its ability to function effectively. In a country as vast as ours, they think that 435 is the most we can handle.

PRO: Brian Frederick

The present size of the U.S. House of Representatives is not sufficient to represent a nation of over 300 million people. The time has come for the House to dramatically increase the size of its membership beyond the 435-seat threshold. When members of the House made a decision to place a permanent ceiling on its size they failed to fully consider the negative implications for representation. It is difficult to fathom that members of the House would have approved a permanent limit on the allocation of seats had they foreseen the prospect that the U.S. population would one day surpass the 300 million mark. The House is first and foremost a representative institution. In order to restore its representational character it is time for the House to be increased to 675 seats. Adopting this change would lead to better representation in four ways. It would: (1) make it easier for House members to stay in touch with their constituents, (2) improve the policy responsiveness of House members, (3) provide better demographic representation, and (4) provide improved representation for geographically based interests. Significantly increasing its size would go a long way toward fulfilling the ideal that the U.S. House is truly the people's House.

Why do I propose 675 seats as the appropriate number? The original decision to impose a limit of 435 seats was arbitrarily made without the use of an empirical formula. However, there is a more systematic way to determine the appropriate size of the House. In most advanced democracies, the lower house of the national legislature approximates the cube root of the nation's population.[1] Comparative legislative scholars have classified this empirical pattern as the cube root law of national assembly size. There is a logic behind this empirical regularity. Every legislative body must balance the trade-off of the need to operate efficiently while providing effective representation to the citizens in their districts.[2] Legislators must communicate with their fellow members and remain in touch with their constituents. If the average number of constituents in a district becomes too large, the legislator will be unable to communicate effectively with constituents. The cube root law projects that the optimal assembly size is determined by the number of seats relative to the ratio of citizens per district that will accommodate these competing demands. Legislatures do not expand without limit or in direct proportion to population increases because such boundless expansion would undermine the effectiveness of the legislature. The size of a legislature tends to increase along with the growth of the population in a country, but at a lower rate.[3] For the first century of the nation's history the U.S. House conformed rather well to this law.[4]

The cube root law provides the most rational formula for balancing the trade-offs involved in determining the size of any legislative body. Not only would it bring the House into alignment with international legislative norms, it would also help restore some balance on the representative side of the ledger between the competing imperatives of representation and legislative efficiency. The House would be well served to return to the policy of increases every ten years linked to the cube root of the nation's population. Enacting such a law would mean that following the 2010 census the House should be increased to approximately 675 members, the projected cube root of the population in that year.

IMPROVING CITIZENS' ACCESS TO THEIR REPRESENTATIVES

Advocates of increasing the size of the House have argued that it would make it easier for representatives to stay in touch with their constituents.[5] Although senators from more populous states tend to be less accessible and less popular than senators from less populated states,[6] until recently there was not much evidence to show that such a relationship exists in House districts. However, a pair of studies I recently conducted established that House members who represent larger constituencies also confront a similar challenge in trying to remain in touch with the citizens in their district. Looking at survey data from the 1980, 1990, and 2000 elections I found that as constituency size increases, citizens are less likely to report having contact with their representative and having met their representative in person.[7] The evidence also demonstrates that citizens are less likely to make an attempt to initiate contact with their representative in larger districts.

Not only is contact between citizen and representative undermined by a larger constituency, but so are citizens' perceptions of legislative responsiveness. Citizens residing in the most heavily populated congressional districts are less likely to believe their representative would be helpful should the need to contact them arise. The same relationship applies when citizens are queried about whether their representative does an adequate job of staying in touch with the people in the district. This relationship is also at work for the approval ratings of House members. Serving additional constituents increases the probability that the representative will be disapproved of by the people in their districts. Future increases in the ratio of citizens per representative seem likely to exacerbate the discontent citizens feel toward their elected representatives in the U.S. House.

As predicted by the cube root law of national assembly size, the failure to increase the size of the House to accommodate dramatic population growth has interfered with channels of communication between representatives and their constituents. Refusal to adjust the size of the chamber as the population continues to expand will further attenuate the connection between citizens and their representatives. Returning to the practice of decennial increases in the size of the House tied to the cube root of the nation's population would enable representatives to be more accessible to citizens and would help citizens feel more connected to their representatives.

IMPROVING POLICY REPRESENTATION

In addition to increasing constituent access to their representatives, a larger House would facilitate better policy representation. Many scholars have argued that as constituencies become larger the probability that a representative will reflect constituency opinion in the district declines.[8] My research has documented that this dynamic is present for the U.S. House as well.[9] Examining the voting patterns of House members at various levels of district population size, I found that a larger constituency creates more policy divergence between constituents and their representatives than would otherwise be the case. The presence of a considerable number of additional citizens in the district has the effect of pushing representatives farther away from the views of their constituents. The result is a voting record that tends to gravitate toward the activist base of party supporters in the district and veers farther away from the median voter than would be the case in a smaller constituency. This outcome was predicted by opponents of the 435-seat limit at the time it was established and appears to have come to fruition. Although the available evidence does not indicate that constituency size is the primary factor that leads to divergence between the issue positions of constituents and their representatives, it does offer support for the proposition that larger constituencies diminish policy representation.

Increasing the size of the of the House to account for population growth in line with the cube root law of national assembly size is not the only solution for remedying the lack of responsiveness of House members to their constituents' policy views, but it would certainly make a contribution toward bridging the divide that presently exists. If the average House district population size continues to expand, the prospect for greater divergence between constituency preferences and policy responsiveness will be heightened. Since the larger the size of a district's population the less likely representatives are to reflect opinions of the majority of their constituents, in smaller, more ideologically cohesive constituencies it will be easier for House members to reflect the policy preferences of the people they represent.

ENHANCING DESCRIPTIVE REPRESENTATION

Another benefit of enlarging the size of the House is that it would improve descriptive representation. The concept of descriptive representation holds that the composition of a legislature ought to reflect the demographic makeup of society. This form of representation matters because members of certain groups may pursue policies that are in the interests of those groups in the policy making process. Furthermore, it may allow for unarticulated interests to be heard in the deliberative process and may give members of groups who have been systematically excluded from full participation in politics—like women and minorities—the chance to demonstrate their ability to participate effectively in the governing process.[10] This country is far more diverse than it was when the 435-seat limit was first imposed. A House consisting of over 200 additional members would better accommodate the vast ethnic and racial diversity that currently exists in the United States.

Most House members get elected not by defeating an incumbent but by winning a seat that becomes open either through retirement, resignation, or death. There is a greater likelihood that women will run for and emerge victorious in open-seat races. Women have typically made significant gains in the first election following reapportionment. Under my proposal, after each census the number of new seats apportioned would rise, creating additional opportunities for women and minorities to run successfully for the House.[11] For African Americans and Latinos, less populated congressional districts would make it easier to create majority-minority districts that are likely to elect members of these underrepresented groups.

According to my own research, women and African Americans are particularly supportive of increasing the size of the House of Representatives for this purpose.[12] Doing so could enhance minorities' sense of political trust and efficacy and strengthen the bonds they feel with their elected representatives. The present 435-seat limit delays the entrance of members of underrepresented groups into the House. A larger body would open up new opportunities for women and minorities to serve, resulting in greater numbers of citizens who feel that they have someone in the House of Representatives to look out for their interests.

FACILITATING BETTER GEOGRAPHIC REPRESENTATION

A further justification for increasing the size of the House is that it would enhance representation of geographic interests in the United States. In the decades after the imposition of the 435-seat limit in the House there has been a dramatic shift in the allocation of seats among the states. Some states grow faster than others, and to accommodate this growth they must get additional seats in the House. Since the cap of 435 seats has not been raised, those gains must come at the expense of other states. In the first twelve rounds of reapportionment that occurred from 1790 to 1910 an average of four states lost seats. In contrast, between 1930 and 2000 an average of twelve states lost seats after reapportionment.[13] The number of states that lose seats is likely to increase over the next few decades as population growth in the Northeast and Midwest lags behind the rest of the country.[14] Take New York, for instance. In 1910 it sent forty-three representatives to the U.S. House. In 2000 that number fell to twenty-nine, and some estimate that by 2030 it could drop to twenty-three.[15] The authors of the *Almanac of American Politics* note that "reapportionment is carnage time for New York."[16]

One might be prompted to respond to these figures by noting that fewer seats for Northeastern and Midwestern states is a manifestation of slower population growth than the rest of the county. However, these states have experienced a rise in population, just not at the same clip as the national rate.[17] The New York delegation has fallen by fourteen since the adoption of the 435-seat limit, meaning that the state has lost 33 percent of its representation in the House. Meanwhile, the state's population has gone up by 108 percent over this period. Is it fair for states to continue to lose seats in the House, even as their populations continue to climb, albeit less rapidly than the nation as a whole? A larger House would allow slower growing states to avoid losing seats every ten years and give the states with the fastest growing populations an even greater number of seats following each census.

Even a relatively homogeneous state like Montana illustrates how geographic representation can be enhanced with additional representation in the House. In the aftermath of the 1990 census, Montana lost one of its two seats in the House and now has only one representative for a state of over 900,000 people. This development has made representing the state a much more daunting proposition. In addition to having to traverse one of the most expansive geographical landscapes in the entire country, Montana's sole House member must represent two very different political regions. The state's western half leans Democratic and is economically rooted in the mining and timber industries, while the eastern portion of the state is strongly Republican with an emphasis on ranching and other agricultural interests.[18] Enlarging the House to 675 members would enable states like Montana that possess great geographic diversity to have those geographic interests better represented.

ADDRESSING THE ARGUMENTS OF THE CRITICS

Even critics of increasing the size of the House concede that some benefits would accrue from a larger House. They maintain, however, that these benefits are not worth the costs. Although many of the critics' concerns are valid, none of them rise to the level that would outweigh the positive impact on representation a larger House would produce.

One of the most frequent objections against increasing the size of the House is that it would come at an extra cost to taxpayers and worsen the federal budget deficit.[19] Paying for the salaries and additional staff necessary to support a larger House would undoubtedly be costly, but it would only be a fraction of the overall federal budget. The wealthiest country in the world can certainly afford to provide its citizens a better quality of representation, particularly in an institution that was designed by the framers to be closest to the people.

A second criticism lodged by opponents is that expanding the size of the House would harm the quality of deliberation.[20] It is true that if the House was expanded to 675 seats a smaller percentage of members would have the opportunity to make their voices heard on certain issues, and when they did get the opportunity to participate in debates they might get less time to speak on the House floor. However, this is a problem in the current House of 435 members. Unless the House is dramatically reduced in size the lengthy speeches that occur on the Senate floor are just not practical. Although some members might lose out on the opportunity to speak, members often speak (as avid viewers of C-SPAN can attest) to a mostly empty chamber. Moreover, on many issues plenty of time for debate is often yielded back.

Perhaps the most compelling argument advanced by those opposed to increasing the size of the House of Representatives is that it would lead to a more unwieldy legislative process and would prevent the House from carrying out its basic legislative functions.[21] Although these are legitimate worries, there are strong reasons to believe that an increase in the size of the House will not undermine its legislative effectiveness. The rules of the House are already tightly structured to promote swift passage of most key legislation.[22] If further restrictions are needed to prevent the legislative process from bogging down, then such measures will be adopted. It is up to lawmakers to devise rules that make this outcome possible. If that requires less influence for individual members and a more leadership-dominated institution, the gains that would accrue to representation are worth it. In the final analysis, concerns about legislative efficiency should not be allowed to derail an increase in the size of the House that is so desperately needed to increase the representativeness and responsiveness of what is supposed to be the people's House.

CON: C. Lawrence Evans and Nicholas J. Bell

There is absolutely nothing magical about "435," which since 1929 has been the number of voting members in the U.S. House of Representatives. Indeed, the first House included only 65 members, and throughout the nineteenth century the number of U.S. representatives was periodically increased as additional states entered the Union. Furthermore, the best scholarship suggests that the size of a legislature can be consequential, potentially affecting the interactions that take place between individual constituents and their elected representatives, and perhaps even the quality of deliberation that occurs within the chamber. A larger House, of course, would mean fewer constituents per member. In the U.S. Senate, people living in less populous states are far more likely to have personal contact with their senators and also tend to view them more favorably than do people living in larger states. Perhaps, then, more House members would mean more popular incumbents and better communication between citizens and their elected representatives in Congress.[1] Enlarging the House might result in the election of a greater number of women, African American, and Hispanic legislators, producing a chamber that looks more like the American people. Most Americans clearly believe that there is room for improvement in the performance of their national legislature. In a May 2009 Gallup Poll, almost 60 percent of them disapproved of the way Congress was handling its job. Maybe we can enhance the representative capacity and internal operations of Congress by increasing the size of the House from 435 to 675 voting members.

Or maybe not. While increasing the size of the House would reduce the number of constituents per representative, we believe that any gains from such a change would be more than countervailed by reduced efficiency and deliberative quality in the legislative process and a host of related problems. There are four main reasons for our view: (1) more members means greater difficulty building coalitions, (2) the deliberation that does occur in the House would be undermined, (3) there likely would be an increase in parochial behavior within the chamber, and (4) the logistical hurdles to increasing the number of House members by more than 50 percent would be complicated and expensive. Other less sweeping, but more realistic, reform options would better address many of the concerns that the public has about Congress.

COALITION BUILDING

Although the dramatic rise in partisan polarization on Capitol Hill in recent decades makes many roll-call votes highly predictable (Democrats vote one way, Republicans vote the other, and both sides lambaste their opponents), building coalitions in support of legislation is actually very difficult work. Deals need to be cut between competing interests and policy views, amendments are drafted and offered, leaders in committee and on the floor attempt to persuade wavering colleagues to support their initiatives, procedures must be devised to help glue the majority coalition together, and so on. Very few bills—and probably no major legislation—pass the House without some substantive adjustments at the drafting stage, in committee, or on the floor aimed at securing the votes necessary to prevail. The difficulties of building winning legislative coalitions can be daunting with just 435 members. Increasing the number of lawmakers to 675 would make an already unwieldy legislative process even harder to manage.

Consider the vast array of interests that are potentially thrown into conflict when legislation is offered to reform the nation's health care system. Doctors and health care professionals, insurance companies, small businesses, labor unions, senior citizens, and the working poor would all like to see their ideas reflected in the final bill. While party politics does simplify this vast array of competing interests by grouping certain viewpoints together under one or the other party's program, legislators still need to weigh many divergent demands that do not fall cleanly along partisan lines. The relative importance of these pressures varies a lot from district to district, which is precisely why party and committee leaders must tailor their lobbying tactics to individual members when building coalitions. Increasing the size of the House would vastly complicate these efforts, slowing down the legislative process and promoting gridlock.

An analogy might reinforce our argument. In the game of chess, each player is responsible for coordinating the moves of a king and queen; pairs of rooks, bishops, and knights; and eight pawns. The array of possible moves and strategies in chess is vast, which makes the game very difficult to master and exciting for some. Now increase the number of chess pieces by 50 percent, which is roughly the order of magnitude of an increase in House membership from 435 to 675. Add a second queen to the mix, another rook and bishop, and a bunch more pawns. The game would become much more complex, perhaps even unplayable. An analogous increase in the size of the House, we believe, would make legislative politics far more complex, at times even unmanageable. Given all that is at stake in Congress—health care reform, the economy, climate change, the foreign policy of the United States—it would be unwise to further complicate the already daunting task of building coalitions and forging consensus. Sure, certain major democracies like Germany and the United Kingdom have legislatures with over 650 members, and their parliamentary bodies are able to pass bills. But these countries also are much smaller and less politically diverse than the United States, and for constitutional reasons their legislatures have much less power than does the U.S. Congress.

DELIBERATION

Increasing the size of the House would also undermine the important deliberation that occurs within the chamber. Of course, we need to be realistic about the deliberative capacity of the modern House. Members often make up their minds about major issues fairly early in the legislative process, and much of the "debate" and "discussion" that takes place in the halls of Congress is highly scripted, consisting mostly of position taking before a broader audience of interest groups and voters. Still, the give-and-take that takes place between members, especially in committee, does change minds, generate new ideas, and improve legislation. Not surprisingly, constructive deliberation and debate are most likely to occur when individual legislators are familiar with and trust each other. Unfortunately, members of the current House already do not know each other very well. As former majority leader Richard Gephardt, D-Mo., once observed, "Members are islands. They're very busy, and they often don't have the time to get to know one another."[2] Within an enlarged House, lawmakers would know even fewer of their colleagues and deliberation would suffer.

Consider also the increased demand for speaking time that would characterize a House of 675 members and what that might mean for deliberation. Indeed, in 1961 then Speaker Sam Rayburn claimed that the House was already too large with a membership of 435.[3] The deliberative process in a 435-member House, Rayburn claimed, is often an unwieldy mess. Members of Congress clamor to participate in the legislative process to pursue their goals of reelection, shaping policy, and securing influence on the national political stage. A significantly larger membership would place even more strain on the limited time available for debate in committee and on the floor. More members would demand time to speak on the floor and appear before their constituents on C-SPAN. The committees of the House would have to increase significantly in size or number to accommodate the larger membership. The result would be either fewer opportunities for individual members to participate meaningfully in committee, or the number of televised meetings would have to be greatly expanded, adding to the congressional din that already confuses so many Americans.

PAROCHIALISM

Now consider an alleged advantage of an enlarged House: the closer ties and increased communication that might occur between individual constituents and their elected representatives in Washington. For some, that claim evokes comforting images of regular personal interactions between ordinary citizens and their representatives, more e-mails and other written communications between congressional offices and folks back home, and House members who can be more intimately familiar with the interests and concerns of the people they represent. Unfortunately, these images are far from realistic.

First, based on recent population data, the average House district now includes more than 650,000 constituents, which in fairness is a lot of people for a single person to represent. But even with 675 members, the average district population would still be around 450,000, nowhere near low enough to guarantee representational relationships between individual constituents and their House members that are qualitatively different from the status quo. Still, for the sake of argument, let's assume that the level of meaningful interactions between constituents and members would increase somewhat with an enlarged House and that voters would come to expect (and receive) more responsiveness to their personal concerns and interests from their representatives. What would this heightened responsiveness look like? Let's consult the available evidence.

We know that much of the communication that occurs between citizens and their members of Congress is very parochial. According to surveys, less than 20 percent of constituent contacts with their representatives are to advocate policy views or request information about a legislative matter. The rest are mostly requests for "casework"—that is, assistance in dealing with the executive branch or for some other concrete benefit or favor from the member.[4] Examples of casework include help getting a government job, assistance with Social Security or Medicare benefits, getting copies of government publications, requests for flags that have flown over the Capitol building, and the like.[5] As mentioned, there is some empirical evidence that the likelihood a constituent will contact a House member for such assistance will rise if the chamber is enlarged and districts are made less populous. But would that be an unambiguously good consequence? Time and again, scholars have demonstrated that incumbent House members are almost always reelected (in part) because they do so much casework, which tends to increase their personal approval ratings at home, even though most voters typically disapprove of the performance of Congress as a whole. Do we really want to further enable incumbents to duck responsibility for the collective failures of the House by currying personal favor with constituents via casework and constituency service?

It also is worth noting that smaller-population districts would almost certainly mean more homogeneous constituencies on average for House members and thus more parochialism on policy matters as well. Demographers have shown that while America as a whole is very diverse, there also exists a lot of residential segregation by economic well-being, way of life, and—increasingly—ideological and partisan orientation. The country is diverse, but individual neighborhoods and precincts tend to be fairly homogeneous.[6] Look up and down your street the next time you are at home. Do most of your neighbors appear to vote the way you do? Most likely, the answer is "yes." As district populations grow smaller, this within-constituency homogeneity should increase, fueling parochialism. U.S. senators represent states, which are generally larger and more diverse than are House districts. As a result, senators are forced to confront a wider array of interests within their constituencies on major policy matters, which according to scholars is one reason why their chamber traditionally has been less aggressively partisan than the House. So if House districts are made smaller and presumably more politically homogeneous, then the partisan loyalties of members probably will grow even stronger. Even fewer of them will represent large numbers of Democrats and Republicans. Scholars of Congress often assert that there is a trade-off between rules and procedures that promote constituency parochialism and those that heighten partisan tensions. Interestingly, enlarging the House to 675 members is the one change we can think of that might promote both ill effects simultaneously.

LOGISTICAL ISSUES

Finally, consider the practical logistics of enlargement. Many of the readers of this volume are students in courses related to American government. So imagine that your college or university was mandated to increase the number of enrolled students by 50 percent. Or better yet, imagine that your own family had to immediately grow in size by this proportion. The first questions popping into your head probably would be, "Where the heck are we supposed to put all these people?" and "Who is going to pay for all this?" Similar questions should be posed here.

When so-called "news commentators" and other muckrakers complain about the costs of funding Congress or the amount of money spent on campaigns, advocates for the institution often respond that these sums are really not that large, especially when compared to the $40 billion that Americans spend annually on their pets or the more than $10 billion that is devoted to video games. Fair enough. But it is worth noting that each House office typically employs eighteen full-time staffers. Unless members agree to staff reductions, which is highly unlikely, then personal office staffs will have to increase by over 4,000 employees in a 675-member House. Most likely, enlargement of the House would also would require the hiring of many more committee staffers, especially if the number of panels is increased to accommodate the influx of new lawmakers. Anyone who has visited a congressional office knows that these buildings contain very little excess space. Indeed, most member offices are already crammed full of employees. Almost certainly, a larger House would require the construction of new office buildings on the Capitol complex. Based on surveys, most Americans probably would oppose such expenditures on their elected representatives, further undermining the legitimacy of Congress.

And do not forget about the additional members themselves. Fortunately, the chamber of the House already can seat far more than 435 people. The State of the Union address, which is also attended by the entire Senate, the Supreme Court, most members of the president's cabinet, and a number of other government officials, has long taken place within the House chamber. As a result, the proposed enlargement probably would not necessitate the knocking down of any Capitol walls or the construction of "loft seating" on the floor. But, depending on whether the committees are increased in number or in size, the proposed influx of 240 additional House members would require either a lot more committee and subcommittee rooms—and thus the construction of still more office space—or committee leaders would have to find a way to seat more members in existing rooms which are already overcrowded. Not too long ago, for instance, the two most junior members of the Armed Services Committee had to share the same chair at committee meetings, literally sitting "cheek to cheek," as one later recalled. Frankly, televised nationally via C-SPAN, images like that would probably be enough by themselves to convince right-thinking Americans to revise any initial support for increasing the size of the House.

CONCLUSION

Although adjustments to the size of the House were commonplace throughout the nineteenth century, and there may be certain advantages now to enlarging the chamber from 435 to 675 members, we believe that the downside from such a change would overshadow any benefits. Enlargement would complicate coalition building, undermine deliberation, promote parochialism, and be logistically complicated, to say the least. There are many other reasons to oppose the change that we could have highlighted. For instance, any accompanying increase in committees would mean more panels with smaller jurisdictions, potentially enabling interest groups and other narrow interests to dominate individual panels. A larger House might mean the election of more women and ethnic minorities, but their proportions of the full body might not change very much, mitigating any advances in descriptive representation. Heightened communications between constituents and House members, assuming they occur, could come in the form of stronger demands for pork barrel projects and earmarks for the district. The smaller and more homogeneous House districts that would result from enlargement might make incumbents even safer and, as a result, the chamber less responsive to changes in the public mood. We could go on, but you get the drift. Enlarging the membership of the House would be a lot more trouble than it is worth.

Indeed, there are other, more incremental reforms that might help alleviate the concerns that so many Americans have about the representative capacity of Congress. Most casework and constituency service is actually conducted by staff, rather than members. If the goal is to enhance constituent contacts with House members, one approach would be to increase the funds available to district offices for such purposes, or better yet, to establish a central ombudsman's office for the chamber as a whole staffed by personnel with specialized expertise at solving the problems individual constituents have with federal programs and bureaucrats.[7] Or perhaps committee jurisdictions could be realigned so that there are fewer overlaps and redundancies, enabling citizens to better discern who is responsible for policy successes and failures at the crucial committee stage of the legislative process. Most incumbents are electorally safe because most challengers are woefully underfunded. Rather than building a bunch of new House office buildings or dramatically expanding the funds for staff, perhaps we should take steps to guarantee a minimum campaign war chest for all credible congressional candidates.

And here's one final thought. Maybe the best approach to improving the representative capacity of Congress is to elect better House members, rather than more of them. Most voters do not know very much about their incumbent representatives, much less the challengers that run against them in House campaigns—a level of ignorance that cannot be mitigated by reducing district populations. The essential ingredient to effective representation in any legislature, we believe, is a knowledgeable electorate. Reforms and other structural fixes aside, ordinary citizens need to invest the time necessary to inform themselves about candidates and issues. As James Madison summed up centuries ago, "Knowledge will forever govern ignorance [and] a people who mean to be their own Governors must arm themselves with the power that knowledge gives."[8] But increasing the size of the U.S. House from 435 to 675 seats? Intriguing proposal, bad idea.

10

RESOLVED, the redistricting process should be nonpartisan

PRO: Michael P. McDonald

CON: Justin Buchler

The Constitution clearly vests the power of apportionment—the number of House seats each state receives—with Congress and specifies that the number of representatives a state receives must be proportional to its population.[1] The Constitution is silent, however, about redistricting, the drawing of the boundaries of congressional districts. The Constitution does not say who should draw the boundaries or how they should be drawn, and the task has largely been left to state legislatures. Occasionally in the nineteenth century Congress did provide the states with some general rules. In 1842, for instance, Congress specified that districts should be contiguous (that is, territorially connected) and should elect only one member (some states in those days still used multimember, at-large districts rather than single-member districts). In 1872 Congress legislated that House districts should be made up of "as nearly as possible an equal number of inhabitants." However, Congress generally refrained from involving itself in redistricting, both out of a belief that the Constitution did not grant it that power and because the members thought that exercising such power, even if it were constitutional, would be unwise. As a House report from 1901 explained, allowing Congress to redistrict would open up the prospect of partisan gerrymandering on a national scale. Of course, it was true that state legislatures carried out partisan gerrymandering, "but the division of political power is so general and diverse that notwithstanding the inherent vice of the system of gerrymandering, some kind of equality of distribution results." That is, although drawing boundaries to advantage one party at the expense of another was to be regretted, it was safer to distribute that power to the states so that one party's gain in some states would be counterbalanced by another party's advantage in other states.

The trouble with leaving redistricting to the states, however, was that states varied widely in their practices, particularly in their toleration of population discrepancies between districts. In 1946 these population discrepancies were brought before the Supreme Court in *Colegrove v. Green.* Kenneth Colegrove, a professor of political science at Northwestern University, filed suit against the state of Illinois because the congressional district in which he lived was made up of 914,000 people, while the nearby Fifth District included only 112,000 people. His vote was thus worth one only-eighth as much as the vote of a citizen in the Fifth District, which he insisted was a violation of the Fourteenth Amendment's equal protection guarantee. The Supreme Court disagreed, however, insisting that redistricting was "of a peculiarly political nature and therefore not meant for judicial interpretation." It was the responsibility of Congress or the state legislatures, not the courts, to ensure equal representation.

Sixteen years later, however, the Court famously reversed course in *Baker v. Carr* (1962) and entered the "political thicket" that it previously warned against. *Baker* was precipitated by a challenge to state legislative boundaries in Tennessee, which had not been redrawn since the turn of the century. This was not an isolated problem. Delaware and Alabama had also neglected to redraw state legislative boundaries for the past sixty years, and nine more states had gone three decades since last adjusting their district lines. In some states, the population discrepancy between the largest and smallest state legislative districts was as much as a 100 to 1. In Tennessee, the ratio was about 10 to 1, with urban residents the big losers. The Supreme Court decided in *Baker* that, contrary to its opinion in *Colegrove,* such matters were in fact justiciable—that is, decidable by courts. Two years later, in *Reynolds v. Sims* (1964), the Court ruled that the "one person, one vote" principle required that state legislative districts, including the upper house, must contain roughly equal populations. That same year, in *Wesberry v. Sanders,* the Court ruled that the same principle applied to districts drawn for the U.S. House of Representatives. The courts have been heavily involved in the redistricting process ever since, particularly in policing so-called "racial gerrymandering"—that is, efforts to use the redistricting process to advantage or disadvantage racial and ethnic minorities.

The courts have been much more reluctant to get involved in challenges to political gerrymandering, whether in the form of giving an advantage to one party over the other (a partisan gerrymander) or protecting incumbents of both parties (a bipartisan gerrymander). In *Davis v. Bandemer* (1986), for instance, a sharply divided Court set the plaintiff's threshold so high that it seemed nearly impossible to find a redistricting plan that would not pass constitutional muster. In *Vieth v. Jubelirer* (2004) the Court heard a challenge to a

Republican gerrymander of congressional districts in Pennsylvania and again was sharply divided, with the four most conservative justices arguing that partisan gerrymanders were nonjusticiable and the four most liberal justices arguing that they were justiciable. The critical swing vote in the case was provided by Justice Anthony Kennedy, who agreed with the Court's conservatives that there could be no judicial remedy in this case but held out the possibility that the Court might in the future discover a workable standard that would allow for judicial review of political gerrymanders.

These and other court cases have given states a relatively wide berth in redistricting, so long as they adhere to a strict population equality and don't unconstitutionally dilute the votes of racial and ethnic minorities. Political gerrymandering may not violate the U.S. Constitution, but the question remains as to whether it is a problem that we should seek to remedy. Michael P. McDonald argues that it is, and recommends nonpartisan redistricting as the way to clean up the abuses that result from allowing politicians to draw district lines. Justin Buchler disagrees, arguing that politicians have an incentive to avoid partisan gerrymanders and that the bipartisan gerrymanders that politicians do have an incentive to craft actually benefit voters.

PRO: Michael P. McDonald

In 2000 a young Illinois state senator named Barack Obama challenged entrenched incumbent congressman Bobby Rush in a Democratic primary election. Obama received 30 percent of the vote in the four-way contest. Although victorious, Representative Rush wished to ensure that his opponents would not challenge him in future elections. In the subsequent congressional redistricting in 2001, Rush arranged for his congressional district boundary to be shifted to place Obama's residence in Rep. Jesse Jackson Jr.'s district.[1] His pathway to the U.S. House of Representatives blocked, Obama then used state legislative redistricting to further his political goals. Due to a quirk in timing, Democrats won the right to redraw the Illinois state legislative districts after the congressional districts were drawn. Obama discovered during his primary contest that he was effective at creating biracial electoral coalitions. His old majority African American state senate district was redrawn to include expensive high-rise apartments north of downtown Chicago along Lake Michigan's shoreline. These affluent constituents would later serve Obama well in his 2004 run for U.S. senator and 2008 run for president by permitting him to craft a biracial campaign message and to establish a cadre of wealthy campaign contributors.

Not every politician is Barack Obama. The two other candidates for the 2000 Illinois First Congressional District primary election—Donne Trotter and George Ruby—are not widely known, even though they too were drawn out of Representative Rush's district. Indeed, these sorts of shenanigans played by incumbents are the norm in redistricting.[2] Potential primary and general election challengers are routinely drawn out of districts. Constituents favorable to a candidate are shifted into districts, and those unfavorable are shifted out. Apocryphal stories abound of representatives including specific industries within their districts, ones that they oversee by virtue of a committee assignment and from which they receive campaign donations. Perhaps more amusing, but equally troubling, are instances where representatives insist on including their country club in their district, presumably so that they can continue to receive preferential treatment. Virginia state delegate Ken Plum—a longtime advocate of redistricting reform—said what few elected officials will admit: "elected officials are where they are because they fight to get elected, it is in their nature and we should expect no less during redistricting."[3]

Political parties play these games with district lines on behalf of incumbents, but have other goals in mind as well. Through artful drawing of district boundaries it is possible for a political party to place itself in a better position to control a state legislature or congressional delegation by receiving more seats than its share of votes.[4] The other party's votes can be wasted by stacking their supporters into districts that they will win by an overwhelming margin or cracked across districts that the gerrymandering party will likely win by a comfortable margin.[5] Opposition incumbents often find themselves drawn into a district with another incumbent, forcing a primary match-up or compelling one of the incumbents to retire or move into a new district.

The framers of the Constitution could not reach consensus on how to administer national elections, particularly voting qualifications, so they delegated the authority to the states in Article I, Section 4.[6] Still, the founders recognized the mischief that could be played through manipulation of electoral laws, including redistricting. The pejorative term *gerrymander* derives from an oddly shaped 1812 state legislative district signed into law by Massachusetts governor Elbridge Gerry that a political cartoonist likened to a salamander, or a "Gerrymander." James Madison, the chief architect of the U.S. Constitution, worried that "Whenever the State Legislature had a favorite measure to carry, they would take care so to mould their regulations as to favor the candidates they wished to succeed."[7] Madison himself was the target of a gerrymander engineered by Patrick Henry, who manipulated Virginia's congressional district lines in an attempt to prevent Madison from being elected to Congress.[8]

The rallying cry for redistricting reformers is that voters should pick representatives, representatives should not pick voters. Indeed, limits on the obvious self-interest and the accompanying abuse of power exercised during redistricting have been incrementally increasing over the past half-century. Redistricting authorities are constrained by federal courts, the federal government, and state constitutional amendments or legislative action. Extension of regulation of redistricting seems likely given these precedents.

Ironically, a lack of redistricting ushered in greater regulation of the process and shifted control of redistricting away from state legislatures. During the first half of the twentieth century, many state legislatures refused to conduct redistricting because doing so often shuffles constituents around, breaking the link between representatives and their familiar constituents that helps them get reelected. One such state was Tennessee, which had not redistricted in sixty years. As a result, district populations became unbalanced or "malapportioned" between fast-growing urban areas and slow-growing rural areas. This situation suited many rural Tennessee legislators just fine. Ultimately, the U.S. Supreme Court took action in the landmark 1962 case *Baker v. Carr*,[9] in which the Court for the first time recognized that redistricting was "justiciable"—that is, not a political issue outside the Court's sphere—and put the Tennessee legislature on notice to conduct a redistricting or else they would do so for them. Later in that decade, a series of court cases forced many state legislatures to carry out redistricting in a timely manner following the decennial census in order to equalize districts' populations.[10]

Initially, scholars expected to see a significant reduction in partisan gerrymandering following the "one-man, one-vote" rulings,[11] but this goal was not realized. As political scientists Andrew Gelman and Gary King note, "population equality guarantees almost no form of fairness beyond numerical equality of population."[12] The deficiency of equal population standards—and others such as compactness—is that they allow too many different district configurations to meaningfully constrain gerrymandering. Moreover, as another pair of scholars argues, practice makes perfect. Redistricting authorities learn how to gerrymander despite legal constraints when they are required to draw districts every decade.[13] Indeed, some of the most egregious abuses, such as carving a street block out of a district that just happens to contain a potential challenger's home, are enabled by creating districts with perfectly equal population, which requires drawing district lines at such fine levels of geography.

A constraint placed upon how states can redistrict—one that has had considerably more success in constraining how lines are drawn than the Court's equal population rulings—is the Voting Rights Act of 1965 and its many extensions. Just as political parties had learned how to waste votes of the opposition party, white politicians discovered that redistricting could be used to deny minorities an opportunity to elect a candidate of their choice by arranging districts to dilute the voting strength of minorities. If a state or locality violates the Voting Rights Act, the Department of Justice and the federal courts are granted oversight authority to force a state or locality to draw a more acceptable map. If such a map is not forthcoming, the courts are empowered to draw a map of their own. The Voting Rights Act has been credited with the election of thousands of minorities to federal, state, and local offices since its inception.[14]

In 1986 the U.S. Supreme Court ruled that partisan gerrymandering is justiciable. However, although there have been many maps challenged on partisan gerrymandering grounds, the Court has only overturned one.[15] The thorny issue is that the swing justice on these 5–4 decisions, Justice Anthony Kennedy, has not found a standard to his liking that identifies when a partisan gerrymander occurs.

These Supreme Court cases illustrate that state legislatures cannot simply draw whatever districts they may like. The U.S. Constitution and federal law provide some intrusive oversight of the redistricting process, dictating when redistricting must occur and specifying some requirements as to how districts are to be drawn. Although states are provided great discretion how they may draw districts, there are instances where federal courts have actually drawn districts. Following the 2000 census, courts adopted congressional maps in Colorado, Maine, Minnesota, Mississippi, New Hampshire, New Mexico, Oklahoma, Oregon, South Carolina, and Texas.[16] The debate, then, is not whether state legislatures should have sole redistricting authority; they don't. Rather, the debate is over how much politicians should be constrained while they redistrict and, in the extreme, whether they should have any authority whatsoever.

The way that redistricting takes place varies greatly among the states.[17] There are states such as Arizona and California that do not permit politicians to draw districts, while in others such as Illinois and Virginia there are no holds barred. Some states impose criteria in addition to the federal requirements, such as drawing compact districts, drawing districts blind to partisan or individual candidate interests, fostering district competition, respecting existing political and geographic boundaries, and respecting communities of interest. Most states use the regular legislative process to draw their congressional and state legislative districts. Others use a commission as the sole authority (e.g., Arizona), an adviser to the legislature (e.g., Iowa), or as a place of last resort if the regular legislative process fails to produce a map (e.g., Texas for its state legislative districts).

The United States is exceptional in that it is the only country in the world where politicians have a role in redistricting. Every other advanced democracy that must draw districts uses a nonpartisan bureaucratic commission.[18] Members of these commissions, like the Parliamentary Boundary Commission for England, must adhere to a strict code of conduct to prevent the appearance of partisanship in their decision making. They make revisions to district boundaries following a set of standards, and their deliberations and recommendations are publicly available.[19]

Two states use a commission system that comes close to how other countries redistrict. Voters in Arizona adopted a redistricting commission in 2000 and California voters followed suit in 2008, in both cases through the ballot initiative process. Both states select members to the redistricting commission through a complicated vetting process that attempts to weed out political insiders. They draw districts according to a strict set of criteria, they actively seek public input, and their meetings are held in public. Still, even in these states, legislative leaders retain some say. They choose who may serve on the commission from the pool of vetted candidates.

Not all commissions are models for reform in the United States. Reformers do not consider Iowa's model an attractive reform model, even though Iowa's commission is often heralded as following the bureaucratic model used in other countries. The state's commission is a nonpartisan support staff known as the Legislative Service Agency (LSA). The difference is that the LSA only serves in an advisory capacity to the Iowa legislature, which has the final authority and may reject the LSA's proposed maps. Commissions used in other states are sometimes called "independent" from the legislature, even though elected officials or their hand-picked lieutenants serve on these commissions.[20] In these states, self-interest is not removed from the process because politicians still have a direct say in how districts are drawn.

It is too soon to tell if these reform model commissions in Arizona and California produce maps that are different from those produced by other states since, as of this writing, only Arizona's commission has actually drawn maps.[21] Commissions are often enacted along with a set of redistricting criteria to guide their map drawing, and there has been an explosion of state litigation over these criteria in recent decades.[22] There is an upper limit on the number of states that will adopt redistricting reform since states seldom adopt this reform through means other than a ballot initiative. However, there are states where redistricting may yet go to voters either for a first time or to amend an existing commission to provide for greater independence, so it is likely that in the near term the redistricting authority of state legislatures will continue to be eroded, either by more states adopting truly independent commissions or by courts vigorously enforcing the proliferating criteria.

What shape may this redistricting reform take? Good government groups such as the League of Women Voters and Common Cause generally advocate a set of four guiding principles:

1. **Independence.** Districts should be drawn by commissioners who are as removed from political influence as possible. This may be achieved by a vetting process that removes elected officials, lobbyists, legislative employees, immediate family members, and anyone else who may have a vested interest in district lines. Commissioners may not run for offices in the districts that they draw.

2. **Criteria.** The commission should be given a set of specific criteria to guide the drawing of districts. In the extreme, these criteria are envisioned to be mechanical in nature, thereby giving the commission very little discretion as to how districts will be drawn.

3. **Public Input.** The commission should accept input and solicit maps from the public. When combined with a strict set of criteria, public input can lead to a form of competition whereby the map that scores best on the criteria will be adopted by the commission.

4. **Transparency.** The commission should operate in meetings open to the public. This avoids backroom deals and maps that are thrust upon the

public at the last minute without public input. If subsequent court action is necessary, commission deliberations can provide clues as to the intent behind a map.

If the goal of this reform model is to take the politics out of redistricting, why not adopt a map with districts that look like squares, or some other compact shape? Better yet, why not program a computer to draw the districts with this goal in mind? As appealing as this mechanical approach may sound, there are surprisingly many difficulties in implementing it. Understanding these problems reveals why human decision making is inevitably required during redistricting.

The first problem is that people do not align themselves on a regular grid. There are densely populated urban areas and sparsely populated rural areas with suburban areas in-between. Since districts must be of equal population, their geographic sizes must be unequal. For even a modestly sized state, there are more feasible ways of drawing districts than there are atoms in the universe. Fitting districts together to achieve even a simple goal like district compactness is an extremely complicated mathematical partitioning problem, and there is no guarantee that a computer is able to sort through all possible maps to find the optimal solution in a finite amount of time.[23] Adding more criteria, such as respecting existing political boundaries, almost always makes things more complicated.

A commission can escape from the impossible quest for perfection by adopting a suboptimal map. This may work especially well where a commission accepts public input to keep the commission honest in looking at a wide range of alternatives. This is effectively how the New Jersey state legislative redistricting commission worked during the post-2000 census redistricting. The tie-breaking member selected by the New Jersey Supreme Court, Princeton political science professor Larry Bartels, issued a set of criteria and told the political parties he would vote for the map that best satisfied his criteria. The two parties were then placed in a competition to produce the map that would best attain the stated goals. The political parties might still try to gain advantage, but only at the peril of having the other party's map chosen. In this approach, the self-interest of the political parties is harnessed to produce a more equitable map, even if that map is not the absolutely best possible map. More generally, allowing the public at large to submit maps would place further pressure on the political parties to devise more equitable maps. Indeed, there is no guarantee that a party's maps might win such a contest.[24]

Another problem is that the criteria may have particular political biases to them. For example, if Democrats are concentrated in urban areas of a state—at

80 percent of all persons—and are intermingled with Republicans in rural areas—at 35 percent of all persons—then a redistricting plan that emphasizes compactness will result in a Republican gerrymander. Democrats living in urban areas will be inefficiently concentrated into districts they win overwhelmingly and distributed across rural districts that they have little chance of winning. In this "second order bias" effect, ostensibly neutral criteria may have a predictable political effect.[25]

A solution to this particular problem is to balance what one scholar calls "process-based regulations," such as compactness and respect for existing political boundaries, with "outcome-based regulations," such as political fairness or competition.[26] States such as Arizona and Washington, for instance, require districts to be politically competitive and the overall map to be politically balanced.

A problem is that once these criteria are piled upon one another, it is virtually impossible to optimize all criteria simultaneously. A redistricting commission must be given discretion to balance competing goals, and there is the rub. Give a commission too much discretion, and any map may be justified. Give it too little, and second-order bias may result.

The solution to this dilemma returns us to why commissions are preferred to state legislatures when drawing districts. If reasonably neutral actors can be selected to serve on commissions to draw districts, their deliberations observed in public meetings, and their actions monitored by the courts if necessary, then it should be possible to draw districts reasonably removed from the excesses observed when representatives draw their own districts in state legislatures.

The same level of oversight to prevent abuse of redistricting is difficult to achieve when politicians draw their districts. Supreme Court Justice Antonin Scalia argues that it is impossible to determine "legislative intent" in legislatures.[27] When large assemblies use majoritarian voting rules, motivations can be hidden within logrolling deals between members. Given that a legislator's primary motivation is to get reelected, legislators should be assumed to act in their self-interest during redistricting.[28] Their self-preservation instincts may thus be camouflaged within the many deals cut between members in backrooms. Short of kicking the bums out of office, which is difficult to do when legislators manipulate district lines to help themselves win elections, there is no way to hold a legislature accountable during redistricting.

If the United States is exceptional in that it is the only advanced democracy where legislators draw their own districts, it is also exceptional in that redistricting is litigated far more in the United States than in any other country.[29] Beyond removing the abuse that follows when legislators draw their own districts, following the rest of the world may have other benefits. Less money may be wasted on litigation as politicians stop seeking to gain political benefit through gerrymandering or trying to substitute a gerrymander with one of their own through court action. Citizens may have more confidence and trust in a redistricting system in which citizen input is actively solicited and actions are taken in public for all to see and understand, rather than in the backrooms where it often currently occurs.

Experimentation with redistricting reform is just beginning in earnest, now that Arizona and California have adopted processes that promise true independence from the legislature. The genius of the American federal system is that it permits such experimentation at the state level. How can commissions be devised to be truly independent of the legislature? Should commissions have mandates to achieve broad goals, or should they adhere to specific criteria? Should a tournament approach be employed that opens the process to wide public participation? These promising experiments in redistricting reform should continue and the results monitored to answer how best to implement reform. One thing is clear: the past demonstrates that politicians have done a poor job of policing themselves, so reform is necessary. Taking redistricting authority away from politicians and placing power into neutral commissions will prevent the most egregious abuses witnessed during redistricting.

CON: Justin Buchler

Reform advocates argue that partisan elected officials should not be permitted to redraw district lines because they face a conflict of interest. Clearly, partisan officials have an *interest* in how district lines are drawn. However, that does not mean that they have a *conflict* of interest, which only occurs when an agent charged with carrying out a task has incentives to carry out that task in a way that is detrimental to the principal, which in this case is the voting public. So, in order to determine whether or not there is a conflict of interest, we must examine partisan officials' incentives, voters' interests, and the degree to which they conflict. While partisan gerrymanders are harmful to voters, partisan officials have incentives not to attempt them. Instead, they have incentives to enact bipartisan gerrymanders. That bothers many reform advocates because bipartisan gerrymanders prevent competitive elections. However, a bipartisan gerrymander, by promoting partisan and ideological representation, serves voters' interests more effectively than a plan that promotes competitive elections. Thus partisan officials face no conflict of interest because they have strategic incentives to do precisely what is in voters' best interests.

PARTISAN OFFICIALS' INCENTIVES

Broadly defined, a gerrymander is a redistricting plan aimed at achieving a political objective, and all redistricting plans have a political objective. Thus any plan can be called a gerrymander. Three types of gerrymanders warrant attention here: the partisan gerrymander, the bipartisan gerrymander, and the competitive gerrymander. A partisan gerrymander is a plan in which one party attempts to maximize the number of seats it wins. In a bipartisan gerrymander, the two parties agree to create safer seats for each party by making Democratic districts more Democratic and Republican districts more Republican. A competitive gerrymander maximizes the number of districts in which there are equal numbers of Democratic and Republican voters to promote competitive elections.

Consider, first, the partisan gerrymander. Suppose an electorate has twenty-one Democrats and twelve Republicans, and that they must be divided into three districts of eleven people each. If the Republicans were to attempt a partisan gerrymander, they would group the voters as follows: District 1 (eleven Democrats), District 2 (six Republicans, five Democrats), and District 3 (six Republicans, five Democrats). By giving themselves majorities in two districts, the Republicans can theoretically win two out of three seats, even though they only have roughly one-third of the population. This plan, if successful, would distort the electorate's preferences. However, note the words *theoretically* and *if successful*. If just two voters switch their allegiance for some reason, Democrats can win all three seats because the Republican majorities in Districts 2 and 3 are so narrow. This is more than just a hypothetical danger. In 1974, the Watergate scandal caused an attempted Republican partisan gerrymander in New York to backfire dramatically by allowing Democrats to win seats that were supposed to be narrow Republican majorities.[1] When a party attempts a partisan gerrymander, a small shift in public opinion can cost many seats, and partisan elected officials are sufficiently historically informed and risk-averse that self-interest prevents egregious partisan gerrymandering.

Perhaps the most vilified modern redistricting plan was the one passed by Texas in 2003 under the guidance of Tom DeLay, which reformers use as an exemplar of why partisan officials shouldn't be allowed to redraw district lines. However, even that plan is far from an egregious partisan gerrymander. After the 2000 U.S. Census, the Democratic-controlled Texas state legislature and Republican governor failed to agree on a plan, so a panel of judges essentially maintained the previous plan, giving the Democrats seventeen out of thirty-two U.S. House seats from the state. The 2002 election gave the Republicans control of the state legislature for the first time in years, and they capitalized by redrawing district lines in a notorious mid-decade procedure. Under the new plan, the 2004 election gave the Republicans twenty-one out of thirty-two House seats. The process of passing that plan was unusual, not merely from a timing perspective, but because it involved such amusements as Democratic state legislators literally fleeing the state in order to deny a quorum in the legislature, thereby postponing passage of the plan in a poor-man's filibuster. While the procedure that produced the plan was difficult to defend, the plan itself was another matter. The 2002 district lines gave the Democrats 53 percent of the House seats, even though the Texas electorate was majority Republican. The DeLay plan ultimately gave the Republicans 66 percent of the U.S. House districts from Texas. Which was a better representation of the Texas population? Consider the statewide election results from the years preceding the DeLay plan, which can be used to measure the partisan composition of the state.[2]

As Table 10-1 shows, the DeLay plan had a Republican bias, but by most measures that bias was smaller than the Democratic bias of the court-drawn plan. Using the 2002 Senate race as a baseline, the DeLay plan and the court plan were essentially equally biased (the difference is rounding error), and

Table 10-1

Bias and the Texas Redistricting of 2003

Year	Office	Republican two-party vote	Democratic two-party vote	Court plan bias	DeLay plan bias
2000	President	64%	36%	17 points	2 points
2000	Senate	67	33	20 points	1 point
2002	Governor	59	41	12 points	7 points
2002	Senate	56	44	9 points	10 points
2002	Lieutenant governor	53	47	6 points	13 points
2002	Attorney general	58	42	11 points	8 points

Source: Texas Secretary of State.

using the 2002 lieutenant governor race as the baseline, the DeLay plan had a stronger bias than the court plan. However, by every other measure, the bias of the DeLay plan was smaller than that of the court plan. While it was procedurally unusual to redraw district lines mid-decade, thus understandably angering Democrats, the result of having partisan officials redraw the lines was a *reduction* in partisan bias. This is to be expected because the risks of attempting partisan gerrymanders are sufficiently high for the dominant party that, contrary to the fears of reform advocates, partisan officials rarely attempt to create an egregious bias.

Instead, since partisan elected officials are risk-averse, they are more likely to draw bipartisan gerrymanders, as they did in California after the 2000 U.S. Census. In the 2000 election, Democrats won thirty-two out of fifty-two U.S. House seats in California, and the 2000 U.S. Census gave California an additional seat. However, despite the fact that Democrats controlled both houses of the state legislature and the governor's office, they made no attempt at a partisan gerrymander. Instead, they passed a bipartisan gerrymander that eliminated competitive districts, made Democratic and Republican seats safer, and left the partisan ratio essentially unchanged. In 2000 George W. Bush and Al Gore were separated by less than ten points in the two-party vote in fifteen of California's U.S. House districts. In 2004 Bush and John Kerry were separated by less than ten points in only five districts. However, the partisan ratio remained essentially unchanged. In 2002 the Democrats won thirty-three out of fifty-three House seats, which is essentially the same proportion they won before redistricting. Partisan officials rarely attempt serious partisan gerrymanders. They are more likely to attempt bipartisan gerrymanders because they don't want to run the risk of losing too many seats for their parties, they want to make their own seats safer, and those with progressive ambitions want to create safe House seats for which they will eventually run.

VOTERS' INTERESTS

Partisan officials have incentives to draw bipartisan gerrymanders. That only constitutes a conflict of interest if voters have an interest in a different type of plan. Reform advocates believe that voters' interests would be better served by a competitive gerrymander. If so, then partisan officials face a conflict of interest. So do bipartisan gerrymanders really hurt voters? Reformers, like Samuel Issacharoff,[3] ask us to imagine if Coke and Pepsi carved up the country into districts in which only Coke is sold and districts in which only Pepsi is sold, based on the strange idea that elections are like markets. Issacharoff suggests that allowing partisan officials to redraw district lines knowing that they will create bipartisan gerrymanders is no different. Of course, a bipartisan gerry-mander is more like placing Coke drinkers into one set of districts and Pepsi drinkers into another set, then allowing districts to collectively choose what they drink. It would seem odd to suggest that Coke drinkers in this system are prevented from drinking Pepsi just because they prefer Coke, but that is pre-cisely what this market analogy does. The fact that an election is a collective choice suggests that we should group people in ways that will allow them to make collective choices that satisfy the maximum number of people.

So what specific interests do voters have in a redistricting plan? Consider the following two interests. Voters have a collective interest in a state delegation with a partisan balance that reflects the partisan balance of the state electorate, and they have an interest in giving as many voters as possible a representative whose opinions reflect their own. Competitive gerrymanders undermine both interests.

If a state is 60 percent Democratic, a redistricting plan that produces a 60 percent Democratic delegation is better than a plan that produces a 60 percent Republican delegation. So what type of redistricting plan minimizes partisan bias? Empirically, the more competitive districts there are, the greater the par-tisan bias is.[4] Bipartisan gerrymanders do a much better job of ensuring pro-portionality than competitive gerrymanders. This may seem counterintuitive, but to understand why, consider a state evenly split between Democrats and Republicans, divided into two districts. The competitive gerrymander would be to make each district a microcosm of the state. The bipartisan gerrymander would be to create a homogeneously Democratic district and a homogeneously Republican district. If an evenly divided district has a 50 percent chance of electing a candidate of either party, then the competitive gerrymander has a 25 percent chance of electing two Democrats, a 25 percent chance of electing two Republicans, and only a 50 percent chance of producing a delegation that actu-ally reflects the state's preferences. On the other hand, the bipartisan gerry-mander would deterministically give the state the fifty-fifty delegation that it should have.[5] Bipartisan gerrymanders ensure partisan representation; com-petitive gerrymanders undermine partisan representation.

The second interest voters have is in electing representatives whose opin-ions match their own. Advocates of competitive elections argue that bipartisan gerrymanders cause two related problems—they create legislative polarization and foster discrepancies between the opinions of voters and their representa-tives. There is an intuitively appealing theory underlying such claims. A com-petitive general election might pull the candidates toward the ideological center of the district. In a district dominated by voters of one party, there won't be a competitive general election, so candidates in such districts may simply move to the extremes to win the primary. Thus it has become a mantra for reform advocates to blame the increase in congressional polarization on bipartisan gerrymanders. Furthermore, if we assume that voters are not themselves polarized, then that polarization is a distortion of voters' preferences, so by promoting polarization bipartisan gerrymanders foster discrepancies between the positions of voters and their representatives.

However, the data do not support such claims. Consider the following histograms, showing the ideologies of representatives to the U.S. House in the 83d (1953–1954) and 109th (2005–2006) Congresses. There is nothing unique about these Congresses. Scholars point to the 1950s as a period of depolarization and the 2000s as one of hyperpolarization, and these two Congresses are representative of their periods. The scores are DW-NOMINATE scores, where negative scores indicate liberalism and positive scores indicate conservatism.

The 83d Congress had a large number of centrists, as Figure 10-1 shows. However, the 109th Congress had very few centrists and a large number of

Figure 10-1

DW-NOMINATE Scores for 83d Congress

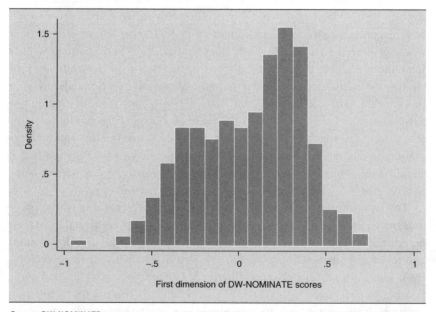

First dimension of DW-NOMINATE scores

Source: DW-NOMINATE scores are computed by Keith Poole, and available at http://www.voteview.com

Figure 10-2

DW-NOMINATE Scores for 109th Congress

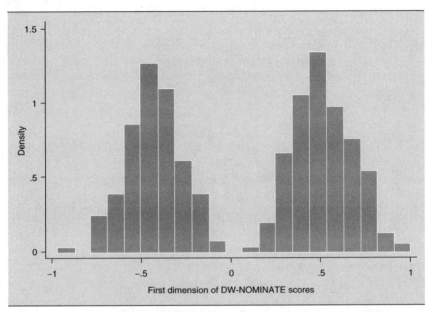

Source: DW-NOMINATE scores are compiled by Keith Poole, and available at http://www.voteview.com

extremists, as shown in Figure 10-2. There was a steady progression through-out the post–World War II period that produced the now famously polarized Congress. If reform advocates are to be believed, then this trend has occurred because partisan officials have systematically eliminated competitive districts, thus removing incentives for anyone in Congress to adopt moderate positions. This proposition has been empirically debunked,[6] and it is relatively easy to see why. If bipartisan gerrymanders had been responsible for the disappearance of moderates, then what would we see if we just looked at representatives from marginal districts? Consider members of Congress who represent districts in which the presidential candidates were separated by less than ten points in the two-party vote. If bipartisan gerrymanders had been responsible for the disap-pearance of moderates, then these legislators should be just as moderate in the 109th Congress as in the 83d Congress—there should just be fewer of them in the 109th Congress. Figures 10-3 and 10-4 are histograms like Figures 10-1 and 10-2, except that they only show the ideologies of members of Congress from marginal districts in the 83d and 109th Congresses.

Figure 10-3

DW-NOMINATE Scores for Marginal Members, 83d Congress

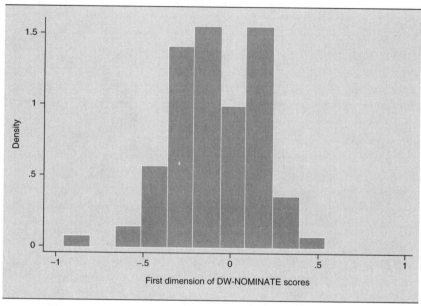

Source: DW-NOMINATE scores are computed by Keith Poole, and available at http://www.voteview.com

If bipartisan gerrymanders had been responsible for the disappearance of moderates, then representatives from marginal districts in the 109th Congress would have been just as moderate as representatives from marginal districts in the 83d Congress—there would simply have been fewer of them in the 109th Congress. However, as we can see in Figures 10-3 and 10-4, that is not the case. Just like the rest of Congress, members from marginal districts have become more polarized, so we cannot blame polarization on the presence of fewer marginal districts. In fact, marginal districts haven't even been disappearing! Figure 10-5 shows the proportion of U.S. House districts in each presidential election in which the two major-party candidates were separated by less than ten points in the two-party vote.

The number of competitive districts fluctuates over time, but Figure 10-5 hardly paint a picture of partisan officials systematically destroying competition through bipartisan gerrymanders. In fact, there were actually *more* marginal districts in 2004 than in 1952, yet polarization was much more pronounced in the 109th Congress than in the 83d. While bipartisan gerrymanders do occur, as they did in California after the 2000 U.S. Census, their

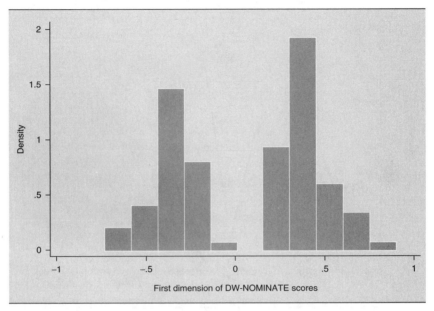

Figure 10-4

DW-NOMINATE Scores for Marginal Members, 109th Congress

Source: DW-NOMINATE scores are computed by Keith Poole, and available at http://www.voteview.com

frequency and effect have been dramatically overstated by reform advocates. Marginal districts have not been disappearing, and even if they had, members of Congress from the remaining marginal districts are more polarized now than members from marginal districts in the 1950s. Therefore, while there are many reasons to be troubled by the increasing polarization in Congress, we clearly cannot blame that polarization on bipartisan gerrymanders.

So allowing partisan officials to redraw district lines is not responsible for polarization. We now move on to the second part of the competition-ideology argument. Proponents of competitive elections argue that competitive elections yield legislators who are more ideologically representative of their constituents than are legislators who win by landslides. There are several related problems with that line of reasoning. First, even in competitive districts, candidates must win a primary before getting to the general election, so even in competitive districts, candidates don't just appeal to the median voter because of the wide gap between the preferences of primary voters and general election voters. Second, remember that a bipartisan gerrymander requires

Figure 10-5

Percentage of House Districts That Are Marginal

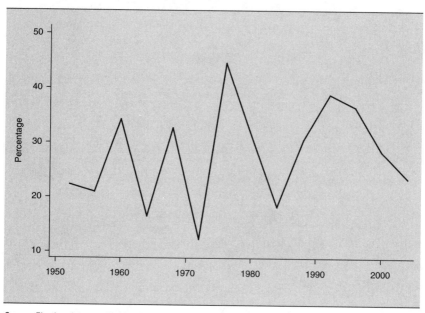

Source: Election data provided by Gary C. Jacobson.

drawing homogeneous districts, and a competitive gerrymander requires drawing politically diverse districts. When districts are politically diverse, that is precisely when we see the biggest gap between the preferences of the primary voters and those of the general election voters. Since bipartisan gerrymanders involve homogeneous districts, they ensure that the gap between the primary and general electorates is as small as possible. Thus bipartisan gerrymanders force candidates to adopt policy positions that are as similar as possible to as many constituents as possible.[7] Furthermore, a politically diverse district ensures that no matter which candidate wins, and no matter what platform the winner proposes, a large number of constituents will disagree with it. Thus it should be no surprise that, empirically, it is in competitive districts that voters are most likely to disagree with the platforms of their representatives.[8] Bipartisan gerrymanders, by definition, create more homogeneous constituencies, so bipartisan gerrymanders are more likely to elect representatives who are ideologically similar to their constituents than competitive gerrymanders.

CONFLUENCE OF INTERESTS

Partisan elected officials have strategic incentives to enact bipartisan gerrymanders. A bipartisan gerrymander is also the type of redistricting plan that
most benefits voters by giving them partisan and ideological representation,
and we cannot blame polarization in Congress on bipartisan gerrymanders.
Thus partisan officials have strategic incentives to draw lines in precisely the
same way that benefits voters. They do not face a conflict of interest; they face
a confluence of interest, because competitive elections are in neither the constituents' interests nor partisan officials' interests.

It should be noted that there may be other considerations. Some might
object to allowing partisan elected officials to redraw district lines because they
may attempt to lock minor parties out of the process. However, we have a two-
party system because of Duverger's law—a simple plurality rule electoral system tends to produce a two-party system, so even if partisan officials had
incentives to eliminate marginal districts that would have little effect on third
party prospects because they are unlikely to win, regardless of how district lines
are drawn. Similarly, some reformers are concerned with the possibility of corruption. In fact, competitive elections have the potential to spur one of the
most commonly feared forms of corruption—*quid pro quo* exchanges of campaign contributions for favors. An incumbent in a marginal district has more
need for campaign money than an incumbent from a safe district, so it stands
to reason that drawing more marginal districts would *increase* legislators' willingness to engage in certain acts of corruption. Competitive elections are in
nobody's best interests, so the fact that partisan officials are unlikely to promote them does not indicate a conflict of interest. It indicates a confluence
of interest.

RESOLVED, the Senate should represent people, not states

PRO: Bruce I. Oppenheimer

CON: John J. Pitney Jr.

Not every high school student takes a class in civics or government anymore, but even those who don't seldom graduate without hearing words to this effect somewhere along the line: "The framers of the Constitution created the House of Representatives to represent the people and they created the Senate to represent the states." Students who took government may have delved into *The Federalist Papers,* a series of newspaper articles that Alexander Hamilton, James Madison, and John Jay wrote to persuade the country to ratify the Constitution in 1787 and 1788. They may even have read *Federalist* No. 62.

In that essay, which was published in New York's *Independent Journal* on February 27, 1788, Madison explained and defended the Senate's place in the proposed constitutional system as "giving to the State governments such an agency in the formation of the federal government as must secure the authority of the former." Not only was each individual state empowered by the Senate to defend its sovereignty, Madison added, but so were the states as a whole. For that reason, "the equal vote allowed to each State" in the Senate "ought to be no less acceptable to the large than to the small States; since they are not less solicitous to guard, by every possible expedient, against an improper consolidation of the States into one simple republic" ruled exclusively by a national government.

The truism that the House represents the people and the Senate represents the states has more than *Federalist* No. 62 going for it. Even in 1790, the most populous state, Virginia, had nineteen representatives and Delaware, the least populous, had only one. By 2010, Delaware still had one and California, the largest, had fifty-three. All of these representatives—then and now—have been elected by the people. In contrast, until the Seventeenth Amendment was added to the Constitution in 1913, senators were chosen by their state legislatures. Since 1913 senators have been chosen by voters, but Virginia, Delaware, California, and every other state still have two senators each.

Strong evidence, to be sure, but strong enough? Consider: if the framers' goal was to have the Senate represent the states, then why did they give each state two senators instead of one—that is, why did they risk the possibility that a state's two senators will cancel each other out (as in practice they often do) by voting against each other on important issues? And why didn't the Constitution authorize each state to instruct its senators how to vote on issues that came before Congress? Or to recall senators when they voted their own minds instead of giving them six-year terms designed to insulate them from pressure from their states? For that matter, why did the framers provide that senators' salaries would be paid by the federal government, not by the various state governments? And why did the Constitution give the Senate unique responsibilities in making important national decisions—whether to ratify treaties and to accept or reject Supreme Court nominees—that have nothing to do with the states?

Questions such as these make plain that the framers designed the Senate with multiple purposes in mind, which included but were not confined to representing the states. The question presented in this debate, however, is about the present and the future, not the past: that is, whether the Senate *should* represent people, not states.

To this resolution, Bruce I. Oppenheimer boldly says yes, and John J. Pitney Jr. firmly says no. Both acknowledge the unusual constraint placed on a wide-ranging consideration of this issue by the "equal suffrage" clause in Article V of the Constitution, which says that "no State, without its Consent, shall be deprived of its equal Suffrage in the Senate." Interestingly, Pitney, who favors equal suffrage, sees a possible way around this clause and Oppenheimer, who opposes equal suffrage, is resigned to its immutability.

PRO: Bruce I. Oppenheimer

The resolution defining this debate assumes something that has not been accurate since the adoption of the Seventeenth Amendment in 1913, and may never have been accurate. The Senate does represent people, not states. Arguably, it always has represented people, not states. But it represents them in a skewed, inefficient, and unequal manner because two senators represent the residents of each state, regardless of the state's population.

The extent of the inequality of representation of people residing in the different states has increased over the history of the Republic, just as James Madison predicted at the Constitutional Convention when he opposed apportioning the Senate by giving equal representation to each state. In 1790 a majority of the Senate could be elected from states with 30 percent of the nation's population. Today it requires less than 18 percent. With a population approaching 37 million, California's two senators represent nearly seventy people for each one that their Senate colleagues from Wyoming represent. No powerful democratic legislature is as malapportioned, judged by the "one person, one vote" standard, as the U.S. Senate is.

In the course of this essay, I will argue the following: first, the Senate may always have been meant to represent people, not states; second, the Seventeenth Amendment removed any doubt about whether the Senate represents people or states; third, the problems that equal representation of residents in states with highly varied populations creates are numerous and undesirable; fourth, the population-based House of Representatives does not compensate for the biases that the Senate creates; and fifth, little, if anything, can be done to correct this significant shortcoming of American constitutional design.

IS SENATE APPORTIONMENT A SYMBOL OF FEDERALISM?

Many people accept the idea that the Senate represents states because it is apportioned with an equal number of senators for each state. Senate apportionment is thereby assumed to function as a symbol of federalism. Accordingly, the apportionment scheme must have been designed to institutionalize a position for states in the national government.

There is some support for this view in statements articulated at the convention describing the composition of the Senate as an acknowledgment of the sovereignty of the states. And in *Federalist* No. 62, Madison argues that it makes sense for the legislature to represent both individuals and states, with the House of Representatives and the Senate, respectively, performing these functions. (Madison, however, was arguing for ratification of the Constitution, not because he believed in the apportionment basis of the Senate.) In fact, however, the delegates in Philadelphia rejected a number of proposals to link senators more closely to their states, including having them paid by the states and being subject to recall by the states. If anything, the delegates' expectation was that senators would be "national" legislators, not parochial like House members, and not responsive to state interests. The primary parameters for the Senate were that it be a small, elite body, insulated from the impulse of popular majorities. Equal representation of all states was as much, if not more, a consequence of the delegates' desire to limit the Senate's size than it was to provide the same representation for each state. Awarding additional Senate seats to more populous states would have resulted in a larger body than the framers thought desirable.

In the mid-1960s the Supreme Court ruled that all state legislatures must be apportioned on the basis of population,[1] but excepted the Senate from this population-based apportionment requirement because of its linkage to the principle of federalism. However, there are several reasons to doubt the Court's interpretation of why the Senate has equal apportionment for each state. First, it is unnecessary for federal systems of government to provide for equal representation of units within the national legislature. Representation can be given to the units without requiring equal representation. Indeed, that is what occurs in most other federal systems that have bicameral legislatures. Subnational governing units are the basis on which representation is assigned, but all units do not receive the same number of representatives. Second, the claims that states possess some residual sovereignty that requires equal representation status in one chamber of the national legislature and that the original federal compact gives states a sacrosanct status are flawed. Aside from the original thirteen states, none of the others have prior independent existence apart from territorial status as defined by the U.S. government. Often, the establishment of states was the subject of political bargains and partisan advantage, not some prior governing community of interest or geography. Even the borders of several of the original thirteen states have been altered since the adoption of the Constitution. Kentucky and West Virginia were once part of Virginia, and the area that became Maine was part of Massachusetts. Preserving preexisting sovereignty in the representational basis of the U.S. Senate because of prior attachment to these governing units is hardly supported by the historical record of the formation of states.

THE SEVENTEENTH AMENDMENT

Suppose we concede for the sake of discussion that the Senate was originally designed to represent states, not people, and that the equal representation of all states and the indirect election of senators by state legislatures, and not by the people, is sufficient evidence to substantiate that claim. The Seventeenth Amendment clearly undercuts the continuing basis of the contention. If indirect election by state legislatures provided the proof that the Senate represented states, not people, then the change to direct election of senators means that since 1913 the Senate has represented the people of the states and not the state governments. The Seventeenth Amendment formally transferred electoral accountability from state legislatures to the people.

The problem is that the apportionment basis of the Senate and the distribution of population across the states have resulted in grossly unequal representation that has far-reaching and undesirable effects not just in terms of representation but also in terms of Senate elections, influence within the Senate, and the way the Senate makes public policy. Moreover, the framers could not have envisioned how skewed Senate representation would become. Living in a country with a population of three million people, the delegates to the Constitutional Convention did not imagine that little more than two centuries later a single state would have a population twelve times greater than that. And, as mentioned above, the magnitude of the deviation of Senate representation from a one person, one vote standard has increased markedly over the years and continues to do so. Accordingly, my concern is less with the untenable claim that the Senate represents states, not people, than with how unequally it represents people and with the empirical and normative consequences that Senate apportionment has for governing.

THE NEGATIVE CONSEQUENCES OF SENATE REPRESENTATION

The obvious starting point for examining the unfairness of Senate representation is a quantitative one. The contrast between residents of Wyoming and California has already been alluded to. As the political theorist Charles R. Beitz has maintained: "The meaning of quantitative fairness has become a settled matter: it requires adherence to the precept 'one person, one vote.'"[2] It is not merely that the Senate deviates from this standard, it is the extent of the deviation. The differences from state to state are not a few residents or votes, or even a few thousand or a few hundred thousand, but millions. And these differences have consequences. Residents in small states receive quantitatively and qualitatively better representation than residents in large states. Although residents in U.S. House districts in different-sized states all have roughly equal access to their representatives, those in small states have much better access to their U.S. senators than those in more populous states. It was only a slight exaggeration during the 2008 presidential campaign to say that every resident of Delaware had met Sen. Joe Biden and felt that they knew him personally. The close to 37 million residents of California could not make a similar claim about their two senators. Moreover, what is true for residents is also true for interest groups within the states and their access to their senators.

This difference in access leads to a normative concern with fairness. It is not just that the votes of individuals in small states count more in determining the composition of the Senate. The bigger problem is that Senate apportionment carries with it inequality in access. Individuals and groups in small-population states find it easier to communicate their preferences to their senators, to meet with them, and to have a personal relationship. Importantly, because racial and ethnic minority populations are concentrated in the populous states, those demographic groups are among those most negatively affected by the unequal representation of the Senate.

As Frances E. Lee and I have demonstrated in our book *Sizing Up the Senate,* Senate apportionment also affects Senate elections in unequal ways.[3] Senators in small-population states tend to win by larger margins, need to raise far less money, and are free from electoral accountability on more issues because their states are less diverse. Large-state senators must raise money constantly and in much greater amounts. They have less time to focus on the concerns of their constituents and to pursue influential positions within the Senate. It is no accident that Senate floor leadership positions since the 1970s have been dominated by senators from small-population states: Robert Byrd of West Virginia, Robert Dole of Kansas, George Mitchell of Maine, Trent Lott of Mississippi, Tom Daschle of South Dakota, and Harry Reid of Nevada. They are the senators with the time to seek and exercise the power that leadership positions provide.

Perhaps the antidemocratic effects of Senate apportionment would be an acceptable cost of U.S. constitutional design if they were limited to representation, access, the expense and competitiveness of elections, and the influence of senators. But the effects go beyond these to the very basis of politics: who gets what, when, and how.[4] One of the major consequences of requiring all states to have two senators regardless of population is that the people in smaller states receive more funds per capita from the federal government than those in larger states. When the Senate passes legislation that establishes a formula for distributing federal funds to the states, the formula in program after program gives small states a disproportionate share of funding, even when one controls for state program need. Whether it's transportation, community development, environmental quality, housing, education, or employment, small states receive a disproportionate share of federal dollars primarily because of the influence the U.S. Senate has over the design of those programs. Of course, any apportionment method will have biases. Even the fairest set of rules is never neutral. Some benefit more than others, even when the same rules are applied to all players. The one person, one vote standard that governs the apportioning of the House of Representatives and the state legislatures is no exception. But the apportionment scheme of the Senate, unlike the one person, one vote standard, does not meet the test of fairness.

WHY THE HOUSE DOESN'T COMPENSATE FOR SENATE INEQUALITY

Some might argue that the beauty of the U.S. Constitution, with its checks and balances, is that the House of Representatives—which is apportioned on the basis of one person, one vote—countervails the unequal effects of Senate representation. A careful examination of that argument quickly uncovers its flaws. In terms of access, elections, and internal influence, the House cannot compensate for the Senate. Should we expect that a House member from California, who has roughly the same number of constituents as the single House member from Wyoming, will be able to compensate in terms of representational access for the fact that California's two senators have so many more people to represent than the two senators from Wyoming do? And how can the House members do anything about the fact that Senate campaigns in populous states are so much more expensive and are on average more competitive than those in small states? Nor is the House or its members likely to have much sway over which senators have the time to compete for positions of leadership.

Even when it comes to the design of legislation, the idea that the House will correct for the biases caused by Senate apportionment is not borne out by the facts. It's incorrect to assume that the House offsets Senate policy decisions that favor residents in the less populous states. After all, no bill can become law unless it is first passed in identical form by both the House and Senate before being sent to the president. One might think that the population-based House would not allow the Senate to design formulas that give disproportional funding to small-population states and underfund the most populous states. But House members are more concerned with federal dollars going to their individual districts than with the overall distribution of program funding to states. In bargaining with the Senate, many House members are willing to accept the biases of Senate funding formulas in exchange for including individual projects for which they can claim credit in their districts.

Moreover, even though the House normally passes programs with population-based funding formulas, it must then bargain with the Senate in conference. At best, House conferees get the Senate to adjust its formula so that the small state bias is not as great as in the Senate version of the legislation. But that still leaves the final version of the bill with a formula that rewards residents in the small states at the expense of those in the populous states. In fact, the Senate wins nearly three-quarters of the time when it negotiates with the House over formulas. Frequently, this type of legislation contains a minimum guarantee provision that entitles every state to at least one-half of 1 percent of the total funds. This provision alone means that the thirteen least populous states will receive more than their fair share of funds. And the minimum guarantee is just one feature that gets written into legislation that results in the skewed distribution of funds.

In sum, the belief that through the brilliance of constitutional design the House of Representatives will automatically correct for the biases that result from Senate apportionment is a myth.

WHAT CAN BE DONE?

The good news contained in this essay is that the Senate represents people, not states. The bad news is that it does so unfairly and that the magnitude of the unfairness is increasing. That leads us to even worse news. Very little can or is likely to be done about the situation. Unlike the decision to amend the Constitution to provide for direct election of senators, changing the apportionment basis of the Senate is not subject to the normal amending process. Article V of the Constitution, which addresses the amending process, says that "no state, without its consent, shall be deprived of equal suffrage in the Senate." It is hard to imagine circumstances in which any state that benefits from the current scheme would grant that consent. Also, despite its obvious lack of fairness, Senate representation is hardly the type of issue that is likely to result in a great public outcry. (Ironically, the electoral college's deviation from the one person, one vote standard is quite modest compared with that of Senate apportionment. But there is nearly continuous public concern about its lack of fairness.) Even if the American public were better educated about the unequal consequences of the Senate's representational scheme, one would not expect the American people to protest what many view as the most undemocratic feature of the Constitution.

Perhaps the only means available to ameliorate the degree to which Senate representation deviates from the one person, one vote standard would be to divide some of the most populous states into several states. And one can only imagine the controversies that such a move might engender.

The Senate, as it has since 1913 if not before, will continue to represent the people, not the states. But it will continue to do so unequally and with negative consequences for the people and for the ideal of American democracy.

CON: John J. Pitney Jr.

"Nothing is either good or bad save alternatives make it so," said economist Procter Thomson. To show that the Senate should represent people instead of states, one cannot merely point out shortcomings of the current system. It is also necessary to compare that system with alternatives. That is where the case for fundamental change runs aground. To paraphrase Winston Churchill, having two senators per state is the worst possible arrangement except for all the others.

The question of alternatives has a whiff of improbability, since Article V of the Constitution forbids any amendment that would deprive any state of equal representation in the Senate without its consent. Some legal writers, however, have suggested ways around the Equal Suffrage Clause, such as a two-part amendment that would first abolish the clause and then restructure the Senate.[1] For the sake of argument, then, let us assume that radical reform is possible. What forms could it take?

The first is simply to do away with the Senate, as a few progressives have suggested.[2] This sentiment is understandable because the chamber's procedures have sometimes enabled a minority of members to thwart liberal measures. At other times, however, it has done the reverse, much to the liberals' relief. When the Newt Gingrich–led House of Representatives tried to roll back government regulation, an environmental lobbyist said: "Thank God for the Senate. I never thought I'd be saying that."[3]

Bicameralism aids in policy deliberation. The presence of two chambers may complicate the lawmaking process, but it also provides more chances to debate the merits of legislation. A relevant argument or datum that goes unnoticed in one chamber may get a look in the other. The scrutiny of a second set of eyes makes it more likely that troublesome provisions will come to light. One Senate staffer told legal scholars Victoria F. Nourse and Jane S. Schacter: "Sometimes no one is focusing on the text. Thank God for a bicameral legislature. Things can happen quickly, in the dark, in the long bills where no one has seen it."[4]

In this light, it is not surprising that there is scant support for a unicameral Congress. Assuming that the Senate stays, we must now ask how it could represent population. Weighted voting would be the simplest approach. Under this system, each state would still elect two senators, but each senator's vote would equal half the state's population. Instead of having one vote each, a California senator would have 18.4 million (half the state's population) while a colleague from Wyoming would have about a quarter-million. Weighted voting would give the bigger states more say without requiring changes in state election laws, or even the addition of any desks in the Senate chamber.[5]

Though it may sound appealing at first, weighted voting would involve great problems. One is that it would enable a small number of senators to rule the chamber. According to 2008 census estimates, the nine largest states comprise more than half the nation's population, meaning that a weighted voting scheme could give control of the chamber to a mere eighteen senators. Under a cloture procedure requiring a 60 percent vote, it would still take only twenty-six senators (from thirteen states) to overpower their colleagues. These figures represent an extreme case, since the eighteen or twenty-six senators would not always have a common interest. But even under other scenarios, a minority of senators would typically prevail, and a large number would seldom have a chance to affect the outcome of a vote. This arrangement would exclude much of the country from the coalitions and compromises that create the law.[5]

Another problem is that weighted voting would do nothing to change the Senate's composition.[6] One criticism of the institution is that members of historically disadvantaged groups have had difficulty winning Senate races. At the time of his election to the presidency, Barack Obama was the only African American senator. By contrast, African Americans made up 9 percent of the membership of the House, and held key positions of power. Under weighted voting, Senator Obama would have had more power in roll calls, but he would not have had more African American colleagues.

If weighted voting is out of the question, then people-based representation would entail an enlargement of Senate membership, with the size of each state's delegation corresponding to its share of the national population. A key practical question is how many more seats would be necessary. A modest increase (say, fifty more) would do little to meet a one person, one vote standard and would hardly justify the great trouble it would take to amend the Constitution. A serious expansion would require the Senate to grow to about 435 members, or as big as the House has been for nearly a century. And even that number would fall short of the reformers' ideals. Although the courts mandate that all House districts *within* a state have roughly equal populations, there are large disparities *among* the states. Because each state must have at least one House member, and because state populations vary so widely, it is impossible to devise 435 equal districts.[7] Montana has nearly twice as many people as Wyoming, yet each has one member. California's population is sixty-nine times greater than Wyoming's, yet its House delegation is only fifty-three times larger. A smaller chamber would have even more severe anomalies, so if the Senate were to be adequately representative of people instead of states, it would have to be at least as large as the current House—and preferably larger.

There are several reasons why a bigger Senate would not be a better Senate.

First of all, deliberation would suffer. Granted, the quality of debate in today's Senate is often mediocre, leading many observers to sneer when they call it "the world's greatest deliberative body." Nevertheless, in their authoritative analysis of congressional deliberation, Gary Mucciaroni and Paul J. Quirk find that floor debates in the Senate are better informed than those in the House, with more substantiation of claims and rebuttals.[8] This difference stems from the relative sizes of the two bodies. The Senate can afford to let each of its hundred members speak at length about the merits of policy. With more than four times as many members, the House must ration floor time much more stingily. In the House, Mucciaroni and Quirk find, "most speeches are very brief, ranging from one to five minutes in length; speakers generally do little more than state their positions and recite their side's scripted talking points. For the most part, speakers do not respond directly to other speakers—for example, to make and answer criticisms."[9] If the Senate doubled, tripled, or quadrupled in size, it would have to abandon its tradition of extended debate, substituting recitation for deliberation.

Second, expanding the Senate would make it more rancorous. Although the ideological differences between Republican and Democratic senators have widened, and their debates have sometimes taken on a hard edge, the Senate remains a more civil place than the House. The shouting matches and walkouts that have marred House politics in recent years have not been a part of Senate life. Once again, size helps account for the difference. Senators are much more likely to know a given colleague in their chamber than are House members. Personal relationships thus temper policy conflicts. In the House, as Ross K. Baker says, social distance loosens political restraint: "House members, like air crews dropping bombs on an enemy they cannot see, take a more cold-blooded view of partisan warfare. . . . The rules of engagement in the Senate are largely personal; in the House they are distinctively partisan."[10]

Third and most important, increasing Senate membership would have the paradoxical effect of reducing the number of senators who really matter. Among one hundred senators, power is widely dispersed, and each can play a meaningful role. The more members a chamber has, however, the harder it is to give everyone free rein, and the more likely it is that a small subset will take charge. As James Madison put it: "[In] all legislative assemblies the greater the number composing them may be, the fewer will be the men who will in fact direct their proceedings."[11] In the middle of the twentieth century, the House put great power in the hands of key committee chairs, or "barons." During the 1970s, the focus of influence shifted to the leaders of the majority party.

When ideological gaps are wide and rancor runs hot, this concentration of power means that members of the minority party have little say. In 1986, when Democrats were in their fourth straight decade of control, Rep. Henry Waxman, D-Calif., said: "If we have a united Democratic position, Republicans are irrelevant."[12] Specifically, the majority's leaders can use procedural rules to block the minority from offering amendments or otherwise influencing the content of legislation. In 1993 Rep. Gerald Solomon, R-N.Y., grumbled: "Every time we deny an open amendment process on an important piece of legislation, we are disenfranchising the people and their Representatives from the legislative process."[13] When Republicans controlled the House for a dozen years after the 1994 election, Democrats complained that they had become the voiceless minority. After party control switched again in 2006, incoming Rules Committee chair Louise Slaughter, D-N.Y., said of the outgoing GOP majority: "They really had disenfranchised about half of the American citizens."[14] Although it may have been a stretch to speak of "disenfranchisement," members of the minority party could plausibly argue that their status had left their constituents with much less effective representation than people in majority-party districts.

Despite pledges of change, the new majority acted just like the old one, only more so. In the 110th Congress, a Brookings Institution study found, a "pattern of tighter, more centralized control—which began more than two decades ago under Democratic rule and then intensified under Republican majorities, especially after the 2000 election—continues unabated."[15] With Slaughter now chairing Rules, Republicans lodged the same complaint that Democrats had made a few years before. Rep. Tom Price, R-Ga., expressed the Republican lament: "We all represent essentially the same number of people. When the majority does not allow a certain Member or Members to offer amendments or to offer their best ideas, what they do is disenfranchise nearly half of the American people."[16]

If the Senate were larger, it would have to tighten its procedures, enabling the majority to overpower the minority. As with the House, some Americans would have legislators who could actually legislate, while others would not.

In addition to the sheer number of senators, we must also consider the manner of their selection. At-large elections, in which Senate candidates would run statewide, could not work in the larger states. California has fifty-three House seats, and if it chose that many senators on a statewide basis, its voters would have a preposterously difficult task: few would be able to name them all, much less appraise their performance. As a practical matter, then, population-based representation would mean dividing all but the smallest states into Senate districts. Accordingly, Senate elections would come to resemble House elections, a development that would damage the Senate's accountability.

In this context, accountability means that officials are subject to serious review by the electorate, and that they can lose their jobs if they perform poorly. Accountability hinges on two conditions. First, voters must have access to full and accurate information about what the officials are doing. Second, they must have a real choice in the next election, featuring credible challengers who can get their message out and who have a chance of defeating the incumbent.

Voters can currently gain more information about their senators than their House members. National publications and broadcast news organizations frequently run stories about senators, sometimes from a critical perspective. Individual House members are much less likely to make the national news. Reporters regard the average senator as more important and newsworthy than the average House member because each is one of 100 instead of one in 435.

Senators also tend to receive more scrutiny on their home turf. True, scholars have found that a senator generally gets only a little more coverage from a typical local paper than a House member.[17] But except in the states with a single House member, Senate constituencies include more media organizations. A New York senator must deal with the state's fifty-three daily newspapers, along with dozens of television and radio news operations. House members work in a different media environment. The New York City market includes many congressional districts, so while the *Times, Post,* and *Daily News* amply cover their senators, they give little space to an average local House member. Elsewhere in the state, House districts may encompass just a handful of newspapers and broadcast stations. Most of these local news shops do not have Washington bureaus, and even where they once did they are closing them.[18] As a result, much local coverage of House members' Capitol Hill activity comes from press releases. In such cases, the only other major sources of information are the members' own newsletters and Web sites.

In aggregate, then, senators face a greater volume of scrutiny from their state press than House members get from their district press. Many of the stories about senators are puff pieces, but some are hard-hitting, and thanks to the Internet, a voter anywhere in a state can access this coverage. If the Senate were more like the House, senators would find it easier to duck.

House members often escape the genuine competition that accountability requires. They consistently enjoy a higher reelection rate than senators, and districting explains at least some of the difference. There has long been controversy about gerrymandering, the practice of drawing districts so as to favor one party or the other. When it works, gerrymandering can provide safe districts to the dominant side. And even without gerrymandering, many House seats would still be uncompetitive. Certain locales tend to have high concentrations of Republicans or Democrats, rendering those districts virtually unwinnable for the other party.[19] Moving the Senate to a district system would thus take a large number of seats out of play.

It would also hurt the quality of Senate challengers. In each election, dozens of House districts go uncontested: even in the hotly fought 2008 election, twenty-seven candidates won without a major-party opponent. Of the House challengers that do emerge, many are weak candidates with little experience and few resources. Senators are much less likely to go unopposed (only one did in 2008) and are more likely to face credible challengers. Why? Constituency size is part of the answer. States with more than one House district will have a bigger pool of potential candidates. (Under the Constitution, any qualified resident of a state may run for any of its House seats, but in practice it is usually hard to win without local roots.)

Personal calculation is another reason for the difference. Running for office, especially against an incumbent, is a tough, costly venture. No sensible person will do it lightly. When deciding whether to make the race, potential candidates must weigh both their chance of victory and the value of the office. (Notwithstanding Gov. Rod Blagojevich's infamous description, I define "value" as power and prestige, not dollars and cents.) If the chance of victory is too remote, or if the office does not seem worth the effort, good potential candidates will probably bow out. As we have seen, a district system would mean a number of uncompetitive seats, which would draw few serious contenders. Moreover, expanding the Senate would dilute the value of each seat. Instead of being one of 100 members in an institution with widely dispersed power, a senator would now be just one of 435 in an institution where power rested with the top leaders and where minority-party members scarcely mattered. A diminished prize would mean a diminished field of contestants.

This discussion has assumed that a Senate with population-based representation would resemble the U.S. House. It is possible to imagine other alternatives. In a party list system, such as Israel uses for the Knesset, voters nationwide would cast a ballot for parties instead of individuals, and each party would get seats in proportion to its share of the vote. But such ideas would not only change the Senate but unravel the entire basis of American federalism and electoral politics. They are in the realm not of speculation but of political science fiction. Even the district system that we discussed is improbable: in addition to the constitutional questions, there is also the matter of public reluctance. The last thing American voters crave is more politicians. But at least it lies at the outskirts of plausibility.

So let us review. Restructuring the Senate to represent the people rather than states would render the institution less deliberative, less civil, and less accountable. It would make Senate elections less competitive. It would also tend to give greater power to the majority party, thus depriving minority-party senators of the leverage they currently have and leaving their constituents without an effective voice. In short, it would make the Senate less democratic, not more.

12

RESOLVED, Senate Rule XXII should be amended so that filibusters can be ended by a majority vote

PRO: Steven S. Smith

CON: Wendy J. Schiller

Thomas Jefferson was not at the Constitutional Convention; he was in Paris serving as the American minister to France. According to a famous story, when Jefferson returned he had dinner with his fellow Virginian George Washington and asked him why the convention had created the Senate. Washington answered Jefferson's question with a question of his own: "Why did you pour that coffee into your saucer?" "To cool it," Jefferson replied. "Even so," said Washington, "we pour legislation into the senatorial saucer to cool it."

The story is almost too good to be true, and some scholars doubt its veracity. But Washington's reputed description of the Senate as a patient, deliberative, "cool" body in contrast to the impulsive, rapid-response, "hot" House of Representatives is consistent with certain constitutional features of the two chambers. The Senate is less than one-fourth the size of the House of Representatives (100 members, as compared with 435), so fewer rules are needed to organize its work. Senators' six-year terms are three times longer than the two-year terms served by representatives, so they feel less pressure to rush through their work in time for the next election.

For these reasons, students of Congress have always thought it appropriate that the rules of the House favor focused, organized debates on proposed legislation and that the rules of the Senate favor diffuse, individualistic debates. In the 109th Congress, for example, 84 percent of all bills that were considered by the House came to the floor under closed rules (that is, rules that allowed for no amendments). In contrast, any Senate bill is open to amendment during floor debate, even if the subject of the amendment is "nongermane"—that is, it deals with a different subject than the bill itself.

The House also restricts the length of debate on each bill, sometimes to no more than an hour or two, with those favoring and opposing a piece of legislation often given no more than a few minutes each to make their case so that others who wish to be heard can have their say. The Senate places no restriction at all on how long a senator may speak. One use—or, some would argue, abuse—of this privilege is the filibuster. A senator who strongly opposes a bill but lacks the votes to defeat it is free to speak for a long while, then yield the floor to another senator who shares the same views, and so on until the bill is almost literally talked to death without ever being voted on.

In 1917 the Senate created Rule XXII in an effort to limit filibusters. The rule provided that the Senate could invoke cloture—that is, bring an end to the debate on a bill and clear the decks for it to be voted on—by a two-thirds vote of those voting on the motion. Perversely, senators began filibustering more than ever, especially southerners when bills involving civil rights were debated. South Carolina senator Strom Thurmond spoke against the Civil Rights Act of 1957 for twenty-four hours and eighteen minutes—the all-time record. (Yes, Thurmond thought of that—he spent the morning in the Senate steam room to purge himself of water.)

Summoning a two-thirds vote to invoke cloture was not impossible—for example, the Senate voted for cloture after a fifty-seven-day filibuster against the Civil Rights Act of 1964—but it was harder than most senators thought it should be. In 1975 the Senate reduced the vote needed to invoke cloture to three-fifths of all senators. Yet use of the filibuster soared once again, from an average of one every couple years in the 1950s to more than fifteen per year in the 2000s. Threats to filibuster have become so common that they seldom need to be executed in order to be effective. If opponents of a bill can prove in advance that they have enough votes to block cloture, then those in the majority won't even bring the bill to the floor lest the other business of the Senate go undone. Although Senate rules provide that a bill passes if a simple majority of the senators voting on it say aye, the filibuster-based reality is that any important bill needs sixty votes.

Arguing for the resolution that Rule XXII should be amended, Steven S. Smith makes the case for lengthy but not unlimited Senate deliberation. Specifically, he proposes that the three-fifths rule be modified so that after every day or two of debate, the size of the majority needed to invoke cloture would be reduced. Wendy J. Schiller, citing both the constitutional mission of the Senate and the positive ratio of benefits to costs in the way filibusters actually have functioned, opposes modifying Rule XXII.

PRO: Steven S. Smith

In December 2008, the president and the House of Representatives agreed to a bill to provide loans to U.S. automakers. The bill died in the Senate on a 52–35 vote, eight short of the three-fifths majority, sixty votes, needed to close debate and bring the bill to a vote. Twelve senators did not bother to vote (one seat was vacant). Their votes were effectively no votes because Rule XXII provides that cloture must be supported by three-fifths of senators "duly chosen and sworn," whether or not they vote.

The 2008 experience is commonplace. A House majority, Senate majority, and the president supported the bill, all the requirements for enacting legislation anticipated by the framers of the Constitution. The bill died because of a Senate rule and practice that has emerged in the more than two centuries since ratification of the Constitution and the first Congress. Throughout the Senate's history, bills have died by the hand of a Senate minority despite the support of congressional majorities and the president, but using the filibuster to kill legislation has become much more common in recent decades.

In this essay, I contend that filibusters undermine democratic accountability and are inconsistent with the Constitution. Senate Rule XXII should thus be reformed so that minorities can no longer indefinitely thwart majorities.

THE EXPANDED USE OF FILIBUSTERS AND CLOTURE

The problem of obstructionism by filibuster has become much more severe than at any time in the Senate's history. Counting filibusters is not easy. The filibustering senators often deny that they are filibustering. Moreover, newly started filibusters and many threatened filibusters kill or delay action on a bill without senators having to appear on the floor of the Senate to debate the bill. Majority party leaders merely move on to other legislation. Moreover, cloture motions are sometimes used by the majority leader to prevent nongermane amendments that would be in order otherwise. Nevertheless, the number of cloture motions, shown in Figure 12-1, gives a fairly clear measure of the prevalence of filibustering as an obstructionist strategy.

The number of cloture votes—and filibusters—moved from a rarity to commonplace in the 1970s and has continued to grow since then. Once the major civil rights battles of the 1960s were over and southern Democrats began to join Republicans more frequently against the expanded bloc of liberal Democrats in the early 1970s, filibusters—usually by the conservative bloc—and cloture motions—usually offered by the Democratic majority leader—became common. Republican control of the Senate (1981–1986, 1995–2001, 2003–2006)

Figure 12-1
_____

Number of Cloture Votes in the Senate, 1919–2008

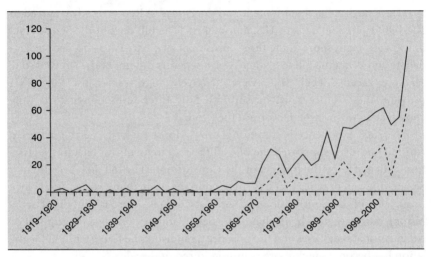

Sources: Norman J. Ornstein, Thomas E. Mann, and Michael J. Malbin, *Vital Statistics on Congress, 2008* (Washington, D.C.: Brookings, 2008), 129; www.senate.gov/pagelayout/reference/cloture_motions/110.htm#result_key.

Note: Attempted is solid line, successful is dashed line.

did not change the basic pattern. At nearly any time in the last two decades, some measure was being held up by a filibuster or threatened filibuster.

RESPONSES TO THE COMMON ARGUMENTS IN FAVOR OF SUPERMAJORITY RULE

The case for retaining the right to filibuster under Senate rules rests on four propositions. The first is that minorities have interests that would be trampled by majorities without the special supermajority threshold established under Senate Rule XXII. The second is that the delay and compromise required to obtain supermajority support for legislation creates better legislation with broader support. The third is that rules should be difficult to change, and the current rule ensures that. The fourth is that the hard-earned experience of more than two centuries supports the other three propositions.

I will respond to the four propositions in reverse order.

History

The framers of the Constitution and its principal defenders in *The Federalist Papers* emphasized the different term of office, method of selection, and formal powers of the Senate and the House of Representatives, but said nothing about the two houses operating under different parliamentary procedures. They were silent on the subject of the filibuster. The Constitution provides that each house can determine its own rules; the rules that the two houses might develop were not discussed.

The Senate filibuster practice is the byproduct of historical accident and brass-knuckle politics, not careful consideration and deliberate choice. In the House of Representatives and most parliamentary bodies, there is a motion on the previous question. In those institutions, the motion is in order at most times and, if adopted, forces a vote on the issue at hand. The motion allows a majority of legislators to end debate, act on the issue, and move to other business.

Until 1806, the Senate had a previous question motion that was seldom used, but in that year the Senate overlooked the motion when codifying its rules for the first time. With no recorded discussion of the previous question motion, the motion disappeared from the Senate's rules. Thus, without so much as a question or comment, the Senate lost the rule that allowed a majority to get a vote on a bill.

The absence of a rule limiting debate was not a problem for the Senate at first, but within a couple decades it became obvious that the absence of a debate limit facilitated obstruction by extended debate. The filibuster emerged during debates over slavery and prompted calls from many prominent senators, including Daniel Webster, Henry Clay, and Henry Cabot Lodge, for a rule that allowed a Senate majority to bring a matter to a vote. Southern senators, seeking to block antislavery and later pro–civil rights legislation, came to defend the filibuster as vital to minority rights and continued to do so through most of the nineteenth and twentieth centuries.

On several occasions in the nineteenth and twentieth centuries, a Senate majority sought to modify the rules to create a means for limiting debate but was blocked by a filibuster or threatened filibuster. Only on two occasions, in 1917 and in 1975, did the minority relent to pressure to allow a significant reform. In 1917 the first cloture rule was adopted so that two-thirds of senators voting could close debate. The 1975 rule reduced the threshold to three-fifths of senators duly sworn, except for measures affecting the Senate rules, for which the two-thirds threshold was retained.

Thus a rationale for a supermajority threshold for limiting debate cannot be found in the Constitution, *The Federalist Papers,* early Senate practice, or even in the views of the most prominent senators of the eighteenth and nineteenth centuries. Rather, the practice emerged by accident and has been retained by virtue of the ability of minorities to filibuster reforms. The rationale for the filibuster developed as minority partisans justified their opposition to rules changes that would put them at a disadvantage.

To be sure, the framers of the Constitution and the authors of *The Federalist Papers* addressed the issue of minority rights. The protection of minority rights was to be found in creating a bicameral Congress and a separate presidency and judiciary, all selected by different means and for different terms, so that it was unlikely that any faction or party would dominate all branches of government. The Bill of Rights was quickly added to the Constitution upon its ratification to further reinforce minority and individual rights. At no time during the early years of the Republic did the Senate's internal rules figure in thinking about how to limit the ability of majorities to act. To the contrary, both the House and Senate were assumed to act by simple majority rule.

The lesson of hard-earned experience of the Senate is not that a supermajority threshold is in the interest of the Senate or the nation. Rather, the lessons are that (1) it is unreasonable to expect minorities to voluntarily concede parliamentary advantages to the majority, and (2) senators can rationalize both simple- and supermajority rules with alacrity. Upon a change in party control of the chamber, senators appear to exchange their speeches on the pros and cons of majority rule across the center aisle. Only a few diehards seem to be able to maintain a consistent attitude about majority and minority parliamentary rights. I can think of no current senator who has served in both the majority and minority party who has done so.

Rules

The Senate filibuster can be used to defeat more than legislation; it can be, and often is, used to defeat a change in the rules. Thus filibuster reform can be filibustered, which makes Rule XXII self-perpetuating. This is a particularly pernicious feature of Senate practice.

Two features of Senate practice, neither anticipated by the framers of the Constitution, combine to make changes in Senate rules difficult. First, the current Senate rule requires a two-thirds majority of senators present and voting to close debate on a resolution to change the Senate's standing rules. This provision of Rule XXII is often neglected in discussions of filibuster reform. Second, a more frequently recognized feature is that the Senate considers itself to be a continuing body that does not have to approve its rules at the start of each new Congress. This is a byproduct, it is argued, of the fact that two-thirds of the Senate continues to serve from one Congress to the next. Because the standing rules merely continue from one Congress to the next, the parliamentary advantage rests with senators seeking to preserve old rules. Any proposed change can be filibustered, and the two-thirds threshold for overcoming a filibuster is always a potential obstacle to changing the rules.

The Constitution provides that "each house may determine the rules of its proceedings" (Article I, Section 5), but, it is reasonable to argue, a Senate that cannot get to a vote on its own rules is hardly able to determine its own rules. Even sixty-six senators—a fraction short of two-thirds of the one hundred senators—may not be able to get a vote on a resolution to change the Senate's rules. An effort to create a new standing committee or limit the number of subcommittee assignments a senator may acquire can be blocked by a filibuster that requires sixty-seven votes to overcome. In contrast, the second act of the House of Representatives in each new Congress is to adopt its rules, often with amendments to previous rules, as it does by a simple majority vote under traditional parliamentary procedure.

Parliamentary rules represent a balance of competing values such as stability and flexibility. The Senate's two-thirds threshold is a high threshold that favors stability, but it is wrong to think that this outcome is the result of a careful balancing of interests at some early point in the institution's history. Rather, at the time the cloture rule was first adopted in 1917, 128 years after the Senate first convened, there was no way to limit debate as long as a senator sought recognition and kept talking. Thus senators favoring some limitation on debate had to make a large concession to those few senators who wanted either no threshold or a high threshold in order to get any rule at all. Brass-knuckle politics, not careful deliberation, set the two-thirds threshold as well.

Large Majorities and Compromise

Sometimes we get lucky and acquire good rules despite the short-term political calculations that produced them. In the case of the cloture rule, some of its advocates insist, we got lucky because the supermajority threshold forces the development of a broader consensus on controversial matters, which is good for maintaining a peaceful society. This argument is a stronger one than an alternative defense of the filibuster—that filibusters have killed much bad legislation. Both arguments ignore a very ugly history.

Race-related legislation—antislavery, civil and voting rights, antilynching measures, and many others—have been the single most common target of filibusters, particularly before the 1970s. If the filibuster serves minority rights, it is only in the narrow sense of a Senate minority. For 150 years, the filibuster protected a policy status quo that suppressed basic human rights in the most fundamental ways. It is hard to see how to weigh the bad bills on other subjects that were killed by filibuster against that horrific legacy on race.

While race-related bills have been the most common targets of filibusters, they constitute less than a seventh of all filibustered bills. Many other important bills have been killed by filibuster or threatened filibuster. The 1917 rule change was precipitated by a filibuster of the "armed ship bill," legislation favored by the president that would have allowed the American merchant vessels to arm themselves in defense against German U-boats.

The effects of the filibuster, and the threat of a filibuster, are so pervasive in the Senate that they are hard to quantify. Rather than being reserved for matters of "constitutional" significance, as was sometimes argued in the mid-twentieth century, filibusters now are used regularly for legislation as well as judicial and executive nominations. Moreover, rank-and-file senators threaten to filibuster bills in order to get leverage with leaders, committee chairs, and other colleagues on otherwise unrelated legislation. In fact, filibusters have become all-purpose hostage-taking devices.

Protecting Minorities

There is no doubt that the Senate's cloture rule protects Senate minorities. There are three responses to this argument.

First, it plainly is not true that the substantial *Senate* minority required to obstruct action is necessarily a substantial *national* minority. In principle, senators from the twenty-one smallest states, constituting just over 11 percent of the U.S. population, can prevent a three-fifths majority from closing debate on regular legislation. Senators from the seventeen smallest states, constituting just over 7 percent of the population, can prevent the two-thirds majority required to invoke cloture on legislation affecting the rules. These percentages have been shrinking as more of the U.S. population is found in urban areas in the largest states.

Second, important political minorities *within* states, including demographic minorities identified by race, occupation, age, or some other division, do not win protection from minority rights in the Senate's parliamentary rules unless elected senators represent their interests. There is nothing in the way that we elect senators—plurality, statewide elections—that gives us any reason to think that a Senate minority is any more likely to represent those interests than a Senate majority. In practice, such demographic minorities may be integral to the political coalitions for either majority or minority factions and parties in the Senate.

Third, because senators from the same state frequently represent different parties and political views, there is nothing in the protection of Senate minority rights that preserves the rights of a minority of states. It is true, of course, that antislavery legislation in the nineteenth century was opposed by southern senators, who feared that their state would hold a minority of Senate seats and needed the filibuster to protect their region. In modern America, senators from the same state often are divided on issues and cloture motions. Very seldom are the rights of states at issue on cloture motions.

Perhaps most perniciously, the filibuster and threatened filibuster have become the everyday tools of the minority party. Because the majority party seldom has three-fifths, let alone two-thirds, of Senate seats, the minority party is able to block much of the majority party's legislative program. Indeed, most cloture votes in recent decades have produced partisan divisions, with majority party senators voting for cloture and minority party senators voting against cloture. Rather than encouraging consensus building, the filibuster has contributed to sharpened partisanship and legislative stalemate. The protection of minority rights has withered to the protection of temporary Senate minority parties.

DO SENATE RULES REFLECT THE WISHES OF THE MAJORITY?

The ultimate argument in favor of the current Rule XXII is that it is favored by most senators. If so, whatever the arguments against the filibuster might be, it might be argued that a majority of senators should have the right to structure their rules as they please. The record does not justify this argument.

The most important problem in assessing support for reform of Rule XXII is that the Senate cannot obtain a direct vote on a reform resolution if cloture cannot be invoked first. Nevertheless, it is clear from journalists' and senators' accounts that at various times a majority favored reducing the threshold but was blocked by a determined minority. In many other cases, the majority did not bother to pursue a proposal because it knew that a two-thirds majority could not be obtained.

A recent argument holds that a simple majority of senators always had the means to change the rules but have not availed themselves of the opportunity to make further changes in Rule XXII. The means can be called an "unorthodox rules change." A ruling of the presiding officer to change a rule (technically, an interpretation of a rule) is supported by a majority that votes to table the appeal of the ruling. Because a motion to table cannot be filibustered, it provides the means for the majority to impose its will if it has a cooperative presiding officer.

As a practical matter, the unorthodox rules approach often is not viable and therefore is no measure of majority preferences. The possibility that an angry minority will object to every unanimous consent request and force votes on every motion—going "nuclear," in Senate jargon—would so slow the Senate that even senators who favor limiting debate do not favor reforming the rules by that means. The minority and perhaps some majority senators also would observe that the approach directly undermines Rule XXII, which provides a supermajority means for gaining cloture on rules.

REFORM

Rule XXII should be amended so that it secures lengthy deliberation while still allowing action on a bill by a determined majority. Specifically, I favor a cloture procedure that provides for a sliding scale of votes, starting with the threshold of three-fifths of senators voting (sixty if all are voting) and ratcheting down the threshold every day or two so that, after a week or two, the majority could obtain a vote on the legislation or rules change. This would allow plenty of time for debate and for minority senators to persuade the public and their colleagues of the virtue of their position. But if they fail to persuade, then the majority would be able to rule, as the framers intended and as democracy requires.

CON: Wendy J. Schiller

> When a Senator desires to speak, he shall rise and address the Presiding Officer, and shall not proceed until he is recognized, and the Presiding Officer shall recognize the Senator who shall first address him. No Senator shall interrupt another Senator in debate without his consent. . . .
>
> —Rule XIX of the Standing Rules of the Senate, Section 1(a)

A mazing as it seems, any of the one hundred U.S. senators can use their right to be recognized on the Senate floor to indefinitely or permanently delay legislation in the U.S. Congress. The "right" to filibuster is not actually written anywhere in the Senate rules themselves; rather, it comes from the strategic use of the right to speak on the Senate floor. U.S. senators realized early on in the nation's history that if they objected to a measure, whether it was a piece of legislation or even a change in the Senate rules, they could simply stand up, be recognized, and talk for as long as they wanted to prevent the Senate from taking a vote on the measure. The existence of the filibuster has given rise to the practice of seeking unanimous consent to move forward on any legislation in the Senate. The Senate majority leader goes to the Senate floor and asks for unanimous consent to proceed to the consideration of a bill, amendment, or executive nomination. Based on the power to speak, any senator has the right to object to the motion to proceed and, in doing so, delay the business of the Senate.

If a majority of the members of the House of Representatives passes a bill, and a majority of the Senate supports the bill, it makes logical sense that the bill should pass. A filibuster stands in the way of that majority momentum, and as such, one could argue that it is patently unfair, and worse, undemocratic. However, in this essay I argue that the filibuster is an essential part of the democratic function of the Senate and should be preserved, albeit with stronger enforcement.

THE CONSTITUTIONAL MISSION OF THE U.S. SENATE

Congress was created as a bicameral (two-branch) legislature whose mission was to represent all the people. The reason the framers of the Constitution created two parts of the legislative branch was to maximize representation but minimize the probability that a majority could sweep through Congress and pass harmful or irresponsible legislation. They allowed the House of Representatives to grow in size as the nation's population grew, by adjusting the number of members apportioned to each state after every census. In the 1920s, Congress itself decided to limit the size of the House because it had grown too large to be effective and responsive to constituents. The more members a legislature has, the more bills, speeches, and motions it must consider. Over the years, the House has reorganized itself into a majority party, committee-based institution because that is the only way it can accommodate all its members. Key to controlling business on the House floor has been the ability to move the previous question—that is, to effectively close debate with a majority vote. With the growth of political parties and partisanship, this device essentially allows the majority party members to ride roughshod over the minority party members, and in a large chamber it leaves minority party members with little to no power.

In contrast, the framers did not allow the number of senators apportioned to each state to change with population growth; the only way that the Senate grew in size was with the admission of new states into the Union. The framers were aware that by permanently limiting each state to only two senators, the Senate itself would remain a small chamber where senators would be forced to face each other to deliberate the merits of a bill. James Madison wrote a letter to George Washington on April 16, 1787, in which he explained that senators should stay in office longer than House members; that they should be reelected at different times to make sure to leave a majority of continuing members in office after each election; and that, as a result, "the negative on the laws might be most conveniently exercised by this branch."[1] Madison elaborated on this argument in *Federalist* No. 62, where he wrote that there is a tendency for "single and numerous assemblies, to yield to the impulse of sudden and violent passions, and to be seduced by factious leaders into intemperate and pernicious resolutions."[2] By keeping the Senate small, and making sure that a majority of senators were never up for reelection at the same time as each other, or with the House of Representatives, the framers gave the Senate the task of slowing down the legislative process.

The combination of small chamber size with equal apportionment in the Senate gave senators the sense that they were all equal to one another, as opposed to the House, where members from larger states had a sense of power over their smaller-state colleagues. In the early part of the nation's history, the Senate dealt mostly with issues of land expansion, commerce, and trade, and although there was conflict, it rarely rose to the level where filibustering was deemed necessary. The onset of the conflict over slavery brought with it far more contentious debate in the Senate, and more delay and obstruction. After the Civil War ended, the issues of Reconstruction, industrialization, and trade politics gave rise to more frequent and extended use of the filibuster tactic.

It took until 1917 before the public demands on the Senate, and Congress more generally, led senators to adopt some restrictions on debate. The use of the filibuster had defeated a bill that was important to President Woodrow Wilson, so he made it his mission to campaign throughout the country for the Senate to adopt "cloture," which was a procedure for shutting off debate. He argued that having the right to shut off debate in the Senate, and allow legislation to be voted on by a simple majority, was a matter of national security. The Senate responded by passing a rule that allowed sixteen senators to file a cloture motion to close off debate; if two-thirds of senators voting approved the motion, then debate would be limited to one hour per senator. For opponents of the filibuster, the first cloture reform was a hollow victory because the high bar it set (two-thirds of the Senate) was very difficult to meet. But in 1975, after decades during which the filibuster had been used to prevent or slow the passage of civil rights legislation, the Senate refined the cloture rule to require only three-fifths of the Senate to shut off debate.

The three-fifths number (sixty senators) is a supermajority threshold. There are two reasons the Senate requires this higher number. First, majority party control of the Senate is achieved when fifty-one senators agree to caucus together as a party. Typically a majority party has between fifty-one and sixty members, and therefore the sixty-vote requirement means that the majority party must win over some members of the minority party in order to end debate on a bill. By setting the bar higher than a simple majority, cloture can only be achieved when there is genuine national consensus on a proposal. Second, the House of Representatives is a simple majority institution, and in order to slow the House down, or even block its actions, the Senate needs to preserve the power of the minority. Setting the number of votes required to shut down a filibuster considerably higher than a simple majority accomplishes this goal.

THE FILIBUSTER AS A TOOL FOR ADVOCACY

The strongest argument against preserving the filibuster is that it can be used for antidemocratic purposes. Even James Madison conceded as much in *Federalist* No. 62, in which he wrote that the Senate's power to slow down the legislative process might be "injurious."[3] Certainly, one has to agree that when southern senators filibustered civil rights legislation in the 1930s, 1940s, and 1950s (before finally losing their battle to obstruct in the 1960s) they were using the filibuster to deny fundamental human rights. However, at the same time, one must also agree that those southern senators were giving voice to what they perceived to be a majority of their constituents' views, however wrongly held. In other words, the southern senators were using their power as individual senators to represent their constituents. It should be noted that at the same time, powerful southern committee chairmen in the House of Representatives were using their majority committee power to stall or block the same legislation. The division over civil rights was deep and profound, and it is not at all clear that it was the procedural mechanism of the filibuster in the Senate that stood in the way of civil rights legislation.

Opponents of the filibuster always seek out the most offensive examples of its use to argue that it should be eliminated. But where there is truly a majority consensus, in Congress and among the public at large, most filibusters do not succeed. In truth, the goal of a filibuster is not always to kill a bill, amendment, or nomination. Frequently, senators use the power of delay to draw attention to a local issue in their state or raise an ideological issue, present the minority party viewpoint, or extract some benefit from the president. The filibuster has been used in a wide-ranging set of ways by senators seeking to assert their own power as well as represent their state. For example, in the 1890s Louisiana's two senators went to the Senate floor to filibuster a major trade bill because it lowered the import taxes on raw sugar; sugar cane was one of Louisiana's major economic industries, and the senators wanted to protect their industry from cheaper imports. They did not succeed in raising the import tax, but they did succeed in preserving a federal subsidy—called a bounty—for the domestic sugar industry that laid the foundation for the modern version of crop subsidies.

A century later, in 1987, Nevada's freshman senator Harry Reid began his campaign to filibuster any bill that appropriated funds to allow the Department of Energy to dump nuclear waste at Yucca Mountain. Senator Reid became Senate majority leader in 2007, but at every step of his rise up the political ladder, he has always insisted on blocking the Yucca Mountain proposal. As of 2009, no nuclear waste material has been deposited in Yucca Mountain.[4] Granted, there is a national interest in finding somewhere to house the waste that is generated by nuclear power plants, but why do the residents of Nevada have to be the recipients? Since they are outnumbered in the House of Representatives, the Senate is their only refuge to fight this plan. Without the filibuster, they would have no way of protecting their interests.

Sometimes, senators use the filibuster to draw attention to an economic hardship in their state and try to get some relief. In October 1992, New York senator Alfonse D'Amato, a Republican, spent more than fifteen hours straight filibustering a bill because it did not include a provision to protect a typewriter plant in his state that employed 875 workers.[5] Although the filibuster was ultimately unsuccessful, Senator D'Amato was using the ability to block a bill to put pressure on the parent company of the plant as well as the federal government to find a solution for his constituents.

If it were not for the power to filibuster, how could an ordinary citizen, company, or state stand up for its own interests in a majority-structured system of government? In the House of Representatives, the majority party only grants the minority permission to present its alternative legislation on the House floor if the majority is certain it has the votes to defeat the minority's alternative. In the Senate, the majority party has the power to bring up the bills it wants to pass on the Senate floor, but any senator from the majority or minority party can offer an amendment to that bill or, in the extreme, filibuster it. The filibuster in the Senate provides a crucial opportunity for senators in the minority party to offer their views or to force the majority party to consider their alternatives.

THE PARTISAN ABUSE OF THE FILIBUSTER

One of the consequences of the increase in partisanship in Congress over the past two decades is that senators from the minority party have used the filibuster to score political points rather than to take a principled stand based on individual beliefs or constituents' economic interests. The filibuster has also been used much more frequently to block judicial nominees, from district court to the Supreme Court, based on their perceived ideological positions on issues such as abortion, gun control, and the right to privacy. To some, this use of the filibuster violates the principle of an independent federal judiciary appointed by the president. The Constitution calls for the president to make such appointments with the advice and consent of the Senate. The original intent of the framers was to encourage the president to work with the Senate in making his judicial appointments, but it has long been understood that the fundamental choice remained his to make. Senators in the modern era have taken advantage of their power to filibuster to stop judicial nominees with whom they disagree, rather than stopping them based on inadequate qualifications to sit on the federal bench. Senators from both parties are guilty of this abuse of the filibuster, and it has occurred under both Democratic and Republican Party control of the Senate.

In 2005 then majority leader Bill Frist, R-Tenn., announced a proposal to abolish the right to filibuster judicial nominees by changing the Senate rules. Senator Frist made the case that senators had been abusing the right to filibuster and violating separation of powers by obstructing Republican president George W. Bush's right to appoint members of the federal judiciary. Although his critique was directed at Democratic senators, there were senior Republican senators who remembered doing the same thing to Democratic president Bill Clinton during the 1990s. In response, a group of fourteen senators—seven from each party—joined together to object to any limitation on the right to filibuster. Sen. John McCain, R-Ariz., a leader in that group, explained that the compromise was reached because "there was a group of us that thought the institution, and the very fundamentals of the institution, were at stake."[6] The Senate eventually agreed to a compromise that formally protected the right to filibuster, but informally senators agreed that they would not do so on judicial nominees except in "extraordinary circumstances."[7] This incident shows that senators are cognizant of the value and power of the filibuster, and also that it is not a tool to be used lightly or capriciously.

MAKING THE FILIBUSTER A MORE COSTLY ENDEAVOR

The solution to the abuse of the filibuster lies not in abolishing it but in enforcing the basic requirements of extended debate. Sen. Strom Thurmond, then a Democrat from South Carolina, held the record for the longest filibuster ever recorded; in 1957 he talked for twenty-four hours and eighteen minutes against Republican president Dwight Eisenhower's Civil Rights bill. Recall the earlier story of Senator D'Amato, who spent fifteen hours on his feet to filibuster a bill in 1992; that was the sixth-longest filibuster in history. Both of these filibusters required the expenditure of an enormous amount of time and energy on the par of the protesting senator.

How many stories do you hear today of senators pulling all-nighters to filibuster a bill or amendment? The answer is very few. Instead, senators can merely raise the threat of objecting to a bill to signal that they *might* actually talk long enough to delay it, and their demands are considered by their colleagues. Given that the filibuster has now been reduced to a mere sentence or two voicing an objection to a motion, it is no wonder that we have come to believe it is at the heart of all legislative delay. In fact, the abuse of the power to filibuster stems from the failure of the Senate as a whole, and the majority party leadership specifically, to enforce the basic requirement that a filibuster consists of *extended speech*.

The U.S. Senate today has a legislative workload that is unparalleled in its history; and, in addition to their legislative responsibilities, senators are expected to meet with government officials and key constituents as well as raise funds for their next reelection campaign. They literally no longer have the time to stand on the Senate floor and talk, much less listen.

If the only way a senator could filibuster a motion was to come to the Senate floor, stand up, get recognized to speak by the presiding officer, and start talking without stopping, we would most certainly see a drastic drop in the number of supposed filibusters. Senators would only engage in filibustering when it was vitally important to his or her constituents, or if the issue was one that he or she cared deeply about on principle. Opponents of the filibuster argue that trying to enforce the extended speech aspect of the filibuster is an unrealistic solution. They argue that the majority leader is elected by the senators from his or her party, and no majority leader would be willing to risk the wrath of his fellow senators by forcing them to stand up and talk indefinitely. But that answer does not hold up well in light of history; plenty of majority leaders have enforced the filibuster and kept their jobs. If the cost of filibustering increased, then a senator would be less likely to use this tactic to delay the Senate's business, and that would most certainly make the job of majority leader easier and increase the productivity of the U.S. Senate.

Therefore, I recommend that the right to filibuster a bill, amendment, or nomination be preserved in the U.S. Senate under one condition: any senator who claims to have an objection be forced to come to the floor and speak openly and publicly to his or her colleagues. From the time that the majority leader makes a motion to proceed with a bill or judicial nomination, a senator shall have two legislative days to come to the floor; that window shall be reduced to one legislative day in the case of an amendment. These windows of time are necessary to allow senators who are traveling to return to the Senate to make their case. If the senator does come in person to filibuster, the standing sixty-vote threshold to invoke cloture and shut off debate shall remain in effect. If he or she fails to show up on the Senate floor to voice his or her objection, the Senate majority leader can move forward, without requiring unanimous consent or a Senate vote to do so.

The Senate was designed to be a bulwark against hasty and rash decision making by the federal government. The framers of the Constitution knew that they were taking a risk by giving a centralized government ultimate power over each state; they split the legislative branch in order to maximize the venues where citizens could have their voices heard and their interests addressed. In the House, it is the voice of the majority that rules the day, but in the Senate each senator has an equal power to voice dissent. The filibuster provides an essential incentive for Congress to achieve compromise among the competing interests, opinions, and ideologies that characterize American democracy.

13

RESOLVED, the president should be granted a line item veto

PRO: Michael Nelson

CON: Robert J. Spitzer

In December 1873, President Ulysses S. Grant submitted his annual message to Congress (what we call today the State of the Union address), suggesting that Congress consider a constitutional amendment that would "authorize the Executive to approve of so much of any measure passing the two Houses of Congress as his judgment may dictate, without approving the whole." Empowered to approve some parts of a bill while negating others, the president would be able to "protect the public against the many abuses and waste of public moneys which creep into appropriation bills and other important measures." Armed with such power, the president could ensure that the nation's budget would be balanced and its money well spent.

Congress paid no heed to Grant's recommendation, but presidents kept asking. Rutherford Hayes, Chester Arthur, and Grover Cleveland were among the late-nineteenth-century presidents who pleaded with Congress to grant them an item veto. In 1938, by which time all but nine states had endowed the governor with a line item veto, President Franklin Roosevelt pressed Congress to give him the same sort of item veto power on appropriations bills that he had exercised while he was governor of New York. Roosevelt recognized that there was "a respectable difference of opinion" as to whether such a grant of power required a constitutional amendment, and told members of Congress that he would leave to them the decision about whether to pursue a statutory or constitutional route. The House of Representatives obligingly passed a bill that granted FDR's wish, but the Senate refused to go along.

As the federal budget grew ever larger, the drumbeat for the item veto intensified. Congressional spending, critics maintained, was filled with waste.

Appropriations bills were laden with the pet projects—what the critics derided as "pork"—of individual legislators: $250,000 for the National Cattle Congress in Waterloo, Iowa; $500,000 for the Teapot Museum in Sparta, North Carolina; $1 million for a Waterfree Urinal Conservation Initiative; $50 million for an indoor rainforest in Coralville, Iowa; and so on. Armed only with the blunt instrument of the normal veto, the president was allegedly compelled to assent to pork barrel spending that he and the public would otherwise reject. Give the president a precise scalpel, though, and he could carefully carve away the wasteful spending, leaving only the meritorious and necessary portions of a lean budget. The item veto would make the appropriations process more accountable and more economical.

During the 1980s, support for the line item veto increasingly became identified with the Republican Party. In 1984 Republicans endorsed it in their party platform, and President Ronald Reagan pleaded for one in every State of the Union message of his second term. Frustrated at congressional inaction, some conservative Republicans even flirted with the idea that the president had an inherent item veto authority, although President George H. W. Bush eventually backed away from that radical notion. When the Republicans finally gained control of the House of Representatives in 1994, they promptly moved to fulfill the campaign promise—articulated in their "Contract with America"—to give the president a line item veto in order "to restore fiscal responsibility to an out-of-control Congress." By a largely party-line vote of 232 to 177, the House approved the item veto, and the Senate followed suit, passing the legislation by a better than two-to-one margin. On April 9, 1996, Democratic president Bill Clinton, bucking his party, signed the bill into law, explaining that it "gives the president tools to cut wasteful spending, and, even more important, it empowers our citizens, for the exercise of this veto or even the possibility of its exercise will throw a spotlight of public scrutiny onto the darkest corners of the federal budget."

President Clinton began to exercise his newfound power in 1997, using it to cancel eighty-two budgetary items. Among the canceled items was a section of the Balanced Budget Act that appropriated money for hospitals in New York City and a provision in the Taxpayer Relief Act that gave a tax break to potato farmers in Snake River, Idaho. Rudy Giuliani, then mayor of New York City, and representatives of the affected hospitals and hospital workers took the Clinton administration to court, as did representatives of the potato farmers. Their cases were consolidated by a federal judge. On June 25, 1998, just two months after hearing oral arguments in the case, the Supreme Court announced its verdict, striking down the line item veto.

The Court's verdict did not settle the question of whether a line item veto was desirable. Michael Nelson and Robert J. Spitzer disagree on this matter. Nelson argues that a constitutional amendment granting the president a line item veto will help to reduce wasteful spending and will make the president and Congress more responsible and accountable for their actions. Spitzer, in contrast, argues that a line item veto would do little or nothing to erase the deficit or make spending more rational. Instead, it would just empower the president and weaken Congress, exacerbating the worrying trends of contemporary American politics.

PRO: Michael Nelson

One thing is for sure: giving the president line item veto authority will require a constitutional amendment. The unhappy story of the last two major attempts to empower presidents not to spend money that Congress wanted them to spend proves that.

The first attempt came in the early 1970s, when President Richard Nixon claimed that, as head of the executive branch, he already had all the authority he needed to "impound" funds that Congress had appropriated for programs he didn't like. Impoundment was a kind of de facto line item veto. Other presidents had done similar things, but Nixon took impoundment to an extreme. One year he impounded 7 percent of domestic appropriations, and on another occasion he tried to dismantle an entire federal agency, the Office of Economic Opportunity, by ordering its acting director to spend none of the funds that Congress had budgeted for it.

Both of the other branches of the federal government slapped the president around for these actions. Overriding the Watergate-weakened Nixon's veto, Congress passed the Impoundment Control Act of 1974. The act required both the House of Representatives and the Senate to approve any impoundments proposed by the president within forty-five days. If either house chose not to do so, the impoundment would not take effect. In early 1975, the Supreme Court ruled unanimously in *Train v. City of New York* that Nixon's unilateral impoundments exceeded his office's constitutional authority.

The second attempt at a line item veto took flight during the 1980s and culminated in the Line Item Veto Act of 1996. During the Ronald Reagan and George H. W. Bush administrations, as federal budget deficits soared, both Republican presidents urged Congress to create a line item veto power that would enable the president to sign some parts of a newly enacted money bill while vetoing others. Although they didn't get anywhere, Republican candidates made the line item veto a prominent part of their politically successful "Contract with America" in the 1994 congressional elections and enacted the veto into law soon after they took control of Congress. Democratic president Bill Clinton, who had enjoyed the line item veto power during his 12 years as governor of Arkansas, enthusiastically signed the legislation, even though the Republican Congress had delayed its effective date from April 9, 1996, when Clinton signed it, until January 1, 1997, in the hope that the GOP's presidential candidate would win the 1996 election.

The Line Item Veto Act of 1996 allowed the president to sign a spending or tax bill passed by Congress and then, within five days, to "cancel in whole" any item in an appropriations bill (or, more to the point, in the committee reports that accompany such a bill); to void any new entitlement program or expansion in an existing entitlement program; and to strike down any new tax break aimed at one hundred or fewer beneficiaries. If Congress wanted to restore a canceled item, it would have to pass a "disapproval" bill within thirty days of the president's action. If the president then vetoed the disapproval bill, a two-thirds majority of both houses would be needed to override that veto. In 1997 Clinton used the line item veto to cancel eighty-two provisions in eleven laws, ranging from $15,000 for a new police training center in Arab, Alabama, to $30 million for an air force program to intercept an asteroid in space. Congress overrode thirty-eight of the cancellations, all of them contained in a single military construction bill. In all, Clinton's use of the line item veto saved $869 million in spending and tax breaks. Congressional overrides of his vetoes voided another $1.1 billion in savings that he sought.

The government of New York City, which objected to Clinton's veto of a spending item related to the Medicaid program, and the Snake River (Idaho) Potato Growers who were upset about the loss of a legislative item that gave farmers' cooperatives a capital gains tax advantage, were among those who challenged the constitutionality of the Line Item Veto Act of 1996. On June 25, 1998, in the case of *Clinton v. City of New* York, a six-member majority of the Supreme Court agreed with them and voided the act.

Justice John Paul Stevens, writing for the majority, ruled that line item vetoes are "the functional equivalent of partial repeal of acts of Congress" even though "there is no provision in the Constitution that authorizes the President to enact, to amend, or to repeal statutes" after they have become law. Stevens and his colleagues grounded their ruling in the "presentment clause" contained in Article I, Section 7, of the Constitution, which states: "Every Bill which shall have passed the House of Representatives and the Senate, shall, before it become a Law, be presented to the President of the United States," who has ten days, not including Sundays, to either sign it, veto it, or take no action (in which case the bill becomes law if Congress is still in session but does not become law—that is, it's "pocket-vetoed"—if Congress has adjourned). The Court's message was plain: whether the president signs, vetoes, or ignores a bill, the Constitution requires that he sign, veto, or ignore it in full, not item by item.

Clearly, both unilateral executive actions (like Nixon's impoundments) and merely legislative actions (like the Line Item Veto Act of 1996) do not pass constitutional muster in the judgment of the Supreme Court. Nor, it seems likely, would a similar bill cosponsored in 2009 by Republican senator John McCain of Arizona and Democratic senator Russell Feingold of Wisconsin. I have no quarrel with the Court's judgment on these points. But the

Constitution that the Court has properly interpreted is not written in stone. It can be amended to grant the president the line item veto, and I urge that such an amendment be added, preferably one that follows the outline of the 1996 act by allowing the president to veto: "(1) any dollar amount of discretionary budget authority; (2) any item of new direct spending; or (3) any limited tax benefit" within five days of signing a bill and allowing Congress to overturn such a veto by a two-thirds vote.

One argument for an item veto constitutional amendment is grounded in the same presentment clause on which the Court based its decision to overturn the Line Item Veto Act. To the delegates at the Constitutional Convention of 1787, the phrase "[e]very bill . . . presented to the President" meant "every short bill, straightforward in its meaning." Short, straightforward bills were the only kind legislatures passed at the time. The idea that the president should either accept or reject such bills in their entirety remained sensible during the early years of the Republic when, for example, the only appropriations bill passed by the first Congress in 1789 was 142 words long. Short, straightforward bills continued to be the norm for quite a while thereafter. Bills passed by the 80th Congress (1947–1948), for example, were on average one-eighth as long as those passed by the 104th Congress (1995–1996).

Today, as a matter of course, Congress handles appropriations through earmark-laden "omnibus" bills that run more than one thousand pages and, it's safe to say, are read (much less understood) in their entirety by exactly none of the senators and representatives who vote on them. Such a bill is a cut-and-paste aggregation of scores of what the framers would have considered individual bills. In addition, modern bills often are riddled with "riders"—that is, amendments that have nothing to do with the general purpose of the legislation, like an anti-abortion rider to a defense appropriations bill. To keep up with these changes in the modern legislative process, modern presidents need to be able to treat each of these bound-together parts as a freestanding whole, just as the framers intended. And to do that presidents will need a change in constitutional language that modifies the presentment clause.

A second argument for a line item veto amendment is that the practice has been well tested in the states. Justice Louis Brandeis famously described the states as "laboratories of democracy" where ideas for making government better can be tried out and tested to see if they work. Ideas that pass the test, he predicted, would be adopted by other states and even by the federal government.

By this standard, the line item veto has passed with straight As: governors have the item veto in forty-three of the fifty states, including a strong majority of the states in every region of the country and all nine of the largest states: California, New York, Texas, Florida, Illinois, Pennsylvania, Ohio, Michigan, and Georgia. The states' experience with the line item veto has been long: the first state (Georgia) included one in its 1865 constitution, and by 1915 most states had adopted it. The experience of these states remains positive. A recent survey of current and former governors—sixty-seven Republicans, fifty Democrats, and one independent—found that 69 percent of them described the line item veto as "a very useful tool in helping balance the state budget," and 92 percent believed that "a line-item veto for the president would help restrain federal spending." Former governor Hugh Carey of New York, a Democrat, described the line item veto as an "antidote for pork." His Republican colleague, former governor William L. Weld of Massachusetts, said: "Legislators love to be loved, so they love to spend money. The line-item veto is essential to enable the executive to hold down spending."

Presidents of both parties who previously served as governor are among those who have enthusiastically shared that view, including Democrats Grover Cleveland and Franklin D. Roosevelt of New York, Woodrow Wilson of New Jersey, and Bill Clinton of Arkansas, and Republicans Rutherford B. Hayes of Ohio, Ronald Reagan of California, and George W. Bush of Texas. Some scholars argue that the line item veto has not made much difference in the states. But how credible is that argument in the face of such strong and positive testimony by those who have actually wielded the power?

A third argument for the line item veto turns on its ear the usual attack— namely, that it will increase presidential power at the expense of Congress. The truth is that the president's power to selectively enforce new laws passed by Congress already has soared in recent years through the use of signing statements. In these statements, which became a prominent tool of presidential power under Ronald Reagan, mushroomed under George W. Bush, and continue to be employed by Barack Obama, the president signs a bill but accompanies his signature with a statement declaring certain provisions void because they allegedly infringe on the office's constitutional authority. Adopting a line item veto would shrink the unilateral power of signing statements by giving Congress a way to hit back with a vote to overturn the line item vetoes that usually would take their place.

Along the same lines, the item veto will make the president responsible for spending decisions that he currently can evade. Without the item veto, presidents typically sign bills loaded with "earmarks" (that is, honeybee factories, Mormon cricket control grants, bridges to nowhere, and similar programs that members of Congress insert into bills to benefit their constituents or major campaign contributors at public expense) and other wasteful items by saying the Constitution allows them no choice: to get the 90 percent of a bill that's good they have to accept the 10 percent that's bad.

That's a cop-out that only absence of the line item veto allows. One of the main reasons the Constitutional Convention entrusted the entire executive power of the new federal government to the president is that the delegates accepted Pennsylvanian James Wilson's argument that only a person, not a committee-style executive, could be held responsible for executive actions. That kind of responsibility-assigning doesn't happen now, but it would if the president, empowered with the line item veto, no longer could claim that his hands were tied when it came to vetoing the wasteful provisions of generally good bills. And the modern era of massive budget deficits (only briefly interrupted during the late 1990s) cries out for additional constitutional tools that public pressure can force presidents to use to place restraints on narrow spending and tax breaks. Will the item veto alone cure excess federal spending? Not at all. But its presence in the Constitution will foster a culture of restraint in Washington in which every decision to sign a bill, instead of ending public and media debate, will trigger a whole new debate about which items in the bill the president should veto in the five days (not counting Sundays) that follow.

Considering how good an idea a line item veto constitutional amendment is, how realistic are its chances of being enacted? Let's face it: amending the Constitution is really hard if the issue is controversial. The flip side of saying that an amendment requires passage by two-thirds of both houses of Congress and ratification by three-fourths of the state legislatures is that an amendment can be stopped in its tracks by one-third plus one of either the House or the Senate or by thirteen of the fifty states' ninety-nine legislative houses. (Except in unicameral Nebraska, for a state to ratify a constitutional amendment, both its house and senate have to approve it.)

But how controversial is the line item veto? Much less controversial than most proposed amendments. Remember, forty-three states already have it in their own constitutions, five more than the thirty-eight states needed to ratify. These states range from hyper-blue bastions like Hawaii, New York, Illinois, and Delaware (four of Obama's best six states in 2008) to ultra-red bulwarks like Wyoming, Oklahoma, Utah, Idaho, and Arkansas (five of McCain's best six.) Former president Clinton's endorsement of the idea means that recent presidents of both parties have favored the item veto, which should keep Congress from polarizing along partisan lines on the issue. Both major-party presidential nominees in 2008 crusaded against earmarks (the likeliest target for item vetoes), and Obama stepped up this campaign when he became president. Public opinion polling in early 2009 showed that the greatest threat to Obama's popularity was voter concern about deficit spending. At the five-month mark of his administration, a *New York Times*/CBS News poll found that although 63 percent still approved of the job Obama was doing as president, a worrisome 60 percent thought he had not "developed a clear plan for dealing with the current budget deficit."

As noted earlier, the item veto won't solve all our budget woes—critics of the idea are right about that. But it sure will help.

CON: Robert J. Spitzer

The president's call for item veto powers was both emphatic and familiar. In his message to Congress, the president asked for the power to veto parts or items of bills presented to him by Congress to "protect the public against the many abuses and waste of public moneys which creep into appropriations bills and other important measures."[1] Since President Ulysses S. Grant made this request to Congress in 1873, many presidents have echoed his sentiments: "give me the authority to strip special interest spending and earmarks out of a bill"[2] with an item veto, President George W. Bush proposed in 2006.

It should come as no surprise that presidents would seek greater power over legislation. But would a presidential item veto actually lead to spending reductions or to the elimination of wasteful or unnecessary spending, and is such a power consistent with the separation of powers system designed by our Constitution's framers? The answer to both these questions is "no."

THE ITEM VETO IS INCONSISTENT WITH THE FOUNDERS' INTENT

The president's existing veto power, as set out in Article I, Section 7 of the Constitution, requires the president either to sign or veto each bill as passed and presented by Congress. The presidential veto power was extensively debated at the Constitutional Convention of 1787, but there was no discussion of giving the president the power to veto parts of bills. Nevertheless, there's good reason to believe that the idea was known to them. The nation's first president, George Washington, who also presided at the Constitutional Convention, wrote in 1793: "I give my Signature to many Bills with which my Judgment is at variance. . . . From the nature of this Constitution, I must approve all parts of a Bill, or reject it in toto."[3] While Washington seems to regret his inability to separate desirable from undesirable provisions of a single bill, his acknowledgment that he does not have the power to do so (even if the term *item veto* was not known at the time) strongly implies his recognition that such a power could exist.

Further evidence that the founders were familiar with the notion of an item veto is that they actually debated the two chief reasons that are typically offered in support of giving the president an item veto: the attachment of nongermane riders (provisions added to bills that are of a different subject than the bill to which it is attached) to legislation and the practice of combining appropriations into "omnibus" appropriations bills that do not list specific appropriation items. As early as the mid-1600s, members of the British House of Commons had begun to add riders onto legislation in a controversial process then called "tacking." America's political leaders were well aware of this practice, as they debated it during the Constitutional Convention when they discussed whether the House of Representatives should be given sole power to originate money bills.[4] The Constitution's founders also discussed the relative merits of attempting to limit appropriations (i.e., money) bills to single subjects. (They rejected the idea.)

Contrary to the arguments of item veto supporters, early appropriations bills were by no means limited to single subjects. The nation's first appropriations bill, passed in 1789, was an omnibus measure that incorporated the entire budget, made up of four lump sum dollar amounts for the Department of War, the civil list, pensions for invalids, and prior government expenditures. Similar omnibus appropriations were enacted in the 1790s.[5] Omnibus appropriations have long been criticized. Obviously, they are a means by which Congress tries to avoid a veto. Yet presidents like omnibus bills, too, because they give the president and the executive branch great discretion to decide how to spend the money appropriated by Congress, since the law does not stipulate specific items of spending. In other words, both Congress and the president benefit from the enactment of omnibus appropriations—a fact often ignored in the item veto debate. As we will see, presidents in fact have great ability to shape appropriations priorities without resort to an item veto.

THE ITEM VETO IS NO REMEDY FOR EXCESS SPENDING

The image of a fearless president, selflessly standing alone against wasteful and extravagant congressional spending, is widely held. Yet the estimates of experts suggest that this reputation is mostly undeserved. There are three reasons why a president with an item veto might well use it in a way that would have no net effect on overall spending. First, presidents would most likely use an item veto to increase political leverage over Congress, by threatening or using the item veto to block the projects of opponents or by withholding item vetoes on supporters' pet projects. Second, presidents love pork barrel spending no less than members of Congress do. Third, even a zealous, veto-minded president would find relatively few item veto–eligible provisions.

A study conducted by the General Accounting Office (GAO) in 1992 examined estimated budget savings achievable through an item veto for a six-year period. The initial result of the study reported estimated savings as high as $70 billion—an impressive-sounding number. Yet the head of the GAO later admitted that these findings were wildly inaccurate, and that actual budget savings for the six-year period would probably have been $2–3 billion at most, and in fact could have been "close to zero."[6] Budget specialist Louis Fisher also examined the data, and concluded that an item veto could actually result in an *increase* in government spending,[7] an argument made by others, including in 2006 by then Congressional Budget office director Donald Marron. Why an increase? According to Marron, an item veto would "simply shift spending priorities to those favored by the president."[8] Congress expert Norman Ornstein argues that a presidential item veto would accelerate political deal making between members of Congress trying to protect budget items at veto risk and the president, who would now be in a position to promise *not* to item veto provisions in exchange for political support. For their part, members of Congress would, if anything, be tempted to insert even more spending items into legislation in the hopes that some would survive item veto scrutiny.

Any budget savings from an item veto would likely be small. About three-quarters of the federal budget is made up of appropriations that are nondiscretionary, meaning that the money must be spent by law or contract, such as cost-of-living increases in Social Security benefits, government contracts to build new weapons systems for the military, and interest payments on the national debt. None of these nondiscretionary spending items would be subject to an item veto. Moreover, there is one real-world example of a limited presidential item veto in action. In 1996 Congress granted the president a limited power to excise items in certain types of spending bills (called "enhanced rescission"). President Bill Clinton used this power in 1997 to excise eighty-two spending provisions (before the Supreme Court declared the power unconstitutional in 1998) for a total savings of about $355 million for fiscal year 1998—about .2 percent of that year's total budget.[9]

There's another problem with the image of the president as sole protector of the public purse: presidents are as interested in "pork barrel" spending—government programs also called "patronage," "distributive," or "earmark" spending that target some specific project or purpose that usually involves the creation of jobs—as members of Congress. A study of presidential policy making in Congress from the 1950s through the 1970s found that presidents proposed more distributive, pork barrel–type spending bills to Congress in presidential election years than at any other time. The likely reason? To help the president and his political party win votes in an election year.[10]

Finally, and perhaps most importantly, a comparison of the actual budget records of presidents and Congress shows that it is presidents who are more prone to push for big spending, not Congress. In eleven of sixteen years from 1977 to 1992, presidents requested more in spending than the amount approved by Congress.[11] In other words, presidential spending requests are usually greater, not less than the amount Congress actually approves. This pattern has continued throughout the 1990s and 2000s. The pattern of greater congressional penny-pinching is seen in another way. Since 1974, presidents have had the power to issue budgeting "rescissions"— that is, to recommend that specific items of spending already enacted into law be rescinded. Congress then has forty-five days to act on the rescission requests. Congress may also recommend rescissions. From 1976 to 2005, presidents proposed about $73 billion in rescissions to Congress (amounting to .5 percent of total budgets), which approved about a third of them. During the same time period, Congress proposed twice as much rescission cutting—$142 billion; of that, 85 percent was passed and approved by the president.[12]

These findings are consistent with Ornstein's conclusion that "any honest review of the historical record suggests that Congress has been more careful over the near 200-year history of this country with public money than Presidents have."[13] Members of Congress are, and always have been, keenly interested in legislation that funds special projects benefiting their home states and districts. Some of these are worthy, some are not. But the idea that presidents are somehow indifferent to special interest legislation is simply false. President George W. Bush provides a recent case in point.

Like his predecessors, Bush not only requested an item veto but regularly chastised Congress for its wasteful, free-spending ways, reserving special criticism for Congress members' insertion of "earmarks" in legislation. Yet in his fiscal year 2009 budget proposal to Congress, Bush inserted literally thousands of earmarks, including such items as funding for fish hatcheries, highway paving, harbor dredging, construction of an air traffic control tower in Michigan, research on the fundamental properties of asphalt, monitoring of the red snapper fish population, rural transportation research, a fruit-growers dam project, research on the emerald ash borer beetle, and many, many others.[14] These may all be worthy projects, but they are the same kinds of "pork barrel" programs for which members of Congress are regularly criticized. The lesson is quite simple: presidents are pork-loving politicians too.

THE EXISTING PRESIDENTIAL VETO IS A POTENT POWER

The idea that presidents need an item veto carries an often-unstated assumption: that the president's existing veto powers are somehow inadequate as a way to influence the bills Congress passes, and that without an item veto the president is powerless to force Congress to alter specific items within bills. These assumptions are also false.

The existing veto power is, in fact, a potent political weapon for presidents. Throughout American history, presidents have vetoed over 2,500 bills. About 93 percent of vetoes subject to override (not including pocket vetoes, which cannot be overridden) have been upheld, an impressive batting average that shows that Congress rarely succeeds in overriding the presidential veto decision. Veto use has accelerated over time: from George Washington through Abraham Lincoln, presidents employed a total of only fifty-nine vetoes. Veto use increased exponentially thereafter, and the typical modern president casts dozens of vetoes, a clear indication of the power's effect. As the earlier quotation from George Washington illustrates, presidents are sometimes faced with the difficult decision of signing or vetoing a bill that may contain both worthy and unworthy parts. But presidents have effectively used the veto, or the mere threat of a veto, to force Congress to change legislation or excise provisions of bills. The second veto ever used, cast by President Washington in 1797, was just such a veto. In the final days of his presidency, Washington vetoed a military organization bill that contained one provision with which he disagreed: it disbanded two companies of dragoons that Washington believed should have been preserved. In his veto message, Washington cited this specific objection. Congress promptly re-passed the bill, minus the offending provision, and the president then signed the revised bill. Modern presidents regularly follow the same veto strategy.

In addition, the mere threat of veto use has been a key lever for presidents to shape the content and flow of legislation. President George W. Bush cast only twelve vetoes in his two terms (the lowest per year veto average in forty years), but he issued dozens of veto threats on matters including funding of stem cell research, tax cuts, pension plan reform, a ban on the use of torture, congressionally mandated timetables for withdrawal of troops from Iraq, farm legislation, road and bridge construction, and drug benefits. These threats had a major impact in shaping the final legislation that reached Bush's desk. The veto threat is a low-cost, high-potency political tool used by all presidents.

Moreover, the existing veto power has been effective in reducing government spending when presidents chose to use the power in that way. A study of the fiscal consequences of vetoes by Presidents Gerald Ford, Jimmy Carter, and

Ronald Reagan found that Ford averaged annual spending cuts by veto of about $16 billion per year during his presidency, Carter about $6 billion per year, and Reagan about $2.5 billion per year.[15] Admittedly, the veto is not a perfect political weapon for the president, but if the founders had wanted the president to have complete control over the flow of legislation, they could have simply given the power to make laws to the president instead of to Congress.

STATE GOVERNOR ITEM VETOES ARE NO MODEL FOR THE PRESIDENT

Item veto proponents often point out that forty-three of fifty state governors possess some kind of item veto power. This too is an appealing argument, but it is not one that withstands scrutiny as a reason for giving the president similar power. First and foremost, state governments function differently from the national government. Governors obtained item veto powers, beginning after the Civil War, because state legislatures met only briefly each year (as continues to be true in most states), so governors needed greater power to keep their states running. Second, state budget appropriations are normally highly itemized, inviting item veto use, whereas federal government appropriations are not (minimizing the number of item veto opportunities even if the president had such a power). Third, actual studies of state item vetoes reveal that they offer no budgetary panacea. Various studies show no statistical difference between per capita spending in item veto versus non–item veto states; in fact, some studies show more spending in states where governors have the item veto power.[16]

THE ITEM VETO WOULD ONLY FURTHER UPSET THE SEPARATION OF POWERS

The rise of a strong presidency is one of the most well-established features of modern American governance. The presidency of the last century little resembles the presidency of the country's first century. This does not mean that presidents are all-powerful, by any means, but from the rise of a powerful executive bureaucracy to budgeting to war powers, modern presidents dominate American governance in ways that the Constitution's founders could hardly have imagined. The trend toward a stronger presidency may be necessary, even desirable, but there are limits to presidential power that, if exceeded, would rupture the separation of powers/checks and balances system that is the essence of American governance. An item veto power would give the president an unprecedented degree of control over the legislative branch by seriously eroding its lawmaking power. The most important effect of granting an item veto power to the president would not be lower or more efficient government spending but an even more domineering presidency than the one we have today. The keys to responsible budgeting, limits on government spending, and more responsive government lie in constructive engagement between the legislative and executive branches, not in giving the president yet another club with which to flail Congress.

RESOLVED, the government should scale back the outsourcing of government jobs to private contractors

PRO: Charles T. Goodsell

CON: E. S. Savas

Most students know that *democracy* means "government by the people," and many are even aware that it comes from two ancient Greek words: *demos* (people) and *kratos* (rule). Nearly everyone thinks of democracy as a good thing. That's why even tyrannical regimes such as the Democratic People's Republic of Korea (North Korea) try, however preposterously, to brand themselves with the term in their names.

Bureaucracy is a much more modern word, dating only to late-eighteenth-century France. It too means rule, not by the people but by *bureaux*—offices filled with anonymous government officials. Hardly anyone thinks of bureaucracy as a good thing. When a friend tells you that applying for financial aid or getting a parking permit involved dealing with "the bureaucracy," you know he isn't relating a pleasant experience. And when he describes an associate dean as a bureaucrat, he's not paying her a compliment.

Americans don't like bureaucracy, but what don't we like about it? Think of some of the words that come to mind when people talk about bureaucracy: flabby, lazy, unimaginative, impersonal, slow to change, devoted to rigid rules and procedures, bound by "red tape." Words like these suggest that we dislike bureaucracy because we think it doesn't do much of anything. But consider some other bureaucracy-related words that we also commonly use:

meddlesome, intrusive, demanding, arrogant, empire builders, social engineers. These describe a bureaucracy that we think does too much.

In contrast to bureaucracy, most people think positively of private enterprise—the business world. Even when the headlines are filled with corporate bankruptcies and bank failures, we tend to assume that these are exceptions rather than the rule—the rule being that private enterprise operates more efficiently and effectively than government bureaucracies. Not surprisingly, then, when the national agenda turns to reforming bureaucracy, people often look to private enterprise for solutions.

This is where outsourcing comes in. In recent decades, the amount of money spent by the federal government has grown exponentially—from about $100 billion per year in fiscal year 1965 to more than $3.5 trillion in fiscal year 2010 (the government's fiscal year begins in October and ends the following September). Nearly all of that money is spent by the myriad departments and agencies of the executive branch—that is, by the bureaucracy. Yet the size of the federal government's civilian workforce—the so-called "bureaucrats"—has only grown from about 2.5 million to 2.7 million in that same period. Note the contrast: a 3,500 percent increase in federal spending, an 8 percent increase in the number of federal employees.

What is filling the gap between spending and employment? Inflation offers only part of the answer: in today's dollars, that $100 billion federal budget in 1965 would have been about $675 billion—still a lot less than the actual $3.5 trillion. Another part of the answer involves improved technology. For example, a Social Security Administration employee with a computer processes a lot more monthly checks to retired senior citizens than she did when she was working with file cards. Still another is the rise in grant programs to state and local governments, in which Washington supplies money to these units of the federal system and imposes guidelines for how to spend it. Largely because of grant programs, the number of state and local government employees has risen from about seven million in 1965 to about eighteen million today.

Outsourcing is yet another strategy that the federal government has used to spend a lot more money without drastically increasing its workforce. Outsourcing involves the government contracting with private enterprise to do part of its work. There's nothing new about outsourcing—for example, the army has always bought its weapons from privately owned businesses rather than building its own munitions factories. But the scale of federal outsourcing has grown dramatically in recent decades. Even some prisons are run by corporations funded by government contracts.

Charles T. Goodsell is concerned that outsourcing has gone too far and that, in the words of the resolution for this debate, "the government should scale back the outsourcing of government jobs to private contractors." He is concerned that these contractors are less accountable for their performance than government employees, and that they seldom deliver on their promise of greater efficiency and effectiveness. In opposing the resolution, E. S. Savas sees multiple advantages in outsourcing that in his view far outweigh the disadvantages.

PRO: Charles T. Goodsell

When I first taught American government in the 1960s, an issue sometimes discussed was whether bureaucracy is a fourth branch of government. Clearly this is not true, as it is responsible to the three constitutional branches. Yet its employment and expenditures, when compared to the legislature, executive, and judiciary, loom very large. Today, students could just as easily wonder if *government outsourcing* is not another branch of government—for in size it is now of the magnitude of direct public administration by government employees.

The national government employs 2.7 million civilian civil servants. Studies have shown that this number is not much different than the total number of nongovernmental workers employed by federal contractors and under federal grants. The Department of Defense, the largest and most prolific contracting agency in Washington, augments its civilian workforce by 39 percent this way. During the aftermath of our country's 2003 invasion of Iraq, at some points civilian contract employees actually outnumbered the troops there.

As for the fifty states and 88,000 local governments, more than 40 percent of their combined budgets go to contractors. Many cities and counties outsource routine services such as trash collection and tree trimming, but also life-and-death matters like child welfare, mental health, and care of the homeless. Other activities occasionally contracted out are street repair, snow plowing, code enforcement, waterworks, libraries, cemeteries, tax assessment, and the preparation of payrolls. The city of Weston, Florida—population 62,000—has no bureaucracy at all! Every administrative function is contracted out to businesses or other governments; exactly three employees work for the city—the city manager, assistant city manager, and city clerk.[1]

There is nothing wrong with contracting out, per se. It has been done since the birth of the country, when the colonial post office contracted haulers to transport the mail and tax collection was farmed out to private individuals paid on commission. Governments everywhere need to buy all kinds of things from contractors, from paper clips to computers to submarines. The outsourcing of services, the focus of this debate, is often the most efficient and practical step for a government when it temporarily needs specialized resources or requires help from professionals available only in the marketplace. But what we have today is far different than seeking pragmatic solutions to occasional skill shortages. It is now orthodox thinking in the nation's executive corridors, legislative halls, and public administration classrooms that a modern government cannot and should not try to operate without handing over a huge portion of its duties to the corporate sector. This approach to governance could be characterized as public administration by private capitalism.

The outsourcing movement springs from many sources. Pro-market, "neoliberal" political thinking in the Western democracies of the world assumes that mass privatization is the only answer to corrupt, bloated government bureaucracies. Pro-business, antigovernment Republican administrations like those of Ronald Reagan and George W. Bush deliberately sought to diminish the role of public authority in welfare and regulatory policy while serving the interests of large corporations. The centrist Democratic administrations of Jimmy Carter and Bill Clinton wanted to downsize the number of federal employees to appear conservative, while at the same time expanding middle class and environmental programs via contracts. Public administration scholars, enthralled by the new public management movement and a business-inspired, market-oriented, and economics-influenced take on the public sector, champion third-party, networked delivery of services as the wave of the future.

Then, after 9/11, Washington policy makers became grimly determined to launch huge new governmental undertakings quickly to protect the homeland and launch wars against terrorism. Government outsourcing expanded astronomically for intelligence gathering inside and outside the country. Vast amounts of manpower were needed to back up two military invasions and a subsequent attempt to reconstruct the invaded lands. Federal spending on contracts, which stood at $177 billion in 1998, rose to $203 billion in 2000, $377 billion in 2005, and $532 billion in 2008.

There are four reasons why this onslaught of contracting out is bad for the country and must be reversed, or at least reined in. The first is that this vast reliance on outsourcing is, on a net basis, *wasting billions in taxpayer dollars.* Many will be surprised to hear this, since as Americans we are taught from the cradle onward that government can never be as efficient as business. The reasons given are that private enterprise is the only place where material incentives motivate people and where competition exists to induce cost-cutting and innovation. The only incentive for government bureaucrats, we are told, is to last until they can retire from deadbeat bureaucracies whose main goal is to secure more appropriations each year.

These views ignore two realities. First, a great many government employees work where they do not just for material rewards like pay and promotion, but because of the public importance of what they do. They feel a calling to work for all of us, by fighting neighborhood crime, battling forest fires, managing national parks, working for clean air and streams, teaching in public schools, entering the diplomatic service, and combating child abuse. Second, almost all government agencies do not simply accept a bit more appropriations each year, but strive ardently to figure out how to respond to urgent and rising public needs in the face of chronic shortages of people and money.

If government is short on people and money, why not go ahead and contract out government work to the private sector? The reason is that it will often cost more, especially in the long run. Contractors have to make money. That is why they are open for business. Moreover, they want to make as much money as possible; and if they can negotiate quietly with a government procurement office to be the only bidder considered for a contract, so much the better. That indeed is what often happens. Approximately 40 percent of federal contract dollars are awarded without competitive bidding. The biggest federal contractors, namely Lockheed Martin, Boeing, Raytheon, Northrop Grumman, General Dynamics, United Technologies, and General Electric, obtain between 60 and 95 percent of their contract income from sole-source contracts. This relative absence of competition means profits can be good, very good. Revenues can also be inflated by high "administrative overhead" costs, which can escalate almost without limit under cost-plus contracts. These cover high salaries for CEOs, handsome bonuses for managers, and the expenses of K Street lobbying firms and Beltway branch offices. It is not surprising, then, that a study by the Senate Select Committee on Intelligence discovered an interesting fact: while the average annual cost of one federal employee, including all benefits, is $126,500, the equivalent average outlay per federal contract employee is $250,000.[2]

Further, the inherently lucrative business of government contracting can become an absolute bonanza if politically greased sweetheart arrangements can be exploited. An example is Halliburton's relationship to the Bush administration during the early phases of the Iraq war. This well-connected corporation, formerly headed by Dick Cheney, was approached while the invasion was being planned to provide support services to the troops. It was awarded, without competition, a blanket, open-ended, ongoing contract to supply food, build facilities, and provide nonmilitary services to the occupying forces. Between 2002 and 2005 more than $14.5 billion was paid to the company and its subsidiaries. Of this amount, $1 billion—more than the total annual budgets of most of the nation's government agencies—was found by auditors to be questionable. Subsequent investigations uncovered many quality problems, like charging jacked-up prices for items sold to service personnel, allowing undrinkable water to be given to contract laborers, and installing shoddy circuitry in showers that electrocuted some soldiers.

There is a second reason why the egregious turn to contracting out should be turned around. It *loosens external control over what the government does.* The essence of our republican form of government is that the basis of rule is the people themselves, exercised through the mechanisms of representative government from above and direct citizen voice from below. When the actions of government are outsourced, however, these democratic mechanisms of control are replaced by negotiations over the terms of a contract. This legal instrument, by specifying the work to be done and its anticipated cost, becomes the only platform of accountability. Short of cancelling the contract, intervention by political executives and legislative committees is reduced to post hoc investigation. The lack of public knowledge of the contract's terms or even existence cuts off citizen voice. Governance is handed over to commercial organizations possessing legally privileged information while operating under the compelling aura of state sponsorship.

To be sure, there are various degrees to which popular control is sacrificed. The extreme case is the "hollowed out" government that does practically everything by contract. Weston, Florida, is the pure case. Partial examples are EPA's Superfund, NASA's space-station cargo program, and the Department of Energy's nuclear security program. The most common and subtle form of loosened control, however, is when the process of contract procurement loses its integrity. Sometimes the procurement function is itself contracted out to private firms, as we shall see. The more common situation is for contract administration to become a formalistic sham because of political pressure for quick action or too few trained procurement personnel. The writing of statements of work, the negotiation of price and fee structures, and the monitoring and evaluation of contract activities are complex and technical tasks that must be in the hands of professionals. Unfortunately, in a tight-budget, downsized situation, their value is often underestimated, with the result that the numbers and expertise of these professionals diminish. Only about 29,000 procurement personnel exist in the entire federal government, and it is their responsibility to watch over an estimated 7.7 million contractual transactions annually.[3] That works out to an average of 266 transactions a year for each procurement officer.

Experiences at the Department of Homeland Security (DHS) illustrate how an inadequate procurement staff and a hollow government can hurt. When DHS was created by consolidating twenty-two existing agencies in 2003, it turned to government contractors to organize the department. But DHS did not have sufficient contract professionals to do the procurement, and as a result it entered into an interagency contract with the Department of Veterans Affairs (VA) to do it for them. The VA proceeded to hire Booz Allen Hamilton, a McLean, Virginia, consulting firm and major federal contractor, to staff temporarily DHS's Information Analysis and Infrastructure Protection offices. But

DHS was not informed enough to give Booz Allen clear guidance as to what it wanted, and as a result the consulting company proceeded on its own, at times without a written contract. After two years DHS attempted to take control of Booz Allen's activities but found them so greatly expanded that the department did not have the capacity to manage the situation. The department's only recourse was to continue using the firm as de facto administrator of the intelligence program. This went on for two more years, with costs under the cost-plus contract mushrooming upward each year.[4]

DHS also illustrates how multiple layers of contractors can lead to loss of control. When Congress determined that post-9/11 airport screening would be performed by government employees and not outsourced, the department contracted with NCS Pearson, an educational testing company, to recruit and assess people. Pearson found it could not handle the job and proceeded to hire 168 subcontractors. Some of these then hired outside consultants, adding yet another level of complexity. Assessment centers were set up at 150 hotels around the country, creating a far-flung network of operations. Costs started to mount, and in one year estimates multiplied sevenfold. Department of Defense auditors and the Department of Transportation's inspector general conducted investigations and unearthed many unsubstantiated charges, such as $525 for an airport shuttle trip; $1,180 for twenty gallons of coffee; and $3,500 for renting 140 surge protectors. A "complete breakdown of management controls" had occurred, according to the inspector general's report.[5]

The third problem with an excessively outsourced government is that it *creates new and less detectable opportunities for unethical conduct.* Moral lapses have always occurred in government, of course. Age-old examples like bribery, kickbacks, and conflicts of interest tended to involve people in separated organizations or even different parts of society, which made their existence more noticeable to watchdog groups and oversight committees. In the heavily outsourced state, however, collusive parties operate for all practical purposes in one tightly knit, melded workforce where relationships can be private.

An unusual glimpse into the intimate world of government contracts is afforded by an extensive piece of investigative reporting in 2009 by the *Washington Post.*[6] Two central figures are present in this saga. They are the director of a start-up technology center in the army's Communications and Electronics Command (CECOM) at Fort Belvoir and the female corporate liaison for a small technology contractor in Alexandria named Enterprise Integration, Inc. (EII). The two met at a military technology conference in Hawaii and soon became close friends. They frequently lunched together at EII offices and sailed together on the Chesapeake Bay. A contract valued at $600,000 was soon awarded by the Fort Belvoir center to EII. The following year a second, larger contract was in the works, and in violation of federal procurement regulations its director gave his friend at EII advance information and, allegedly, allowed her to help write its statement of work.

Word of their collusion finally leaked out, however, and EII management told the woman her time at the company was running out. The center director thereupon warned the company that if she were fired they would get no more CECOM contracts. She was dismissed anyway, and a stop order was imposed on the current contract. A few months later the CECOM center awarded a replacement contract, this time to BearingPoint Corporation, which happened to be headed by the owner of the sailboat used by the contracting friends. The number two lead on the contract was the female half of the sailing partnership. Army auditors and attorneys became suspicious of these developments and relationships and conducted an investigation. It was quashed, but a second one followed that resulted in a decision to fire the center director. He retired before it was carried out, however, and left the government with full benefits. Soon he found a new job with a Washington-area contractor. When interviewed by the *Post* reporter, he flatly denied any wrongdoing, and declared his behind-the-scenes interaction on the EII contract was perfectly normal—"It happens all the time," he said.

The fourth and final reason for scaling back on contracting out is that it *can invade the heart of exclusive governmental authority.* The United States and the fifty states are sovereign within their respective spheres and exercise ultimate authority in them. Their constitutions confer this supreme author-ity, laying the basis of a government of laws. It follows that by definition sovereign authority must be exclusively retained by government and cannot be transferred to private parties.

Certainly governments can elect to have their sovereign authority exercised by outside parties, but so as not to delegate activities intimately identified with its majesty they should pick and choose. In 1998 Congress enacted a statute that includes a definition of what powers are "inherently governmental."[7] Although not necessarily a perfect definition, it is a starting point. Included in it are: the exercise of discretion in applying federal authority to bind the United States; diplomatic and military actions; judicial proceedings; the man-agement of contracts; acts that significantly affect the lives, liberties, or prop-erty of private persons; and activities that determine or control the employees and property of the government.

Using this list as a standard, are there currently or recently outsourced activities that fall into these categories? The answer is definitely yes—many. Contracting out the management of government contracts binds the United States and is moreover specifically mentioned. Contracts to assassinate terrorists, administer foreign aid projects, engage in street patrols in Iraq, direct torture practices at Abu Ghraib, and collect foreign intelligence for the United States are clearly a part of the diplomatic and military realms. The outsourcing of armed police functions and the management of prisons, both of which occur at the state level, could be construed as involvement in judicial activity. Contracting out of functions that significantly affect the lives and liberties of private persons have occurred at the federal level, such as the collection of delinquent taxes, administration of the Freedom of Information Act, and involvement in NSA and FBI monitoring of citizen communications. As for determining and controlling government employees, outsourcing commonly occurs in recruitment, background checks, the writing of job descriptions, to-hire recommendations, overtime approval, and acceptance of completed work.

To summarize, much-needed reform is needed in the contracting out practices of American government. We must pull back on and regulate better the outsourcing of government jobs to private contractors. In its present state of excess, the practice wastes vast sums of taxpayer money, removes government programs from adequate external control, creates new opportunities for unethical conduct, and invades realms of public authority that should by law not be transferred to private parties.

What specific reforms would help swing the pendulum of outsourcing back to a more acceptable position? Strong interest currently exists to do just that in the Obama presidency, the U.S. Senate, the Department of Defense, and the Commission on Wartime Contracting in Iraq and Afghanistan. While most of the problem rests at the federal level of government, state and local governments should be considering reforms as well. Some proposed ideas:

- When new programs are being considered at all levels of government, direct agency administration should at least be initially considered the preferable means of implementation.

- The outsourcing of military duties in war zones, the direction and evaluation of government employees, and the process of procurement should, wherever possible, be retained by or returned to government hands.

- Blanket, open-ended, and sole-source contracts should be kept to an absolute minimum, and made allowable only under waiver at a higher level or in emergencies.

- Vigorous steps should be taken to recruit, train, and retain greater numbers of competent procurement professionals in government.

- Procurement professionals should carefully negotiate, monitor, and evaluate not just prime government contracts but subcontracts as well. Close scrutiny must also be given to contract renewals, extensions, and cost reauthorizations.

- "Revolving door" employment moves between agencies and their contractors should be banned for one year following separation from the other type of employer.

These reforms won't solve every problem—few reforms do. Nor will they—or should they—eliminate all outsourcing. What they will do is reduce the harm that results when a potentially good practice is carried to an extreme and becomes bad for democratic government.

CON: E. S. Savas

To think of outsourcing as giving government jobs to contractors is mistaking the elephant's tail for the elephant. There are two issues: the work itself and the transfer of that work from public to private employees. Outsourcing is an important way to get the public's work done efficiently and effectively. This is the goal of public administrators, not keeping jobs in one set of hands or another. The large part of the elephant, the work, will be discussed first, then the transfer.

THE CONCEPTS BEHIND OUTSOURCING

It's curious. We go to great lengths to protect the public against monopolies: the Sherman and Clayton Anti-Trust Acts, the Justice Department's antitrust unit, and public service commissions in every state are all designed to protect the public against monopolies—but only against *private* monopolies. The presumption is that *public* monopolies will unfailingly act in the *public* interest. But that's naive. Public monopolies will inevitably favor their own interests, just like private monopolies. The problem is systemic; monopolies such as the post office, public schools, and city bus systems were created routinely and unthinkingly in the past before it became apparent that monopoly agencies cannot always be relied on to function in the public interest. The explosive growth of public-employee unionism in the mid-twentieth century greatly exacerbated the monopoly problem.

Organizations like these that face little or no competition tend to become fat, dumb, and happy: fat, meaning overstaffed with too many employees;

dumb, meaning blissfully unaware of innovations or potential improvements; and happy, meaning content with the present, pleasant arrangement. But even such an organization encounters an occasional upstart who is fired by the desire to do things better, or it gets an inspired new head who manages to make much-needed changes, albeit with a Herculean effort.

The antidote for monopolies is competition. Outsourcing can be considered simply a way to introduce competition in the delivery of government services. Not all public services lend themselves to competition—for example, some aspects of national defense—but wherever possible we should aim to eliminate monopolies and opt for competition. Instead of scaling back outsourcing, government should expand it whenever it is in the public interest.

The post office offers an interesting example. To get around the limitations of traditional government services, it was made a separate government-owned corporation, which was still unsatisfactory. Faced with growing competition from UPS and Federal Express, however, it gradually adopted some changes in a struggle to improve efficiency.

The preferred policy is not *out*sourcing but *competitive* sourcing, where the public agency competes against the private sector on a level playing field. This may or may not lead to outsourcing; it depends on who wins the competition. If the public agency can provide the same or higher level and quality of service at a lower cost to taxpayers than a private bidder, it retains the work. If the situation is reversed, the private firm is awarded a contract and the work is outsourced. In any case the crucial factor is competition. If the government activity is new, however, then outsourcing, not competitive sourcing, is required because the government lacks in-house capability and would have to start a new, in-house unit to do the work.

Of course, even a public agency immune to competitive pressure is not immune to other pressures. An aroused public can complain to its elected officials about poor service and high taxes, but this pressure is difficult to transmit down through the bureaucratic layers; the pressure is buffered, muffled, and dissipated. Thus budget reductions and large improvements, for example, are notoriously difficult to effect in a public body.

The monopoly nature of many government activities is not the only reason why government performance is often inferior to private-sector performance. James Q. Wilson points out in his book *Bureaucracy* that managers in government are severely constrained in their ability to buy and sell products or hire and fire people; they are not free to manage according to what best achieves efficiency or productivity in their agency.[1] It is no wonder that they outsource to try to harness the efficient performance possible in market-driven organizations.

Ownership, or rather the lack of it, is another reason why government performance is often found wanting compared to the private sector. Aristotle figured this out in about 350 B.C., in the founding document of political science, *Politics, Book 1.* He said: "That which is owned in common by the greatest number has the least care devoted to it." In other words, if everyone owns it, nobody takes care of it. The experience of government-owned vehicle fleets illustrates this. As a New York City official, I found that 15 percent of our garbage trucks were out of service awaiting repairs, while the corresponding figure for private garbage haulers was only 5 percent. If your livelihood depends on your trucks, you cannot afford to buy more than the minimum number you need, and you will take good care of them. Outsourcing captures this incentive for good performance. Let's see what happens to "Government Motors," the successor to General Motors, now that "everybody," through the U.S. government, owns it.

WHY OUTSOURCE?

Governments routinely purchase *goods* from the private sector: airplanes, police cars, pencils, asphalt, potatoes, computers, etc. Outsourcing involves purchasing *services* from the private sector: tree pruning, trash collection, vehicle repairs, building maintenance, security guards, food service, etc. Many private firms outsource such chores to firms that specialize in this work. Indeed, outsourcing is even more common in the private sector than in government; private buyers find it better and less expensive than using their own employees because doing it themselves would detract from their core function. Government should emulate successful private companies and do more outsourcing, purchasing from for-profit firms for ordinary commercial services and from nonprofit or for-profit organizations for social services and elementary education, for example. It is worth noting that global outsourcing has reduced inequality: abject poverty declined in China and India due to outsourcing of manufacturing and information services.

Governments typically outsource for many reasons, but these are the leading ones:

1. To save money because market pressures tend to enforce efficiency, and the contractor is free of most of the constraints and distracting influences that hobble public managers.

2. To take advantage of skills lacking in the government's own workforce, for example, outsourcing technical computer work or staffing new programs with required specialists.

3. To be able to expand or contract a service in response to changing demands and availability of funds; the size of a government agency cannot be changed easily.

4. To avoid large capital outlays; the contractor has the necessary capital equipment, so government spending under a contract is constant, predictable, and spread out over time.

5. To capture economies of scale regardless of the size of the jurisdiction, because the contractor can spread his costs over many customers and achieve economies that smaller jurisdictions cannot.

THE EXTENT OF OUTSOURCING

One measure of the value of outsourcing is its use. Many surveys have been conducted, and their gist can be summarized as follows: virtually every government in the United States outsources services,[2] and more than two hundred different services are provided by contractors to local governments alone.[3] The value of contract services rose by 65 percent from 1996 to 2001 and exceeded $400 billion.[4] The fraction of city services provided exclusively or in part by municipal employees declined while the amount of outsourcing increased between 1988 and 1997.[5]

Among the most commonly contracted municipal services, in order of frequency, are towing away and storing vehicles (by 83 percent of local governments), legal services, refuse collection and disposal, building security, street repair, emergency ambulance service, labor relations, and data processing (by 15 percent of local governments).[6]

HOW TO OUTSOURCE

Whether buying goods or services, government must be a smart buyer. When government engages in competitive sourcing or outsourcing, it must: (1) specify what it wants to buy and the service standards to be achieved, (2) attract qualified bidders, (3) conduct a fair and efficient bidding process, (4) evaluate bids and award the contract to the best private competitor or keep the work in the agency if the latter offers better value, (5) plan the employee transition (if outsourcing), (6) monitor contractor performance, (7) have a procedure in place to resolve any conflicts,[7] and (8) be prepared to terminate the contract in case of unsatisfactory performance.

OUTSOURCING IS EFFICIENT

Detailed information on outsourcing's efficiency comes from hundreds of studies comparing public and private provision of common municipal services. The easiest and least expensive studies (and least persuasive) are telephone surveys of government officials; these show overwhelming satisfaction with outsourcing. Another class of studies compared the same set of services in a jurisdiction before and after outsourcing, while other studies looked at services, such as bus operations, before and after outsourcing in multiple jurisdictions. These before-and-after studies showed cost reductions ranging from 20 to 50 percent. The most authoritative, compelling, costly, and rare studies are cross-sectional, econometric analyses that compare cities using municipal employees with cities that outsourced that same service. The services studied were solid-waste collection, street construction, street cleaning, building custodial services, traffic-light maintenance, payroll processing, and tree pruning. Municipal costs were 37 to 96 percent higher, except for payroll processing, where the costs were equal.[8]

The most studied service is solid waste collection. Of eight major studies in the United States, Canada, and Switzerland, all—except one with serious errors that disqualify it—are consistent with the conclusion that the price of outsourced collection is significantly less than the cost of municipal collection.[9]

The federal government's experience with outsourcing is illuminating. From 2003 through 2007 it conducted 1,375 public-private competitions involving 50,989 employee positions. Private firms won only 17 percent of the competitions and the federal agencies won 83 percent, but the entire process resulted in total estimated net savings of $7.2 billion regardless of who won.[10] This illustrates the value of introducing a competitive climate: the agencies had to improve to retain the work.

The differences in performance do not arise because the people who work for government are somehow inferior to those in the private sector; they are not. The difference is the result of forces and incentives in one environment and not the other, as discussed above. Nor is the difference generally due to lower wages or benefits in the private sector, but to more efficient organization and management of the work—that is, doing it with fewer but often better-trained workers.

Economist Barbara Stevens summarizes the operational reasons she found for the observed difference: "[I]n the majority of public agencies, the concepts of clear, precise task definitions and job definitions, coupled with easily identifiable responsibility for job requirements, are not enforced as vigorously as in the majority of private enterprises. It is this difference that appears, in general, to be responsible for the very significant public sector–private sector cost differences."[11]

In summary, "[A] general consensus exists that [outsourcing] can save money in most services and that private operations are generally more efficient than their public-sector counterparts."[12] Research has moved beyond the question of comparative efficiency to how best to manage outsourcing.[13]

Some critics assert that outsourcing encourages corruption, as contractors make campaign contributions to ensure favorable consideration or bribe public officials to obtain contracts. In fact, corruption is symmetrical: public officials steal money and engage in fraud even when no contractors are involved, and public employee unions make campaign contributions to gain favorable treatment in the form of higher wages and more costly fringe benefits at public expense.

Of course, contractors are not always better than government agencies. Every situation is unique and requires a competitive comparison to select the best option, public or private, not a mindless choice of one or the other.

OUTSOURCING AND PUBLIC EMPLOYEES

The biggest barrier to outsourcing is concern about current government employees and the strong, sometimes violent opposition of their unions. Many practical approaches have successfully addressed these legitimate concerns. Contractors may be required to offer jobs to current public employees even if they do not need so many to do the work; if the contract period is long enough, attrition will reduce the number of excess workers. Gradually outsourcing portions of the work also allows normal attrition to reduce the number of affected employees. San Diego did this with its buses. Workers were reassigned to different routes, and no one lost a job. This approach is applicable to many services. Moreover, better job opportunities are often available for workers who choose to leave the security of a government job and go to work for the private contractor after outsourcing. For example, workers in technology jobs that were outsourced ended up on better career paths, made more money, and were happier in their private-sector jobs.[14] Job enrichment is experienced by a manager whose work is upgraded by outsourcing: for example, instead of running a department that maintains parks, he or she makes sure that parks are maintained. This is analogous to an automobile executive who advances from managing the production of windshield-wiper motors to managing acquisition of the motors; the manager can decide to make or to buy the motors or to do some of each. It is a step up in responsibility and rewards.

A major study by the National Commission on Employment in 1989 found that 93 percent of affected employees were satisfactorily taken care of through one or the other of these methods and only 7 percent lost jobs as a result of outsourcing.[15] Note that the public does not believe that public employees should be exempt from economic forces that result in job losses in the private sector.

CONTRACTING IN WAR ZONES

No discussion of outsourcing can ignore the scandals reported in contracting for services in a war zone such as Iraq. Competitive procedures are short-circuited, overpayment is common, monitoring is limited, and corruption may be rife. It is difficult, however, to find competing, qualified contractors willing and able to work as civilians in these circumstances, and they must be hired urgently because soldiers' lives are at stake. And what is the alternative? Use trained troops to obtain, deliver, and prepare food for meals, and manage mess halls? Or to import, store, and distribute supplies? Or to build and maintain bases and housing for our military? Or to guard high-level local officials who operate in treacherous settings and are targeted by al-Qaeda?

If not using trained troops for such functions, should the military have a corps of civilian employees doing such work? But such needs rise and fall and differ from time to time and place to place, and therefore a permanent corps makes little sense. In these circumstances outsourcing is the best of several poor options. Textbook contracting procedures as described above are a valid goal that can rarely be realized on the battlefield.

PRISON PRIVATIZATION

The corrections commissioner of New York City once said to me: "Basically I run a hotel, providing living accommodations and meals; it's just more difficult than usual to check out in the morning." At a time of growing problems in American prisons, the president-elect of the reform-minded American Correctional Association joined forces with businessmen and investors to form the Corrections Corporation of America, confident that they could design and run better prisons. This is now the premier private prison company, operating prisons in the United States and abroad.

Outsourcing critics decry private prison management. They acknowledge that some savings may be realized, but their main objections are that prisons are "inherently governmental" and that private jailers may violate the human dignity of prisoners. Alas, both public and private guards sometimes engage in appalling behavior. Riots by abused illegal immigrants at a detainee center run by Esmore Correctional Services in Elizabeth, New Jersey, in 1997 led the Immigration and Naturalization Service to cancel the contract and Esmore to fire the responsible employees. Contrast this with the 1971 riot in New York's Attica Correctional Facility, a state-run prison. Nine guards and twenty-eight inmates were shot to death by state troopers in a situation ineptly handled by public officials. The punishment? One trooper was indicted for reckless endangerment, and after twenty-seven years of court battles the state agreed to pay $24 million to relatives of the inmates and guards killed in what the New York State Special Commission on Attica described as one of "the bloodiest one-day encounters between Americans since the Civil War."[16] So much for that argument.

CONCLUSION

Properly carried out, outsourcing—or, more accurately, competitive sourcing—is a good public-administration strategy for government, taxpayers, service recipients, and workers. It should be used wherever it is practical, cost-effective, and better than public provision.

RESOLVED, the terms of Supreme Court justices should be limited to eighteen years

PRO: Steven G. Calabresi and James Lindgren

CON: Ward Farnsworth

Among the "repeated injuries and usurpations" of King George III detailed in the Declaration of Independence was the complaint that "He has made Judges dependent on his Will alone, for the tenure of their offices." In doing so, the rebellious colonists believed, the king was violating a fundamental principle of English law and liberty, as laid down in the Act of Settlement of 1701. In previous centuries, judges served at the pleasure of the king (*durante bene placit*), and when the king died the judge's term ended. One of the achievements of the Glorious Revolution of 1688 was that judges now served during good behavior (*quamdiu se bene gesserit*) and could be removed only if they were convicted in a regular judicial proceeding.

Many of the state constitutions drafted in the immediate aftermath of the Declaration included a provision that judges would, in the words of Virginia's constitution of 1776, "continue in office during good behavior." At the Constitutional Convention in 1787 there was much debate over who should appoint federal judges—some thought they should be selected by the legislature and others preferred that they be appointed by the executive—but nobody disagreed that judges should serve "during good behavior." In *Federalist* No. 78, Alexander Hamilton stressed that the "good behavior" provision of Article III, Section 1 ("The Judges, both of supreme and inferior Courts, shall hold their Offices during good Behavior") was among the least objectionable and most important provisions of the Constitution. To the extent that critics of the document took aim at this provision, it was evidence "of the rage for objection which disorders their imaginations and judgments." Having judges serve during good behavior, Hamilton argued, was essential to preserve the independence and integrity of "the least dangerous" branch.

Legal scholars disagree, however, about what the framers meant by "good behavior." According to many scholars, the clause means that the only way that judges can be removed is through impeachment, which is authorized by Article II, Section 4: "The President, Vice President, and all other civil Officers of the United States shall be removed from Office on Impeachment for, and Conviction of, Treason, Bribery, or other High Crimes and Misdemeanors." Of the seventeen federal officers who have ever been impeached by the House of Representatives (seven of whom were convicted by the Senate), ten were federal judges, including, in 1805, Supreme Court Justice Samuel Chase. A few scholars argue, in contrast, that the framers of the Constitution intended that judges could be removed for misbehavior without being impeached so long as due process was followed.

Whatever the framers' original intent, it is clear that today "good behavior" is widely construed to mean that federal judges may serve for life so long as they do not commit an impeachable offense. The most important question is not what the framers intended but rather whether the framers' handiwork meets the needs of the twenty-first century. Steven G. Calabresi and James Lindgren answer this question sharply in the negative. They argue that the framers were wrong to think that life terms—as opposed to fixed terms of a specified length—were essential to judicial independence and strength; and even if they were right in the context of the late eighteenth century, they are wrong in the context of our own times. To return to the levels of judicial turnover that the framers took for granted requires setting a limit on the amount of time federal justices serve, at least on the Supreme Court. Ward Farnsworth rejects that argument. The framers, he says, got it right: life tenure makes not only for a more robust, independent judiciary but also for a more stable legal system.

PRO: Steven G. Calabresi and James Lindgren

Life tenure for high government officials is generally a feature of monarchies and aristocracies, and it is not to be found in any modern constitutional democracies other than ours. In the modern world, we associate life tenure with communist dictatorships, like those in Cuba or in the People's Republic of China. Some religious leaders like the supreme Ayatollahs of Iran or the Pope also effectively hold their offices for life.

The Western world generally rejected life tenure as a result of the Enlightenment's rejection of feudalism. Life tenure, like the inheritance by kings and nobles of their offices, was seen as being an outdated feature of feudalism. Life tenure persists in the United States for Supreme Court justices, but it is striking that no other modern Western democracy gives life tenure to its equivalents of our Supreme Court justices. Not a single one. And of the fifty states, only one—Rhode Island—gives its state Supreme Court justices life tenure. Life tenure for U.S. Supreme Court justices stands out like a sore thumb to any modern-day scholar of comparative law.

Compounding the problem, recent U.S. Supreme Court justices have been taking advantage of life tenure to stay in office longer and retire at an older average age; as a result, vacancies on the Supreme Court are occurring less frequently. From 1789 to 1970, justices stayed on the Supreme Court for an average of 15 years, they retired at an average age of 68, and vacancies on the high court arose on average once every 2 years. Since 1970, however, justices have stayed on the Court for an average of 25 years, they retired at an average age of seventy-eight, and vacancies on the high court have arisen on average only once every 3 years.

We think this development is a big problem, and as a remedy we propose a constitutional amendment that would provide that each of the nine Supreme Court justices serve a single eighteen-year term. A new justice would be appointed every two years in odd-numbered years. Our term limits amendment would push Supreme Court tenure, retirement ages, and the length of time between vacancies back toward the average numbers that have prevailed for most of American history. Our reform proposal is not radical but is instead a Burkean change that would restore Supreme Court tenure to the way it used to be—while also bringing American practice into conformity with that of other Western democracies.

We offer ten reasons in support of our proposed amendment.

The first reason to get rid of life tenure for Supreme Court justices is that it violates the cardinal principle of the Declaration of Independence and of the Enlightenment: all men and women are born politically equal and free. The

Declaration begins in its second paragraph with the words: "We hold these truths to be self evident, that all Men are created equal." It goes on to say that government derives its "just Powers from the Consent of the Governed." No one is born to be a king, a nobleman, a serf, or a Platonic guardian. Everyone is born politically equal to everyone else, which leads to the principle of one person, one vote. This is why the Declaration points the way toward democratic majoritarian governance.

Life tenure for Supreme Court justices, given the enormous power those justices have, is grossly and offensively anti-egalitarian and thus undemocratic. It is premised on the idea of an aristocracy, that some men and women are naturally better at governing than everyone else. Once appointed, these natural aristocrats ought to rule us until they die—at least as to important matters of law, philosophy, and religion. Defenders of life tenure might respond that it is necessary for us to have an extreme version of judicial independence, but no other country in the world agrees, nor do forty-nine out of the fifty states. Rule by life-tenured Supreme Court justices is almost as offensive as rule according to the divine right of kings. In America, the lowest common man or woman is equal to a king, and they are also equal to a Supreme Court justice. That is why most decisions ought to be made by letting everyone vote so the majority can have its way.

The principle of political equality—of one person, one vote—is imperfectly followed in the U.S. Constitution since it is violated by the existence of the Senate, the electoral college, and the fifty states, but it is still a bedrock ideal of our polity. When the average tenure of Supreme Court justices jumps from about fifteen years to over twenty-five years, and when vacancies on the Court start occurring only once every three years instead of once every two years, then the Supreme Court becomes much less accountable to the American people than it once was. Democracy requires that Supreme Court justices ultimately follow the election returns, as has been asserted both in the press and by Yale political science professor Robert Dahl. Life tenure for U.S. Supreme Court justices is unequal and undemocratic. It makes them too unaccountable to the American people and much more unaccountable than they were for most of our history before 1970.

Second, life tenure for Supreme Court justices undermines the Constitution because it makes the Supreme Court far more powerful than the framers meant it to be—too powerful, in fact. The current life-tenured Supreme Court is a threat to liberty and to the rule of law. The Declaration of Independence says that we are endowed by our "Creator with certain unalienable Rights [and] that among these are Life, Liberty, and the Pursuit of Happiness." Not only are men and women born equal, they are also born free, and it is the obligation of government to secure that freedom. The framers sought to secure freedom by separating and dividing power both horizontally among the three branches of the national government and vertically between the federal government and the states.

When life-tenured Supreme Court justices start staying on the Court for ten years longer than they have historically and vacancies on the Court open up substantially less frequently than they used to, it takes a lot longer to correct the Court's errors through the appointment process. The concentration of power we currently see in the Supreme Court is anticonstitutional. Many people base their votes for president in significant part on their preference for Supreme Court appointments. The president and the Senate are less important than they used to be and are becoming a kind of electoral college for the really important job of picking Supreme Court justices.

The American separation of legislative, executive, and judicial powers grew out of the Aristotelian idea that the optimal regime in practice was a mixed regime that combined the energy of monarchy, the wisdom of aristocracy, and the common sense of democracy. Our framers, however, saw to it that our monarchical president and our aristocratic Senate and Supreme Court were popularly selected—as is the people's chamber, the House of Representatives—thus making "We the People" the ultimate master in the U.S. version of the mixed regime. The trend since 1970 of lengthening Supreme Court tenure is making the U.S. constitutional regime much more aristocratic and much less democratic than it used to be. Long Supreme Court service disrupts the Aristotelian balance of the U.S. constitutional regime as it functioned from 1789 to 1970.

Moreover, the problem may soon get a whole lot worse as life expectancies increase. How will we feel about life tenure for Supreme Court justices when it starts to mean service for forty or fifty years? Even with justices serving 25 and 30 years, however, a life-tenured Supreme Court is a threat to liberty and is an anticonstitutional concentration of power in an unaccountable entity.

Third, term limits for Supreme Court justices are necessary if the famous American system of checks and balances is to work for the Supreme Court. In theory, impeachment could check and balance the Supreme Court, but in practice it is "a scarecrow," as Thomas Jefferson called it, because no Supreme Court justice has ever been removed from the Court by impeachment. Constitutional amendments could in theory check and balance the Supreme Court, and four amendments have been adopted overturning Supreme Court opinions, but in practice new constitutional amendments are almost impossible to pass. The only workable check and balance that Congress and the president have on the Supreme Court (beyond complaining to the press) is the appointment process, and that is being rendered obsolete by increases in the life expectancy of Supreme Court justices.

Fourth, term limits and staggered terms for Supreme Court justices are needed to prevent some presidents from getting many more appointments to fill than other presidents get. For example, Presidents William Howard Taft and Warren G. Harding made ten appointments to the Supreme Court during the early twentieth century, while serving only seven years combined as president. In contrast, President Woodrow Wilson, who was president between Taft and Harding, made only three appointments to the Court during his eight years in office. Similarly, Richard Nixon appointed four justices in his five and a half years as president, while Jimmy Carter appointed none in his entire four-year term. Some presidents get to fill lots of seats and others get no appointments at all or only a few. This problem of hot spots—where a lot of seats suddenly open up in a few years—is best solved with staggered terms and term limits.

Fifth, the absence of term limits and staggered terms creates a powerful incentive for strategic retirement. Justices try to—and often succeed—in retiring when an ideological soul mate occupies the White House. Our research shows that strategic retirement—and even dying in office while making a vain effort to outlive a president you disagree with—is a major fact of life on the Supreme Court. This is unseemly, and it undermines the rule of law by causing the public to perceive the justices as being merely politicians in robes. The way to end strategic retirement by Supreme Court justices is with term limits. Any replacement for a justice who retires early should be able to fill only the remaining years of the retiring justice's term. Strategic retirement ought not to be rewarded with a new full eighteen-year term.

Sixth, life tenure on the Supreme Court leads to shirking in the form of laziness, boredom, and associated problems that economists call "agency costs." The current long-serving Supreme Court hears half as many cases, about eighty a year, as the 150 cases a year that it heard twenty-five years ago. This nearly 50 percent reduction in output roughly coincides with a doubling of the justices' staffs from two law clerks per justice in 1968 to four law clerks per justice today. The failure to hear and decide more cases also comes in the face of a dramatic increase in the number of cases the Court is being asked to hear. When confronted with these figures, it is hard not to wonder if there is some shirking going on.

Our proposal for term limits in part grows out of the experience one of us, Professor Steven G. Calabresi, had clerking on the Supreme Court during the 1987–1988 term. He concluded that all five justices then on the Court with at least fifteen years of service, except for Justice John Paul Stevens, were to some degree shirking. These four justices, Chief Justice William H. Rehnquist and

Justices William J. Brennan, Thurgood Marshall, and Harry Blackmun, were in his opinion shirking by relying heavily—indeed, excessively—on their law clerks. In some cases, the justices were not even in their offices for an appropriate number of hours in the day. During this same period of time, Justice Byron White was continuing to work hard, but he was bored by the job and cynical about the importance of each individual case. In contrast, Justice Stevens and the then-newer justices Sandra Day O'Connor, Antonin Scalia, and Anthony Kennedy were all working hard. Thus personal observation and common sense, together with the numbers cited above, combine to suggest that there is a problem with shirking on the Supreme Court that is associated with life tenure for the justices—a problem that would be corrected by term limits.

Seventh, there is an additional agency cost associated with life tenure beyond shirking, which is that the justices may find themselves increasingly tempted to aggrandize judicial power. The growth of the Imperial Judiciary since 1970 has directly coincided with the increase in average tenure of the justices' terms. If power corrupts, and absolute power corrupts absolutely, so too will substantial increases in the length of judicial tenure. Our Supreme Court justices are enormously powerful individuals, and they have assumed a dramatic role in recent years—legalizing abortion on demand and deciding a presidential election are just two examples.

Eighth, there is a serious problem with mental decrepitude on the Supreme Court. Some older justices have been seen to fall asleep on the bench during Court sessions—some more than once! Some justices in recent decades have stayed on the Court, propped up by their law clerks long past the point when they were able to function well in the job. Justices Brennan, Blackmun, and Marshall are examples on the liberal side, while former chief justice Rehnquist is an example on the conservative side. Brennan and Marshall were physically too frail to function in their later years, while Justice Blackmun was cognitively overtaxed. Rehnquist stayed on the Court with throat cancer for almost a year until his death, during most of which time he was unable to do his job. These episodes are far from unique, as historian David J. Garrow has documented.[1] An eighteen-year term limit would have eliminated almost all the past problems of mental decrepitude that have been documented without the arbitrary unfairness of a maximum age limit. Thus term limits also make sense as a way of eliminating mentally and physically decrepit justices in a society where life expectancies are constantly increasing.

Ninth, we believe that life tenure and the increasing gap between vacancies has made the confirmation process far more contentious than it otherwise would be by raising the stakes associated with each new Supreme Court appointment. When the average length of service of a Supreme Court justice goes up from about sixteen years to about twenty-five years, political actors in the White House and the Senate will devote a lot more in the way of resources to try to influence Supreme Court appointments. That is a major reason why we have recently seen such contentious confirmation processes, as in the cases of Robert Bork and Clarence Thomas. The nominations of John Roberts and Samuel Alito led to national political campaigns almost akin to those waged by presidential candidates. Sonia Sotomayor's nomination elicited less controversy only because Democrats held such a huge majority in the Senate that a filibuster was out of the question. Term limits for Supreme Court justices should lower the stakes associated with each individual Court appointment, thus leading to a more civil, less contentious selection process.

Tenth, and finally, the current system of life tenure gives presidents a powerful incentive to appoint the youngest plausible nominee they can find, thus extending their influence over the Supreme Court for decades to come. Experienced nominees who are in the prime of their careers and are in good health, like Judge Jay Harvie Wilkinson of the Fourth Circuit or Judge Diane Wood of the Seventh Circuit, may not be nominated because they are nearing age sixty and thus probably too old to last for three or four decades on the Supreme Court. This is an insane way to pick people to serve on the Supreme Court. If we had an eighteen-year term limit for justices, presidents would not hesitate to name a sixty-year-old to the Supreme Court because that person could reasonably be expected to function well to age seventy-eight; there would be nothing gained by nominating a forty-five-year-old instead. In contrast, the current system creates a powerful incentive to name people who are too young to do the job well.

In conclusion, the Supreme Court plays a bigger role today than ever before in its history, but its members are less accountable, less checked, and less balanced than ever before. At three previous times in our nation's history, turnover on the Court was so slow that Congress felt compelled to act. In 1837 the size of the Supreme Court was expanded from seven to nine justices; in 1869 judicial retirement was encouraged by instituting pensions for retiring justices; and in 1937 justices became eligible for senior status, allowing them full pay while keeping an office and being relieved of most of their duties. Each time Congress acted to resolve a crisis in judicial tenure by making structural changes in the Court or in the retirement system. Rather than dealing with the problem of excessive tenure—as we did three times before—most current opponents of term limits want to stick their heads in the sand and deny that there is even a problem.

Our solution is eighteen-year, nonrenewable terms that are staggered with one seat on the Court opening up every two years. This reform is fundamentally a Burkean constitutional change that would merely restore the norms for Supreme Court service that prevailed in this country between 1789 and 1970. Far from being revolutionary, term limits for the Supreme Court would return things to the way they used to be, just as the two-term limit on the president returned things to the way they had been before Franklin D. Roosevelt. The United States ought not to be governed by a gerontocracy of Supreme Court oligarchs like the leadership cadre of the Chinese Communist Party. It is high time that we impose a reasonable system of term limits on the justices of the U.S. Supreme Court.

CON: Ward Farnsworth

I defend life tenure for Supreme Court justices, and oppose fixed terms for them, on two main grounds. First, by slowing down the rate of turnover on the Court, life tenure puts a useful brake on political majorities who want to change fundamental legal doctrines by filling the Court with justices who will do their bidding. Fixed terms of eighteen years, by contrast, would guarantee every two-term president the power to dramatically remake the Court—a result that would destabilize the law and place too much trust in the judgment of short-term majorities. Second, term limits would add to the political character of the Court's work; they would turn Supreme Court nominations into an explicit spoil of every presidential election, and might well increase the justices' sense of obligation to carry out the views of the presidents who have nominated them. Some of these arguments have a speculative quality, but then so do the arguments in favor of fixed terms, and this counsels in favor of leaving well enough alone.

FASTER AND SLOWER LAW

It is natural to think of life tenure mostly as a feature of the justices' working conditions—a measure meant to improve their performance by insulating them from worries about what they will do after they leave the bench. But the length of their terms also dictates how often openings on the Court arise and thus how quickly electoral majorities can remake the Court and so produce tectonic shifts in the law. It might fairly be said that Americans live under two types of law: fast-moving and slow. The faster law is made by members of Congress, state legislators, and other political actors who face elections every few years. The slower law mostly is made by a committee of officials known as

Supreme Court justices. Since the justices keep their jobs for a long time, it takes a long time to replace them if the public doesn't like what they do. The Supreme Court is thus conservative—not in the modern sense of being "right wing," but in the traditional sense of being slow to change. The most fundamental decisions in our legal life are put on a track that requires a sustained expression of public will before they can be reversed.

The Supreme Court's case law on federalism provides a good example. A sea change in that area of law took place in the 1990s; the Court made small but important steps to enhance the rights of the states and limit the powers of the federal government. That shift was not caused by any quick or transitory change in public mood. It was the result of twelve consecutive years of Republican control over the White House (and resulting appointments to the Court), plus the presence of a holdover from the Nixon years (William Rehnquist). The Court's work thus came to reflect, in a slightly delayed fashion, certain national preferences that were durably expressed through the political process. Major shifts in the Court's jurisprudence tend to be of this character, sometimes changing from generation to generation but rarely from year to year.

The value of the Court as a slow lawmaker is that it resists short-term or even medium-term majoritarian judgments so that long-term majorities can prevail. Changing the slower law takes a long time, and this frustrates many people. My debate opponent Steven G. Calabresi, for instance, who has described abortion as murder, believes that the need to get *Roe v. Wade* reversed is "*the* biggest issue implicating law and morality today."[1] Abolishing life tenure would make reversing *Roe* easier. Maybe that is a good thing, and maybe it isn't; in any event, everyone should have a clear sense of the stakes in this debate. Every generation has its unpopular Supreme Court decisions. The question is whether we should take structural steps to make those decisions easier to undo.

No doubt there are some who would prefer that all sorts of decisions by the Supreme Court be made easier to reverse. On the right there are those like Robert Bork (who wants to make censorship easier) and on the left those like Mark Tushnet (who feels that "progressives and liberals are losing more from judicial review than they are getting").[2] Both are dismayed by the Supreme Court's frustration of their projects, and both clamor for more public control over the law the Court makes. But most people are more cautious than that, and rightly so—and this is one reason why the movement for fixed terms has not picked up steam. Speeding up the rate of change at the Supreme Court would create winners and losers, but it is hard to be sure who they would be, and in the meantime most Americans enjoy a combination of expansive liberties and social stability that makes them understandably risk-averse.

Here is a last way to put the point. Having justices serve for eighteen years would guarantee every two-term president at least four appointments to the Court: the ability to create a near-majority, which easily could become a majority with the addition of an interim appointment or the presence on the Court of a like-minded justice appointed fifteen years before. This can happen already, but it usually doesn't. The question is whether we should ensure that it always does. I am skeptical. A two-term president may reflect a single national mood, and there is value in a Court that cannot be remade by one such gust. We should be slow to assume that the country would be better off if the same ideological fads that can elect a two-term president were to regularly produce decisive changes in the Court's membership as well.

THE SUPREME COURT AS A POLITICAL SPOIL

Apart from slowing the pace of fundamental legal change, life tenure also makes the process of appointment to the Court less explicitly political than it would be with fixed terms of eighteen years.

First, fixed terms would facilitate the work of interest groups trying to influence the composition of the Court. If justices served terms of eighteen years, one no longer would speak of the *possibility* that the winner of a presidential election might make appointments to the Court. Every winner would be guaranteed two of them. The stakes for the Court in every campaign thus would be higher than they currently are; interest groups would see larger expected returns from pressuring candidates to make and keep promises about how they would use their two nominations if elected. Fixed terms also would make it easier to coordinate pressures further in advance. Everyone would know years ahead of time when the next vacancy will arrive and what seat will be involved. Campaigns to have it filled would begin far in advance, just as a new political campaign begins as soon as the prior one ends. Depriving pressure groups of a clear target, as life tenure does, makes it harder for them to organize their efforts and concentrate their energies.

A second and related drawback of fixed terms is that they might well increase the justices' sense of obligation to carry out the wishes of whoever appointed them. If everyone knows that two seats on the Court are a spoil the president won fair and square, those seats may be regarded as his to fill in a stronger sense than we currently see, and his nominees may feel more pressure to carry out the president's agenda. The justices will be Republican appointees or Democratic appointees in a more explicit sense than they now are. Some may therefore view their own roles in a manner a little more political and less lawlike.

Finally, fixed terms resemble the arrangements in the legislative and executive branches of the government and so may cause justices to think of themselves as political officeholders in a more traditional way than they now do. Indeed, some of the proposals for fixed terms are pitched expressly as efforts to make the Court more responsive to popular will. New justices will be familiar with the rationale of such a plan if it is enacted; they will understand that they are serving fixed, limited terms precisely in order to keep the Court accountable to current political values. The implication is that the justices are supposed to give effect to those values and to popular sentiment when they make their decisions—but this is just how we don't want them thinking about their jobs when it comes time to decide cases. The justices negotiate all the time between their own preferences and the pressure exerted, sometimes weakly, by the legal materials in front of them. We should hesitate before taking any measure that would increase even a little the justices' sense that their charge is political.

SOME FURTHER REPLIES TO CALABRESI AND LINDGREN

Calabresi and Lindgren suggest that life tenure is a pre-Enlightenment feature of the Constitution associated with dictatorships and feudalism. This is a terribly overheated claim. Life tenure's most famous defender was Alexander Hamilton in *Federalist* No. 78, who had perfectly rational grounds for his views; he wanted to maximize the independence of the judicial branch. The result has hardly resembled a dictatorship, and in practice the eighteen-year terms that the authors propose would often not be all that different from what we now have. The most recent justice to step down was David Souter, whose term lasted nineteen years. Most specious of all is the claim that "Rule by life-tenured Supreme Court justices is almost as offensive as rule according to the divine right of kings." Yes, almost—except that Supreme Court justices are nominated by an elected official (the president), confirmed by elected officials (the Senate), are subject to impeachment, can only decide litigated cases, don't command an army, and make decisions that can be overridden by popular amendment.

Calabresi and Lindgren point out that other countries don't have life tenure for *their* Supreme Court justices, and argue that we should be "bringing American practice into conformity with that of other Western democracies." One could say the same thing about the Second Amendment; a private right to bear arms is almost unheard of in the constitutions of other countries. The civil jury rarely appears in advanced countries outside the United States either; nor does capital punishment. Do Calabresi and Lindgren believe we should enact constitutional amendments to end these practices? I doubt it; and so I greatly fear that the appeal to a worldwide consensus serves the same function here that it often does in legal argument: it is an argument made only when it helps bolster a conclusion reached on other grounds.

Calabresi and Lindgren also contend that life tenure "violates the cardinal principle" of the American polity—that "all men and women are born politically equal and free." Why? Because life tenure "is premised on the idea of an aristocracy, that some men and women are naturally better at governing than everyone else." I know of no advocate of life tenure who holds the view the authors describe. The premise just quoted certainly was not the basis for Hamilton's endorsement of life tenure; the closest he came was to say that good justices—the ones who combine "the requisite integrity with the requisite knowledge"—are hard to find, and that life tenure might help attract them to the bench.

Calabresi and Lindgren also note that the Court hears fewer cases than it used to; they suggest that this means the justices are "shirking," and that the problem is caused by life tenure. It is true that between 1988 and 1998 a great drop did occur in the number of cases the Court decided by full opinion—from 146 to 83 (and now holding constant at around the latter number). But in 1998 the average age of the justices was three years *less* than it was in 1988; and in 1998 there were only two justices who had served for more than eighteen years, compared with four in 1988. In other words, the reduction in the size of the Court's docket happened during a period when the justices as a group were becoming younger and more junior.

The authors also suggest that life tenure causes the justices to seize more power, citing the Court's abortion cases and *Bush v. Gore* as examples. Yet the majority in *Roe v. Wade* consisted of only one justice who had been on the Court for more than eighteen years, and six who been there for less than that, including four who had joined in just the previous five years. The majority in *Planned Parenthood of Southeastern Pa. v. Casey,* which reaffirmed *Roe,* likewise included just one justice who had been on the Court for more than eighteen years. In *Bush v. Gore,* two members of the majority had been there for more than eighteen years (Sandra Day O'Connor was in year nineteen). In short, the cases that Calabresi and Lindgren believe are problematic power grabs cannot be attributed to justices serving on the Court too long. If those cases are evidence of "aggrandizement," there is no reason to think that eighteen-year terms would help matters.

Calabresi and Lindgren maintain that life tenure has made confirmation hearings too contentious, suggesting that "the nominations of John Roberts and Samuel Alito led to national political campaigns almost akin to those waged by presidential candidates." The comparison is ludicrous; the confirmations of those justices were relatively low-key affairs that bore no resemblance in any sense to presidential campaigns. To be sure, the nominations of Robert Bork and Clarence Thomas were characterized by genuinely acrimonious hearings that were socially divisive. But those hearings were controversial because both nominees held views that were controversial. Does anyone think that the Bork nomination would have been a more pleasant and collegial experience if he had been nominated to serve for "only" eighteen years?

Finally, Calabresi and Lindgren say that life tenure puts pressure on presidents to pick the youngest plausible nominees they can. So it might seem in theory, but again the facts do not bear out their claim. It is true that Clarence Thomas was nominated at an unusually young age (forty-three), but Ruth Bader Ginsburg was sixty years old when she was nominated; Stephen Breyer was fifty-six, John Roberts was fifty, Samuel Alito was fifty-five, and Sonia Sotomayor was fifty-five. Harriet Miers, whose nomination was made and withdrawn in 2005, was sixty. The typical age of nominees in recent times is about the same as ever, and is not notably young.

CONCLUSION: THE CLAIMS OF THE STATUS QUO

Life tenure has practical consequences. But a recurring problem in debates about life tenure is that most claims about the details of those consequences (and the consequences of any alternatives) are speculative. Terms of eighteen years would cause more frequent turnover than we now see; this may or may not have good or even noticeable effects on the Court's output. Fixed terms might decrease the intensity of the politics that surround the confirmation process, or might make it worse. They would even out the chances for presidents to make nominations, a good thing, but they might cause justices to feel more responsibility to the parties who chose them, a bad thing. They would reduce the risks of strategic retirement and mental decrepitude, but then so would the simpler solution of age limits—and in any event it's far from clear that either of those problems is great as a practical matter.

There is much to be said for leaving the Constitution alone unless it is clear that revising it would create net benefits. Our current arrangements, which most would say have served the country tolerably well for over 220 years, are entitled to some respect on that ground alone. The costs of readjusting to a new order, and the risk that it will be worse than the old, are worth incurring only if it is clear that the expected gains are large. Those who wish to end life tenure for Supreme Court justices have a high standard of proof to satisfy, and Calabresi and Lindgren have come up short.

RESOLVED, the United States should adopt an "emergency constitution" to preserve civil liberties in an age of terrorism

PRO: Bruce Ackerman

CON: Patrick O. Gudridge

National emergencies have always been the bane of civil liberties. When people fear for their safety they become more willing to give up some freedoms in the name of greater security. Freedom of the press, freedom of speech, freedom of movement, freedom of association—all are at risk when the government is fighting a war deemed vital to the nation's security. If, during wartime, "loose lips sink ships," then lips must remain sealed. Letters must be censored, conversations and Web traffic monitored, and secrets kept.

Americans like to think of the courts as the guardians of civil liberties, but the judiciary's record during national emergencies is spotty at best. During wartime, federal courts have generally deferred to the government, waiting until after the emergency has passed to step in to protect civil liberties. Not until after the Civil War, for instance, did the Supreme Court, in *Ex parte Milligan* (1866), belatedly reject the Lincoln administration's claim that it could try civilians for treason in military tribunals even where civil courts were open and functioning. During World War II the Supreme Court, in *Korematsu v. United States* (1944), infamously acquiesced in the Roosevelt administration's internment of Japanese Americans after the bombing of Pearl Harbor.

One of the most profound and difficult questions that a republic faces is how to respond to emergencies that threaten its national security. "Are all the laws, but one, to go unexecuted, and the government itself to go to pieces, lest that one be violated?" was the question Abraham Lincoln posed in the message he delivered to a special session of Congress on July 4, 1861. The purpose of the message was to justify the extraordinary actions he had taken during the preceding three months without congressional approval, including the suspension of habeas corpus and the arrest of rebel leaders who were held without trial in military prisons. His actions, "whether strictly legal or not," he told Congress, had been thrust upon him by "public necessity."

Lincoln's sentiments echoed those of another celebrated American apostle of liberty, Thomas Jefferson, who shortly after leaving the White House explained to a friend that "strict observance of the written laws is doubtless *one* of the high duties of a good citizen, but it is not *the highest*." In Jefferson's view, "The laws of necessity, of self-preservation, of saving our country when in danger, are of higher obligation. To lose our country by scrupulous adherence to written law, would be to lose the law itself, with life, liberty, property and all those who are enjoying them with us; thus absurdly sacrificing the end to the means."

In ancient Rome, explicit allowance was made for national emergencies by creating a system of temporary dictatorship. In times of crisis, when the normal governing arrangements were insufficient to protect the republic, certain government officials were empowered to grant an individual temporary and almost absolute power over the republic. The dictator was limited to a six-month term; according to Machiavelli, a great admirer of the Roman system, "if any of them arrived at the dictatorship, their greatest glory consisted in promptly laying this dignity down again." So long as he did not alter or subvert the republic, the Roman dictator had virtually unlimited powers over his countrymen. He could draft every Roman man into the military, he could arrest and fine men, he could even "execute summarily and without appeal."

The United States has no such system of "constitutional dictatorship," as Clinton Rossiter famously titled his 1948 book, *Constitutional Dictatorship: Crisis Government in the Modern Democracies,* which, not coincidentally, was rushed back into print immediately after the terrorist attacks of September 11, 2001. (The new edition's cover displays the two towers of the World Trade Center belching smoke and superimposed over a ripped Constitution.) However, the threat to the nation posed by terrorism has forced an intense national debate and soul-searching about what, if any, allowances or adjustments should be made to our regular constitutional system in order to combat terrorism. Bruce Ackerman argues that an "emergency constitution" may actually be the best way to preserve civil liberties in an age of terrorism. The alternative, he believes, is that the Constitution will be redefined, albeit without formal amendment, to become a warrant for more expansive executive power and less protection of civil liberties. Patrick O. Gudridge counters that Ackerman's cure is worse than the disease, and urges us to trust instead in the ordinary constitutional processes that have preserved civil liberties in this country for more than two centuries.

PRO: Bruce Ackerman

President Barack Obama no longer talks about the "war on terror." But he has failed to develop a new framework to define the challenges before us. The "war on terror" has led us down a blind alley. We need to design an "emergency constitution" to respond to future terrorist incidents. We must act now, before the next attack. Without a new system of checks and balances, our institutions will predictably respond with panic reactions that pose a serious risk to our civil liberties.

But first, why is it a mistake to declare "war" on terror?

Terrorism is merely the name of a technique: the intentional attack on innocent civilians. But war isn't a technical matter: it is a life-and-death struggle against a particular enemy. We made war against Nazi Germany, not the V-2 rocket. Once we allow ourselves to declare war on a technique, we open up a dangerous path, authorizing the president to lash out at amorphous threats without the need to define them. There are tens of millions of haters in the world, of all races and religions. All are potential terrorists, and all the rest of us are at risk of being linked to one or another terrorist band.

There is a second big flaw. By calling it a war, we frame our problem as if it involved a struggle with a massively armed major power. But modern terrorism has a very different genesis. It is more a product of the unregulated marketplace than massive state power.

We are at a distinctive moment in modern history: the state is losing its monopoly over the means of mass destruction. And once a harmful technology escapes into the black market, it's almost impossible for government to suppress the lucrative trade completely. Think of drugs and guns. Even the most puritanical regimes learn to live with vice on the fringe. But when a fringe group obtains a technology of mass destruction, it won't stay on the fringe for long.

The root of our problem is not Islam or any ideology, but the free market in death. If the Middle East were magically transformed into a vast oasis of peace and democracy, fringe groups from other places would rise to fill the gap. We won't need to look far to find them. If a tiny band of extremists blasted the Federal Building in Oklahoma City, others will want to detonate suitcase A-bombs as they become available, eagerly giving their lives in the service of their self-destructive vision.

This is a very serious problem, but it is not illuminated by war talk. Even the greatest wars in American history have come to an end. When Abraham Lincoln or Franklin Roosevelt asserted extraordinary war powers over American citizens, everybody recognized that they would last only till the Confederacy, or the Axis, were defeated. But the black market in weaponry—aka the war on terror—will never end. Whatever new powers are conceded to the commander in chief in this metaphorical war, he will have forever.

A downward cycle threatens. After each successful attack, the president will extend his war powers further to crush the terrorists—only to find that a very different terrorist band manages to strike a few years later. This new disaster, in turn, will create a popular demand for more repression, and on and on. Even if the next half-century sees only three or four attacks like September 11, this pathological political cycle will prove devastating to civil liberties by 2050.

The root of the problem is democracy itself. A Stalinist regime might respond to an attack by a travel blockade and a media blackout—leaving most of the country in the dark, going on as if everything were normal. This can't happen here. The shock waves will ripple through the populace with blinding speed. Competitive elections will tempt politicians to exploit the spreading panic to partisan advantage, challenging their rivals as insufficiently "tough on terrorism," and depicting civil libertarians as softies who are virtually laying out the welcome mat for our enemies. And so the cycle of repression moves relentlessly forward, with the blessing of most of our duly elected representatives, regardless of political party.

Our traditional defense against such pathologies has been the courts. No matter how large the event, no matter how great the panic, they will protect our basic rights against our baser impulses. Or so we tell ourselves—but it just isn't true.

The courts haven't adequately protected us in the past, and they won't in the future. The Supreme Court upheld the long-term detention of Japanese Americans during World War II, and they have failed to protect Americans this time around. Consider the case of Jose Padilla, an American citizen, who was seized as an "enemy combatant" a few months after September 11. He had arrived at O'Hare Airport in civilian clothes and without any dangerous weapons. But Attorney General John Ashcroft went on television to charge him with plotting to attack an American city with a "dirty bomb." The government soon abandoned this charge, but continued to hold Padilla in a military brig for more than three years. His lawyers quickly went to court to force the government to prove its case against him. But time after time, they lost in the lower courts.

Their final appeal to the Supreme Court also proved disappointing. By the time Padilla's case reached the high court, the government had transferred Padilla to face unrelated charges in criminal court. Since he had now been released from the brig, a majority of the Court dismissed his case from its docket. Justice Anthony Kennedy recognized that the case raised "fundamental issues." Nevertheless, he and his fellow justices refused to review the lower court's sweeping decision, which upheld the president's power to seize Padilla at O'Hare Airport.

This means trouble after the next attack. With the lower court's decision in *Padilla v. Hanft* on the books, the president can use it as a precedent to sweep hundreds or thousands of American citizens into military detention camps. After several more years of litigation, perhaps the Supreme Court will finally have the courage to guarantee Americans their right to a trial by a jury, with all the protections of the Bill of Rights. Or perhaps not. Perhaps they will uphold the president's power, as commander in chief, to detain suspected terrorists indefinitely in a never-ending "war on terror." Or—and this is most likely—perhaps the Court will split the difference, and tell the president that he can throw Americans into endless military detention so long as he complies with a very watered-down version of due process.

Which leads to some obvious questions: Why should we be gambling our freedom on how a crisis-driven Supreme Court will decide some future Padilla case? Isn't it far better for us, as citizens and legislators, to strike a sober balance between security and liberty in the coming century?

We require an "emergency constitution" that allows for an effective short-term response to major terrorist attacks but prevents politicians from exploiting momentary panic to impose long-lasting limitations on liberty. Given the clear and present danger, it makes sense to tie ourselves to the mast as a precaution against deadly enticements. To check the descent into despotism, our eighteenth-century framers created a system of checks and balances, and we should continue this worthy tradition. My proposal adapts our inherited system to meet the distinctive challenges of the twenty-first century.

First and foremost, the emergency constitution should impose strict limits on unilateral presidential power. Presidents should not be authorized to declare an emergency on their own authority, except for a week or two while Congress is considering the matter. Emergency powers should then lapse unless a majority of both Houses votes to continue them—but even this vote is valid for only two months. The president must then return to Congress for reauthorization, and this time a supermajority of 60 percent should be required; after two months more, the majority should be set at 70 percent; and then 80 percent for every subsequent two-month extension.

The design of this "supermajoritarian escalator" responds to the distinctive problem posed by modern terrorism. When terrorists attack, it's hard to say what will come next. Perhaps the terrorists were just lucky, and they have already shot their load. Perhaps they have prepared for one or two other sneak attacks. Or perhaps the country is in for a long, tough struggle against a deeply entrenched network. There is really no way to know.

The emergency constitution gives the security services the short-run tools it needs to find out, and to disrupt the networks it discovers. At the same time, it regularly forces our political leaders to ask whether these extraordinary measures are really necessary. Except for the worst terrorist onslaughts, this supermajoritarian escalator will terminate the use of emergency powers within a relatively short period.

Defining the scope of emergency power is a serious and sensitive business. At its core, it involves the short-term detention of suspected terrorists to prevent a second strike. Nobody should be detained for more than forty-five days, and then only on reasonable suspicion. Once the forty-five days have lapsed, the government must satisfy the higher evidentiary standards that apply in ordinary criminal prosecutions. And even during the period of preventive detention, judges should intervene to protect against torture and other abuses.

What is more, detainees should be amply compensated if they later turn out to be innocent. This is a matter of simple justice. When the state takes a person's property to build a highway, the Constitution requires the payment of "just compensation." Similarly, our law provides monetary payments to felons who establish that they were falsely convicted. The case for compensation is stronger here. After all, falsely convicted felons have the right to a jury trial and all the other benefits of the Bill of Rights. In contrast, emergency detainees were seized for forty-five days merely on the basis of a reasonable suspicion of their criminal involvement. They are even more deserving of compensation when it turns out they were innocent.

But there is more than simple justice involved. Fair compensation—say $500 for every day in captivity—will create financial pressures on the authorities to complete their investigations expeditiously, and discharge those who have been caught in the security round-up by mistake. A substantial payment won't adequately compensate detainees for the disruption of their lives and the indignities of their imprisonment. Nor will it salve the agony of loved ones who anxiously fear that their relatives have been trapped in a Kafkaesque maze. But compensation will help innocent people patch together their lives when they emerge from prison, and it will demonstrate that the government recognizes the special sacrifices they have made in the ongoing campaign against terrorism.

We are now in a position to sum up three basic principles organizing the emergency constitution. The first is the supermajoritarian escalator. This authorizes political leaders to take decisive action, but constantly encourages a return to normalcy. The second is a strictly limited forty-five-day period of preventive detention. This allows the security services to disrupt suspicious networks but forces them to come up with more convincing evidence in an expeditious fashion. The third requires fair compensation for the unlucky people who have been swept into the security net. More than money is involved—the payment helps remove the stigma that would otherwise be associated with their unjust detention as "suspected terrorists."

In speaking of an emergency constitution, I don't mean to be taken too literally. Nothing I propose requires formal constitutional amendment. The emergency constitution can be enacted by Congress as a framework statute governing responses to terrorist attack. But this won't happen unless we can conduct a constitutional conversation in the spirit of our eighteenth-century founders.

In offering up my proposals, I'm not building from the ground up. I'm seeking to develop ideas and practices that are already in common use. The newscasts constantly report declarations of emergency by governors responding to natural disasters—and though this is less familiar, American presidents regularly declare emergencies in response to foreign crises and terrorist threats. My aim is to develop these well-established practices into a credible bulwark against the presidentialist war dynamic.

The aim is to provide a framework that will channel the panic following a terrorist attack into a new constitutional direction. In the aftermath of catastrophe, we will no longer turn on the television to see the president pledging himself to a further escalation of the "war on terror." We will hear a different message:

> My fellow Americans, as we grieve together at our terrible loss, you should know that your government will not be intimidated by this terrorist outrage. This is no time for business as usual, but for urgent action. I am asking Congress to declare a temporary state of emergency that will enable us to take aggressive measures to prevent a second strike, and seek a speedy return to a normal life, with all our rights and freedoms intact.

We are in a race against time. It takes time to confront the grim constitutional future that lies ahead; and more time to separate good proposals from bad ones, to engage in a broad-based public discussion, and for farsighted politicians—if there are any—to enact a constitutional framework into law. During all this time, terrorists will not be passive. Each major attack will breed further escalations of military force, police surveillance, and repressive legislation. The cycle of terror, fear, and repression may spin out of control long before a political consensus has formed behind a constitution for an emergency regime.

Then again, we may be lucky. Only one thing is clear: we won't get anywhere if we don't start a serious conversation.

CON: Patrick O. Gudridge

Tsunamis, wildfires, earthquakes, tornados, hurricanes; automobile accidents, airplane crashes, subway wrecks; crime waves, gang wars, insurgencies, acts of terrorism, outright wars; market collapses, bank failures, massive job layoffs; scandals; global warming—disastrous events like these claim or should claim the immediate attention of those who can do something to prevent or mitigate or manage them. Emergencies are emergencies, however, not only because they require immediate attention but because they prompt changes in standard ways of proceeding. All of us who drive cars know that if we hear sirens and see oncoming vehicles with flashing blue or red lights we slow down, pull over, and get out of the way. We alter the way we drive because it's the right thing to do, because we don't want to be involved in an accident ourselves, and because we are aware of adverse legal consequences that might follow if we don't respond appropriately. Emergency circumstances often endure longer and are more complex, of course. The work required in New Orleans in the wake of Hurricane Katrina, even if all proper steps had been taken in advance, likely would have proceeded on an emergency footing for months. Wars can extend over many years. Terrorist incidents sometimes are not just particular horrors or emergencies of the moment but parts of larger, connected sequences of events that demand longer-term and more extensive changes in standard operating procedures.

In many cases, questions arise as to whether circumstances really count as emergencies, and whether officials who are supposed to be first responders reacted too slowly, too incompletely, or too aggressively. Longer-term, harder to describe emergencies—an "age of terrorism," for example—obviously increase the difficulties officials face in deciding whether or how to act. Months after December 7, 1941, did wartime urgencies really require officials to relocate large numbers of American citizens and other legal residents of Japanese origin to internment camps? Was it really necessary, in the wake of September 11, 2001, to round up large numbers of men of Arab descent and hold these individuals incommunicado indefinitely?

Perhaps trying to think hard about emergencies is a dead-end exercise. Emergency circumstances, it is sometimes said, are exceptional and need to be dealt with independently of any general rule. Advance planning becomes beside the point. From this point of view, the only pertinent question is, who decides? Whoever is in charge determines what's done. Writing in Germany in the 1920s, Carl Schmitt declared: "Sovereign is he who decides on the exception."[1] This famous formula raises several important questions. How do we decide what is an emergency, a crisis that justifies suspending the usual rules that regulate official actions? Is every administrative exercise of discretion an emergency action because, by definition, it does not involve the application of a general rule? If we suspend some of the usual rules, what prevents them all from being suspended?

Schmitt himself was careful. He drew a distinction between "constitutional laws"—by which he meant specific provisions of a written constitution—and the constitution as such—by which he meant a prior choice about the basic form of government. Emergency acts—official responses to states of emergency—could displace "constitutional laws" but must respect the constitution as such. If a constitution reflects a widespread public commitment to a parliamentary republic (for instance, as in Germany, after the collapse of monarchical government following World War I), then emergency acts must be enacted by parliament. But that still leaves a problem: for Schmitt, political events of great moment—he would later point to Adolf Hitler's rise to power in the 1930s—could become new constitutional acts, providing new allocations of authority and therefore new bases for judging emergency acts. New actors and new understandings would rule—and new, potentially awful emergency measures might be legitimated, regardless of prior political understandings.

Some have argued that in the United States, elections are the fundamental institution that justify or reject official emergency measures.[2] "We the People" decide the propriety of emergency acts and hold accountable officials who take charge (or fail to take charge). From this perspective, the 2004 election might be thought of as a referendum on President George W. Bush's responses to the terrorist attacks of September 11, 2001. However, election results reflect a multitude of factors—not surprisingly, since they aggregate the choices of millions of voters. People make choices about who to vote for president on the basis of many different considerations, including factors that may have little to do with public policy. Moreover, a president has many policies. Consider the Bush administration's prosecution of the Iraq war, its establishment of the Guantanamo prison camp, its aggressive interrogation techniques (arguably tantamount to torture), and its secret surveillance. Were all of these programs in some sense ratified by the 2004 election? Was the margin of victory in 2004 clear enough to count as ratification, or was it too close to count as a meaningful public verdict? How do we decide what is too close?

Bruce Ackerman takes a different tack. He draws on the familiar American idea of checks and balances and proposes both recognition of executive discretion and a program of legislative involvement. Ackerman's scheme starts with the suggestion that Congress enact a statute in advance of any particular emergency that would grant officials the authority to detain individuals on "reasonable suspicion" for an extended but statutorily specified period of time (forty-five days) after a terrorist attack and an executive declaration of a state of emergency. On the model of a South African constitutional provision, Ackerman also proposes that this grant of executive discretion expire within a relatively short time unless renewed by a legislative supermajority, itself good for only another short time, with every subsequent renewal requiring a greater supermajority.

Bruce Ackerman is not Carl Schmitt. He is less interested in justifying emergency powers than in setting real limits on such powers. Ackerman would grant power in order to restrain it. He proposes, for example, that detained individuals be paid just compensation. He prohibits torture and racial profiling. He recognizes a right to counsel, and a judicial hearing of real substance in advance of any detention beyond the initial forty-five days. He acknowledges the importance of judicial review in maintaining the integrity of his structure and endorses lawsuits against officials who behave abusively. His aim, quite clearly, is "to preserve civil liberties in an age of terrorism."

Ackerman nonetheless misses the mark. He seeks to avoid difficult problems of definition by restricting relevant emergencies to "actual attacks" and their aftermaths, and by setting up a political process—the renewal votes—meant to bring to an end emergency authority. But why would officials who think of themselves as first responders in emergency circumstances want to participate in this process? If the crisis persists past the first time period, officials seeking extensions would likely be required by Ackerman's system to disclose to skeptical members of Congress the details of official efforts and the resulting failures as well as successes. Why would executive officials run the risks of confusion, compromise, and controversy that accompany the legislative process? Why would they accept the compensation requirements, counsel rights, and torture limits? Why not follow a course akin to the one that Vice President Dick Cheney sometimes plotted: act unilaterally, disclose little, and rely on results to trump constitutional niceties or political objections? Ackerman deploys judicial review to enforce his system, but is this enough to constrain determined executive officials playing upon public fears?

Naked disregard, however, may not be the real problem. The plausibility of the Ackerman scheme depends on a view of crises as short-run events. He envisions as prototypical sequences of individual terrorist attacks rather than an "age of terrorism." However, officials might not agree, and might persuade their legislative overseers that terrorist risks are pervasive and persistent. They might contend, therefore, that preventive detention is not enough, that the right course might require elaborate systems of surveillance, operating more or less continuously across very large populations. Fearing the political consequences of "the next attack," Congress might find it prudent to agree and reauthorize detention repeatedly, extend states of emergency indefinitely, or bolster executive powers of surveillance or other counterterrorist responses. The legislative history after September 11, 2001—for example, the votes renewing the USA PATRIOT Act and adopting the Military Commissions Act—suggests that this is a very real danger. Politics as usual might well reduce Ackerman's plan to an empty gesture. Or worse.

During Ackerman's emergency periods, officials will acquire broad freedom of action. Not quite anything goes—no torture or racial profiling, for example—but Ackerman plainly assumes that officials will sometimes act in ways that are inconsistent with usual understandings of individual rights. For example, the Bill of Rights, even in the face of all the safeguards that Ackerman includes, might well be read as denying Congress the power to authorize mass preventive detention solely on the basis of reasonable suspicion. Ackerman tolerates preventive detention but seeks to cabin the risk of "normalization," of constitutional degradation—the possibility that "whatever it takes" might become the "new normal." How can we be sure that his policy of segregation would work? Emergency periods, we've just seen, might prove politically easy to extend and, as a result, the limiting line might appear to fade over time.

Is it really necessary to conceive of emergencies as outside the scope of our usual thinking about constitutional rights and government powers? Why not judge official emergency measures within the terms of ordinary constitutional law? Ackerman has depicted law as "a blunt instrument" that "hacks the complexities of life into a few legal boxes." He also believes that judges, even if they sometimes think outside boxes, tend to proceed by creating "clouds of obscurity."[3] He's not entirely consistent, perhaps—his own proposal seeks to define a new "box" and relies heavily on judges. More importantly, ordinary constitutional law is not quite what Ackerman depicts it to be—it is more complicated, but also more effective than the alternative that he proposes.

Consider the most famous discussion of states of emergency in American constitutional law. Writing in the depths of the Great Depression, Supreme Court Chief Justice Charles Evans Hughes announced: "Emergency does not create power. Emergency does not increase granted power or remove or diminish the restrictions imposed upon power granted or reserved. . . . [E]mergency may furnish the occasion for the exercise of power."[4] These sentences, on first reading, are puzzling, and almost nonsensical read together. Doesn't the third sentence subvert the first two? Doesn't the third supply a vocabulary—the language of "occasions"—that allows emergency actors to ignore the first two sentences? *No.* Hughes instead stressed the second of his sentences. He insisted that emergency measures must accommodate important interests that would be adversely affected—only then could it be said that the emergency measures were consistent with constitutional norms.

Supreme Court justices—and other constitutional interpreters—use variants of this idea all the time. For example, in the majority opinion in *Boumediene v. Bush* (2008), Justice Anthony Kennedy ultimately concluded that a congressionally provided military commission procedure was not an adequate substitute for constitutionally protected judicial review of Guantanamo detention. Kennedy noted that the Court's majority was "sensitive to . . . concerns" that habeas corpus proceedings might in some circumstances unduly interfere with "other pressing tasks" of the military personnel whose time and attention the courts would command in the course of judicial proceedings. But in the case at hand, he found, "[t]he Government presents no credible arguments that the military mission at Guantanamo would be compromised if habeas corpus courts had jurisdiction to hear the detainees' claims." The shortcomings of the military commission proceedings challenged in the case, therefore, could not be defended as responses to real military needs. Kennedy thus left open the possibility that other commission procedures restricting individual rights, perhaps responding to different circumstances, might nonetheless be constitutionally allowable.

Legal analysis like this is not helpfully described in terms of "boxes" or "clouds," the dismissive terms used by Ackerman. Such analysis is instead a common method in constitutional thought that dramatically reduces the risk of oversimplification. We know, as Ackerman stresses, that recent Supreme Court decisions like *Boumediene* dealing with post–September 11 detention efforts are at one level equivocal. They leave room for congressional revision and recognize the force of government concerns and the possible success of government arguments in subsequent proceedings. At the same time, the Court repeatedly underscores the importance of the individual interests at stake. Official claims to a free hand, to wide latitude, are rejected.

It is important not to claim too much. The World War II Japanese American internment camps ultimately closed in the wake of close judicial scrutiny—but later rather than sooner, after Supreme Court justices and other judges had repeatedly deferred to the claimed discretion of executive officials. Civil liberties also only slowly acquired greater protection over the course of the cold war, at the cost of quite a few ruined lives. The post–September 11 detention policies are not yet entirely past history. Ackerman is not wrong to worry about the costs of long-run processes.

However, once we recognize that responses to extraordinary occasions—good and bad—are part and parcel of our accumulated constitutional culture, we also recognize that the long term may matter much even in the short term.

Some emergencies—the cold war or the war on terror—may continue indefinitely and we may need to confront and constrain official actions over and over. Even in true short-term emergencies, though, we draw upon our history of past responses, either to put particular approaches to use once again or to repudiate them and proceed differently.

Korematsu v. United States (1944)—the Supreme Court decision most associated with judicial deference to the internment of Japanese Americans in World War II—was in one respect irrelevant the day it was decided. *Ex parte Endo*—issued simultaneously with *Korematsu*—effectively closed the camps, reading the statute that authorized internment as acknowledging that U.S. citizens already found to be loyal were constitutionally "not-internable." As it happened, and as the justices knew, most camp residents fell within this category. *Korematsu* nonetheless has a rich subsequent history—as an occasion for eloquent outrage and for criticism of the judiciary's failure to closely scrutinize the government's detention scheme. It was also one of several cases, we have learned, in which government lawyers, aware of the weakness of the supposed facts they were alleging, wrongly failed to inform judges that government officials themselves knew their national security arguments in favor of internment were factually dubious. This wrongdoing ultimately triggered judicial and congressional condemnation.[5] *Korematsu* lives in infamy, and lives vividly, as one point of departure among many within the repertoire of inquiries, histories, and values that together supply the working tools of our constitutional thinking.

This accumulated repertoire—some call it our "constitutional culture"—enables us to address hard cases as well as easy ones, emergencies and non-emergencies alike. We therefore already possess the constitutional capacity to think hard about terrorism, influenza pandemics, disastrous natural phenomena, economic collapses, and the risks as well as benefits of responses our government's officials might undertake. Emergencies—sometimes regarded as exceptions to general rules—are occasions for use of our ordinary constitutional thinking. Ackerman's emergency constitution offers us no equivalent means of acknowledging our commitment to civil liberties at the same time that we respond to emergency circumstances.

RESOLVED, residents who are not citizens should be granted the right to vote

PRO: Ron Hayduk

CON: Stanley A. Renshon

The conventional narrative of American history accents the progress the nation has made in the area of civil rights, especially with respect to the right to vote. In the first half of the nineteenth century, states dropped property qualifications so that all adult, white males could vote. The Fifteenth Amendment, enacted after the Civil War, promised African American males the right to vote, and the Nineteenth Amendment, ratified in 1920, gave women the suffrage. In 1964 the Twenty-fourth Amendment abolished the poll tax, and in 1971 the Twenty-sixth Amendment lowered the voting age to eighteen.

However, two areas of American politics do not readily fit this familiar narrative of progress. The first is the denial of voting rights in many states to felons and ex-felons. To be sure, most of these state laws date to the nineteenth century, and the number of states that disenfranchise ex-felons who have completed their sentences has dropped markedly since the early twentieth century. Still, the number of felons and ex-felons who cannot vote has grown markedly in recent decades, in large part because what counts as a felony has expanded, and so have incarceration rates. In Maryland, for example, the loss of voting rights is triggered not only by heinous crimes such as rape and murder but also by lesser crimes such as "shipment of alcoholic beverages to an unlicensed person," "misrepresentation of tobacco leaf weight," "misrepresentation by refrigerator contractors," being "an accessory after the fact to a felony," "sodomy," "possessing fireworks without a license," and "intentionally removing/defacing/obliterating [a] serial number."[1] Because of the ongoing "war on drugs," drug offenders constitute about one-third of convicted felons.

As a result, more than five million Americans are disenfranchised by felony convictions—about 2.5 percent of the voting-age population. And among African Americans the disenfranchisement rate is over 8 percent, three times the national average. About one in every seven black males in the United States is disenfranchised by these laws

Some progress has been made in softening these laws—in 2005, for instance, the governor of Iowa issued an executive order giving ex-felons the right to vote, and the same year Nebraska lifted its lifetime ban on ex-felons in favor of a two-year waiting period. But there has been little or no change on another front: the movement to grant voting rights to permanent residents who are not citizens. In the nineteenth century noncitizens were often permitted to vote in the United States. In fact, offering voting rights was one way that states attracted new immigrants. But in 1926 the last state—Arkansas—stamped out immigrant voting. Although in recent decades a few localities have permitted noncitizens to vote, efforts to grant this right have generally failed, even in liberal bastions like San Francisco.

For the vast majority of Americans, the connection between voting and citizenship is fundamental, almost part of the natural order of things. In his essay, Ron Hayduk asks us to rethink that connection in view of the rapidly changing demographics of the nation, and particularly the growing proportion of immigrants who are noncitizens. In California, for instance, about 20 percent of the voting-age population is excluded from voting because of the citizenship requirement. The ban on voting by noncitizens not only makes American voting rates (which are calculated using voting-age population as the denominator rather than voting-eligible population) look much worse than they really are, but, according to Hayduk, raises troubling questions of representation and fairness. Stanley A. Renshon, however, implores us to think about the lasting damage that would be done to our concept of citizenship if we were to decouple citizenship from voting. Granting noncitizens the vote is not like extending the suffrage to previously excluded groups such as women or African Americans, he says, but is instead an abandonment of core American values. The question that Hayduk and Renshon pose for the reader, then, is whether immigrant voting rights are properly understood as part of the new frontier in the ongoing struggle to end discrimination and extend civil rights, or whether they are instead a perversion of the civil rights agenda and an affront to fundamental American principles.

PRO: Ron Hayduk[1]

> They who have no voice nor vote in the electing of representatives do not enjoy liberty, but are absolutely enslaved to those who have votes.
>
> —Benjamin Franklin

> The rule of citizens over noncitizens, of members over strangers, is probably the most common form of tyranny in human history.
>
> —Michael Walzer

The idea of allowing noncitizens to vote may sound odd or outlandish. For most Americans, voting is the essence of citizenship. But it was not always so; nor need it be so in the future. In considering the case for immigrant voting rights, there are three things to keep in mind:

1. *It's legal.* The Constitution does not preclude it and the courts—including the Supreme Court—have upheld voting by noncitizens. Noncitizens have enjoyed voting rights for most of U.S. history and continue to do so today.

2. *It's fair and beneficial to all.* There are moral and political reasons to restore immigrant voting, including our commitment to equal rights and the benefits that accrue to all community members, citizen and noncitizen alike.

3. *It's feasible.* Noncitizen voting is making a comeback in the United States and across the globe.[2]

Americans are usually surprised to learn that immigrants enjoyed voting rights for most of our history and throughout the vast majority of the country. In fact, from 1776 to 1926, forty states and federal territories permitted noncitizens to vote in local, state, and even federal elections. Noncitizens also held public office, such as alderman, coroner, and school board member. Voting and holding office promoted civic education and citizenship while also facilitating the political incorporation of immigrants. The notion that noncitizens should have the vote is older, was practiced longer, and is more consistent with democratic ideals than the idea that they should not. Curiously, this 150-year history has been eviscerated from national memory.

Nor is immigrant voting merely a relic of the distant past. Noncitizens currently vote in local elections in over a half-dozen cities and towns in the

United States, most notably in Chicago's school elections and in all local elections in six towns in Maryland. In addition, campaigns to expand the franchise to noncitizens—primarily in local elections—have been launched in more than a dozen other jurisdictions during the past decade, including in New York, Massachusetts, the District of Columbia, California, Maine, Colorado, Minnesota, Wisconsin, Connecticut, Vermont, New Jersey, and Texas.

Moreover, the effort to expand the franchise to immigrants is not particular to the United States; it is a global phenomenon. Nearly fifty countries on nearly every continent allow resident noncitizens to vote at various levels in the host countries' elections, with most countries adopting such legislation during the past three decades. Often this is on a reciprocal basis within groups of affiliated nations—for example, within the Nordic Passport Union or between Portugal and its former colonies. Several European countries, most notably Sweden, Denmark, Norway, and Ireland, allow any resident noncitizen to vote in regional and national elections. Belgium, Austria, and Hong Kong are among the latest nations to take steps to enfranchise noncitizens.

THE CASE FOR IMMIGRANT VOTING

Contemporary campaigns for immigrant voting rights are part of a broader movement for immigrant and human rights. A truly universal suffrage is the linchpin of the broader effort to make government representative of and responsive and accountable to all the people. To achieve these ends, immigrant rights advocates employ many of the same moral and political arguments that were used in past struggles to expand the franchise to previously excluded groups, including African Americans, women, and young people.

In many respects, federal, state, and local governments already treat noncitizens—both legal residents and undocumented individuals—like other community members. The most obvious example is that all residents must pay income taxes regardless of their immigration status. In fact, contrary to popular belief, most immigrants pay more in taxes than they receive in benefits and contribute positively to the nation's economy.[3] Immigrant households paid an estimated $133 billion in taxes to federal, state, and local governments—from property, sales, and income taxes—and the typical immigrant pays an estimated $80,000 more in taxes than they receive in federal, state, and local benefits over their lifetimes.[4]

Noncitizen immigrants, or resident aliens, work in every sector of the economy, own homes and businesses, attend colleges and send children to schools, pay billions of dollars in taxes each year, make countless social and cultural contributions, are subject to all the laws, participate in every aspect of social life, serve in the military, and even die defending the United States, but they are without formal political voice. You see them in every walk of life and neighborhood; they are teachers, students, firefighters, police officers, nurses, doctors, small-business owners, entertainers, construction workers, gardeners, and domestic workers.

One of the basic tenets of democratic theory is that the legitimacy of government rests on the consent of the governed. Members of democratic communities are obliged to obey the laws to which they are subject because they participate in selecting those who govern them. This notion is enshrined in the rallying cry for the American Revolution, "No taxation without representation." Denying voting rights to permanent residents violates this fundamental precept of American democracy.

Democracy means rule by all the people, not merely some of the people. Otherwise, as the experience of African Americans and women demonstrates, those who are excluded from participating will be subject to discrimination and oppression. "When a substantial number of [a society's] inhabitants are excluded from the body politic and have no meaningful way to petition for a redress of grievances through the electoral process," Joaquin Avila points out, the result "of such exclusion is a political apartheid."[5] Although voting is a crude democratic instrument for transmitting political preferences, it is ultimately an essential means to ensure elected officials are responsive to people's interests and values.

Voting rights are not intrinsically tied to citizenship. Recall that voting was originally restricted to white, male property owners. Women and post–Civil War African Americans were citizens yet were denied voting rights until 1920 and 1965, respectively. Voting rights were tied to gender and race rather than citizenship. Similarly, citizens between the ages of eighteen and twenty were excluded from voting until passage of the Twenty-sixth Amendment. In short, voting rights have always been linked to questions about who should be included and excluded in the polity, and being a citizen has never been sufficient to decide who should be granted the right to vote.

From the colonial period until the late nineteenth century, voting by non-citizen immigrants was common throughout most of the United States and was generally not controversial. Wisconsin developed a formula in 1848 allowing aliens who "declared" their intent to become citizens the right to vote. The Wisconsin formula became a model for other states and Congress. Jamin Raskin describes how this model—the declarant alien qualification—helped to weaken the objections of nativists and nationalists by recasting how alien suffrage was conceived and practiced. Alien suffrage was now seen more clearly to be "a *pathway* to citizenship" rather than a substitute for it; a kind of "pre-citizen voting."[6]

During Wisconsin's constitutional convention, foreign-born delegates argued successfully "that when a foreigner left his old life behind and traveled thousands of miles to start a new life in Wisconsin, that effort alone was more than adequate to demonstrate his loyalty and commitment to Wisconsin."[7] Similarly, foreign-born soldiers who fought in the Civil War pointed to their wartime sacrifices in making a compelling case that they could be trusted with the vote.

After the Civil War and during Reconstruction, alien suffrage spread in the South and West with the growing need for new labor. Many new states and territories used voting rights as an incentive to attract new immigrant settlers and as a pathway to citizenship.

If immigrant voting was so prevalent in the nineteenth century, why was it eliminated? The short answer is fear. Fear about what newcomers—who spoke different languages, practiced different religions, and had different cultural habits—might mean for America. Even in the nineteenth century, the anxiety about immigrants periodically led to a curtailing of immigrant voting rights. During the War of 1812, for instance, the spread of alien suffrage was slowed and even reversed because of political leaders who raised the specter of foreign "enemies." Prior to the Civil War, many in the South opposed immigrant voting because they feared that many of the new immigrants were opposed to slavery. In fact, one of the first planks in the Confederate constitution was to exclude voting to anyone who was not a U.S. citizen.

The dramatic rollback of immigrant voting rights began in the late nineteenth and early twentieth centuries, when large numbers of Southern and Eastern European immigrants came to the United States. These newer immigrants, coupled with the rise of mass social movements and third parties such as the Populist, Labor, and Socialist parties, were seen as a threat to the dominant political and social order. The anti-immigrant backlash that culminated after World War I led to the gradual elimination, state by state, of the long-standing practice of extending voting rights to noncitizen residents.

Noncitizen voting rights were abolished at the same time that other restrictive measures were enacted by political elites in both major parties, including literacy tests, poll taxes, felony disenfranchisement laws, and restrictive residency and voter registration requirements. As a result, voter participation dropped precipitously from highs of nearly 80 percent of the voting-age population in the mid- to late nineteenth century down to 49 percent in 1924. Additional legislation drastically reduced the flow of immigrants into the United States and limited the proportion of non–Western European immigrants. These changes had profound effects in shaping the ethnic and racial composition of the United States. The civil rights movement swept away many of these obstacles to voting and also established antidiscrimination laws. But the American Dream is still out of reach for many immigrants, who remain political outsiders and consequently suffer discrimination and exploitation.

Today, about one in five people in the United States is an immigrant or a close relative of an immigrant. More than 25 million adults are barred from voting because they lack U.S. citizenship. In many places immigrant political exclusion approximates the level of disenfranchisement associated with African Americans before the Voting Rights Act of 1965. Noncitizen adults comprise over 10 percent of the adult voting-age population in seven states and the District of Columbia, and more than 20 percent of all Californians. If these noncitizens were enfranchised, they could wield decisive power in state races. At the local level, noncitizens are even more highly concentrated. Adult noncitizens in Los Angeles make up more than one-third of the voting-age population; in New York City, they are 22 percent of adults. In some cities and towns, noncitizens make up 40 to 50 percent—or more—of all voting-age residents. Their taxation without representation challenges basic democratic notions that government rests on the consent of the governed and "one person, one vote."

The rising number of noncitizens challenges democratic ideals not only because immigrants are excluded from formal political participation, but also because they are all too often relegated to the lower social order. Noncitizens are more likely to score lower on nearly every social indicator, including working and living conditions, health, education, and safety. According to the Urban Institute, one in four low-wage workers is foreign-born, and one in four low-income children is the child of an immigrant. Even though immigrants work more than most other Americans—more hours and often at two or more jobs—large numbers of immigrants and their families have low incomes, lack health insurance, and are "food insecure" (a euphemism for going hungry).

Noncitizens suffer such inequities, in part, because policy makers can ignore their interests. Discriminatory public policy and private practices—in employment, housing, education, health care, welfare, and criminal justice— are the inevitable by-products of immigrant political exclusion, not to mention racial profiling, xenophobic hate crimes, and arbitrary detention and deportation. Denying immigrants local voting rights makes government officials less accountable and undermines the health of our democracy and the legitimacy of our public policies.

Noncitizen voting would extend the visibility and voices of immigrants, which in turn would make government more representative, responsive, and accountable. Winning voting rights could help advance other struggles important to immigrants—and to working people and people of color more generally—from speeding up the naturalization process and enacting comprehensive immigration reform to improving health care and education.

One thing is for sure: immigrants are here to stay. Population projections indicate that, given current family reunification policies, birth rates, and domestic economic arrangements, the foreign born will grow in number and disperse further throughout the United States. Their large and growing numbers make them increasingly important political players, especially at the state and local levels. Although questions remain about the direction U.S. immigration policy will take, there is little doubt that how immigrants will be incorporated—socially, politically, culturally, economically—will remain a burning issue for years to come. It is not a question about whether the millions of immigrants in the United States will be incorporated, but *how* they will be incorporated.

SOME ANSWERS TO COMMON OBJECTIONS

The most common objection to immigrant voting is that noncitizens already have access to the vote—by becoming citizens. As New York City mayor Michael Bloomberg argued, "the essence of citizenship is the right to vote, and you should go about becoming a citizen before you get the right to vote."

Most immigrants want to become U.S. citizens, but the average time it takes to naturalize is eight to ten years, or longer. Mario Cristaldo, born in Paraguay and a resident of the District of Columbia since 1994, said, "I invite anyone who says we don't want to become citizens to navigate the [immigration] system. It is not easy." In addition, not all immigrants are eligible to become U.S. citizens, unlike in earlier times when almost everyone who came to the United States was able to naturalize. It used to be a much easier and faster process. Today, millions of people are barred from the pathway to citizenship, including foreign students and people with work visas. Even were the citizenship process to be speeded up significantly—which is highly unlikely in our post–September 11 world—there are still strong reasons for treating noncitizen voting rights and an expedited citizenship process as complementary rather than mutually exclusive goals. By promoting civic education and political engagement, noncitizen voting can help immigrants become better citizens.

Others object that immigrants are ill prepared for voting and possess limited knowledge of U.S. laws, customs, and values. However, specific knowledge is not a prerequisite for political participation. If it were, many native-born citizens should be disenfranchised since they would routinely fail tests of even basic political knowledge, as survey research has consistently shown. Such objections are eerily reminiscent of rationales previously used to disenfranchise women, African Americans, and youth.

Some contend that granting noncitizens voting rights would reduce incentives for immigrants to naturalize and cheapen the meaning of citizenship. Daniel Stein, executive director of the Federation of American Immigrant Reform, a Washington, D.C.–based organization that supports stricter immigration controls, argues: "No one should be given the franchise without taking the Pledge of Allegiance. If you divorce citizenship and voting, citizenship stops having any meaning at all."

This objection is misplaced, however, because there are many rights and privileges besides voting that immigrants gain when they naturalize. Among these are petitioning for relatives to come to the United States, traveling abroad, obtaining government benefits, and gaining employment. Pending and proposed legislation would permit residents to vote in municipal and/or state elections but not federal elections, leaving plenty of incentives to naturalize. Important distinctions between citizens and noncitizens would remain. What would change is the silencing of noncitizens.

CONCLUSION

Contemporary campaigns for immigrant voting focus on restoring voting rights at the local level rather than the state or federal level. Most contemplate only granting voting rights to those who are here legally, such as permanent residents or "green card" holders. For example, legislation in New York City, Massachusetts, Connecticut, Maine, and Wisconsin would enfranchise only documented immigrants in local municipal elections. A ballot proposal in San Francisco in 2004 would have granted voting rights only in school board elections, though it would have allowed all noncitizens—both documented and undocumented—to vote (the proposal was narrowly defeated, 51 percent to 49 percent).

The debate about immigrant voting does not therefore need to be an all or nothing proposition. One can be opposed to granting immigrant voting rights in federal elections yet favor it in school board or municipal elections, particularly in localities in which there are as many noncitizen residents as there are citizen residents. How representative is a school board if the parents of 60 percent of the students attending the school are excluded from voting? Similarly, one might reasonably distinguish between those who are permanent alien residents and those who are in the United States illegally. The moral claims of the former are arguably stronger than those of the latter.

Reasonable people may differ, too, about tactics. Is it better to push for incremental reforms at the local level or will these smaller reforms at the local level undermine the broader movement for immigrant voting rights? But the debate about tactics should not obscure the fundamental moral question at stake in this debate.

Granted, there are well-meaning representatives at every level of government, but good fortune should not play a role in democratic elections and governance. Voting is a crucial mechanism to ensure government that is truly of the people, by the people, and for the people. Immigrant rights are the great civil rights battle of our day and noncitizen voting is the suffrage movement of our time. The burgeoning movement to create a truly universal suffrage invokes America's past and future as an immigrant nation. Restoring immigrant voting rights would update our democracy for the twenty-first century. By granting resident noncitizens the right to vote, we would make history, again.

CON: Stanley A. Renshon[1]

Voting is an iconic embodiment of American civic life. Other than standing for public office, American citizens have no stronger collective civic obligations than those that flow from their ability and responsibility to help shape community policy. The vote is a primary vehicle for exercising those civic responsibilities. That is why the extension of the vote to all the country's citizens has historically been a critical measure of America's progress toward living up to its democratic ideals.

Voting is also an essential marker of full community membership in a democratic republic. In choosing to enter into the naturalization process, immigrants demonstrate an interest in becoming full members of the American national community as well as a willingness to spend the time and effort necessary to do so. In accepting an immigrant as a full citizen at the end of that process, the community affirms that full membership. In linking the vote to full membership, the community further affirms that new members have shown the requisite attachment and commitment to be trusted with helping to make community decisions.

Every state in the United States bars noncitizens from voting in national or state elections. In 1996 President Bill Clinton signed a bill into law that made it a crime for any noncitizen to vote in a federal election. Indeed, the association of voting with citizenship is so deeply ingrained in American political culture that it is included as a factual question of basic political knowledge in the only major nationwide civics test given to American students.

The reader is therefore entitled to wonder why proposals for allowing noncitizens to vote merit much attention. The answer is that in recent years a concerted and growing effort has been made to gain acceptance for the idea that the United States should allow new immigrants to vote without becoming citizens.

It is tempting to dismiss the call for noncitizen voting as an idea that is not likely to get very far. After all, when such a proposal was introduced in the New York City Council, even the generally liberal editorial page of the *New York Times* endorsed Mayor Michael Bloomberg's view that voting is "the essence of citizenship" and that "Extending the most important benefits of citizenship to those who still hold their first allegiance to another country seems counterproductive."[2]

Dismissing this movement, however, would be a mistake. It has had some local success and, as a result, several municipalities in the United States currently allow noncitizens to vote in local elections. The best known of these is Takoma Park, Maryland, which introduced the practice in 1992. In Massachusetts the cities of Amherst, Cambridge, and Newton have approved measures to allow noncitizens to vote in local elections, but these ordinances require approval of the state legislature, which has not yet acted favorably on these proposals. Legislation to allow new immigrant noncitizens to vote has been introduced in a number of major cities, including Washington, D.C., San Francisco, and New York City, as well as in several states, such as Minnesota, Texas, and most recently Maine. Boulder, Colorado, recently introduced a measure to allow noncitizens to serve on city boards and commissions. And in City Heights, California, all residents are able to vote for members of the City Planning Commission, whether or not they are citizens.

TONING DOWN THE RHETORIC

Heated rhetoric and hyperbole accompany much of the advocacy around this issue. For instance, one advocate writes that noncitizen voting is "normatively *imperative* from the standpoint of fairness and ensuring our democratic institutions operate with the consent of the governed." Another asserts that not allowing noncitizens to vote is "a form of tyranny."[3]

Proponents repeatedly describe noncitizens as "disenfranchised." The problem with this emotionally loaded word is that it is inaccurate as a description of noncitizens who are not legally able to vote. *Webster's Dictionary* defines disenfranchised as: "to deprive of a franchise, of a legal right, or of some privilege or immunity; *especially:* to deprive of the right to vote." Of course, as it currently stands, noncitizens have no legal right to vote; that is precisely what advocates are trying to obtain for them. It follows, then, that they are not disenfranchised.

Another word one frequently encounters in connection with noncitizen voting is *discrimination*. The word has a customary meaning and hence a connotation. The word's primary meaning is defined in the Encarta dictionary as "treating people differently through prejudice: unfair treatment of one person or group, usually because of prejudice about race, ethnicity, age, religion, or gender." The word *distinguish* is probably a fairer, more accurate word that doesn't load the deck in favor of a particular normative framework. To discriminate is wrong, but to distinguish is to raise legitimate questions or to make analytic distinctions, without racial or ethnic prejudice.

A staple of some noncitizen voting advocates is the accusation that those who have qualms about their proposals are anti-immigrant or worse. It is difficult to assess the legitimacy of critics' arguments if they are caricatured and summarily dismissed as illegitimate. That accusation is a way of attempting to discredit both the argument and the person making it, and of avoiding debate. It reflects a view that there are not serious and legitimate concerns about the proposed policy of allowing noncitizens to vote. If one believes this, as advocates apparently do, then prejudice is a simple and readily available alternative explanation.

ARGUMENTS FOR NONCITIZEN VOTING

Advocates of noncitizen voting make many arguments for what would be a radical political change. These arguments seem reasonable. To advocates they are compelling. Yet a closer look suggests they are neither.

It is only fair, advocates say, since noncitizens already pay taxes. That argument assumes that noncitizens get nothing for their taxes and need the vote to compensate for that. However, the truth is that immigrants from most countries enjoy an immediate rise in their standard of living because of this country's advanced infrastructure—for example, hospitals, electricity, and communications.

Advocates assert that voting provides an ideal way for new immigrants to learn about their new country. Yes, but the fallacy of that argument is the assumption that there are not other, less damaging ways to do so. No law bars noncitizens from learning democracy in civic organizations or political parties. No law keeps them from joining unions or speaking out in public forums. Indeed, no law bars them from holding responsible positions within all these groups. In all of these many ways, legal residents can learn about their new country and its civic traditions. Voting is not the only means to do so, and may not even be the best, since it requires little knowledge of the issues or their context to just pull a lever.

What of representation? Isn't it bad for democracy and against democratic principles to have so many people unrepresented? That condition is temporary and easily remedied; *every* legal resident can apply for citizenship. Second, the very fact that advocates, and this includes some who hold public office, push noncitizen voting undercuts the argument that this group's interests are not represented. No smart politican ignores potential new supporters. This country is a republic, not a democracy. We depend on our representatives to consider diverse views. The views of legal noncitizen residents are no exception. The more such persons take advantage of the many opportunities to participate in our civic and political life, the more likely it is that their voices will be heard.

TAKING CITIZENSHIP SERIOUSLY

All of the proposals to offer noncitizens the right to vote—whether for local, state, or national elections; for legal residents or all residents; immediately or only after three months, six months, or longer—suffer from a major defect: few of the proposals require much, if any, preparation for exercising this responsibility.

If noncitizen voting is implemented, new noncitizen voters would not have to demonstrate "an understanding of the English language including the ability to read, write, and speak words in ordinary usage in the English language." They will not have to demonstrate "a knowledge and understanding of the fundamentals of the history and of the principles and form of government of the United States." They will not have to demonstrate that they are of "good moral character" by not, for example, having been convicted of a felony. They will not have to take an oath of allegiance to the United States and renounce allegiance to any foreign country. And they will not have to have been in residence in the United States for five years and for a minimum of thirty consecutive months before naturalization.[4]

These requirements are, of course, those that accompany the naturalization process by which legal immigrants become citizens. Abandoning all of them in order to give noncitizens the right to vote puts advocates in the paradoxical position of requiring far less for noncitizen than for citizen voting. Moreover, all of the citizenship requirements—knowing English, knowing about American history and government, having "good moral character," having spent an ample amount of time in the United States in order to better know and understand it, and being willing to commit yourself publicly to your new home while symbolically placing your allegiances to your old country in a position of lesser prominence—seem to be basic, appropriate, and legitimate requests to make of those who want to join the American community and shape its destiny through the vote.

Technically, even legal immigrants are nationals of their country of origin until they formally go through the naturalization process. Psychologically, it is unrealistic to expect that new immigrants will arrive with strong feelings of emotional attachment to the United States. And factually, it is incorrect to assume that an immigrant who has just arrived has anything more than the most rudimentary knowledge and experience of cultural and civic life here.

THE "OTHER COUNTRIES DO IT" BANDWAGON

Advocates of noncitizen voting tout the fact that other countries allow legal immigrants to vote in local elections. The implication is that "everyone is doing it," and the United States should join the bandwagon. The reality is far more complicated.

As it turns out, noncitizen voting rights do not follow one model, but many. Some states allow noncitizen voting only for a limited group of nationals, and not for aliens in general. Many states impose residency requirements. Countries like Portugal, Denmark, and the United Kingdom allow some noncitizens to vote in their national elections but impose nationality as well as residency requirements.

Advocates of noncitizen voting fail to inform their audiences that many of the countries impose residency requirements that are not significantly different from those required to become a full-fledged citizen in the United States. For example, in two of its nine cantons, Switzerland allows legal immigrants to vote in local elections, but only after being in residence there for five years. In Uruguay it's fifteen years. In Venezuela ten-year residents can vote in local elections. In the Netherlands and Chile it's five years. In Finland it's four years. In Norway, Portugal, and Korea it's three years. When the Federal Republic of Germany considered the issue of noncitizen voting, which did not pass, it required eight years of residence and a residence permit. It's true that Ireland allows noncitizens to vote in local elections after a residency of six months and New Zealand does so after a year, but these are the exceptions, not the rule.

The European Union (EU) has adopted policies to grant nationals of other member states the right to vote and run for office in local elections. Yet keep in mind that these exceptions to the rule are only for nationals of the EU, and then only for local and not regional or national elections. The right to automatically stand for office and vote in local elections is not granted to non-EU immigrants. Indeed, only five of the pre-2004 EU's fifteen states automatically give voting rights to non-EU citizens, and in several cases these are only for each other's citizens. Andre Blais and his colleagues studied the voting require-ments of sixty-three democratic countries and found that forty-eight of them (76 percent) restricted the right to vote to citizens.[5]

In short, everyone is not doing it, and those that are vary substantially in what they allow, when, and by whom. Of particular importance to the debate in the United States are two limitations imposed on noncitizen voting by those that allow some form of it: nationality and residence.

THE NONCITIZEN NONVOTING PROBLEM

Almost all of the myriad benefits claimed for noncitizen voting rest on a major assumption: that noncitizens will take advantage of the opportunity if it is presented. If, where noncitizen voting is allowed, the number of noncitizens who register to vote is small, or if those who do register don't actually vote, then almost all of the claimed benefits of noncitizen voting and for which so much would be sacrificed ring hollow indeed.

Noncitizen voting has been tried in a number of places that keep fairly good statistics. The results do not support claims that great benefits will follow from noncitizen voting because even where they are legally able to vote, noncitizens don't register in substantial numbers, and those who do register don't vote. In the 1994 and 1998 EU elections, for instance, the rates of noncitizen voting were 5 percent and 9 percent, respectively. Or, to put it another way, 95 percent and 91 percent of those who could vote did not.

We can look to Takoma Park, Maryland, where legal and illegal immigrants have been able to vote since an enabling law was passed in 1991. In 1995, 20 out of 195 (10 percent) of aliens who were registered actually voted; in 1997 the figure was 71 out of 287 (25 percent); in 1999 it was 41 out of 334 (12 percent); in 2001 it was 41 out of 475 (9 percent); in 2003 it was 14 out of 460 (3 per-cent); in 2005 only 23 noncitizens out of 460 registered voted (5 percent); and most recently, in 2007 only 10 registered noncitizens voted. In a special election also held in 2007 to fill a vacancy in one of Takoma Park's six voting wards, "officials took extra steps to get the word out. They mailed a notice, in Spanish and English, to every home. They sent a second notice to every registered voter," yet not one noncitizen voted.[6]

It is well to keep in mind that these Takoma Park figures only represent the number of noncitizens whom advocates were able to register and not the num-ber of noncitizens who could have registered but chose not to do so. Moreover, as the number of noncitizens that advocates were able to register went up, the number of noncitizen voters declined.

If the vote won't be used, how can it provide the many benefits that advocates allege? None of the long list of benefits claimed for allowing noncitizens to vote is possible if they don't actually vote.

Moreover, if immigrants and noncitizens won't use their vote, why should the American community incur the damage to its civic culture that would accompany the decision to allow noncitizens to vote? What would it mean to the legitimacy of elections and their results if a large infusion of noncitizens were to decide or even shape the outcome of an election or an issue? Would that result be accorded the same level of legitimacy that accrues to even controversial decisions? Imagine, as a thought experiment, the extra strains on election legitimacy if noncitizen voters had been instrumental in deciding the 2000 presidential election in Florida between Al Gore and George W. Bush in favor of either. The winner's supporters would have exalted, the loser's supporters would have seethed, and the legitimacy of the results would have surely been contested even more than they were.

NATURALIZATION AS AN ATTACHMENT PROCESS

Immigrants come to the United States for opportunity and freedom. Many give up a great deal in doing so. They leave behind the comfort of families, cultural familiarity, and a substantial part of their own personal experience. Their motivations for immigrating must obviously be very strong.

In making this trip, many immigrants already exhibit many of the psychological traits that make for success and help define American culture. They are willing to take chances and they are willing to work hard. They are determined to make a better place for themselves and their families, and are optimistic that they can do so. They are already, in many psychological respects, Americans.

Americans reasonably expect that new immigrants will, over time, become at home with the language, familiar with how the culture works, conversant with the political customs and practices through which the national community shapes its future, and develop an emotional attachment to their new county. The question for American policy is how can we best help immigrants acquire these basic building blocks of an American identity?

One vehicle to help accomplish this purpose is the naturalization process, one of the few socialization experiences that all immigrants who become citizens go through as a group. As such, it is an important, but poorly utilized, opportunity for a collective bonding experience.

Each of the five elements of the naturalization process—residency, good character, language facility, civics knowledge, and affirmation—are essential elements in helping immigrants become Americans. You cannot really learn about America without living here. You cannot understand or take part in America without understanding its language. And you cannot begin to form the more enduring attachments to the national community that you have asked to join without first taking an affirmative step in that direction. For all these reasons, naturalization as a requirement of citizenship and voting is not so much a series of hurdles to surmount, but an essential part of becoming American.

Noncitizen voting has a strong potential to weaken and degrade the process of becoming an American citizen. In a post 9/11 age, the United States still commits itself to becoming the home of millions of new immigrants every decade, and this means that facilitating the emotional attachment of these new immigrants is important and serious business. Anything that could damage or retard that process, as noncitizen voting is likely to do, should be avoided. In the end, we do immigrants—and this country—no favor (indeed, we are likely to do damage) by erasing the distinction between immigrants and citizens. The United States, like other democracies, requires members who are not only familiar with its customs, practices, and history, but also who care about and take responsibility for that community—its institutions, traditions, and fellow members. What else could be the basis for common purpose, given diverse cultural and ethnic perspectives, in these difficult, dangerous, and complex times?

RESOLVED, the government should require national service for all youth

PRO: Robert E. Litan

CON: Tod Lindberg

On April 21, 2009, President Barack Obama signed into law the Serve America Act. After being introduced in the House of Representatives on March 9, the bill had sailed through both houses, passing by a 321–105 vote in the House and a 79–19 vote in the Senate. In Washington that is about as close to bipartisan domestic policy making as it gets. Underscoring the bipartisan support for the bill, it was cosponsored by the liberal Democratic senator Ted Kennedy and the conservative Republican senator Orrin Hatch.

During the 2008 presidential campaign, national service was one of the few things upon which Democrat Barack Obama and Republican John McCain seemed to agree. Indeed, every recent president, Democrat and Republican alike, has called for and then signed into law legislation promoting national service.

In 1988 George H. W. Bush's campaign for the presidency was punctuated by frequent invocations of "A Thousand Points of Light," the many community organizations that Bush said "are spread like stars throughout the Nation, doing good." Right after his inauguration, Bush created the Office of National Service in the White House and launched the "Points of Light Foundation," which sought to promote voluntarism and community service. The following year he signed into law the National and Community Service Act, which authorized funding for the Points of Light Foundation and created the Commission on National and Community Service, which was charged, among other things, with promoting and funding service-learning in schools through Serve America (later renamed Learn and Serve America). In his last year in office Bush cooperated with legislators from both parties in fashioning the National Civilian Community Corps (NCCC).

The concept of national service also played a prominent part in Bill Clinton's successful run for the presidency in 1992. In his first year in office, President Clinton signed into law the National and Community Service Trust Act. The act established the Corporation for National and Community Service, which merged the newly created Commission on National and Community Service with an older government agency called ACTION. The latter dated from the Nixon administration and housed VISTA (Volunteers in Service to America), formed in 1964 as part of the Johnson administration's War on Poverty, as well as several volunteer programs for senior citizens that were created during the Nixon administration and that are known today as Senior Corps. At the heart of Clinton's 1993 law was the creation of AmeriCorps, a program that provides a small stipend, health care benefits, and college aid to individuals willing to give a year of their life to national service. As of 2009, more than half a million Americans had served in AmeriCorps.

Several months after the terrorist attacks of September 11, 2001, George W. Bush used his State of the Union address to call on Americans to volunteer in their communities for four thousand hours during their lifetimes and proposed a 50 percent expansion of AmeriCorps. The day after the address Bush created the USA Freedom Corps. Housed within the White House, its task was to serve as a "coordinating council" that would work to "strengthen our culture of service and help find opportunities for every American to start volunteering." The following year Bush signed into law the Strengthen AmeriCorps Program Act, which nearly doubled the number of AmeriCorps positions.

The Serve America Act that Obama signed into law in 2009 more than tripled the size of AmeriCorps, expanding the number of AmeriCorps jobs to 250,000 over the next eight years. In addition, the act created the Vet Corps, which was designed to enable military veterans to serve other veterans. Four other service corps were created as part of the expansion of AmeriCorps, including the Clean Energy Service Corps, which will train AmeriCorps workers to install solar panels and weatherize low-income homes, and the Healthy Futures Corps, which will use AmeriCorps volunteers to improve health care access for low-income communities. The act also included provisions that are aimed at increasing opportunities for unpaid volunteers.

The many national service and voluntarism acts passed during the past two decades are a testament to the allure that national service has for many Americans. But although both parties have embraced national service and voluntarism, there are sharp differences in the ways Republicans and Democrats typically approach the issue. Republicans have tended to prefer promoting unpaid, part-time voluntarism, such as the first President Bush's Points of

Light Foundation, whereas Democrats have generally opted for government-subsidized, full-time service programs on the model of AmeriCorps. Although Bush did back the expansion of AmeriCorps in 2003, four years later his administration proposed to slash funding for one of the AmeriCorps programs (AmeriCorps NCCC) from $27 million to $5 million and hoped to abolish it altogether. Even the 2009 Serve America Act was less bipartisan than it seemed. In the House all but one of the 104 dissenting votes were cast by Republicans (70 Republican House members voted in favor), and in the Senate all nineteen "no" votes were cast by Republicans (22 Republicans voted for it). Moreover, when the House voted on the version of the bill that the Senate had amended, only 26 Republicans voted in favor and 149 voted against, whereas Democrats approved it unanimously.

One of the provisions of the original House bill that came under severe attack from Republicans was section 6104, which created a "Congressional Commission on Civic Service." The bipartisan commission was tasked with exploring "whether a workable, fair and reasonable mandatory service requirement for all able young people could be developed and how such a requirement could be implemented in a manner that would strengthen the social fabric of the nation." The provision was dropped in the Senate version of the bill, so we don't know what the commission would have decided. But the following debate between Robert E. Litan and Tod Lindberg gives us a good idea of what the arguments on both sides would have been. Litan maintains that national service is not only workable and fair but would strengthen the nation in innumerable ways. Lindberg, on the other hand, sounds the alarm about the dangerous consequences of having government mandate service. Indeed, Lindberg suggests that even voluntary programs like AmeriCorps may well entail subtle forms of political coercion.

PRO: Robert E. Litan[1]

The United States has, from time to time, had a military draft, but has never had a permanent "universal service" requirement that could be fulfilled by military or nonmilitary service. This is understandable given our Constitution, which emphasizes rights more than responsibilities.

National public service youth programs, which are of relatively recent vintage, have been entirely voluntary. In 1961 President John F. Kennedy persuaded Congress to create and fund the Peace Corps, a voluntary program primarily for college graduates to promote America's image abroad and to give motivated young people opportunities to help lift peoples abroad out of poverty. President Bill Clinton extended the Peace Corps idea to addressing problems here at home by creating the AmeriCorps program, providing another way in which young Americans could volunteer for a limited time to serve their country. In 2002 President George W. Bush created USA Freedom Corps, which was designed to facilitate volunteer organizations, such as the Peace Corps and AmeriCorps, to place over two million Americans a year in some kind of formal national service (75,000 in full-time AmeriCorps programs). The president also called on every American to give two years over the course of their lives to some kind of service. Shortly after he became president, Barack Obama signed into law the Edward M. Kennedy Serve America Act, which abolished USA Freedom Corps but expands AmeriCorps and helps Americans find volunteer opportunities at a new Web site (www.serve.gov). President Obama also has proposed that students have access to additional federal support for college if they volunteer to participate in a recognized form of community service.

If these various volunteer programs (military and nonmilitary) seem to be working, why should policy makers now consider *requiring* some form of national service, either after high school or college graduation? Below I provide multiple answers, but first I outline how a universal service program might work.

UNIVERSAL SERVICE: A BRIEF GUIDE

Universal service would require qualified individuals to *choose,* at an appropriate time in their lives, whether to serve in the armed forces or in some eligible civilian capacity. Military experts agree that volunteers make better soldiers. Putting all four million of our high school graduates each year into some kind of military service would not only be highly expensive, but very likely would significantly weaken the morale and fighting ability of those who truly do want to be in the armed forces.

Since the armed service "option" is well understood, having been in place since the United States went to an all-volunteer army shortly after the Vietnam War, I concentrate here on the design of a civilian service program, outlining several of the more important issues and how they might be resolved. Doing so requires trading off costs against achieving various social objectives; accordingly, there is no single "best" program.

Who Should Serve?

I would propose to give every individual a choice of when to begin service, either upon graduating from high school or college (two or four year), but no later than some cutoff age (say twenty-five). Allowing individuals to delay serving until after they graduate college would deliver more value to the nation, since those individuals would have greater skills at that point in their lives. But creating a two (or three) tier program (counting community college graduation) would reduce the extent to which the civilian program would expose individuals to others from different socioeconomic, racial, and ethnic backgrounds who are performing their service at the same time. I would be willing to accept that cost, others might not.

What should be done with the currently excessive number of high school dropouts—by some estimates, as high as one-third of any age cohort? It will be especially difficult to integrate individuals with few skills, and some with criminal backgrounds, into a national service effort. My view is that these individuals nonetheless should not be exempted from national service, but instead be assigned to duties suitable to their skill level and that service be structured to motivate them to improve their lives, and ideally to return to complete high school.

How Long?

If the civilian option had parity with the military option, the length of the service would be two years. (Military duty also includes six years of follow-on inactive duty, subject to call back, which I ignore for the present purpose.) For reasons of cost, I would favor a shorter service period for civilian service: one year.

What Kinds of Service Would Qualify and How Much Should It Pay?

I favor a broad definition of eligible activities, to include any work that serves the national interest. Government-provided jobs should be a last resort, for individuals who have not found qualifying jobs on their own or through a wide range of nonprofit organizations that I would expect to be created if a national service program were in place. The rough model here is the method draft boards used to assign conscientious objectors to service—to medical assistant jobs in the services themselves or to other private or public sector jobs deemed to suit the national interest—but only with more imagination. Fortunately, programs like AmeriCorps and the Peace Corps have been around for years, and I would expect them to expand to provide a variety of jobs for those performing their national service.

Should Individuals Serving in Civilian Capacities Be Required to Serve Away from Home?

One of the potential purposes of a national service requirement is to expose youth to a broad range of individuals from other socioeconomic backgrounds, ethnic groups, and races, and to put them in settings where they must work and learn from, and ideally make friends with, each other. The armed services are the ideal in this regard. But it achieves this ideal primarily by requiring participants to live together, in dormitory (to be charitable) settings, away from home. A similar degree of "social blending" in civilian settings can probably only be achieved through similar away-from-home dormitory living arrangements.

A military-style program for civilian service would also be the most expensive. Clearly, it would cost far less if individuals were allowed to carry out their service in their home communities, and to live at home—while retaining the option to serve elsewhere, in jobs provided or approved by government. But the cost savings also carry the price of sacrificing some or much of the benefits of social blending.

One compromise would be to allow participants to live at home, but require that the form of service bring them into regular contact with others, from different backgrounds, principally with the beneficiaries of the programs. Think here of teachers' aides in schools, or retirement homes serving largely minority or low-income populations.

There is no perfect solution to this important issue of residence. It is one of many where trade-offs between cost and other objectives inevitably would have to be made.

THE CASE FOR UNIVERSAL SERVICE

I suspect that few Americans oppose offering youth the ability to *volunteer* for the kind of work that would count as civilian service. But many more will legitimately ask why the government should *compel* young people at some early point in their lives to perform such service, either military or nonmilitary. I believe there are several reasons for doing so, with full recognition that on grounds of principle—that the government should never force anyone to do anything against their will if they have done nothing "wrong"—others can and will disagree.

The strongest argument in favor of some form of mandatory service for a limited period, either after high school or college graduation, is one grounded in fundamental fairness. It is appropriate on grounds of efficiency and effectiveness that we now have an all-volunteer army. But it is hard to defend the fairness of a policy that encourages a select few young people, many from low-income families who otherwise might have limited employment prospects, to defend our nation from continuing national security threats, and thus possibly to bear the ultimate sacrifice (losing one's life), without asking all other youth to provide any service at all to the nation.

Second, universal service would establish firmly the notion that with rights come responsibilities. Admittedly, this has not been the prevailing ethic in this country, where the Constitution guarantees all citizens certain rights—free speech, due process of law, freedom from discrimination, voting, and so forth—without asking anything much of them in return beyond paying taxes and the occasional jury service. But why shouldn't citizens be required to give something to their country in exchange for the full range of rights to which citizenship entitles them?

Third, universal service could provide much-needed "social glue" to an American society that is growing increasingly diverse—by race, national origin, and religious preference—and where many young Americans from well-to-do families are able to grow up and go to school in hermetically sealed social environments. Twenty years ago, when the United States was much less diverse than it is now and is going to be, the editorial page of the *Wall Street Journal* (of all places) opined that mandatory service would constitute a "means for acculturation, acquainting young people with their fellow Americans of all different races, creeds, and economic backgrounds."[2] Those same words are as compelling today as they were when they were written. A civilian service program would help sensitize young men and women, at an especially impressionable point in their lives, to the concerns and experiences of others from very different backgrounds and give them an enduring appreciation of what life is really like "on the other side of the tracks."

Fourth, universal service could promote civic engagement, which has steadily declined over the past half-century.[3] Although some individuals who perform service for the required period of time may believe their civic responsibilities will thereby be discharged, many others are likely to develop an added appreciation for helping others that should change the way they lead the rest of their lives—for the better.

Finally, young people serving in a civilian capacity would help satisfy unmet social needs well beyond those associated with homeland security: improving the reading skills of tens of millions of Americans who cannot now read English at a high school level; improving blighted neighborhoods; and assisting in the provision of social, medical, and other services to the elderly and to low-income individuals and families.

COUNTERING THE OBJECTIONS

Admittedly, there are legitimate objections to imposing universal service. I believe they are overstated, however, and must, in any event, be balanced against the benefits of mandatory national service. I believe the benefits exceed the drawbacks, but recognize that others can and will more heavily weight the objections and come out with a different view.

First, there is the philosophical objection to any form of government compulsion and the temporary loss of liberty it entails. The response to this argument is that citizens also owe a responsibility to the society that nurtures them and provides the opportunities for them to live the good life.

Second, critics argue that the "work" performed by those serving is menial and not worth the benefits. Other critics contend that by drafting individuals to perform the jobs that are allowed and paying them at substandard wages, the program would exacerbate unemployment. These arguments are inconsistent with each other. If the program is crowding out better-paid workers, those serving are by definition doing valuable work. But I think a more fundamental response is that the work being performed—helping the disadvantaged, the weak, and the elderly, and helping to beautify the country—is not being done enough, or not being done well. In any event, the best protection against the "make work" criticism of universal service is to do what I suggested earlier: decentralize the design of jobs to nonprofits and other excellent government programs (such as AmeriCorps and the Peace Corps) to the maximum extent feasible.

Probably the most serious argument against universal service is its potential budgetary cost. Roughly four million students graduate from high school each year. A good benchmark for costs is to look at the AmeriCorps program. According to official figures from fiscal year 2001, the federal government spent roughly $10,000 annually per AmeriCorps volunteer in that year. Accounting for inflation since then, that cost would be roughly $13,000 today. A plausible assumption is that the states and the private sector added perhaps another $9,000 (a 1995 study by the Government Accounting Office [GAO] estimated that these costs amounted to about $5,500 per person, which accounting for inflation would put current costs at around $9,000). Given the limited enrollment in AmeriCorps—about 75,000 annually—its per person costs may be higher than those for a much larger universal program, which would be able to amortize overhead costs over a much larger population. On the other hand, not all of the AmeriCorps volunteers live in a dormitory setting. If participants in a universal civilian program were to be housed in a dorm-like arrangement, this would raise the cost relative to AmeriCorps.

Balancing these factors, I believe a plausible per person cost is $22,000, which if funded entirely by the federal government would bring the total annual gross cost of the program to about $88 billion annually. From this figure, it would be necessary to subtract the costs of those who already serve in AmeriCorps and the Peace Corps, as well as those high school students who now volunteer for the military. Taking these offsets into account should bring the annual net incremental cost of the program down to the range of $80 billion—admittedly a very large number, especially in light of projected federal deficits of roughly $1 trillion per year through 2020 (and steadily larger deficits thereafter).[4]

One fair way to reduce cost and thereby make the idea of universal service more palatable would be to implement the requirement initially as a lottery, much like the system that existed toward the end of the Vietnam War. Depending on the cutoff point, the program could be sized at any level that the political traffic could bear.

Those who dismiss a universal service requirement, regardless of size, as too costly must consider its benefits. In 1995 the GAO conducted a cost-benefit evaluation of three key AmeriCorps programs and found that they produced quantifiable monetary benefits of $1.68 to $2.58 for every dollar invested. These estimates did not count the nonquantifiable but very real benefits of strengthening local communities and fostering civic responsibility. Nor did they include the broader benefits of added social cohesion that a universal program would entail. On the other side of the ledger, it is possible that there would be diminishing returns to a much broader program than AmeriCorps, and thus at some enrollment level the costs of a universal requirement could exceed the benefits. But even this result—which is hardly assured—would not take account of the nonquantifiable social benefits of a broader program. The bottom line: even a universal service program as large as $80 billion a year likely would produce social benefits well in excess of that figure and thus represent a net economic and social gain for American society.

CONCLUSION

Universal service is an idea whose time may not be quite here, but it is coming. For reasons of fairness and social responsibility, societal needs and social cohesion, universal service is a compelling idea. If adopted, it could be one of the truly transformative federal initiatives of recent times, perhaps having an even greater impact on American society than the GI Bill, which helped educate much of the post–World War II generation. At the very least, universal service should be on the public agenda and actively debated.

CON: Tod Lindberg[1]

In a speech at Ohio State University in June 2002, President George W. Bush identified three reasons he hoped for the emergence of "a culture of service" in America: "service is important to your neighbors; service is important to your character; and service is important to your country." Bush was not making the case for a *mandatory* program, but the three reasons he listed parallel the reasons often cited in support of a program of compulsory national service: (1) the services performed would benefit the community, (2) service would be good for the people performing it, and (3) service would provide government with resources to undertake desirable activities.

The first of these reasons doesn't really amount to a case for a national service program. Rather, it makes a case for assisting those in need. As Bush elaborated, "in the shadow of our nation's prosperity, too many children grow up without love and guidance, too many women are abandoned and abused, too many men are addicted and illiterate, and too many elderly Americans live in loneliness." This is all true. The question then becomes: What is the most effective way to address these priorities? A compulsory national service program deserves consideration here, but such a program would not be the only possible approach. One would have to weigh the pros and cons of various policies in order to reach a conclusion about what might be best.

Likewise, agreement with the proposition that the government needs human resources to undertake important activities does not translate automatically into a case for national service. The government might compel or encourage service, but it also might simply hire more personnel or contract out to private companies for their provision. In addition, an examination of trade-offs would certainly be appropriate here: service is good for the country, but it is not the only thing that is good for the country. So, for example, is sound fiscal policy.

One would want to be sure that an expansive new national service program, potentially encompassing all eighteen- and nineteen-year-olds in the U.S. population—more than four million young people—would deliver benefits outweighing the considerable costs such a program would entail.

A more compelling justification for a national service program is the argument that service is good for the person who performs it. Service encourages people to think of others rather than just of themselves and responds to the need people feel for social connection. I agree that people need to think of others, not just themselves, and that there is a common longing for social connection. But I don't think a new program of mandatory national service, in which people must participate, can fulfill that need. Nor do I think that even a *voluntary* national service program, if undertaken on a large scale, can fulfill that need. For even a voluntary national service program runs the risk of acting to undermine the social connections it sets out to create.

The American tradition is rich in the provision of services to those in need. Americans give generously of themselves and their money—in 2006 Americans made some $295 billion in charitable contributions. Americans give much more generously than those who reside in comparably prosperous countries. In 1995, for instance, Americans gave about three and a half times more per person than the French and seven times more than Germans. Americans were 15 percent more likely to volunteer their time than the Dutch and 32 percent more likely than Germans.[2]

The American tradition is also rich in its respect for individual liberty. The nation was founded not on the principle that citizens owe something to government, but on the principle that government owes something to citizens—namely, respect for their "inalienable rights, among them life, liberty, and the pursuit of happiness," in the words of our Declaration of Independence. The framers of the U.S. Constitution sought to create a system that safeguarded American liberties from the twin dangers of too little government (anarchy) and too much government (tyranny).

Liberty means more than doing what you please, however. It also means respect for differences. The United States is a nation of law, but because of our constitutional protections and the American view of the rights that underlie them, the law goes only so far in telling people what they have to do. The opinions and preferences of people differ, and so do their circumstances. People will flourish best when they are free to assess their own circumstances (where they are) and desires (where they wish to be) and settle on a course of action accordingly (how best to get from where they are to where they wish to be). Government does not generally use the power of law to apply a one-size-fits-all approach to how people should live their lives.

We may all agree that giving to others, either our labor or our money (the fruit of our labor), is good not only for those who receive but also for the givers, because of the sense of social connection that giving fosters. We may even think everyone should want to feel that sense of social connection. We may think we know, in short, where people *wish to be* (whether they themselves know or not). But we are asking for serious trouble if we don't take into account the particular circumstances from which each person begins and respect their choices about how to get where they want to go.

Here is an example that I hope will illustrate the problem. In April 1998, Vice President Al Gore released his income tax return for the previous year. Total taxable income on the joint return for 1997 was $197,729. The Gores paid a total of $47,662 in federal taxes, but listed charitable contributions for the year at a grand total of $353.

Republicans pounced: Gore was a charity cheapskate. The Republican National Committee issued a press release. Conservative columnists snickered. Nor was the furor confined to conservative media. As Stacy Palmer of the *Chronicle of Philanthropy* was quoted in *USA Today,* "Certainly a lot of other Americans in that income bracket have found ways to dig deeper in their pockets." Or as Joe Breiteneicher of the Philanthropy Initiative, which advises wealthy people on giving, was quoted in the same story, "It's remarkable. It's hard not to give away more than $300 a year." The *New York Times* noted that the Gores' charitable contributions for 1997 amounted to "less than two-tenths of 1 percent of their income."

Shouldn't Al Gore—or, for that matter, anyone with taxable income of nearly $200,000—give more than $353 to charity? Most of us would say "yes." But a little context is in order here. Household income is not the same as great wealth. Gore was not nearly as wealthy as he was prominent. His May 1998 financial disclosure form listed assets between $770,000 and $870,000, all of them highly illiquid: a house and farm in Carthage, Tennessee; a house in Arlington, Virginia; and leasing rights to zinc mined on the Carthage property. Uncharacteristically for a person at Gore's income level, he owned no stocks or mutual fund shares and so missed out on the bull market of the 1990s.

True, in terms of income the Gores were very well-off compared to most Americans. But as it happens, the vice president also had some considerable expenses in 1997, some recurring, some unusual. Gore had three children then attending expensive private schools, one at college and two in high school. He incurred some $100,000 in legal bills in connection with a Justice Department investigation (which exonerated him) into Democratic campaign finance irregularities. To pay part of them, he borrowed money from a bank. In addition, in July 1997 Gore's oldest daughter was married in a ceremony followed by a reception for three hundred guests at the vice president's residence. In short, if one takes Gore's after-tax income of about $150,000 and starts subtracting, one can arrive at a negative number in a hurry.

It's also worth noting that 1997 was an aberration. The previous year, the Gores donated some $35,000 in royalties from a book by Mrs. Gore to charity. More broadly, one would be hard-pressed to argue that either Al Gore or Tipper Gore was somehow derelict in their contribution to public life, broadly construed. For example, in 1997 Tipper won the Hubert H. Humphrey Civil Rights Award for "selfless and devoted service to the cause of equality" as a result of her advocacy for the homeless and for the rights of the mentally ill. And, of course, Al would go on to share the Nobel Peace Prize for 2007 for his work on climate change.

I, for one, therefore cannot reach the conclusion that the Gores should have given more to charity in 1997 than they did (except on the grounds of political prudence). Should Gore have pulled one of his children out of private school for the year in order to have $20,000 to tithe? Should he have stiffed his lawyers or skimped on legal representation? Should he have encouraged his daughter and her beau to elope? What the Gore case shows, and the reason I have belabored it, is that the real-world circumstances of individuals or families do not always fit neatly with generalizations about what people "should" do.

This is not to deny that service is good. President Barack Obama may be right that "nothing is more powerful than when you enlist the skill and talent and passion of the American people on behalf of helping others."[3] But even if service is good, is the failure to serve always bad? Are we really so arrogant as to say to four million people a year that they must devote their lives and livelihoods for two years or so to the performance of national service? Including those who have sick relatives to care for or responsibilities for younger siblings; who are single parents or are struggling to support a family; who have a family business to learn to manage successfully in order to preserve the jobs of employees in turn trying to support their own families; who have opportunities unique to their youth and highly perishable, perhaps as athletes or performers? Well, maybe we are as arrogant as that. But in that case, we should set aside the justification that fulfilling a compulsory national service requirement is good for the individuals performing it, because in these cases it may not be.

Perhaps there can be a way for people in special circumstances to petition to be excused from participation. But seriously: an exemption for those who win football college scholarships en route to careers in the NFL? Will you have to produce your sick relative at the local office of the National Service Bureau to prove that you are not fabricating a need for care? Such an opt-out provision would have to be extraordinarily intrusive in order to ensure that it was not being abused by people who believe they have better opportunities elsewhere.

As well they may. We should not be too casual about what we give up with a compulsory national service system: in the vast majority of cases, two years of productive labor in the private sector economy. An employer hires people when doing so will enable the employer to make more money. A compulsory national service program will incur not only the large direct costs of supporting those performing their service as well as administration, supervision, and overhead, but also the opportunity cost of the forgone productive labor.

In addition to the macroeconomic loss, many individuals will feel this sense of lost opportunity acutely. They may be accordingly reluctant to think that supposed benefits of service in the form of a sense of social connection compensate for the loss.

The military draft is an example of a compulsory (though not universal) national service program. It is also an example of a bad public policy. There may be instances, such as world war, in which the survival of the nation depends on conscription, and so the alternative to a draft is a worse policy still. But in anything but such an extreme case, the ill effects far outweigh the benefits. The problem, put simply, is that too many draftees would rather be elsewhere. Their heart is not in it. They feel coerced, and in many cases they act accordingly: they comply (under threat of court-martial) with the requirements imposed upon them, and that's that. A compulsory national service program, while it would no doubt draw out the best in some people, would breed cynicism rather than a sense of social connection or idealism in others.

As it stands, the U.S. military is a large-scale *voluntary* service program, and that has something to teach us as well. There are many good reasons to join the Marine Corps. There are also many reasons one might not want to. For those who make the latter decision, there is a price to pay (admittedly, typically small): a deficiency in comparison with those who have worn the uniform, and therefore presumably have been willing to risk their lives in service to their country. It is not quite "bad" not to have served in uniform. But neither is it quite as "good" as having done so.

The question of service has become politicized by the state's promotion of it, even if it is not compulsory.

We have two different contexts here: that of a draft and that of an all-volunteer force. But the voluntariness is not dispositive. One cannot say that the compulsory system is politicized in a way that the voluntary system escapes. They are both politicized, in that they set a state standard for good service that implicitly invites the judgment that those who do not serve are wanting.

We can't do without a military. We therefore have to live with the problem of the distinction between those who served in it and those who did not. But we do not *need* a new large-scale civilian service program administered by the state, compulsory or not. We do not *need* to create a world in which the state says "service is good"—thereby implying that a failure to perform it according to the fashion prescribed by the state is bad.

Of course service is good. Americans obviously think so. The United States, as Everett Carl Ladd has demonstrated, has "an unusually expansive and demanding sense of citizenship." As individualists, Americans believe that "the citizen has responsibilities for the health and well-being of his society that extend far beyond his relationship with the state."[4] Hence, as we have seen, Americans volunteer and give at very high rates. That's because they want to. American individualism has always been grounded in a dense social fabric. We need connections with others in order to be fully ourselves.

However, the circumstances of different lives, or of a single life over the course of time, call forth different solutions to the problem of social connection. There is no political solution to this problem, only the possibility of its politicization by the state, transforming something that we do for fulfillment of our heartfelt desires into something we do to avoid the sanction that follows from not doing so. To the extent we are acting only to avoid sanction, we won't satisfy that longing anyway.

In the name of promoting social connection, proponents of national service propose, in effect, to colonize a part of the social field, the impulse to serve and give, that is constituted precisely by the felt need for social connection. I doubt that the state is up to the task. It is possible the result will be benign. It is also possible that young people (and others) will begin to approach service through the state in much the fashion of children approaching the vegetables on their plate: they will eat them because they think they have to.

The issue under consideration here is the coercive power of the state. There can be no doubt about state coercion in the case of a compulsory program. Making a program voluntary, however, does not end the question of coercion but rather transforms it into a question of the state's influence on a person making a decision about whether to serve—and whether that influence is undue. For most proponents of a program of national service, their most important premise is that it is a good thing for young people to serve. So it is, and not just for young people. Unfortunately, however, the sense of social connection that makes service a good thing for those performing it will be the first casualty of a program in which what is really moving people to serve is the coercive power or undue influence of the state.

19

RESOLVED, the federal government should ensure that no firm is too big to fail

PRO: Lawrence G. Baxter

CON: Terence M. Hynes

The United States of America is arguably the most capitalist nation in the world. Public opinion surveys show that Americans have an exceptionally strong belief in the virtues of the free enterprise system. Socialism has been a weaker political force in the United States than almost anywhere else in the world. Many Americans seem instinctively suspicious of government interventions in the marketplace. The tax burden in the United States is lower than in most other advanced industrial societies. Judged by a host of indicators, including child care, vacation time, sick leave, health care, and job training, the American welfare state is less generous to its citizens than the welfare states in other rich, Western nations.

Yet there is another side to the American political tradition. Americans' faith in markets and entrepreneurship coexists with a deep distrust of big business and greedy corporations. A Gallup survey administered in June 2009 found that only 16 percent of respondents said they had "a great deal" or "quite a lot" of confidence in big business. Contrary to what one might think, Americans' lack of confidence in big business is not a result of the spectacular collapse of large financial institutions and automobile companies in 2008 and 2009. A Gallup poll taken three years earlier, in June 2006, produced essentially identical results. Nor can lack of trust in big business be attributed to an undifferentiated cynicism about all aspects of American politics; 82 percent said they have a great deal or quite a lot of confidence in the military, 59 percent said the same about the police, and 51 percent expressed a high level of confidence in the presidency. And, more to the point, 67 percent said they have a great deal or quite a lot of confidence in small business. Scale clearly matters to most Americans.

Granted, distrust of big business is generally not as deep-seated as distrust of big government. Since 1965, Gallup has regularly asked people whether big business, big labor, or big government poses the "the biggest threat to the country in the future." Big government has always come out on top, though since the mid-1980s big business has invariably run a strong second. (Over the past fifteen years the number identifying labor as the biggest threat has not exceeded 10 percent.) Most Americans, however, don't see a need to choose between the dangers posed by big government and big business. Instead, they see big government and big business as allied forces. A Rasmussen Reports survey conducted in April 2009, for instance, found that seven in ten Americans, Republicans and Democrats alike, believed that big business and government worked together against the interests of consumers and investors.

The fear of concentrated economic power is nothing new in American politics. Among the most titanic political struggles in the first half of the nineteenth century was the war waged by President Andrew Jackson against the Second Bank of the United States. Although often described as a national bank, it was in fact a privately owned corporation in which the federal government's money was deposited. Jackson refused to recharter the bank because, as he explained in his farewell address, it was endowed with "immense capital and peculiar privileges," which enabled it to "exercise despotic sway" over the nation's economic life. Jackson took pride in having slain the "monster bank," but he warned his countrymen that "the spirit of monopoly . . . and exclusive privilege" had "struck their roots . . . deep in the soil" and it would require continual vigilance on the part of the citizenry to "check its further growth."

Jackson's warnings against monopoly power and special privileges resonated even more profoundly in the late nineteenth century as Americans came to grips with the development of industrial capitalism and the accompanying emergence of mammoth companies, such as the banking empire of J. P. Morgan, John D. Rockefeller's Standard Oil, and Carnegie Steel. The populist and progressive response to the growth of these gigantic corporations took two forms. One approach was to use big government to regulate big business, an argument made most forcefully by Herbert Croly in *The Promise of American Life* (1909). The underlying problem, from this perspective, was not the scale of corporations but an outdated Jeffersonian tradition that prevented Americans from embracing a central government that was powerful enough to regulate corporations, which were seen as an inevitable and even beneficial product of capitalism. The second approach was to "smash the trusts" and to restore a political economy premised upon competition among small or medium-sized producers, a view espoused forcefully by the lawyer (and future Supreme Court justice) Louis Brandeis. In his influential tract *Other People's Money and How the Bankers Use It* (1914), Brandeis dissected the "curse of bigness," particularly the concentration of wealth and power in the banking industry that forced citizens to approach the "money lords" on bended knee. Decentralizing economic power, in this view, was an essential step toward attaining "the New Freedom."

Is bigness a curse, as Brandeis had it? If so, should government take steps to lift the curse? Or do economies of scale make bigness a virtue, an essential part of a vibrant capitalist economy? These perennial questions of American political economy have taken on added urgency in light of the federal government's massive bailout of many of the nation's leading financial institutions. The bailout has prompted many observers, including Federal Reserve chairman Ben Bernanke and the previous two Fed chairmen Alan Greenspan and Paul Volcker,[1] to ask whether some firms are too big to fail, at least in a political sense if not in a strictly economic one. This important debate is joined by Lawrence G. Baxter and Terence Hynes. Baxter agrees with Brandeis that, particularly in the banking industry, bigness is a curse that requires aggressive government action. Hynes disagrees, suggesting instead that bigness is a virtue, an engine of economic prosperity as well as a marker of success in a competitive capitalist economy.

PRO: Lawrence G. Baxter

When a corporation becomes "too big to fail"—in other words, when we have to use government money in order to prevent it from going bankrupt because the consequences of bankruptcy would be too economically or socially disruptive—our economic and regulatory systems have failed. The result is a system of private enterprise subsidized by government and, ultimately, by taxpayers. This is contrary to the fundamental principles of our economy and ultimately is damaging to the general welfare. It is the responsibility of the federal government not to let this happen.

Throughout the spectacularly successful "American Century," large-scale economic enterprise was celebrated as a monument to the efficiency of twentieth-century modern capitalism. By the end of the century, American capitalism reigned triumphant over the alternatives of communism and socialism. Americans enjoyed a standard of living that rivaled those in the world's most affluent nations. The United States had integrated its economy earlier than any other large capitalist system and reaped the benefits of the efficiencies that large-scale production and distribution can supply. Big business seemed to be both the natural consequence and cause of the "economies of scale" and "scope" that we have been taught are the advantages of large firms and huge markets. Costs of production and distribution could be spread over larger operations and numbers of potential customers, reducing the unit cost of each product or service for everyone. Efficient credit markets—mortgages, credit cards, and home equity and student loans—combined to produce a vibrant market of consumers eager to enjoy the benefits of lower costs and easy availability.

It is little surprise, therefore, that we all grew to love "bigness." "Bigger is better" became our mantra. As part of this culture, ever-larger industrial combinations have generally been welcomed as an inevitable result of a mature and complex economy. An economy dominated by very large corporations offered so many benefits that by 1998 virtually every merger application was being approved by the federal government.[1] In 1984, just one generation ago but already a time when the banking industry was described as "highly concentrated," sixty-four banks held 50 percent of banking resources.[2] According to SNL Financial, by 2008 the top ten banks alone controlled almost 50 percent of the all deposits in the United States. In the broader economy, a steady increase in industrial concentration has been taking place since the early 1980s, partly in response to new technology developments, such as e-commerce, but primarily as a result of a wave of mergers and acquisitions.[3] In 1987 the Fortune 100 companies (i.e., the nation's one hundred largest by revenue) accounted for nearly 28 percent of the gross domestic product (GDP). By the end of 2008, they accounted for more than 46 percent.[4]

Over the last several decades, few people doubted the desirability of these developments. Arguments questioning whether corporations have become too large were dismissed as knee-jerk, shortsighted, or "too parochial for words."[5] CEOs impatiently dismissed questions about the size of their organizations, suggesting that only weaklings cannot manage great organizations.[6] Recent events, however, have shown that the consequences of economic gigantism can be ruinous. We cannot let public policy be dictated by chutzpah and self-interest. Evidence to support the contention that the benefits flowing from extremely large companies tend to outweigh the risks is never cited, nor is it likely to be because the evidence tends to suggest that the opposite is true.

The seemingly inexorable march toward behemoth businesses should be arrested for four reasons. First, assumptions about the benefits of bigness are shaky at best. Second, those who benefit from unrestrained bigness inflict its costs on society while often escaping the burden of these costs. Third, the laissez-faire policy permitting unrestrained corporate growth creates a taxpayer-financed category of banking, commercial and industrial "zombies" that are neither profitable nor subject to a market discipline that would otherwise ensure their demise. Finally, unrestrained growth in corporate power has the potential to undermine democracy. Let us examine each of these concerns in turn.

First, bigger is not always better, even for the businesses concerned. Amidst the prosperity of a consumer society, the idolatry of bigness—E. F. Schumacher famously called it "gigantism" and his followers have applied the term "macrophilia"—blinded us to its economic and social costs.[7] The costs to the businesses themselves are often underestimated, sometimes even concealed. These are known as "diseconomies of scale," and they are generated by the increasing inefficiencies incurred as organizations become very large. It is true that technology, communications, and management techniques have all improved considerably, enabling better management across larger scale and distance and lower unit costs across broader markets. But the costs associated with complexity of scale can outrun benefits. Extremely large banks, for example, do not display obvious advantages in profitability over their smaller counterparts; indeed, their performance has on average declined when they exceeded a certain size.[8]

There are reasons why efficiency declines rather than increases as firms grow beyond a certain size. Most of these extremely large companies are the products of huge mergers between companies that have themselves undergone a process of rapid growth through recent prior mergers. Amidst the hasty "due diligence" processes that precede merger announcements, savings are overestimated and costs are underestimated. Employees are displaced, herded through hasty "cultural transformations" to acclimate them to the new owner, and sidetracked with all the technical and operational requirements for making their new, combined company work. Valuable employees are lured away by competitors. Old technology systems are often inadequate for the new scale of operations, and investment in new technology is underestimated or even avoided. Frustrated customers tax the resources of service departments as they try to get garbled records corrected. Corporate executives who were once capable in smaller roles are often unable to manage much larger ones. Perhaps most important of all, the opportunities for failure increase exponentially with the complexity of the new combination, particularly if the combination is rapid as is required by the cost savings promised upon announcement of the merger. Larger companies necessarily have greater coordination needs than their predecessors. New departments, more widespread locations, different products and customer demographics, and larger and more widespread employee groups—all have to be coordinated. These new frontiers and points of intersection within the newly combined company each create new opportunities for something to go wrong.

So the assumption that bigness is an inherent economic virtue is highly questionable. Yet this alone would not justify creating government policies to restrict corporate growth. After all, one of the unchallenged virtues of the capitalist system is market discipline. One might expect that the share prices of increasingly inefficient organizations would decline—and this does indeed occur. Shareholders can thus be left to police the size of firms.

The costs of excessively large businesses, however, are reflected in more than just declining values for the corporations in question. As the great financial crisis of 2007–2009 sharply demonstrated, when very large organizations collapse or threaten to fail the costs are not absorbed by shareholders alone but are instead borne by everyone. Market mechanisms have proven inadequate to confine the costs of failure to those who have caused it.

Let me be concrete. During 2008 and 2009 we witnessed the dramatic collapse of major organizations, all once celebrated for their scale and efficiency. General Motors, Chrysler, AIG, Bear Stearns, Lehman Brothers, and Wachovia are the best-known American examples. Other countries have their own examples as well: for instance, the giant United Kingdom mortgage company, Northern Rock. In Iceland, the entire economic and financial system imploded when highly leveraged and speculative deals between Icelandic and European banks went sour.

Every one of these failures has required massive governmental support in order to prevent further, more damaging collapse by other companies and industries. In many cases the failing institutions have been forced by the government to merge, with substantial government assistance, into yet larger organizations, creating even greater vulnerability for taxpayers and other organizations connected to the "white knights" that "rescued" the failing companies. In other words, the costs of the failure of these institutions have been externalized to the public in the form of taxpayer-backed government assistance. As cynics have put it, we have privatized the profits while socializing the risks.

Behemoth institutions have become exempt from the ordinary processes of bankruptcy. The cost to the government and taxpayers of liquidating such institutions is either so great or so unforeseeable that they have been propped up with government loans on terms no private source of capital could match. The reason given for adopting this course of action rather than simply letting the normal process of bankruptcy take its course is that the failure of such institutions would have serious systemic consequences for other institutions and for the economic system as a whole. For instance, when Lehman Brothers was allowed to fail in September 2008 there were instant global and systemic effects: credit dried up overnight, precipitating the very worst moments of the great recession. Policy makers learned that Lehman Brothers was too big to fail.

What is scary is that the list of organizations considered too big to fail is not a short one. In 2004 two leading central bankers published a book warning of the dangers of this growing list: in 1983 the list contained the eleven largest U.S. banks; by 2001 the list included the top twenty.[9] Another 2004 estimate placed that number considerably higher, at thirty-four.[10]

So we are left with a growing list of companies that are too big to fail and probably too big to manage. In other words, our modern economy is becoming populated by a growing portfolio of what many commentators have called "zombie" organizations: too big to fail and too big to make profits for shareholders (as opposed to their highly paid executives). This situation is a far cry from any notion of free enterprise to be found in economics textbooks.

Failing behemoths pose not only an economic problem but a political one. The political influence of large corporations is always large, but their political pressure becomes even more irresistible when politicians are worried that a corporation's economic collapse will reverberate through the economy. They are also able to exercise a disproportionate influence on public perceptions and political behavior because they have a huge reservoir of funds for marketing and political contributions and because the leaders of large corporations and the lobbyists they hire are very influential in the formulation of public policy.

Charles E. Lindblom described this phenomenon as the "privileged position of business."[11]

Many very large companies make greater political contributions than are made by entire industries.[12] Some of the biggest political contributors were the same companies that received massive government assistance to bail them out: General Motors, Chrysler, Citigroup, Bank of America, and Goldman Sachs.[13] A good deal of the money these companies spend on lobbying is meant to influence perceptions about the performance of and risks generated by such organizations.

To sum up, when corporations reach a certain size they negatively affect society in ways that will not be rectified or regulated by market discipline alone. They externalize the costs of their inefficiencies onto the taxpayer. They tend to evolve into the walking dead, adding no net value to the commonweal yet drawing support from it. And they subvert the democratic process.

What can be done about this?

The defenders of "large at whatever cost" offer a potpourri of responses: blame past business decisions ("we won't do it again"); lament past economic policies and government action for this state of affairs ("mistakes were made"); and claim that existing laws provide adequate protection ("no need to change anything this time").

A more sophisticated response is to classify "systemically significant" corporations, particularly those with extensive financial interconnections, into a group that can be separately regulated and, if necessary, liquidated. The real problem, it is argued, is "interconnectedness": governments only bail out firms like Citigroup and AIG because they are so "interconnected" with other institutions. The CEO of Deutsche Bank, one of the few very large banks to survive (only just) the 2008–2009 crisis without a government bailout, has expressed support for the creation of "buffers" that highly "interconnected" institutions would need to have, in the form of additional capital and liquidity reserves, in order to cope with situations where counterparties (i.e., the other parties to the failing institution's contracts) run into difficulties.[14]

However, there is something puzzling about this argument: it appears to deny the point of having a large organization in the first place, namely to extend capital efficiently across a larger base. Banks of all sizes are heavily exposed ("interconnected") with all the others, whether by virtue of participation in the global payments systems, through lending partnerships called loan syndications, or through joint investment underwriting ventures. Interconnectedness necessarily increases with the size and complexity of the financial institution, but it is present with even small institutions. Indeed, the first prominent example of a systemic risk failure—one that has even lent its name to systemic risk as a doctrine—was a relatively small German bank called Bank

Herstatt, which failed in 1974. If buffers are to be increased as the size of the financial institution increases, then the cost of business for those institutions is also going to be increased. As we will see later, this is indeed a promising method of preventing the growth of outsized corporations, but it has consequences that large corporations will not like.

Official versions of this "buffer" policy come in the form of proposals for "systemic risk" or "macroprudential" regulation. Governments around the world, including the United States, have proposed a framework in which certain institutions that are considered "systemically significant" can be so designated by the government, subjected to stricter regulatory requirements (including higher minimum capital reserve requirements), and be placed into liquidation where their failure is possible and the government believes the economy needs protection. In effect, the solution proposed is to designate firms and companies that are too big to fail for special treatment by regulators.

The proposed solution, however, carries its own difficulties. In the first place, it would create a special class of organization that is less profitable (because of its higher capital requirements) and specially protected (because it is too big to fail). Second, as the failure of General Motors and Chrysler demonstrated, a resolution that draws government into ongoing support of private enterprise is something with which we historically have been very uncomfortable. The line between government and private enterprise becomes compromised, and this prompts appropriate concerns about the past failures of statist policies in other countries.

The best way to protect the public from the risk of subsidized industries that start to reduce rather than add to overall welfare is simply to prevent them from evolving to this point in the first place. The government has a responsibility to prevent the growth of corporations to the point where they become too big to fail. This does not mean that government should start tearing apart every large company. Rather, government should not allow a company to *get larger* if to do so would significantly increase the risk that the company will become too big to fail. And where a company has become so large that it needs government assistance in order to stay alive, the government has the responsibility to do what any large private investor would do—impose efficient break-up conditions on the company as a price for the receipt of public funds or other support. In other words, companies on life support, too big to be seized outright, should be dismantled into smaller, more self-sufficient units.

The federal government also has extensive powers to prevent excessive growth. Key regulatory powers are available over banks, which operate at the core of the economy and without the support of which other companies cannot grow. The government is able to impose far-reaching conditions on troubled banks and can even seize them outright. Banks can be prevented from providing finance for mergers that might jeopardize the economic system. The government can also apply supervisory and enforcement powers, as well as adjust the level of deposit insurance premiums that banks pay, to ensure that the risks being undertaken are properly priced and banks are being properly and safely managed. An important proposal before Congress is to permit size-sensitive additional regulation over all financial institutions, and this power would present another tool for averting dangerous growth by large banks. It is all a question of how vigilant the government wants to be.

Through the medium of financial service regulation it is possible to impose brakes on the unrestrained growth of dangerous corporations, both financial and nonfinancial. The great financial crash of 2008 and 2009 has demonstrated that the financial system is central to the health of the overall economic system, both domestically and globally. We cannot afford to neglect corporate developments that imperil the welfare of everyone, and we should demand that government apply a policy that would place behemoth corporations on the defensive, so that the burden remains on them to prove why they should be allowed to continue growing when that growth exposes taxpayers and the general public to the harms of corporate implosion.

CON: Terence M. Hynes[1]

Entrepreneurship and risk taking are the lifeblood of capitalism. A free market economy rewards innovation and prudent investment, while punishing excessive risk and ill-advised business decisions. America's economic history is the story of entrepreneurs, from Henry Ford and Howard Hughes to Bill Gates and Donald Trump, whose creativity and willingness to take risks built highly successful businesses (albeit with some setbacks along the way). Today, American companies such as Ford and General Motors (GM), Microsoft and Dell, and Citicorp and Morgan Stanley are among the global leaders in their respective industries. By allowing capitalism to flourish, the United States has enjoyed unparalleled economic growth and prosperity during the past century.

Nevertheless, the economic turmoil of the past two years has caused some policy makers, academics, and media pundits to suggest that government ought to restrict—or prohibit outright—the growth of such corporate giants. In the wake of government bailouts of automakers GM and Chrysler, and financial institutions such as Bank of America and AIG, critics argue that any firm deemed by the government to be "too big to fail" is, in reality, "too big to exist" because the potential collapse of such a firm poses too great a threat to the broader economy. The recent crisis has also spurred a revival of the populist sentiment that "big business" is bad for America because large corporations wield too much economic and political clout. The proposed solution to these perceived problems is to dismantle America's corporate giants and to impose limitations on corporate growth to prevent their reemergence.[2]

Such draconian action would be fundamentally inconsistent with the capitalist ideology that is at the heart of America's economic system. More than a century of experience has proven that the marketplace—not government fiat—is the best arbiter of the optimum size and scope of private businesses. More importantly, breaking up America's largest companies will not make us more financially secure or insulate the United States from future economic turmoil. To the contrary, government-imposed limitations on the size of U.S. companies will hamstring their ability to compete successfully in an increasingly global economy and, ultimately, reduce rather than enhance America's economic growth and prosperity.

Consider, for example, the "credit crisis" of 2008–2009 that led the federal government to provide billions of dollars in assistance to the nation's largest banks and financial services firms. Placing artificial limitations on the size of financial institutions would not effectively address the conditions that precipitated the crisis. Indeed, the size of those firms was not the cause of the crisis—rather, it came about as a result of a confluence of circumstances.

RISKY MORTGAGE LENDING PRACTICES

The credit crisis of 2008–2009 had its genesis in the housing boom of the 1990s. As home prices soared, mortgage lenders devised new products, including "adjustable rate" mortgages, loans with large deferred "balloon payments," and "subprime" mortgages, which afforded families the opportunity to realize their dream of home ownership or to buy bigger, more expensive houses. In some instances, unscrupulous lenders approved loans for borrowers whose ability to pay was, at best, questionable. The mortgage companies then sold those loans to larger banks and investment firms (thereby passing off the risk associated with loans they had originated). Wall Street firms developed and traded "derivative" securities backed by pools of those high-risk loans, but failed to maintain sufficient capital reserves to protect against potential losses on such precarious investments. The risks inherent in making loans based upon increasingly weaker credit standards were obscured for a time by the continued rise in home values and growing short-term profits. But when the housing bubble (inevitably) burst and housing prices fell, the nation's largest financial institutions were left with billions of dollars in "toxic" assets on their balance sheets. This, in turn, severely impaired their access to funds and forced them to curtail their lending, bringing the credit markets to a grinding halt and triggering government intervention.

INTERCONNECTEDNESS OF MAJOR FINANCIAL INSTITUTIONS

The phrase *too big to fail* is somewhat of a misnomer. The decision by government to assist a large bank or other corporation in distress is not motivated solely by a desire to rescue that particular firm from financial ruin. Rather, government intervenes when the failure of one firm (or group of firms) could have harmful "spillover" effects on other firms and the overall economy.[3] As Federal Reserve Chairman Ben S. Bernanke recently explained:

> Financial institutions are systemically important if the failure of the firm to meet its obligations to creditors and customers would have significant adverse consequences for the financial system and the broader economy. At any point in time, the systemic importance of an individual firm depends on a wide range of factors.... *But size is far from the only relevant consideration.* The impact of a firm's financial distress depends also on the degree to which it is interconnected, either receiving funding from, or providing funding to, other potentially systemically important firms as well as on whether it performs crucial services that cannot easily or quickly be executed by other financial institutions.[4] (emphasis added)

In other words, the federal government chose to bail out Citicorp and AIG not because they were too *big* to fail, but because they were so *interconnected* with other financial institutions, both in the United States and abroad, that the government feared that their collapse could have serious consequences for the national (and global) economy. The Treasury Department has acknowledged that, prior to the recent crisis, it did not fully appreciate the degree to which major financial institutions rely upon one another as sources of short-term borrowing and liquidity.[5] Indeed, the government chose not to rescue an early victim of the crisis, Lehman Brothers. However, Lehman's default on its obligations strained the ability of other institutions to provide funds to one another. As conditions worsened, the government feared a broad "meltdown" of the nation's major banks and injected billions of dollars to stabilize the financial system. The Obama administration has likewise claimed that the virtual "takeover" of GM by the federal government was necessary to prevent massive spillover effects on GM's suppliers and other companies that do business with the automotive industry.

PRIOR GOVERNMENT POLICIES CREATED AN EXPECTATION OF A BAILOUT

A major contributing factor to the credit crisis of 2008–2009 was the widely held perception, based upon prior government policies and actions, that the nation's largest financial and industrial firms will simply not be allowed to fail. Notwithstanding America's belief in a free market economy, the federal government has, on a number of occasions, intervened to prevent the failure of a major company. For example, in 1976 Congress nationalized the Penn Central and other bankrupt railroads in order to prevent an interruption in rail service to the industrial Northeast. In 1979 the government extended $1.5 billion in loan guarantees to Chrysler Corporation, fearing the potential spillover effects of a Chrysler failure on the nation's economy. And in 1984 the Federal Reserve rescued Continental Illinois Bank when its strategy of investing heavily in loans to U.S. energy companies backfired in the wake of a severe downturn in the oil and gas industry.

Although these (and other) government bailouts were perceived at the time as serving the public interest, they established a precedent that gave rise to today's "too big to fail" dilemma.[6] The government's past willingness to prop up companies whose failure might ripple through the nation's economy created an expectation that such assistance would be forthcoming in response to future crises. This, in turn, weakened the incentive of shareholders and creditors to monitor and restrain the level of risk undertaken by financial institutions that are perceived to be "too big to fail." As recent events have shown, the absence of such market discipline, combined with executive compensation schemes that reward short-term profitability rather than longer-term performance, created strong incentives for management to pursue risky (but potentially more profitable) business strategies.

REGULATE BEHAVIOR, NOT SIZE

Given the circumstances described above, a reduction in the *size* of the financial firms involved in the credit crisis of 2008–2009 would have made little difference. The root cause of the crisis was the *behavior* of mortgage lenders (both large and small) seeking to cash in on the housing boom by making increasingly risky loans, of Wall Street firms that issued and traded in "derivative" securities backed only by portfolios of those risky loans, and of shareholders and creditors who failed to restrain such behavior. If Wall Street's ten largest institutions had, instead, consisted of thirty smaller firms, and those firms had engaged in the same pattern of behavior, the result would have been the same, given the extent of the risks being taken, the interconnectedness of all major financial institutions, and the expectation of a government rescue created by prior bailouts. Indeed, government intervention involving a greater number of (smaller) distressed firms could well have been even more complex and expensive.

The "too big to fail" problem cannot be solved by dismantling America's largest financial and industrial firms, or by placing artificial limits on their size.[7] The Obama administration—which has not hesitated to propose intrusive regulatory solutions to other problems (e.g., health care reform)—recognizes that the size of the nation's corporate giants is not the problem. Instead, an effective response must seek to curtail the types of excessively risky behavior that gave rise to the credit crisis, and to restore the market discipline that has been undermined by the perception that government will inevitably rescue large corporations from the consequences of high-risk business strategies. The financial reforms recently proposed by the administration correctly focus on those objectives by, among other things:

- Increasing minimum capital reserve requirements for "systemically important" financial firms (i.e., those whose failure could have cascading effects on the economy).

- Requiring firms that issue high-risk "derivatives" to retain a financial interest in those securities, so that they continue to bear a portion of the risk associated with such investments.

- Giving the Treasury Department new authority to take over any systemically important firm (including nonbanks such as AIG) at an early stage, before its financial problems can threaten interconnected firms or the overall economy.

- Giving the Federal Reserve new authority to regulate the interbank payment, clearing, and settlement processes that create the "interconnectedness" among major financial firms.

- Imposing stricter reporting requirements on systemically important firms to increase the transparency of their operations, enhance the ability of shareholders and creditors to monitor their investments, and restore market discipline of excessive risk taking.[8]

Equally important, the Obama administration has signaled that government will not, in the future, routinely rescue investors and creditors from the economic consequences of the failure, of major financial institutions. Federal Reserve Chairman Bernanke recently told Congress that "[u]nless countervailing steps are taken, the belief by market participants that a particular firm is too big to fail, and that the shareholders and creditors of the firm may be partially or fully protected from the consequences of a failure, . . . materially weakens the incentive of shareholders and creditors of the firm to restrain the firm's risk taking." According to Bernanke, requiring firms that issue derivative securities to retain a financial stake in such securities, increasing big firm transparency, and empowering government to seize and dismantle distressed major financial institutions will spur shareholders and creditors to discourage high-risk behavior by such firms.[9] In urging passage of those reforms, President Barack Obama likewise stated that "[w]e are called upon to recognize that the free market is the most powerful generative force for our prosperity—but it is not a free license to ignore the consequences of our actions."[10]

Overcoming the expectation that failing corporate giants will inevitably be rescued is perhaps the most important step that government can take to restore the proper functioning of a free market economy in America. Every government bailout distorts the natural working of the market by shielding the rescued firm from the consequences of its bad business decisions. Government bailouts also raise fundamental questions of fairness—should public funds be used to assist some firms, but not others? During the course of the credit crisis of 2008–2009, the federal government provided billions of dollars to enable several of the largest financial firms to survive, while the Federal Deposit Insurance Corporation (FDIC) seized and liquidated numerous smaller banks that had become insolvent. The bailout of GM enabled that firm to reduce its debt burden and restructure its operations quickly, without going through lengthy bankruptcy proceedings.[11] The financial resources and political clout brought to bear on GM's behalf conferred on it a substantial advantage over its primary competitor, Ford Motor Company, which has attempted to overcome similar economic challenges without government assistance. Indeed, the 61 percent ownership stake in GM acquired by the federal government as a result of the bailout invites concern that future government policies affecting the automotive industry might be influenced by the government's pecuniary interest in GM. Although one cannot practicably assert that government should never come to the aid of a distressed private firm under any circumstances, both sound economic policy and fundamental fairness support the view that such interventions should be few and far between.

A knee-jerk government response to the recent financial crisis that places artificial limits on the size of financial and industrial companies will not enhance America's prosperity. By stunting the natural growth of firms, society will forfeit the economies of scale and scope that lead to greater efficiency and reduce the cost of products and services. For example, GM markets vehicles under multiple brand names (such as Cadillac, Chevrolet, Buick, and GMC). Each of those divisions benefits from GM's ability to purchase steel and other components, and to conduct research and development (e.g., designing more fuel-efficient engines) for all of its divisions on a collective basis. If government were to decree that GM (or Ford) is too big to fail and must be broken into separate companies based on brand names, each division would be required to perform those functions for itself. The result would be higher costs and higher vehicle prices for consumers.

Placing an arbitrary cap on the assets or revenues of large companies would not make such firms less likely to fail. To the contrary, such regulation could very well sow the seeds of their demise. A large firm with diversified business activities is generally better equipped to survive an economic downturn than an entity with lower revenues derived from a single line of business. Moreover, in a capitalist economy, investors seek those opportunities that offer the greatest return on investment. A firm that is at or near a government-imposed "cap" on assets or revenues has less "upside" potential than a smaller firm that is not constrained by such regulations. Arbitrary limits on corporate growth would encourage investors to sell their shares in firms that had reached the maximum size permitted by government, thereby impairing the access of those firms to capital. Such stagnation would impair the ability of large companies to succeed in the highly competitive global economy and could very well increase the frequency of large corporate failures.

The argument that America's largest corporations should be dismantled because they possess too much economic and political power is unpersuasive. The U.S. antitrust laws do not outlaw size, per se. Rather, those statutes condemn the abuse of market power by such means as price fixing, predatory conduct, and agreements not to compete.[12] America's financial institutions, and industrial companies like GM and Chrysler, do not possess (much less have the ability to abuse) excessive market power. To the contrary, they face intense competition both domestically and abroad—indeed, the root cause of the U.S. automotive industry's economic problems is a steady loss of market share to foreign competitors like Toyota, whose vehicles are increasingly preferred by consumers. Moreover, the Riegle-Neal Banking Act of 1994 already prohibits any bank merger that would result in a single firm holding more than 10 percent of U.S. bank deposits.[13]

The assertion that America's big corporations possess too much political clout reprises the decades-old debate regarding the influence of "special interests" in Washington. The reality is that the financial sector—as well as the health care industry, the energy industry, agricultural interests, and labor unions—are major stakeholders in the U.S. economy. Like those other interest groups, the financial services industry strongly asserts its views with respect to economic policy decisions that may affect it. But the size of the individual firms comprising that industry is not the source of its political power—indeed, collective lobbying by the nation's ten largest banks would be no less effective if they consisted instead of thirty smaller banks acting in concert. Ultimately, the best way to curtail improper influence on the policy making process is to place strict limits on lobbying and campaign contributions, and to elect leaders who possess the courage and integrity to place the public interest first.

RESOLVED, Congress should pass the War Powers Consultation Act

PRO: Nancy Kassop

CON: William G. Howell

To whom belong the powers of war and peace? This question has divided Americans from almost the moment the Constitution was ratified. In 1793 Alexander Hamilton and James Madison, erstwhile allies and collaborators, argued bitterly over whether the president or Congress had the power to declare neutrality. A century later, Sens. John Spooner and Augustus Bacon clashed in a famous debate triggered by President Theodore Roosevelt's foreign policy, with Spooner taking the Hamiltonian ground that "the conduct of our foreign relations is vested by the Constitution in the President" and Bacon adopting the Madisonian position that "Congress and not the President is supreme under the Constitution in the control of foreign affairs." The courts have generally refrained from entering this dispute, judging it to be a "political question" best left to the president and Congress. Judges have thus implicitly agreed with the political scientist Edward S. Corwin that "the Constitution . . . is an invitation to struggle for the privilege of directing American foreign policy."

Article I, Section 8 of the Constitution gives Congress the power to "declare War," to "raise and support Armies," and to "provide and maintain a Navy," while Article II makes the president "the Commander in Chief" and identifies him as the person to "receive Ambassadors and other public Ministers." Treaties are to be made by the president, but with the "Advice and Consent of the Senate," and they go into effect only if two-thirds of senators approve. The framers of the Constitution thus divided powers that in eighteenth-century England were vested almost exclusively in the monarch.

The framers may have intended that control over foreign and military policy be a "joint possession," as Hamilton expressed it in *Federalist* No. 75, but since World War II the powers of war and peace have flowed increasingly toward the executive branch. When the president cannot get a treaty through the Senate, he can fall back on executive agreements in which the Senate plays no role. Congress has not declared war since December 11, 1941, when it declared war on Germany and Italy. Major wars in Korea, Vietnam, and Iraq were all initiated and ended by presidents. Scores of smaller military actions have been taken by presidents in recent years without congressional authorization, including sending troops into Grenada, Panama, Haiti, Somalia, and Bosnia.

Congress has periodically tried to reassert its constitutional powers, most notably in the 1973 War Powers Resolution (WPR), which attempted to limit the president's power to send troops to fight abroad. Passed over Richard Nixon's veto, the WPR requires the president to report to Congress within forty-eight hours of committing troops to combat, and mandates that American troops be brought home after sixty days if Congress has not "declared a war or . . . enacted a specific authorization for such use."

Every president since Nixon has insisted that the WPR unconstitutionally constrains executive power, and each president has refused to comply fully with the law's requirements. The resolution has also been criticized by those who believe that giving the president carte blanche to send troops anywhere in the world, even if only for sixty days, represents an unconstitutional delegation of congressional war power to the president. In recent years, both Clinton and Bush administration officials have embraced the logic of these critics' position to support assertions of presidential control. "The structure of the War Powers Resolution," Clinton's lawyers explained to congressional Republicans in 1994 in defending the administration's intervention in Haiti, "recognizes and presupposes the unilateral Presidential authority to deploy armed forces 'into hostilities or into situations where imminent involvement in hostilities is clearly indicated by the circumstances.'" The ineffectiveness of the WPR in constraining the president or in promoting cooperation between the legislative and executive branches has spurred efforts to find alternative processes that might work better.

One such recent proposal is the War Powers Consultation Act (WPCA) of 2009, which emerged out of the work of a bipartisan commission chaired by two former secretaries of state, Warren Christopher and James Baker III. The commission recommended that the "impractical and ineffective" WPR be repealed and replaced by the WPCA, which would "codify the norm of consultation" between the president and Congress. Nancy Kassop makes the case for the WPCA, arguing that while not perfect, it would help Congress to check executive aggrandizement in military and foreign policy making. William G. Howell counters that the WPCA would be just as ineffective and undesirable as the WPR has been.

PRO: Nancy Kassop

O n July 8, 2008, the National War Powers Commission released its report calling for the repeal of the War Powers Resolution (WPR) of 1973 and the enactment, in its place, of its proposed War Powers Consultation Act (WPCA) of 2009.[1] This bipartisan panel, chaired by two former secretaries of state, James A. Baker III and Warren Christopher, and composed of twelve former, high-level government officials and academics, was charged by the Miller Center of Public Affairs at the University of Virginia to study the contentious issue of war powers, and to report its findings and recommendations. Baker and Christopher, joined by former member of Congress and House Foreign Affairs Committee chair Lee Hamilton, D-Ind., testified in March and April 2008 before the House Foreign Affairs Committee and the Senate Foreign Relations Committee, in advance of the report's public release.[2] Baker and Christopher also publicized their commission's recommendations more widely in opinion pieces published in the *New York Times* and *USA Today.*[3]

To understand why Congress should pass or at least give serious consideration to the WPCA it is helpful to understand the political background and context that preceded it.

For 160 years, presidents and Congress exercised their respective war powers largely as the Constitution provided. Congress declared or authorized wars and the president acted as commander in chief once hostilities had commenced. But that changed with Harry S. Truman's decision in 1950 to invade North Korea on the authority of a United Nations Security Council resolution. The president bypassed Congress in the initiation of this action, leading to its designation as a "presidential war," a concept at odds with the vision of the framers. Little more than a decade later, Lyndon Johnson's foray into Vietnam, based on what now appears to be faulty information that he gave to Congress and expanded over the succeeding years by both Johnson and Richard Nixon into a wider war with 58,000 casualties, provoked sharp public and congressional reactions, grounded in the recognition that the power to take a nation to war had migrated from Congress to the president.[4] The words of the Constitution had not changed, but one branch—the executive—had reached out to grab what the other branch—the legislature—had, in Justice Robert H. Jackson's words, "let slip through its fingers."[5] The third branch—the judiciary—disengaged entirely from this debate, leaving the other two to determine for themselves how to resolve this dilemma of presidential usurpation of Congress's constitutional obligation to determine when to initiate war.

The mid-1970s was a time of a "resurgent Congress."[6] Reacting to the excesses of "the imperial presidency" of the late 1960s and early 1970s, Congress entered an intense period of legislative activity, with the goal of reclaiming many of those powers that had drifted to the president. Foremost among these legislative efforts was the WPR. Its stated purpose was "to fulfill the intent of the framers of the Constitution of the United States and insure that the collective judgment of both the Congress and the President will apply to the introduction of the United States Armed Forces into hostilities, or into situations where imminent involvement in hostilities is clearly indicated by the circumstances." That "collective judgment" was to be achieved by directing that "the President in every possible instance shall consult with Congress before introducing United States Armed Forces into hostilities or into situations where imminent involvement in hostilities is clearly indicated by the circumstances." Other key provisions of the act placed limitations on the president's commander in chief powers, which could be exercised pursuant only to "(1) a declaration of war, (2) specific statutory authorization, or (3) a national emergency created by an attack upon the United States"; required that the president, in the absence of a declaration of war, provide a written report to Congress within forty-eight hours when armed forces are introduced into hostilities; provided for automatic termination by the president of the use of force within sixty to ninety days if Congress had neither authorized it nor declared war or was "physically unable to meet as a result of an armed attack on the United States"; and permitted Congress, by a concurrent resolution (not requiring the president's signature), at any time, even within the sixty-to-ninety-day period, to order the president to remove U.S. forces from hostilities, absent a declaration of war or specific statutory authorization.[7] Congress hoped these steps would ensure its inclusion in decisions to use military force and give it a continuing role in monitoring the president's actions.

Interpretations of the WPR varied widely. Some thought it unconstitutionally restricted executive power, others thought it unconstitutionally expanded presidential authority, while others thought it provided a practical solution that more clearly designated how each branch should carry out its constitutional role.

Any effort to sift through the debate about the WPR must distinguish between offensive and defensive use of military force. The framers of the Constitution were clear about the difference between offensive and defensive use of force: the power to initiate the use of military force for offensive purposes belonged exclusively to Congress. James Madison and Elbridge Gerry acknowledged at the Constitutional Convention that the reason for substituting "declare" for "make" in the war clause (Article I, Section 8, Clause 11) was to leave "to the Executive the power to repel sudden attacks."[8] Madison and Gerry reasoned that a president might need to act defensively in an emergency, before Congress could authorize military action. The framers' concession that a president may employ, on his own, only defensive use of force reinforces the view that the initiation of offensive hostilities was intended to rest with Congress alone.

A common misperception about the WPR is that it is the exclusive definition of the process by which the nation engages in the use of military force. However, it is necessary to distinguish between the constitutional and statutory requirements of this process. The WPR is a statutory enactment that imposes a series of steps (consultation, reporting, and congressional action/inaction) by which the two branches are to carry out their respective constitutional functions of "declaring war" and serving as "Commander in Chief, when called into the actual Service of the United States." As legislation, it can be repealed or revised at any time. Moreover, the resolution is subject to judicial review at any time, and could be found unconstitutional.[9] Not subject to change except through constitutional amendment are the war powers functions that the Constitution allocated to Congress and the president. The WPR attempted to provide a pragmatic process for the two branches to implement the powers given them in the Constitution, but it could not add to or subtract from those powers. The WPR is an ancillary to the Constitution, existing, at best, alongside it but never substituting for it.

The WPR has been law for more than thirty-five years, but every president during that time has called it unconstitutional, and no president has fully complied with its provisions. Few people, if any, would say that it has lived up to its promise. At most, its dwindling number of defenders point to its symbolic value as a constant reminder to presidents that they should seek authorization from Congress when intending to use military force. With only a few exceptions over the last three decades, most presidents have, in fact, sought Congress's approval for use of force, although all have been careful in noting for the record that they were seeking political support from Congress because it was prudent and wise but not because it was constitutionally required.[10] All asserted that they had sufficient constitutional authority on their own to determine when to use military force, and did not need Congress's authorization to proceed. All used language when sending reports to Congress that they were acting "consistent with" but not "pursuant to" the WPR. By submitting reports voluntarily but not pursuant to the law, presidents argued that the subsequent legal obligations of the WPR were not triggered.

The failure of the WPR has spawned many efforts at reform. Among the more notable were the Byrd-Warner Act (1988); Sen. Joseph Biden's (D-Del.)

Use of Force Act (1988); the Combat Authorization Act (1988); and, most recently, H.J. Res 53, introduced in September 2007 by Rep. Walter Jones, D-N.C.[11] None has generated sufficient support for serious consideration. The Miller Center's National War Powers Commission hoped to produce a different outcome by assembling a blue-ribbon panel of members and bringing in respected scholars and former government officials from across the political spectrum for expert advice.

THE WAR POWERS CONSULTATION ACT OF 2009

The Baker-Christopher report makes a conscious effort to learn from the pitfalls of past reform efforts. For that reason, the commission concentrated its efforts on the provisions it believed had a realistic chance of gaining bipartisan legislative support. Three key points guided the commission's work. First, the proposed law should provide "a constructive and practical way in which the judgment of both the President and Congress can be brought to bear when deciding whether the United States should engage in significant armed conflict." Second, the commission acknowledged two opposed "camps" of constitutional interpretation: the "congressionalists" and the "presidentialists." The commission determined at the outset that it would not be fruitful to determine which of these schools was correct and chose to put aside the constitutional question and focus instead on possible areas of agreement.[12] Third, the commission desired to promote consultation between the president and Congress before either branch took action—that is, before Congress declared war or authorized the use of force and before the president embarked on military action.

The main provisions of the WPCA are as follows:

- The president "shall consult with the Joint Congressional Consultation Committee," which is composed of twenty members of Congress, including the majority and minority leaders of both houses and the chairs and ranking members of four House and four Senate committees with foreign policy jurisdiction.

- The president shall submit a classified, written report to the Joint Congressional Consultation Committee before ordering any "significant armed conflict," defined as lasting more than seven days. The act provides for alternative consultation requirements in cases where there is "the need for secrecy or other emergent circumstances."

- The two leaders of the Joint Congressional Consultation Committee shall introduce a concurrent resolution of approval within thirty days after a significant armed conflict begins, if Congress has not declared war or expressly authorized the commitment of U.S. forces. This will be a highly privileged resolution in both houses, and "shall become the pending business of both Houses" and "shall be voted on within 5 calendar days thereafter."

- If the resolution of approval fails, any member of Congress may introduce a joint resolution of disapproval of the significant armed conflict, with similar time deadlines and the same highly privileged status attached to it. This joint resolution will have the force of law if signed by the president or if two-thirds of both houses vote to override the president's veto.

- If the joint resolution of disapproval does not become law, each house may use its internal rules to "specify the effect of the joint resolution of disapproval." This provision is intended to encourage Congress to use its authority to rule out of order, for example, any bill appropriating funds for any part of a specific armed conflict.

- Congress is provided with a "permanent, bipartisan joint professional staff" to assist the Joint Congressional Consultation Committee, and the committee and the staff "shall be provided all relevant national security and intelligence information."[13]

The primary goal of the WPCA was to replace the WPR with an act that would have a realistic chance of being followed in good faith by both branches. Baker and Christopher also concluded that, short of a constitutional amendment or a conclusive judicial resolution of the respective war powers of Congress and the president, neither of which was likely, the best they could do was to provide clear guidelines for consultation and reporting by the president and for specific legislative actions by Congress.

WHY THE WAR POWERS CONSULTATION ACT IS SUPERIOR TO THE WAR POWERS RESOLUTION

The WPCA is an improvement over the WPR for a number of reasons.

First, the WPCA provides a clearer mechanism for consultation than the comparable one that existed in the War Powers Resolution, which did not specify with whom the executive branch should consult. The WPR said that "The President in every possible instance shall consult with Congress," which left considerable discretion to the president about whom to consult and even whether to consult at all. The WPCA, in contrast, directs that "the President shall consult with the Joint Congressional Consultation Committee" before ordering the armed forces into significant armed conflicts.

Second, the WPCA uses the phrase "significant armed conflict," as compared to the WPR's general reference to "hostilities or situations where imminent involvement in hostilities is clearly indicated by the circumstances." The WPCA explicitly defines "significant" as armed conflict lasting more than one week.

Third, the WPCA requires submission of a classified, written report to the Joint Congressional Consultation Committee *before* the president orders or approves any significant armed conflict. In contrast, the WPR required the report within forty-eight hours *after* the introduction of U.S. armed forces into hostilities.

Fourth, the WPCA provides a permanent staff for the Joint Congressional Consultation Committee and requires submission from the executive branch of "all relevant national security and intelligence information." This responded to criticisms of the WPR that (1) there was little institutional support in Congress for facilitating consultation, and (2) there was no guarantee that the executive branch would be forthcoming and complete in the information it provided to Congress.

Fifth, unlike the WPR, the WPCA requires congressional action on a specified time frame: introduction of a concurrent resolution of approval within thirty days after commitment of forces, and a vote in both houses within five days thereafter. It also provides for a joint resolution of disapproval should the concurrent resolution of approval be defeated, and further provides for use of Congress's internal rulemaking authority to determine the effect of the joint resolution should it, too, be defeated. Under the WPA, congressional *inaction* dictated the end of the use of U.S. armed forces, whereas the WPCA requires affirmative congressional action to approve or disapprove of the use of U.S. forces in a significant military conflict.

Sixth, the WPCA remedies, at least in part, the WPR's unintended tendency to enhance unilateral presidential warmaking power. The WPR required termination of the use of U.S. armed forces within sixty to ninety days from the submission of a presidential report, unless Congress acted affirmatively. However, sixty to ninety days was sixty to ninety days longer than any president had previously enjoyed under the Constitution to wage offensive military actions. The WPCA reduces that time, unauthorized by Congress, to thirty-five days, at most. Moreover, no president ever reported "pursuant to" the WPR; thus presidents, by this noncompliance, freed themselves (and disempowered Congress) from any subsequent obligation flowing from the reporting requirement.

Finally, the WPCA is less vulnerable to constitutional criticism than the WPR. Many constitutional analysts believed that the WPR was unconstitutional because it permitted Congress, through a concurrent resolution, to order the president to withdraw U.S. armed forces at any point. These analysts argued that this constituted a "legislative veto," which the U.S. Supreme Court had ruled unconstitutional in *Immigration and Naturalization Service v. Chadha* (1983).[14] In that case, the Court found a legislative veto constitutionally defective because congressional resolutions that negated an executive branch action without subsequent presentment to the president for his signature were "essentially legislative in purpose and effect" but violated "the express procedures of the Constitution's prescription for legislative action."[15] The WPCA avoids this constitutional problem because withdrawal of armed forces can be ordered only by the full statutory process: a joint resolution of Congress that requires a presidential signature or two-thirds of both houses of Congress to override his veto.

WHY SHOULD CONGRESS ENACT THE WAR POWERS CONSULTATION ACT?

The National War Powers Commission is correct in recommending repeal of the War Powers Resolution. It does more harm than good to maintain a law on the books that has been flouted by all seven presidents who have been subject to it and, in the words of the commission, "breeds cynicism and distrust among citizens toward their government."[16]

Admittedly, the War Powers Consultation Act is not perfect. Baker and Christopher concede as much, and have indicated that they are willing to work with Congress to revise and refine their proposal.[17] Its flaws are obvious: (1) it leaves unexamined the constitutional questions (as former representative Lee Hamilton said in the House hearings, "We punt on it");[18] (2) although it clarifies with "whom" in Congress the president must consult (the twenty members of the consultation committee), this leaves out the remaining 515 members of Congress, whom the Constitution charges with decisions of war and peace; (3) it still permits presidents to engage in offensive uses of force, unauthorized by Congress, for up to thirty-five days; (4) the list of exceptions to significant armed conflict, when consultation and reporting are not required, contains the types of military actions that are most likely in a contemporary world (e.g., "limited acts of reprisal against terrorists" or "covert operations"), and have the potential to swallow the rule; (5) the proposal's exhortation to the executive branch to provide "all relevant national security and intelligence information" to the congressional committee carries no guarantee that it will be obeyed, and thus Congress will continue to be at the mercy of the executive branch when it comes to critical information; (6) if two-thirds of both houses are unable to override a president's veto of a resolution of disapproval, then this means that a president may use military force when more than a majority of Congress members disapprove, and it takes only one-third plus one to allow the president to keep troops in the conflict; and (7) Congress already possesses sufficient authority to take every action in the proposal. The proposal is arguably superfluous.

Then, why should Congress pass it? The answer is that the WPCA establishes a political process that can foster the WPR's worthy goal of ensuring that the "collective judgment" of both Congress and the president be brought to bear on decisions to use military force. The WPCA moves closer to an effective war powers decision-making process by acknowledging and improving upon some of the most glaring shortcomings of the 1973 law: (1) the need for a permanent congressional staff working exclusively on war powers matters; (2) exposing publicly the need for cooperation from the executive branch in providing full information to Congress; (3) filling in some of the gaps on consultation (e.g., with whom, when, how often); (4) the need for affirmative legislative action expressing either approval or disapproval of the use of force; and (5) clarification of those specific circumstances when a president may use force defensively, such as "to protect or rescue American citizens or military or diplomatic personnel abroad" or "to repel attacks, or to prevent imminent attacks." This clarification hearkens back to a section that was in the original Senate version of the WPR, but was removed in the final compromise bill that emerged from the House-Senate conference. Commentators have remarked that this deletion was unfortunate, and that the resulting law would have been stronger had this section been retained.[19]

In explaining the WPCA, Baker has emphasized that gaining political support from both branches was at the center of the proposal. When questioned about what penalty, if any, a president would face if he ignored the requirements of this proposal, he replied, "it is diminished political support for a foreign engagement that the President might think is important to the national security of this country because if he does not comply with a law that is as plain and as clear as this one and on the books, then he would suffer the political consequences of not doing so."[20]

The WPCA includes some of the same features that were recommended in another war powers study, this one by the Constitution Project in 2005. Specifically, both urge the requirement for advance approval from Congress for offensive uses of force; both urge the executive branch to supply full information to Congress; and both urge repeal of the WPR and its replacement with legislation that, in the Constitution Project's words, "fairly acknowledges the

President's defensive war powers, omits any arbitrary general time limit on deployments of force, reaffirms the constitutionally-derived clear statement rule for use-of-force bills, and prescribes rules for their privileged and expedited consideration."[21] The WPCA meets each of these criteria.

Thus the National War Powers Commission crafted its legislative proposal with an eye toward pragmatic and realistic suggestions as the foundation for serious, continuing debate and further tinkering. It was born out of careful and methodical study and a clear-headed recognition of the daunting obstacles in front of any effort to bring a measure of discipline to war powers decision making. It deserves Congress's—and our—attention, as a way to move forward, after thirty-five years of disregard for existing law.

CON: William G. Howell[1]

The 2008 National War Powers Commission represents one of the most concerted efforts of the last quarter-century to reform the domestic institutional machinery of war. Rather than lambaste an imperial president and feckless Congress, as so many before had done, the commission sought to offer a more measured tone and constructive voice to ongoing debates about the domestic politics of war. Substantively, the commission aimed to clarify the obligations of presidents and members of Congress during the lead-up to war; to calm the partisan bickering that so often accompanies military deployments; and, crucially, to promote reforms that bipartisan majorities could accept.

The specific changes promoted by the commission are packaged as a legislative proposal: the War Powers Consultation Act (WPCA). The principal objective of the WPCA, which the commission hopes Congress will enact into law, is to augment the quality and frequency of interbranch dialogue. Hence, the WPCA establishes a set of guidelines—some binding, others not—for how the president and Congress ought to communicate with one another during the lead-up to war. As Nancy Kassop explains in her defense of the act, these guidelines are intended to strengthen Congress's ability to extract from the executive branch information about a prospective military venture, but also to require members of Congress to take a clear position, either in support or opposition, on an impending war. The WPCA promises to replace secrecy with forthrightness, obscurity with transparency, happenstance with order.

Even if enacted, the WPCA will not deliver on such promises. The WPCA underestimates the politics that animate interbranch relations during times of war, politics wherein the major cleavages are defined by partisan affiliations rather than institutional loyalties, and wherein the public shows little appetite for punishing elected officials who neglect their constitutional obligations. The act will not materially alter how we as a nation go to war. The WPCA probably satisfies the first requirement of any policy reform, that of doing no harm. But it will not do much good either.

A CRITIQUE

The commission's work intends to serve a single objective: to encourage greater consultation between the federal branches of government. The word appears more than one hundred times in the commission's final report and in the title of its proposed statute. As the commission's members put it, their primary objective is to establish "a constructive, workable, politically acceptable legal framework that will best promote effective, cooperative, and deliberative action by both the President and Congress in matters of war." If we take the commission on its own terms, then, the success or failure of the WPCA unambiguously rides on its ability to encourage each branch of government to share more of its opinions and information about prospective and ongoing military ventures; and, one hopes, that Congress and the president will factor these opinions and information into the decisions they make about war.

It is important to evaluate the WPCA in the spirit in which the commission offers it. Hence, I will not engage the long-standing debate about the dual imperatives during times of war of deliberation on one side and of action on the other. For the purposes of this essay I assume, as the commission does, that increased consultation is an unqualified good.[2] And for the moment, let us further accept the commission's (highly controversial)[3] claims that neither the Constitution itself nor the history of U.S. warfare offers clear insights into the appropriate division of war powers between Congress and the president. I will assume, as the commission does, that all sides in contemporary constitutional debates about presidential and congressional war powers have a reasonable basis for their claims. Finally, I will have nothing to say about the WPCA's prospects of passage. Here again, I will not question the commission's assertion that its members have settled on the legislative initiative with the best chances of becoming law.[4]

Instead, I want to reflect upon whether the WPCA can be expected to alter, in any meaningful sense, the interbranch dynamics that precede military deployments. It is on this possibility, after all, that the commission's final report prides itself. The report repeatedly states the commission's intention to offer a "pragmatic approach" for how Congress and the president can work out their differences about war. As their guiding principle the members of the commission seek to develop a proposal that will "maximize the likelihood" that the president and Congress will more productively consult with one another. The commission has no interest in offering symbolic reform. Rather, the commission's legislative proposal intends to deliver results.

But to deliver results, the WPCA must be self-enforcing. Do not count on the judiciary to ensure the good behavior of either Congress or the president. Although it cites the judiciary's unwillingness to affirm the constitutionality of the War Powers Resolutions as among that statute's central failings, the commission offers no reason to expect things to be any different under the WPCA. The WPCA's success, therefore, depends upon the inclination of both Congress and the president to abide by its central provisions. Will they? I suspect not. And to see why not, one must understand the core motivations that have guided presidential and congressional behavior for at least the last seventy-five years, during which time an avalanche of public expectations and aspirations has fallen upon the White House, and partisan politics regularly trump institutional loyalties on Capitol Hill. The following two subsections therefore reflect upon how presidents first and members of Congress second are likely to respond to a newly enacted WPCA. The promise of change, we shall see, is dramatically overstated.

Presidents

If members of Congress are best thought of as single-minded seekers of reelection, as David R. Mayhew argued thirty-five years ago,[5] then presidents are single-minded seekers of power. Individual presidents may have ulterior motivations: enacting good public policy, undoing the work of their predecessors, responding to a perceived public mandate, securing their place in history. But to accomplish any of these things, presidents need power. And so it is power they seek.

There is a certain virtue, to be sure, in respecting constitutional strictures and, when appropriate, relinquishing power. But neither today's public nor tomorrow's historians—the two audiences that matter most to presidents— show much regard for presidents who, in the face of crisis, cloak themselves in the Constitution and invite deliberation. Rather, both reward the president who refuses to let the Constitution, the corpus of statutory law, or anything else besides disrupt the possibilities for action, for bold leadership, for a rousing insistence that he (someday she) will provide the guidance and energy needed to steer the nation through this moment of peril. Meanwhile, the president who follows the libertarian's counsel during times of crisis can expect to see his public approval ratings plummet and his legacy wither.

Evidence abounds of presidents seeking—not to mention guarding and nurturing—power. Witness them relying upon executive orders, executive agreements, proclamations, and national security directives in lieu of legislation and treaties; building and rebuilding an administrative apparatus around them; emphasizing the importance of loyalty when appointing individuals to the more distant reaches of the federal bureaucracy; issuing signing statements, which allow them further opportunities to re-interpret the meaning of laws; directly engaging the public; and, more recently, invoking the unitary theory of the executive to justify their actions.[6] While different presidents from different parties may advance different policy agendas, all, in one way or another, seize upon opportunities to fortify their influence over the writing, interpretation, and implementation of public policy.

None of this suggests that presidents exercise all the power that they would like. Presidents are seekers of power, not paragons of power. And ample scholarship emphasizes the historical contingencies and institutional constraints that limit a president's ability to exercise his unilateral powers,[7] centralize authority,[8] politicize the appointments process,[9] issue public appeals,[10] or refashion the political universe.[11] Some basic facts about lawmaking further limit the president's ability to have his way: executive orders and executive agreements are not perfect substitutes for laws and treaties; signing statements do not have any legal enforceability; and, as Richard E. Neustadt recognized a half-century ago, the formal powers that presidents retain are entirely insufficient to meet the extraordinary expectations deposited at the White House's doorstep.[12] Even in the policy domain where all observers concede that presidential power reaches its apex—that is, in war—presidents often must confront mobilized opposition within Congress.[13] Presidential power is now contested, as it shall always be. Indeed, should it no longer be, we must stop calling it "presidential."

But a basic point remains: over the nation's history, presidents have managed to secure a measure of influence over the doings of government that cannot be found in either a strict reading of the Constitution or in the expressed authority that Congress has delegated. This, in fact, represents a dominant theme in the scholarship on the emergence of a modern presidency.[14] Article II of the Constitution is notoriously vague. As a practical matter, Congress cannot write statutes with enough clarity or detail to keep presidents from reading into them at least some discretionary authority. And for their part, the courts have established as a basic principle of jurisprudence deference to administrative (and by extension presidential) expertise.[15] It is little wonder, then, that through ambiguity presidents have managed to radically transform their office, placing it at the very epicenter of U.S. foreign policy.

The members of the National War Powers Commission certainly recognize the self-serving ways in which presidents interpret laws. When making their case against the War Powers Resolution, the members point out that "presidents have regularly involved the country's armed forces in what are clearly 'hostilities' under the terms of the statute, while claiming the statute is unconstitutional or not triggered in that particular case." The commission, though, gives us no reason to believe that things will be especially different under their new statutory framework. Nothing about the WPCA fundamentally alters the core incentives of presidents to seize and control the federal government's war powers.

It is of some note, then, that the War Powers Consultation Act offers plenty of ambiguities of its own, each ripe for presidential exploitation. Take, for instance, the requirement that the president consult with Congress in cases of "significant armed conflict." When is an armed conflict "significant"? And does every military deployment represent a "conflict"? Answers to these questions are hardly straightforward. Recall that Harry S. Truman labeled Korea a "police action." In the 1960s, first John F. Kennedy and then Lyndon Johnson insisted that they were deploying U.S. military personnel only to "train and advise" local Vietnamese forces. According to Ronald Reagan, Lebanon was a "rescue and peacekeeping" operation, and Grenada was a mere "rescue" mission. In each of these cases, presidents redefined their actions in ways that allowed them to avoid the very kinds of consultations that the commission now hopes to foster.

Ambiguities, moreover, do not stop here. What, after all, constitutes sufficient "consultation"? Must presidents share all that they know about a foreign crisis? And if not, what are presidents to do when members of Congress either demand too much—or, for that matter, too little—information about military plans? Is the executive branch obligated to track down new information in response to congressional queries? And if so, how much time are the officials charged with this task allowed, and what opportunities do members of Congress have for follow-up?

The ambiguities continue further still. Consider, for instance, the expansive exceptions that the commission grants to presidents under the WPCA. Presidents, for instance, need not consult with Congress about "limited acts of reprisal against terrorists or states that sponsor terrorism." But as former legislators Paul Findley and Don Fraser rightly ask: "Who identifies 'terrorists'? Who defines 'terrorism'? Who determines which are 'states that sponsor terrorism'? Who defines 'limited'? The president alone."[16] And with the freedom to define the law, and powerful incentives to skirt it, it is not at all clear how the WPCA will substantially increase the quality or frequency of consultation between the various branches of government.

As written, presidents can readily claim to honor the WPCA without providing genuine consultation. This does not merely constitute a possible outcome. If past experience is any indication, it is virtually guaranteed. Presidents have powerful incentives to resist sharing intelligence, strategy, or other information that they consider sensitive. And for reasons that the next subsection describes, members of Congress cannot be counted on to force presidents to do much better.

Congress

When presidents flout elements of the WPCA, as they most certainly will, can we expect Congress to do much about it? No. At least not consistently. The WPCA, after all, does not provide Congress with anything that cannot already be found in Article I. Constitutionally, Congress has the power to express its views about a war, either in support or opposition; to demand that the president provide information about either a prospective or ongoing war; to pass other bills to authorize, end, or otherwise govern a war. The fact is, Congress regularly chooses not to exercise these powers at its disposal. A variety of contributing factors explain why. I want to focus, though, on the relevance of partisan politics.

To begin, we need to recognize a basic fact about our nation's legislature: Congress does not act as an institution to fulfill its basic constitutional obligations. Rather, it is members of Congress who do so.[17] And the probability that these members challenge claims about the national interest and the use of military force, demanding that presidents share information and adjust their planning, critically depends upon the alignment of their partisan affiliations. Democrats within Congress regularly and predictably support Democratic presidents, just as Republican members of Congress back Republican presidents. Across party lines, meanwhile, political cleavages regularly rupture.

Recall that Republican members of Congress almost uniformly voted in favor of the 2002 authorization to wage war against Iraq, while Democrats were split evenly. Those Democrats who did break party ranks and support the president, meanwhile, represented districts and states where George W. Bush had performed especially well in the 2000 presidential elections. Persistently and unavoidably, party politics and electoral incentives inform Congress's willingness to stand by the requirements of any constitutional provisions or law, very much including those found in the WPCA.

A variety of factors help explain why partisanship has so prominently shaped the contours of interbranch struggles over military deployments during the modern era. To begin with, the making of U.S. foreign policy hinges on how U.S. national interests are defined and the means chosen to achieve them. This process is deeply and unavoidably political. Only in very particular circumstances—a direct attack on U.S. soil or on Americans abroad—have political parties temporarily united for the sake of protecting the national interest. Even then, though, partisan politics flare as the costs of war mount.

Electoral concerns also play a role. Some members of Congress face electoral incentives to increase their oversight of wars when the opposing party controls the White House. If presidential approval ratings increase when presidents exercise force abroad (as the rally 'round the flag literature suggests),[18] and if high presidential approval ratings redound to the electoral benefit of their copartisans in Congress (as the literature on coattails suggests),[19] then, all else being equal, members' willingness to grant the president broad discretion to exercise force abroad should critically depend upon their partisan identifications.

Issues of trust also fuel partisan fires. In environments where information is sparse, individuals with shared ideological or partisan affiliations find it easier to communicate with one another. The president possesses unparalleled intelligence about threats to national interests, and—despite the dictates of the WPCA—he is far more likely to share that information with members of his own political party than with political opponents. Whereas the commander in chief has at his beck and call numerous agencies that focus exclusively on foreign affairs, Congress enjoys relatively few sources of reliable classified information. Consequently, when a president claims that a foreign crisis warrants military intervention, members of his own party tend to trust him more often than not, whereas members of the opposition party are predisposed to doubt.

My own research with Jon Pevehouse shows that the president's propensity to exercise military force steadily declines as members of the opposition party pick up seats in Congress.[20] In fact, it is not even necessary for the control of Congress to switch parties; the loss of even a handful of seats can materially affect the probability that the nation will go to war. Estimating a wide range of statistical models and datasets on military deployments, we find that the partisan composition of Congress systematically covaries with the frequency with which presidents send troops abroad, the probability that presidents respond to particular crises happening around the globe, and the time it takes for the United States to marshal a response.

The partisan composition of Congress also influences its willingness to formally initiate the kinds of deliberative activities that the commission wants to encourage. According to Linda Fowler, the presence or absence of unified government systematically covaries with the frequency of foreign policy hearings held within Congress. Fowler demonstrates that when the same party controlled both Congress and the presidency during the post–World War II era, the number of hearings about military policy decreased; but when the opposition party controlled at least one chamber of Congress, hearings occurred with greater frequency.[21] Likewise, Douglas Kriner has shown that both congressional authorizations of war and legislative initiatives that establish timetables for the withdrawal of troops, cut funds, or otherwise curtail military operations critically depend on the partisan balance of power on Capitol Hill.[22]

These findings have clear implications for the WPCA. Copartisans within Congress are unlikely to force the president to consult with them more regularly than they already do. Members of the opposition party, meanwhile, may well challenge the president. They will do so, however, not out of a shared sense of duty to defend laws enacted by previous presidents, but because they have powerful political incentives to criticize the opposition presidents who take our nation to war. And because they recognize these political incentives, presidents tend to resist the demands for information sharing that follow.

SOME CONCLUDING THOUGHTS

The commission argues that the War Powers Consultation Act constitutes a "practical replacement of—and improvement on—the War Powers Resolution." The basis for this claim lies in its appeal to common sense and the purported benefits of increased dialogue across the branches of government. I submit, though, that whether a proposal is "practical" critically depends upon whether it conforms to the underlying political incentives of those who would carry it out; and whether there exist political actors who will reliably enforce provisions that presidents, at least, have powerful incentives to disobey.

By underestimating the domestic politics of war, the War Powers Consultation Act is not practical at all. Interbranch contestations over war are fundamentally political, not legal, in nature. And these contestations cannot be legislated away. As James Madison tells us in *Federalist* No. 48—and almost all important insights about presidential power trace back to Madison—we must not place our trust in "parchment barriers against the encroaching spirit of power." Neither laws nor constitutional provisions, no matter how precisely stated, can be expected to set things right. And no statute that overlooks the deeply political incentives that guide members of Congress and presidents will finally restore an appropriate balance of power across the branches of government.

Presciently, the founders anticipated that the proper division of war powers would not be negotiated once and for all. Rather, it would be subject to continued contestation between the branches of government. As Edward Corwin so famously put it, the Constitution issues an "invitation to struggle" over the foreign policy machinery. It's a struggle that no statute, not the War Powers Resolution nor the proposed War Powers Consultation Act, can hope to settle. And it's a struggle that is largely immunized from reforms that do not account for the underlying political incentives of those individuals and parties who participate in it.

NOTES

CHAPTER 1: Article V Should Be Revised to Make It Easier to Amend the Constitution and to Call a Constitutional Convention

PRO

1. Donald S. Lutz, "Toward a Theory of Constitutional Amendment," in *Responding to Imperfection: The Theory and Practice of Constitutional Amendment,* ed. Sanford Levinson (Princeton: Princeton University Press, 1995), 237–274.
2. John J. Dinan, *The American State Constitutional Tradition* (Lawrence: University Press of Kansas, 2009).
3. See Bruce A. Ackerman, "Higher Lawmaking," in *Responding to Imperfection: The Theory and Practice of Constitutional Amendment,* ed. Sanford Levinson (Princeton: Princeton University Press, 1995), 63–88; Stephen M. Griffin, *American Constitutionalism: From Theory to Politics* (Princeton: Princeton University Press, 1996); and David Strauss, "The Irrelevance of Constitutional Amendments," *Harvard Law Review* 114 (2001): 1457–1505. Also see Sanford Levinson, "How Many Times Has the United States Constitution Been Amended? (A) < 26; (B) 26; (C) 27; (D) > 27: Accounting for Constitutional Change," in *Responding to Imperfection: The Theory and Practice of Constitutional Amendment,* ed. Sanford Levinson (Princeton: Princeton University Press, 1995), 13–36.
4. Bruce A. Ackerman, *We the People: Transformations* (Cambridge: Harvard University Press, 1998), 99–252.

CHAPTER 2: Congress Should Restore Each State's Freedom to Set Its Drinking Age

PRO

1. *Time,* July 2, 1984.
2. *South Dakota v. Dole,* 483 U.S. 203 (1987).
3. John Kobler, *Ardent Spirits: The Rise and Fall of Prohibition* (New York: G. P. Putnam, 1973), 180–183.
4. David E. Kyvig, *Repealing National Prohibition* (Chicago: University of Chicago Press, 1979), 2.

5. Herbert Asbury, *The Great Illusion: An Informal History of Prohibition* (New York: Doubleday, 1950), 73–74.

6. See www.ncadd.com/pc_recommendations.cfm.

7. See, for example, Alcohol Policy Information System, "Underage Consumption of Alcohol," at www.alcoholpolicy.niaaa.nih.gov/index.asp (2006); Substance Abuse and Mental Health Services Administration, Office of Applied Studies, "Results from the 2007 National Survey on Drug Use and Health: National Findings" (NSDUH Series H-34, DHHS Publication No. SMA 08–4343, 2008); John Schulenberg et al., "The Problem of College Drinking: Insights from a Developmental Perspective," *Alcohol: Clinical and Experimental Research* 25 (March 2001): 473–477; and D. Allen, D. Sprenkel, and P. Vitale, "Reactance Theory and Alcohol Consumption Laws: Further Confirmation among Collegiate Alcohol Consumers," *Journal of Studies on Alcohol* 55 (January 1994): 34–40.

8. Mark Wolfson, A. C. Wagenaar, and Gary W. Hornseth, "Law Officers' Views on Enforcement of the Legal Drinking Age," *Public Health Reports* 110, no. 4 (1995): 428–437.

9. James H. Hedlund, Robert G. Ulmer, and David F. Preusser, "Determine Why There Are Fewer Young Alcohol-Impaired Drivers," National Highway Traffic Safety Administration, Final Report, DOT HS 809–348 (Washington, D.C.: U.S. Department of Transportation, September 2001), http://204.68.195.250/people/injury/research/FewerYoungDrivers/iv__what_caused.htm#g.%20canadian.

CON

1. James H. Hedlund, Robert G. Ulmer, and David F. Preusser, "Determine Why There Are Fewer Young Alcohol-Impaired Drivers," National Highway Traffic Safety Administration, Final Report, DOT HS 809–348 (Washington, D.C.: U.S. Department of Transportation, September 2001), http://204.68.195.250/people/injury/research/FewerYoungDrivers/iv__what_caused.htm#g.%20canadian.

2. National Highway Traffic Safety Administration, National Center for Statistics and Analysis, *Traffic Safety Facts, Lives Saved in 2007 by Restraint Use and Minimum Drinking Age Laws* (DOT HS 811-049) (Washington, D.C.: U.S. Department of Transportation, November 2008), www.nhtsa.gov.

3. James C. Fell, Deborah A. Fisher, Robert B. Voas, Kenneth Blackman, and A. Scott Tippetts, "The Relationship of Underage Drinking Laws to Reductions in Drinking Drivers in Fatal Crashes in the United States," *Accident Analysis and Prevention* 40 (2008): 1430–1440.

4. Daniel R. Mayhew and Herb M. Simpson, "The Safety Value of Driver Education and Training," *Journal of the International Society for Child and Adolescent Injury Prevention* 8, suppl. 2 (2002): ii, 3–8.

5. Kypros Kypri, Robert B. Voas, John D. Langley, Shaun C. R. Stephenson, Dorothy J. Begg, A. Scott Tippetts, and Gabrielie S. Davie, "Minimum Purchasing Age for Alcohol and Traffic Crash Injuries among 15- to 19-Year-Olds in New Zealand," *American Journal of Public Health* 96, no. 1 (2006): 126–131.

CHAPTER 3: The United States Should Adopt a National Initiative and Referendum

PRO

1. For an overview, see Thomas E. Cronin, *Direct Democracy: The Politics of Initiative, Referendum, and Recall* (Cambridge: Harvard University Press, 1989).
2. Jenny Burley and Francis Regan, "Divorce in Ireland: The Fear, the Floodgates, and the Reality," *International Journal of Law, Policy, and the Family* 16, no. 2 (2002): 202–222.
3. James A. Stimson, Michael B. MacKeun, and Robert S. Erikson, "Dynamic Representation," *American Political Science Review* 89 (1995): 543–565.
4. Michael Murakami, "Desegregation," in *Public Opinion and Constitutional Controversy,* ed. Nathaniel Persily, Jack Citrin, and Patrick J. Egan (New York: Oxford University Press, 2008).
5. Sen. James Eastland, D-Miss., blocked 120 of 121 civil rights bills that came before his committee, which was known as the "burial ground" for civil rights. Robert D. Loevy, *The Civil Rights Act of 1964: The Passage of the Law That Ended Racial Segregation* (Albany: State University of New York Press, 1997).
6. For a related argument, see Mark V. Tushnet, *Taking the Constitution Away from the Courts* (Princeton, N.J.: Princeton University Press, 2000).
7. Examples include *Webster v. Reproductive Health Services* (1989), *Planned Parenthood v. Casey* (1991), and *Gonzales v. Carhart* (2007).
8. Samantha Luks and Michael Salamone, "Abortion," in Persily, Citrin, and Egan, eds., *Public Opinion and Constitutional Controversy,* (New York: Oxford University Press, 2008); D. Granberg and B. W. Granberg, "Abortion Attitudes, 1965–1980," *Family Planning Perspectives* 12, no. 5 (1980): 250–261.
9. Center for Responsive Politics, www.opensecrets.org.
10. Jack L. Walker Jr., *Mobilizing Interest Groups in America* (Ann Arbor: University of Michigan Press, 1991).
11. Tory Newmyer, "Murtha Got Payback in '08," *Roll Call,* January 27, 2009.
12. Barbara S. Gamble, "Putting Civil Rights to a Popular Vote," *American Journal of Political Science* 41, no. 1 (1997): 245–269.
13. Kenneth P. Miller, *Direct Democracy and the Courts* (Princeton, N.J.: Princeton University Press, 2009).
14. Mancur Olson, *The Logic of Collective Action: Public Goods and the Theory of Groups,* rev. ed. (Cambridge: Harvard University Press, 1971).
15. An earmark is an appropriation of funds that can be direct to a specific recipient, such as a business, an organization, or a local government.
16. David Broder, *Democracy Derailed: Initiative Campaigns and the Power of Money* (New York: Harcourt, 2000); Richard J. Ellis, *Democratic Delusions: The Initiative Process in America* (Lawrence: University Press of Kansas, 2002).
17. *Bellotti v. First National Bank of Boston* (1978).

18. Elisabeth R. Gerber, *The Populist Paradox: Interest Group Influence and the Promise of Direct Legislation* (Princeton, N.J.: Princeton University Press, 1999).

19. Arthur Lupia, "Shortcuts versus Encyclopedias: Information and Voting Behavior in California Insurance Reform Elections," *American Political Science Review* (1994): 63–76.

20. See www.nytimes.com/1999/07/07/us/senate-riders-put-some-on-the-inside-track.html?pagewanted=all.

21. John Fund, "Marks for Sharks," Wall Street Journal Online, January 9, 2009, www.opinionjournal.com/diary/?id=110007785.

22. John Haskell, *Direct Democracy or Representative Government? Dispelling the Populist Myth* (Boulder, Colo.: Westview Press, 2001); Alan Rosenthal, *The Decline of Representative Democracy* (Washington, D.C.: CQ Press, 1998).

23. Arthur M. Schlesinger Jr., *The Imperial Presidency* (Boston: Houghton Mifflin, 1973); Matthew A. Crenson and Benjamin Ginsberg, *Presidential Power: Unchecked and Unbalanced* (New York: W. W. Norton, 2007).

24. Theodore J. Lowi, *The End of Liberalism* (New York: W. W. Norton, 1969).

25. Louis Fisher, "Deciding on War against Iraq: Institutional Failures" *Political Science Quarterly* 118, no. 3 (2003): 389–410.

26. American National Election Study data, various years.

27. Alan I. Abramowitz, Brad Alexander, and Matthew Gunning, "Incumbency, Redistricting, and the Decline of Competition in U.S. House Elections," *Journal of Politics* 68 (2008): 75–88.

28. Gary King and Andrew Gelman, "Systemic Consequences of Incumbency Advantage in U.S. House Elections," *American Journal of Political Science* (1991): 110–138.

29. Morris Fiorina with Samuel J. Abrams, and Jeremy C. Pope, *Culture War? The Myth of a Polarized America* (New York: Pearson Longman, 2005); Todd Donovan, "A Goal for Reform: Make Elections Worth Stealing," *PS: Political Science and Politics* (2007): 681-686.

30. Gerber, *The Populist Paradox;* John G. Matsusaka, *For the Many or the Few: The Initiative, Public Policy, and American Democracy* (Chicago: University of Chicago Press, 2004).

31. This is based on requiring the collection of signatures equal to 5 percent of votes cast in the previous presidential election. There were 129,000,000 votes cast for president in 2008.

32. Daniel A. Smith and Caroline J. Tolbert, "The Initiative to Party," *Party Politics* 7, no. 6 (2001): 739–757.

CON

1. For a statutory initiative in California, petitioners must gather signatures equaling 5 percent of the number of votes cast for governor in the preceding election; in Oregon the number is 6 percent. For constitutional initiatives both states require 8 percent.

2. David B. Magleby, *Direct Legislation: Voting on Ballot Propositions in the United States* (Baltimore: Johns Hopkins University Press, 1984), 31.

3. Philip L. DuBois and Floyd Feeney, *Lawmaking by Initiative: Issues, Options, and Comparisons* (New York: Agathon Press, 1998), 49–57.

4. Richard J. Ellis, *Democratic Delusions: The Initiative Process in American* (Lawrence: University Press of Kansas, 2002), 200.

5. Ibid., 201.

6. Lydia Chavez, *The Color Bind: California's Battle to End Affirmative Action* (Berkeley: University of California Press, 1998), 80, 145–146.

CHAPTER 4: Broadcasters Should Be Charged a Spectrum Fee to Finance Programming in the Public Interest

CON

1. See, Adam Thierer, *Media Myths: Understanding the Debate over Media Ownership* (Washington, D.C.: Progress and Freedom Foundation, 2005), 85–104, www.pff.org/issues-pubs/books/050610mediamyths.pdf.

2. Statement of Michael J. Copps before the Senate Committee on Commerce, Science, and Transportation, January 14, 2003.

3. Nobel Prize–winning economist Ronald Coase argued fifty years ago that "The phrase . . . lacks any definite meaning. Furthermore, the many inconsistencies in commission decisions have made it impossible for the phrase to acquire a definite meaning in the process of regulation." Ronald H. Coase, "The Federal Communications Commission," *Journal of Law and Economics* 2 (October 1959): 8–9.

4. See Randolph J. May, "The Public Interest Standard: Is It Too Indeterminate to Be Constitutional?" *Federal Communications Law Journal* 53 (2001): 427–468.

5. See Adam D. Thierer, "Is the Public Served by the Public Interest Standard?" *The Freeman* 46, no. 9 (September 1996): 618–620; William T. Mayton, "The Illegitimacy of the Public Interest Standard at the FCC," *Emory Law Journal* 38 (1989): 715–769.

6. Ford Rowan, *Broadcast Fairness* (New York: Longman, 1984), 39.

7. Ellen P. Goodman, "Proactive Media Policy in an Age of Content Abundance," in *Media Diversity and Localism: Meaning and Metrics,* ed. Philip M. Napoli (Mahwah, N.J.: LEA Publishers, 2007), 370, 374. And there is no reason to believe this situation will change. Writing in 1922, famed journalist Walter Lippmann noted that "it is possible to make a rough estimate only of the amount of attention people give each day to informing themselves about public affairs," but "the time each day is small when any of us is directly exposed to information from our unseen environment." Walter Lippmann, *Public Opinion* (1922): 53, 57.

8. J. H. Snider, *Speak Softly and Carry a Big Stick* (New York: iUniverse, Inc., 2005).

9. Lawrence J. White, "Spectrum for Sale," *The Milken Institute Review,* 2d quarter (2001): 31.

10. See Adam Thierer, "Why Regulate Broadcasting: Toward a Consistent First Amendment Standard for the Information Age," Catholic University Law School *CommLaw Conspectus* 15 (Summer 2007): 431–482, http://commlaw.cua.edu/ articles/v15/15_2/Thierer.pdf; Adam Thierer, "*FCC v. Fox* and the Future of the First Amendment in the Information Age," *Engage,* February 2009, www.fed-soc .org/doclib/20090216_ThiererEngage101.pdf.

11. "By taking some modest fee from commercial broadcasters for their use of the public spectrum in lieu of the public trustee obligation, noncommercial television could be adequately funded to deliver high-quality public service programming." Henry Geller, "Geller to FCC: Scrap the Rules, Try a Spectrum Fee," *Current.org,* October 30, 2000, www.current.org/why/why0020geller.shtml. Also see Henry Geller, "Promoting the Public Interest in the Digital Era," *Federal Communications Law Journal* 55, no. 3 (2003), www.law.indiana.edu/fclj/pubs/ v55/n03/Geller.pdf.

12. Remarks of Norman Ornstein at George Mason University event, "The Gore Commission, Ten Years Later: The Public Interest Obligations of Digital TV Broadcasters in Perfect Hindsight," October 3, 2008, www.iep.gmu.edu/ documents/Ornstein.doc.

13. Paul Taylor and Norman Ornstein, "A Broadcast Spectrum Fee for Campaign Finance Reform," New America Foundation, *Spectrum Series Working Paper* 4 (June 2002), www.newamerica.net/files/IssueBrief5.FreeAirTime.TaylorOrnstein .pdf.

14. Adam Thierer and Wayne Crews, "Just *Don't* Do It: The Digital Opportunities Investment Trust (DO IT) Fund," Cato Institute *TechKnowledge* 35, May 6, 2002, www.cato.org/tech/tk/020506-tk.html.

15. Quoted in Neil Hickey, "TV's Big Stick: Why the Broadcast Industry Gets What It Wants in Washington," *Columbia Journalism Review* (September/ October 2002): 53.

16. See Adam Thierer and Grant Eskelsen, "Media Metrics: The True State of the Modern Media Marketplace," Progress and Freedom Foundation, Summer 2008, www.pff.org/mediametrics.

17. Michael Grotticelli, "Local TV Stations Face Uncertain Future," *Broadcast Engineering,* February 23, 2009, http://broadcastengineering.com/news/local-stations-face-uncertain-future-0223.

18. Ben Compaine, "Domination Fantasies," *Reason,* January 2004, 33.

19. Ibid., 31.

20. Quoted in Krattenmaker and Powe, 314.

21. Pew Project for Excellence in Journalism, "Cable TV," *State of the News Media,* www.stateofthemedia.org/2009/narrative_cabletv_digitaltrends.php?media=7& cat=6/#key6 (accessed November 4, 2009).

22. Ibid.

23. Aaron Smith, "The Internet's Role in Campaign 2008," *The Pew Internet and American Life*, April 15, 2009, www.pewinternet.org/Reports/2009/6—The-Internets-Role-in-Campaign-2008.aspx.

24. Sarah Lai Stirland, "Propelled by Internet, Barack Obama Wins Presidency," *Wired.com*, November 4, 2008, www.wired.com/threatlevel/2008/11/propelled-by-in/.

25. Ibid.

26. Joe Trippi, *The Revolution Will Not Be Televised: Democracy, The Internet, and The Overthrow of Everything* (New York: Regan Books, 2004), 203 (emphasis in original).

27. Ibid.

28. Dan Gillmor, *We the Media: Grassroots Journalism by the People, for the People* (Sebastopol, Calif.: O'Reilly Media, Inc., 2004), xiii.

CHAPTER 5: Political Parties Should Nominate Candidates for President in a National Primary

PRO

1. See www.fairvote.org/?page=27&pressmode=showspecific&showarticle=256 (accessed July 27, 2009). Also see Caroline J. Tolbert and Peverill Squire, "Editors' Introduction: Reforming the Presidential Nomination Process," *PS: Political Science and Politics* 42 (2009): 27–32.

2. William G. Mayer and Andrew E. Busch, *The Front-Loading Problem in Presidential Nominations* (Washington, D.C.: Brookings, 2004).

3. Marty Cohen, David Karol, Hans Noel, and John Zaller, *The Party Decides: Presidential Nominations before and after Reform* (Chicago: University of Chicago Press, 2008). Also see John Aldrich, "The Invisible Primary and Its Effects on Democratic Choice," *PS: Political Science and Politics* (2009): 33–38.

4. Todd Donovan and Shaun Bowler, *Reforming the Republic: Democratic Institutions for the New America* (Englewood Cliffs, N.J.: Prentice Hall, 2004).

5. John H. Aldrich, "A Dynamic Model of Presidential Nomination Campaigns," *American Political Science Review* 74, no. 3 (1980): 651–669.

6. David P. Redlawsk, Caroline J. Tolbert, and Todd Donovan, *Why Iowa? Caucuses, Sequential Elections and Reform of Presidential Nominations* (Chicago: University of Chicago Press, forthcoming).

7. Karen Mossberger, Caroline J. Tolbert, and Ramona S. McNeal, *Digital Citizenship: The Internet, Society, and Participation* (Cambridge: MIT Press, 2008).

8. For these and other turnout data, see Michael P. McDonald, "United States Election Project: 2008 Presidential Primary Turnout Rates," http://elections.gmu

.edu/Voter_Turnout_2008_Primaries.htm (accessed February 3, 2008); Larry Sabato's Crystal Ball Web site, http://www.centerforpolitics.org/crystalball; and Nonprofit Voter Engagement Network, "America Goes to the Polls: A Report on the Voter Turnout in the 2008 Presidential Primary," http://electionlawblog.org/archives/011185.html.

9. Lonna Rae Atkeson and Cherie D. Maestas, "Meaningful Participation, and the Evolution of the Reformed Presidential Nominating System," *PS: Political Science and Politics* 42 (2009): 59–64.

10. Brian Knight and Nathan Schiff, "Momentum and Social Learning in Presidential Primaries," NBER (National Bureau of Economic Research) Working Paper No. W13637 (2007).

11. See Hugh Winebrenner, *The Iowa Precinct Caucuses: The Making of a Media Event,* 2d ed. (Ames: Iowa State University Press, 1998).

12. David P. Redlawsk, Daniel C. Bowen, and Caroline J. Tolbert, "Comparing Caucus and Registered Voter Support for the 2008 Presidential Candidates in Iowa," *PS: Political Science and Politics* 41 (2008): 129–138.

13. Walter J. Stone, Alan I. Abramowitz, and Ronald B. Rapoport, "How Representative Are the Iowa Caucuses?" in *The Iowa Caucuses and the Presidential Nominating Process,* ed. Peverill Squire (Boulder, Colo.: Westview Press, 1989).

14. Knight and Schiff, "Momentum and Social Learning," 18.

15. Christopher Hull, *Grassroots Rules: How the Iowa Caucus Helps Elect American Presidents* (Stanford, Calif.: Stanford University Press, 2007).

16. Caroline J. Tolbert, David P. Redlawsk, and Daniel C. Bowen, "Reforming Presidential Nominations: Rotating State Primaries or a National Primary?" *PS: Political Science and Politics* 42 (2009): 71–79.

17. Steven S. Smith and Melanie J. Springer, eds., *Reforming the Presidential Nomination Process* (Washington, D.C.: Brookings, 2009); Bruce E. Altschuler, "Selecting Presidential Nominees by National Primary: An Idea Whose Time Has Come?" *The Forum* 5, no. 4, art. 5 (2008), www.bepress.com/forum/vol15/iss4/art5.

18. Tolbert, Redlawsk, and Bowen, "Reforming Presidential Nominations."

CON

1. University of Iowa Hawkeye Poll, February 2008, reported in Caroline J. Tolbert, David P. Redlawsk, and Daniel C. Bowen, "Reforming Presidential Nominations: Rotating State Primaries or a National Primary?" *PS: Political Science and Politics* 42, no. 1 (2009): 71–79.

2. Reid Wilson, *The Hill,* June 15, 2009, http://thehill.com/leading-the-news/rnc-poised-to-begin-altering-its-primary-calendar-for-2012=2009=06=15.html. The RNC is poised to begin altering its primary calendar for 2012.

3. Christopher C. Hull reports on media coverage of the 2004 Iowa Caucus in his book *Grassroots Rules: How the Iowa Caucus Helps Elect American Presidents*

(Stanford, Calif.: Stanford University Press, 2007), while Brian Knight and Nathan Schiff carry out a multivariate analysis of the influence of early versus late states in "Momentum and Social Learning in Presidential Primaries," November 2007, NBER Working Paper No. W13637.

4. William G. Mayer, "An Incremental Approach to Presidential Nomination Reform," *PS: Political Science and Politics* 42, no. 1 (2009): 65–69.

5. "On Deadline," USA Today blog, http://blogs.usatoday.com/ondeadline/2008/04/blogosphere-buz.html (accessed April 17, 2009).

6. Gary C. Jacobson and Samuel Kernell, *Strategy and Choice in Congressional Elections* (New Haven, Conn.: Yale University Press, 1981).

7. Marco Battaglini, Rebecca Morton, and Thomas Palfrey, "Efficiency, Equity, and Timing of Voting Mechanisms," *American Political Science Review* 101, no. 3 (2007): 404–429.

8. David P. Redlawsk, Caroline J. Tolbert, and Todd Donovan, *Why Iowa? Caucuses, Sequential Elections and Reform of Presidential Nominations* (Chicago: University of Chicago Press, 2010).

9. Quoted in Charlotte Eby, "Iowa 1, Michigan 0," *Iowa Insider* (2007), www.wcfcourier.com/blogs/eby/?m=200710&paged=2.

10. Bruce E. Altschuler, "Selecting Presidential Nominees by National Primary: An Idea Whose Time Has Come?" *The Forum* 5, no. 4, art. 5 (2008), www.bepress.com/forum/v015/iss4/art5.

11. William G. Mayer and Andrew E. Busch, *The Front-Loading Problem in Presidential Nominations* (Washington, D.C.: Brookings, 2004).

CHAPTER 6: The Electoral College Should Be Abolished

1. Robert A. Dahl, *Pluralist Democracy in the United States: Conflict and Consent* (Chicago: Rand-McNally, 1967), 84.

2. Max Farrand, ed., *The Records of the Federal Convention*, 3 vols. (New Haven: Yale University Press, 1911), 2:500.

PRO

1. See George C. Edwards III, *Why the Electoral College Is Bad for America* (New Haven: Yale University Press, 2004), chap. 2.

2. Darshan J. Goux and David A. Hopkins, "The Empirical Implications of Electoral College Reform," *American Politics Research* 36 (November 2008): 860–864.

3. For a discussion of the 1960 election, see Edwards, *Why the Electoral College Is Bad for America*, 48–51.

4. CBS/*New York Times* poll, May 9–12, 2003.

5. Jack Rakove, "The Accidental Electors," *New York Times*, December 19, 2000, A35.

6. See Robert A. Dahl, *How Democratic Is the American Constitution?* (New Haven, Conn.: Yale University Press, 2001), 50–53, 84.

7. Max Farrand, ed., *The Records of the Federal Convention of 1787*, rev. ed., vol. 1 (New Haven, Conn.: Yale University Press, 1966), 483.

8. Ibid., 447–449.

9. Max Farrand, ed., *The Records of the Federal Convention of 1787*, rev. ed., vol. 2 (New Haven, Conn.: Yale University Press, 1966), 403.

10. I have omitted Washington, D.C., from this analysis; unlike the least populous states, the District of Columbia is not overrepresented in the electoral college.

11. *U.S. Department of Agriculture, 2007 Census of Agriculture*, vol. 1, chap. 2, table 2. (This census occurs every five years.)

12. Edwards, *Why the Electoral College Is Bad for America*, 101–103.

13. Stanley Kelley Jr., "The Presidential Campaign," in *The Presidential Election and Transition 1960–1961*, ed. Paul T. David (Washington, D.C.: Brookings, 1961), 70–72; Daron R. Shaw, "The Effect of TV Ads and Candidate Appearances on Statewide Presidential Votes, 1988–96," *American Political Science Review* 93 (June 1999): 359–360; Edwards, *Why the Electoral College Is Bad for America*, 103–109. Also see Larry M. Bartels, "Resource Allocation in a Presidential Campaign," *Journal of Politics* 47 (August 1985): 928–936; Steven J. Brams and Morton D. Davis, "The 3/2's Rule in Presidential Campaigning," *American Political Science Review* 68 (March 1974): 113–134; Claude S. Colantoni, Terrence J. Levasque, and Peter C. Ordeshook, "Campaign Resource Allocation under the Electoral College," *American Political Science Review* 69 (March 1975): 141–154; Steven J. Brams and Morton D. Davis, "Comment on 'Campaign Resource Allocations under the Electoral College,'" *American Political Science Review* 69 (March 1975): 155–156; Raymond Tatalovich, "Electoral Votes and Presidential Campaign Trails, 1932–1976," *American Politics Quarterly* 7 (October 1979): 489–497; Scott C. James and Brian L. Lawson, "The Political Economy of Voting Rights Enforcement in America's Gilded Age: Electoral College Competition, Partisan Commitment, and the Federal Election Law," *American Political Science Review* 93 (March 1999): 115–131; Daron R. Shaw, "The Methods behind the Madness: Presidential Electoral College Strategies, 1988–1996," *Journal of Politics* 61 (November 1999): 893–913; Daron R. Shaw, *The Race to 270* (Chicago: University of Chicago Press, 2007).

14. Edwards, *Why the Electoral College Is Bad for America*, 109–114.

15. Martin Diamond, *The Electoral College and the American Idea of Democracy* (Washington, D.C.: American Enterprise Institute, 1977), 4.

16. Voter News Service Exit Polls; Gallup News Service, "Candidate Support by Subgroup," news release, November 6, 2000 (based on six-day average, October 31–November 5, 2000).

17. See Eric R. A. N. Smithy and Peverill Squire, "Direct Election of the President and the Power of the States," *Western Political Quarterly* 40 (March 1987): 29–44.

18. Goux and Hopkins, "The Empirical Implications of Electoral College Reform."
19. Michael Hagen, Richard Johnston, and Kathleen Hall Jamieson, "Effects of the 2000 Presidential Campaign," paper presented at the Annual Meeting of the American Political Science Association, August 29–September 1, 2002, 3.

CON

1. Some of the points made in this chapter also appear in my contribution to an online debate on the electoral college: Sanford Levinson, John McGinnis, and Daniel H. Lowenstein, *Should We Dispense with the Electoral College?* University of Pennsylvania Law Review PENNumbra 10 (2007): 156, http://www. pennumbra.com/debates/pdfs/electoral_college.pdf.
2. The term *electoral college* does not appear in the Constitution and is a misnomer. A collegial body is one that meets and deliberates together. The Constitution specifies that the electors are to meet separately in their own states, thus precluding them as a group from operating in a collegial way. Tradition hallows continued use of the term *electoral college*, but the misnomer need not be compounded by capitalization.
3. Bradley Smith, "Vanity of Vanities: National Popular Vote and the Electoral College," *Election Law Journal* 7 (2007): 196–217, provides a cogent demonstration of this point. The following discussion draws in part on Smith's analysis.
4. Ibid., 216.
5. Not as close to inevitable as it should be, however, because of the possibility of a tie in the electoral vote. Congress could and should change the number of House members to an odd number to minimize the possibility of a tie vote in the electoral college.
6. Smith, "Vanity of Vanities," 213–214.
7. Levinson et al., *Should We Dispense with the Electoral College?* (McGinnis, rebuttal).
8. For examples, see Smith, "Vanity of Vanities," 199–200. Two prominent electoral college opponents concede that "the two opposing skews largely cancel each other out." Akhil Reed Amar and Vikram David Amar, "Why Old and New Arguments for the Electoral College Are Not Compelling," in *After the People Vote: A Guide to the Electoral College,* 3d ed., ed. John C. Fortier (Washington, D.C.: AEI Press, 2004), 61.
9. Levinson et al., *Should We Dispense with the Electoral College?* (Levinson, closing argument).
10. See Richard L. Hasen, "Beyond the Margin of Litigation: Reforming U.S. Election Administration to Avoid Electoral Meltdown," *Washington and Lee Law Review* 62 (2005): 937–999.
11. Levinson et al., *Should We Dispense with the Electoral College?* (Levinson, closing argument).

CHAPTER 7: Proportional Representation Should Be Adopted for
U.S. House Elections

PRO

1. Also see Douglas J. Amy, *Real Choices/New Voices: How Proportional Representation Elections Could Revitalize American Democracy* (New York: Columbia University Press, 2002); or David Farrell, *Electoral Systems: A Comparative Introduction* (New York: Palgrave, 2001).
2. Arend Lijphart and Bernard Grofman, eds., *Choosing an Electoral System: Issues and Alternatives* (New York: Praeger, 1984), 7.
3. See Douglas J. Amy, "A Brief History of Proportional Representation in the United States," www.mtholyoke.edu/acad/polit/damy/articles/Brief%20 History%200f%20PR.htm.
4. For more about Cambridge's PR system, see www.cambridgema.gov/election/ Proportional_Representation.cfm.
5. Currently, the main organization promoting PR in the U.S. is FairVote in Washington, D.C., http://www.fairvote.org.

CON

1. Douglas J. Amy, Real *Choices/New Voices: How Proportional Representation Elections Could Revitalize American Democracy* (New York: Columbia University Press, 2002).
2. State legislators draw district lines for themselves and for Congress.
3. See *Baker* v. *Carr,* 369 U.S. 186 (1962); and *Reynolds* v. *Sims,* 377 U.S. 533 (1964).
4. This paragraph is drawn from my essay "Another Missed Opportunity," *Virginia Capitol Connections* 19 (Spring 2009), www.dbava.com/qm_spr_09_web.pdf (accessed June 7, 2009).
5. See John Stuart Mill, *Considerations on Representative Government,* www .constitution.org/jsm/rep_gov.htm (accessed June 9, 2009).
6. See, e.g., "Global Database of Quotas for Women," www.quotaproject.org/ aboutQuotas.cfm (accessed May 27, 2009). Also see European Parliament, "Electoral Gender Quota Systems and Their Implementation in Europe," (accessed May 27, 2009).
7. In some cases, a minority government may form with the consent of the opposition. Still, the point is that the government is created after the people have expressed their electoral choices, not as a result of those choices.
8. See Richard S. Katz, "Electoral Reform Is Not as Simple as It Looks," *Inroads: A Journal of Opinion* (January 1998): 65–72.
9. See, e.g., Gregory Mahler, "Parliament and Congress: Is the Grass Greener on the Other Side?" *Canadian Parliamentary Review* 8, no. 4 (1985).
10. A very telling example of this occurred after the 1994 elections when the Republican Senate stymied the House Republicans' "Contract with America." See,

e.g., Paul Christopher Manuel and Anne Marie Cammisa, *Checks and Balances? How a Parliamentary System Could Change American Politics* (Boulder, Colo.: Westview Press, 1998).

11. For a great discussion of the many dichotomous choices involved in electoral reform, see Katz, "Electoral Reform Is Not as Simple as It Looks."

CHAPTER 8: The "No Cup of Coffee" Rule Should Be Adopted in Washington

PRO

1. Bill Boyarsky, *Jesse Unruh and the Art of Power Politics* (Berkeley: University of California Press, 2007).

2. See http://pollingreport.com/CongJob.htm; also see John Hibbing and Elizabeth Theiss-Morse, *Congress as Public Enemy* (New York: Cambridge University Press, 1995).

3. See Gary C. Jacobson and Michael A. Dimock, "Checking Out: The Effects of Bank Overdrafts on the 1992 Congressional Elections," *American Journal of Political Science* 38 (August 1994): 601–624; Gary C. Jacobson, "The 1994 House Elections in Perspective," *Political Science Quarterly* 111 (Summer 1996): 203–223.

4. Although other, more national factors were more important than scandals; see Gary C. Jacobson, "Referendum: the 2006 Midterm Congressional Elections," *Political Science Quarterly* 122 (Spring 2007). Still, the DeLay and Abramoff problems did tarnish the Republican brand name.

5. Alan Rosenthal, *Drawing the Line: Legislative Ethics in the States* (Lincoln: University of Nebraska Press, 1996), 9 (emphasis added).

6. Peggy Kerns and Susan Huntley, "States Restrict Lobbying Activities," National Conference of State Legislatures *Legisbrief* (August/September 2007), www.ncsl .org.ethics, June 12, 2009.

7. Personal e-mail communication. The NCSL *Legisbrief* on this issue notes changes over time; thus Vermont and South Dakota were previously considered no cup of coffee states but have been removed from the list.

8. Among others, see David Osborne, *Laboratories of Democracy* (Cambridge, Mass.: Harvard Business School Press, 1990).

9. Emphasis added.

10. "Ethics: Giving and Reporting Coffee," NCSL Center for Ethics in Government, March 2008, www.ncsl.org (accessed June 13, 2009). Subsequent figures in this section are drawn from this document or "Legislator Gift Restrictions Overview," noted above.

11. The fourth degree would include great-grandparents, first cousins, and grandnephews/nieces, among others. State regulations range from third degree to seventh degree of consanguinity in setting limits on receiving gifts.

12. Rosenthal, *Drawing the Line*, 121.

13. See Darrell West and Burdett Loomis, *The Sound of Money* (New York: W. W. Norton, 1998); and Gary Andres, *Lobbying Reconsidered: Politics under the Influence* (New York: Longman, 2009).

14. Rosenthal, *Drawing the Line*, 121–122.

15. Senate Ethics Committee, "New Ethics Rules: Gifts and Events," 2009.

CON

1. Public Citizen, Congress Watch, "Recent Public Opinion Polls on Ethics in Government," February 15, 2006, www.citizen.org/congress/govt_reform/ethics/congethics/articles.cfm?ID=14945 (accessed July 8, 2009).

2. Jonathan D. Salant and Kristin Jensen, "Abramoff's 'Equal Money' Went Mostly to Republicans (Update1)," December 21, 2005, www.bloomberg.com/apps/news?pid=10000103&sid=arVHles5cKJc&refer=us (accessed July 8, 2009).

3. Massie Ritsch and Courtney Mabeus, "Casting Off Abramoff," April 7, 2006, www.opensecrets.org/capital_eye/inside.php?ID=210 (accessed July 8, 2009).

4. R. Jeffrey Smith, "A High-Powered Lobbyist's Swift Fall from Grace," *Washington Post*, August 12, 2005, www.washingtonpost.com/wp-dyn/content/article/2005/08 /11/AR2005081101752_pf.html (accessed July 8, 2009).

5. ABC News, "Hastert: No. 1 Recipient of Abramoff Money," May 24, 2006, blogs .abcnews.com/theblotter/2006/05/hastert_no_1_re.html (accessed July 8, 2009).

CHAPTER 9: The Size of the House of Representatives Should Be Increased to 675 Seats

PRO

1. Rein Taagepera, "The Size of National Assemblies," *Social Science Research* 1 (1972): 385–401; Rein Taagepera and Mathew Soberg Shugart, *Seats and Votes: The Effects and Determinants of Electoral Systems* (New Haven, Conn. Yale University Press, 1989); Arend Lijphart, "Reforming the House, Conn.: Three Moderately Radical Proposals," in *The U.S. House of Representatives: Reform or Rebuild,* ed. Joseph F. Zimmerman and Wilma Rule (Westport, Conn.: Praeger, 2000), 135–140; DeWayne L. Lucas and Michael D. McDonald, "Is It Time to Increase the Size of the House of Representatives?" *American Review of Politics* 21 (2000): 367–381; Jeffrey W. Ladewig and Mathew P. Jasinski, "On the Causes and Consequences of and Remedies for Interstate Malapportionment of the U.S. House of Representatives," *Perspectives on Politics* 6 (2008): 89–107.

2. William F. Willoughby, *Principles of Legislative Organization and Administration* (Washington, D.C.: Brookings, 1934); Nelson W. Polsby, "The Institutionalization of the House of Representatives," *American Political Science Review* 62 (1968): 144–168; Kenneth A. Shepsle, "Representation and Governance: The Great Legislative Trade-off," *Political Science Quarterly* 103 (1988): 461–484.

3. Robert A. Dahl and Edward R. Tufte, *Size and Democracy* (Stanford, Calif.: Stanford University Press, 1973).

4. For further evidence, see Taagepera and Shugart, *Seats and Votes,* 175; Lucas and McDonald, "Is It Time to Increase the Size of the House of Representatives," 372; Ladewig and Jasinski, "On the Causes and Consequences of and Remedies for Interstate Malapportionment of the U.S. House of Representatives," 100.

5. Jonathan I. Lieb and Gerald R. Webster, "On Enlarging the House of Representatives," *Political Geography* 17 (1997): 319–329; George Will, "Congress Just Isn't Big Enough," *Washington Post,* January 14, 2001, B7; Brian Frederick, *Congressional Representation and Constituents: The Case for Increasing the Size of the U.S. House of Representatives* (New York: Routledge, 2009).

6. John R. Hibbing and John R. Alford, "Constituency Population and Representation in the U.S. Senate," *Legislative Studies Quarterly* 15 (1990): 581–598; Sarah Binder, Forrest Maltzman, and Lee Siegelman, "Accounting for Senators' Home State Reputations: Why Do Constituents Love a Bill Cohen So Much More Than an Al D'Amato," *Legislative Studies Quarterly* 23 (1998): 545–560; Frances Lee and Bruce I. Oppenheimer, *Sizing Up the Senate: The Unequal Consequences of Equal Representation* (Chicago: University of Chicago Press, 1999); Gary C. Jacobson, "Polarized Opinion in the States: Partisan Differences in Approval Ratings of Governors, Senators, and George W. Bush," *Presidential Studies Quarterly* 36 (2006): 732–757.

7. Brian Frederick, "Constituency Population and Representation in the U.S. House," *American Politics Research* 36 (2008): 358–368; Frederick, *Congressional Representation and Constituents.*

8. Dahl and Tufte, *Size and Democracy,* 84–85.

9. Frederick, *Congressional Representation and Constituents.*

10. Jane Mansbridge, "Should Blacks Represent Blacks and Women Represent Women? A Contingent Yes," *Journal of Politics* 61 (1999): 628–657.

11. James Glassman, "Let's Build a Bigger House; Why Shouldn't the Number of Congressmen Grow with the Population," *Washington Post,* June 17, 1990, D2; Charles A. Kromkowski and John A. Kromkowski, "Why 435? A Question of Political Arithmetic," *Polity* 24 (1991): 129–145; Wilma Rule, "Expanded Congress Would Help Women," *New York Times,* February 24, 1991, E16; Christopher St. John Yates, "A House of Our Own or a House We've Outgrown? An Argument for Increasing the Size of the House of Representatives," *Columbia Journal of Law and Social Problems* 25 (1992): 157–196.

12. Brian Frederick, "The People's Perspective on the Size of the People's House," *PS: Political Science and Politics* 41 (2008): 329–335; Frederick, *Congressional Representation and Constituents.*

13. Kromkowski and Kromkowski, "Why 435," 138, table IV. Calculations through 2000 were updated by the author.

14. Stephen Ohlemacher, "Growing Population Shifts Political Power," Associated Press, December 22, 2005.

15. Vincent B. Thompson, "Projecting Reapportionment," *Indiana Business Review* 40 (2005): 4–6.

16. Michael Barone and Richard E Cohen, *Almanac of American Politics 2004* (Washington, D.C.: National Journal Group, 2003), 1090.

17. Kromkowski and Kromkowski, "Why 435," 139.

18. Brian Nutting and H. Amy Stern, eds., *CQ's Politics in America 2002: The 107th Congress* (Washington, D.C.: Congressional Quarterly Inc., 2001).

19. Morris Silverman, "Better Yet, Reduce the Size of House," *New York Times,* January 14, 1991, A17.

20. Willoughby, *Principles of Legislative Organization and Administration.*

21. Lawrence C. Evans and Walter J. Oleszek, "If It Ain't Broke Don't Fix It a Lot," in *The U.S. House of Representatives: Reform or Rebuild,* ed. Joseph F. Zimmerman and Wilma Rule (Westport, Conn.: Praeger, 2000), 189–190.

22. Barbara Sinclair, *Unorthodox Lawmaking: New Legislative Processes in the U.S. Congress,* 3d ed. (Washington, D.C.: CQ Press, 2007).

CON

1. See Brian Frederick, "Constituency Population and Representation in the U.S. House," *American Politics Research* 36 (2008): 358–381.

2. Quoted in C. Lawrence Evans and Walter J. Oleszek, "If It Ain't Broke, Don't Fix It a Lot," *PS: Political Science and Politics* 31, no. 1 (March 1998): 26.

3. DeWayne L. Lucas and Michael D. McDonald, "Is It Time to Increase the Size of the House?" *American Review of Politics* 21 (Winter 2000): 374.

4. Roger H. Davidson and Walter J. Oleszek, *Congress and Its Members,* 9th ed. (Washington, D.C.: CQ Press, 2004), 141.

5. Ibid.

6. For an accessible treatment, see Bill Bishop, *The Big Sort: Why the Clustering of Like-Minded America Is Tearing Us Apart* (New York: Houghton Mifflin, 2008).

7. On the advantages of an ombudsman's office for Congress, see Morris P. Fiorina, *Congress: Keystone of the Washington Establishment* (New Haven, Conn.: Yale University Press, 1977).

8. James Madison, letter to W. T. Barry, August 4, 1822.

CHAPTER 10: The Redistricting Process Should Be Nonpartisan

1. In the original Constitution, of course, population was calculated not only on the basis of "the whole Number of free Persons" and indentured servants but also on the number of slaves, each of whom was counted as three-fifths of a person. "Indians not taxed" were also excluded from the population count.

PRO

1. John Mercurio, "Between the Lines," *Roll Call,* July 2, 2001.
2. E.g., see Robert Boatright, "Static Ambition in a Changing World: Legislators' Preparations for and Responses to Redistricting," *State Politics and Policy Quarterly* 4, no. 4 (2004): 436–454.
3. Comments to the Fairfax County League of Women Voters, January 24, 2009.
4. For an early examination of "seats to votes" relationship, see Edward R. Tufte, "The Relationship between Seats and Votes in Two-Party Systems," *The American Political Science Review* 67, no. 2 (1973): 540–554.
5. These partisan gerrymandering strategies are discussed by Bruce E. Cain, *The Reapportionment Puzzle* (Berkeley: University of California Press, 1984); and Guillermo Owen and Bernard N. Grofman, "Optimal Partisan Gerrymandering," *Political Geography Quarterly* 7, no. 1 (1984): 5–22.
6. Alexander Keyssar, *The Right to Vote: The Contested History of Democracy in the United States* (New York: Basic Books, 2000).
7. Quoted in Max Farrand, *The Records of the Federal Convention of 1817* (New Haven, Conn.: Yale University Press, 1966), 240–241.
8. Paul J. Weber, "Madison's Opposition to a Second Convention," *Polity* 20 (1998): 498.
9. *Baker v. Carr,* 369 U.S. 186 (1962).
10. Justin Levitt and Michael P. McDonald, "Taking the 'Re' out of Redistricting: State Constitutional Provisions on Redistricting Timing," *Georgetown Law Review* 95, no. 4 (2007): 1247–1286.
11. E.g., see John P. White and Norman C. Thomas, "Urban and Rural Representation and State Legislative Apportionment," *The Western Political Quarterly* 17 (1964): 724–741; Philip Musgrove, *The General Theory of Gerrymandering* (Beverly Hills, Calif.: Sage Publications, 1977); and Gary W. Cox and Jonathan N. Katz, *Elbridge Gerry's Salamander: The Electoral Consequences of the Reapportionment Revolution* (Cambridge: Cambridge University Press, 2002).
12. Andrew Gelman and Gary King, "A Unified Method of Evaluating Electoral Systems and Redistricting Plans," *American Journal of Political Science* 38 (1994): 514–554.
13. Richard G. Niemi and Laura R. Winsky, "The Persistence of Partisan Redistricting Effects in Congressional Elections in the 1970s and 1980s," *The Journal of Politics* 54 (1992): 565–572.
14. Chandler Davidson and Bernard Grofman, eds., *Quiet Revolution in the South: The Impact of the Voting Rights Act, 1965–1990* (Princeton, N.J.: Princeton University Press, 1994).
15. *Davis v. Bandemer,* 478 U.S. 109 (1986). Only the adoption of at-large judicial districts in North Carolina have been overturned under the *Bandemer* standard. See *Republican Party of North Carolina v. Martin,* 980 F.2d 943 (4th Cir. 1992).

16. Michael P. McDonald, "A Comparative Analysis of U.S. State Redistricting Institutions," *State Politics and Policy Quarterly* 4, no. 4 (2004): 371–396.

17. For a comprehensive overview of how redistricting takes place, see Justin Levitt, *A Citizen's Guide to Redistricting* (New York: Brennan Center for Justice at New York University School of Law, 2008), www.brennancenter.org/content/resource/a_citizens_guide_to_redistricting/.

18. See Lisa Handley, "A Comparative Survey of Structures and Criteria for Boundary Delimitation," in *Redistricting in Comparative Perspective,* ed. Bernard Grofman and Lisa Handley (New York: Oxford University Press, 2008).

19. For information about the Parliamentary Boundary Commission of England, see www.statistics.gov.uk/pbc/default.asp.

20. Some call any commission "independent," such as Alan Abramowitz, Brad Alexander, and Matthew Gunning, "Don't Blame Redistricting for Uncompetitive Elections," *PS: Political Science and Politics* 39, no. 1 (2006): 87–90; while others examine the institutions in detail and come to different conclusions (see McDonald, "A Comparative Analysis of U.S. State Redistricting Institutions").

21. I served as a consultant to the Arizona commission during the post-2000 round of redistricting. For an overview of Arizona's experience, see Michael P. McDonald "Drawing the Line on District Competition," *PS: Political Science and Politics* 39, no. 1 (2006): 91–94.

22. Bruce E. Cain, Karin Mac Donald, and Michael McDonald, "From Equality to Fairness: The Path of Political Reform since *Baker v. Carr*," in *Party Lines: Competition, Partisanship, and Congressional Redistricting*, ed. Bruce E. Cain and Thomas Mann (Washington, D.C.: Brookings, 2005).

23. Micah Altman, Karin Mac Donald, and Michael McDonald, "Pushbutton Gerrymanders? How Computing Has Changed Redistricting," in *Party Lines: Competition, Partisanship, and Congressional Redistricting*, ed. Bruce E. Cain and Thomas Mann (Washington, D.C.: Brookings, 2005).

24. For an argument in favor of this approach, see Sam Hirsch, "A Proposal for Redistricting Reform: A Model State Constitutional Amendment," paper presented at the 2009 American Mathematical Society Special Session on "The Redistricting Problem," Washington, D.C., January 8, 2009.

25. Frank R. Parker, *Black Votes Count* (Chapel Hill: University of North Carolina Press, 1990).

26. Adam B. Cox, "Partisan Fairness and Redistricting Politics," *New York University Law Review* 70 (2004): 751–802.

27. Antonin Scalia, *A Matter of Interpretation: Federal Courts and the Law* (Princeton: Princeton, N.J. University Press, 1997).

28. David R. Mayhew, *Congress: The Electoral Connection* (New Haven, Conn.: Yale University Press, 1974).

29. Handley, "A Comparative Survey of Structures and Criteria for Boundary Delimitation."

CON

1. Howard Scarrow, "The Impact of Reapportionment on Party Representation in the State of New York," *Policy Studies Journal Special Issue on Reapportionment* 9 (1981): 937–946.
2. Looking at the total number of votes each party wins in congressional elections across the state is problematic because so many incumbents face weak challengers who cannot even maintain the support of voters in their own party.
3. Samuel Issacharoff, "Gerrymandering and Political Cartels," *Harvard Law Review* 116 (2002): 592–648.
4. David Butler and Bruce E. Cain, *Congressional Redistricting: Comparative and Theoretical Perspectives* (New York: Macmillan, 1992).
5. For elaboration, see Justin Buchler, "The Statistical Properties of Competitive Districts: What the Central Limit Theorem Can Teach Us about Election Reform," *PS: Political Science and Politics* 40 (2007): 333–337.
6. Alan I. Abramowitz, Brad Alexander, and Matthew Gunning, "Incumbency, Redistricting, and the Decline of Competition in U.S. House Elections," *Journal of Politics* 68 (2006): 75–88; Seth Masket, Jonathan Winburn, and Gerald C. Wright, "The Limits of the Gerrymander: Examining the Impact of Redistricting on Electoral Competition and Legislative Polarization," paper presented at the 2006 Annual Meeting of the Midwest Political Science Association; Eric McGhee, *Redistricting and Legislative Partisanship,* Report for Public Policy Institute of California, 2008; Justin Buchler, "Redistricting Reform Will Not Solve California's Budget Crisis," *California Journal of Politics and Policy* 1, no. 1 (2009).
7. Justin Buchler, "Competition, Representation, and Redistricting: The Case against Competitive Congressional Districts," *Journal of Theoretical Politics* 17 (2005): 431–463.
8. Thomas Brunell and Justin Buchler, "Ideological Representation and Competitive Congressional Elections," *Electoral Studies* 28 (2009): 448–457.

CHAPTER 11: The Senate Should Represent People, Not States

PRO

1. *Reynolds v. Sims,* 377 U.S. 533 (1964).
2. Charles R. Beitz, *Political Equality: An Essay in Democratic Theory* (Princeton, N.J.: Princeton University Press, 1989), 141.
3. See France E. Lee and Bruce I. Oppenheimer, *Sizing Up the Senate: The Unequal Consequences of Equal Representation* (Chicago: University of Chicago Press, 1999).
4. Harold Lasswell, *Politics: Who Gets What, When, How* (New York: McGraw-Hill, 1936).

CON

1. Scott J. Bowman, "Note: Wild Political Dreaming: Constitutional Reformation of the United States Senate," *Fordham Law Review* 72 (March 2004): 1017–1051.
2. Timothy Noah, "Abolish the Senate!" *Slate*, November 2, 2000, www.slate.com/id/1006400/.
3. F. Josef Hebert, "GOP Assault on Federal Red Tape Off to Strong Start," Associated Press, March 6, 1995.
4. Victoria F. Nourse and Jane S. Schacter, "The Politics of Legislative Drafting: A Congressional Case Study," *New York University Law Review* 77 (June 2002): 593.
5. See the similar argument about other weighted voting systems in Keith R. Wesolowski, "Remedy Gone Awry: Weighing In on Weighted Voting," *William and Mary Law Review* 44 (March 2003): 1907.
6. Richard Briffault, "Who Rules at Home? One Person/One Vote and Local Governments," *University of Chicago Law Review* 60 (Spring 1993): 410.
7. Jeffrey W. Ladewig and Mathew P. Jasinski, "On the Causes and Consequences of and Remedies for Interstate Malapportionment of the U.S. House of Representatives," *Perspectives on Politics* 6 (March 2008): 89–107.
8. Gary Mucciaroni and Paul J. Quirk, *Deliberative Choices: Debating Public Policy in Congress* (Chicago: University of Chicago Press, 2007), 194.
9. Ibid., 195.
10. Ross K. Baker, *House and Senate*, 4th ed. (New York: W. W. Norton, 2008), 80.
11. Alexander Hamilton, James Madison, and John Jay, *The Federalist Papers*, ed. Clinton Rossiter, with a new introduction and notes by Charles R. Kesler (New York: Signet, 2003), 358.
12. Janet Hook, "House GOP: Plight of a Permanent Minority," *Congressional Quarterly Weekly Report*, June 21, 1986, 1393.
13. *Congressional Record* (daily), March 3, 1993, H975–H976.
14. Carl Hulse, "With Promises of a Better-Run Congress, Democrats Take on Political Risks," *New York Times*, December 27, 2006.
15. Sarah A. Binder, Thomas E. Mann, Norman J. Ornstein, and Molly Reynolds, "Assessing the 110th Congress, Anticipating the 111th," Brookings Institution, January 2009, www.brookings.edu/~/media/Files/rc/papers/2009/0108_broken_branch_binder_mann/0108_broken_branch_binder_mann.pdf.
16. *Congressional Record* (daily), October 2, 2007, H11142.
17. R. Douglas Arnold, *Congress, the Press, and Political Accountability* (New York: Russell Sage Foundation, 2004), 59.
18. Jennifer Dorroh, "Endangered Species," *American Journalism Review* (December/January 2009), www.ajr.org/article.asp?id=4645.
19. John S. Horn, "The District Connection: Competitive Districts and Candidate Quality" (Ph.D. diss., Claremont Graduate University, 2009).

CHAPTER 12: Senate Rule XXII Should Be Amended So That Filibusters Can Be Ended by a Majority Vote

CON

1. Marvin Meyers, *The Mind of the Founder: Sources of the Political Thought of James Madison* (Waltham: Brandeis University Press, 1981), 68.
2. *The Federalist Papers,* ed. Charles R. Kesler and Clinton Rossiter (New York: New American Library, Penguin Group, 1999), 377.
3. Ibid., 376.
4. Coral Davenport, "Beyond Yucca, A Blurry View," CQ Weekly Online, April 27, 2009, 966–972, at http://library.cqpress.com/cqweekly/weeklyreport111-000003103264.
5. David S. Cloud, "Senate Sends $27 Billion Bill Straight for a Veto," CQ Weekly Online, October 10, 1992, 3132–3133, at http://library.cqpress.com/cqweekly/WR102408626.
6. David Nather, "Senate Races against the Nuclear Clock on Judges," CQ Weekly Online, May 30, 2005, 1441–1443, at http://library.cqpress.com/cqweekly/weeklyreport109-000001700754.
7. Ibid.

CHAPTER 13: The President Should Be Granted a Line Item Veto

CON

1. James D. Richardson, *Messages and Papers of the Presidents,* vol. 6 (Washington, D.C.: Bureau of National Literature, 1913), 4197. The first item veto to appear in an American document was in the Confederate constitution of 1861, but Confederate president Jefferson Davis never used the power.
2. "Bush Asks Congress to Approve Line Item Veto," Clear Channel Communications, March 7, 2006, http://www.webcenter11.com (accessed March 8, 2006).
3. Quoted in Robert J. Spitzer, "The Constitutionality of the Presidential Line-Item Veto," *Political Science Quarterly* 112 (Summer 1997): 270.
4. Ibid., 272–273.
5. Louis Fisher, "The Item Veto—a Misconception," *Washington Post,* February 23, 1987, 22.
6. "Statement by Louis Fisher, Specialist at the Law Library, Before the Committee on the Budget, U.S. House of Representatives, 'Line-Item Veto—Constitutional Issues,'" June 8, 2006, 3.
7. Ibid.

8. Congressional Budget Office testimony, statement of Donald B. Marron, acting director, "CBO's Comments on H.R. 4890, the Legislative Line Item Veto Act of 2006," before the Subcommittee on the Legislative and Budget Process, Committee on Rules, U.S. House of Representatives, March 15, 2006, 1.

9. Robert J. Spitzer, "The Item Veto Dispute and the Secular Crisis of the Presidency," *Presidential Studies Quarterly* 28 (Fall 1998): 799–805; "Statement by Louis Fisher," 4.

10. Robert J. Spitzer, *The Presidency and Public Policy* (Tuscaloosa: University of Alabama Press, 1983), 98–100.

11. U.S. House of Representatives, Committee on Rules, "Proceedings of a Hearing of the Subcommittee on the Legislative Process," September 18 and 25, 1992 (Washington, D.C.: Government Printing Office, 1992), 258, 271.

12. Statement of Donald B. Marron, acting director, "CBO's Comments on S.2381, the Legislative Line Item Veto Act of 2006," before the Committee on the Budget, U.S. Senate, May 2, 2006, 2.

13. Quoted in Robert J. Spitzer, *The Presidential Veto* (Albany: State University of New York Press, 1988), 133.

14. Robert Pear, "From Bush, Foe of Earmarks, Similar Items," *New York Times,* February 10, 2008, A1.

15. Spitzer, *The Presidential Veto,* 92–93.

16. These studies are summarized in Andrew Rudalevige, "Deficit Politics and the Item Veto," paper presented at the Annual Meeting of the American Political Science Association, Washington, D.C., August 28–31, 1997.

CHAPTER 14: The Government Should Scale Back the Outsourcing of Government Jobs to Private Contractors

PRO

1. Jonas Prager, "Contract City Redux: Weston, Florida, as the Ultimate Public Management Model City," *Public Administration Review* 68, no. 1 (January–February 2008): 167–180.

2. Walter Pincus, "Conferees Want Hard Look at Contractors," *Washington Post,* December 17, 2007.

3. Partnership for Public Service, *Annual Report,* 2008, 15.

4. Robert O'Harrow Jr., "Costs Escalate as DHS Overruns No-Bid Contracts," *Washington Post,* June 28, 2007, A1, A8.

5. Scott Higham and Robert O'Harrow Jr., "Audit Details High Costs of Contractor," *Washington Post,* June 30, 2005, A1, A12.

6. Robert O'Harrow Jr., "A $191 Million Question," *Washington Post,* August 7, 2009, A1, A6.

7. Federal Activities Inventory Reform Act of 1998, Public Law 105–270, 105th Cong., 112 Stat 2382, Section 5.

CON

1. James Q. Wilson, *Bureaucracy: What Government Agencies Do and Why They Do It* (New York: Basic Books, 1989; preface to the 2000 edition), ix.
2. Jeffrey D. Greene, *Public Administration in the New Century* (Belmont, Calif.: Thomson Wadsworth, 2005), 342.
3. E. S. Savas, *Privatization and Public-Private Partnerships* (Washington, D.C.: CQ Press, 2000), 72–73.
4. Government Contracting Institute, www.ucg.com/govt.
5. Robin A. Johnson and Norman Walzer, "Privatization and Managed Competition: Management Fad or Long-Term Systematic Change for Cities?" in *Local Government Innovation,* ed. Robin A. Johnson and Norman Walzer (Westport, Conn.: Quorum Books, 2000), 172; Jeffrey D. Greene, "How Much Privatization?" *Policy Studies Journal* 24, no. 4 (1996): 632–640.
6. E. S. Savas, *Privatization in the City: Successes, Failures, Lessons* (Washington, D.C.: CQ Press, 2005), 45–46; Jeffrey D. Greene, *Cities and Privatization* (Upper Saddle River, N.J.: Prentice Hall, 2002), 51.
7. Savas, *Privatization and Public-Private Partnerships,* 175–210.
8. Barbara J. Stevens, "Comparing Public- and Private-Sector Productive Efficiency," *National Productivity Review* 3 (Autumn 1984): 395–406.
9. E. S. Savas, "Public vs. Private Refuse Collection: A Critical Review of the Evidence," *Urban Analysis* 6 (1979): 1–13.
10. Annual Privatization Report, 2008 (Los Angeles: Reason Foundation, 2008).
11. Stevens, "Comparing Public- and Private-Sector Productive Efficiency," 405.
12. Greene, *Cities and Privatization,* 51.
13. Phillip J. Cooper, *Governing by Contract* (Washington, D.C.: CQ Press, 2003).
14. Marilyn J. Cohodas, "Outsourcing's Ins and Outs," *Governing* (December 1997): 84.
15. Dudek and Company, "The Long-Term Employment Implications of Privatization," National Commission for Employment Policy, Washington, D.C., March 1989.
16. See http://en.wikipedia.org/wiki/Attica_Prison_riots, July 12, 2009.

CHAPTER 15: The Terms of Supreme Court Justices Should Be Limited to Eighteen Years

PRO

1. David J. Garrow, "Mental Decrepitude on the U.S. Supreme Court: The Historical Case for a 28th Amendment," *University of Chicago Law Review* 67 (2000): 995.

CON

1. Steven G. Calabresi, "How to Reverse Government Imposition of Immorality: A Strategy for Eroding *Roe v. Wade,*" *Harvard Journal of Law and Public Policy* 31 (Winter 2008): 85–92 (emphasis in original).
2. Mark V. Tushnet, *Taking the Constitution away from the Courts* (Princeton, N.J.: Princeton University Press, 1999), 172. Tushnet has also declared that if he were a judge he would do what he could to advance the cause of socialism. See "The Dilemmas of Liberal Constitutionalism," *Ohio State Law Journal* 42 (1981): 411, 424.

CHAPTER 16: The United States Should Adopt an "Emergency Constitution" to Preserve Civil Liberties in an Age of Terrorism

CON

1. Carl Schmitt, *Political Theology: Four Chapters on the Concept of Sovereignty* (Cambridge: MIT Press, 1998), 5. The best general survey of thinking about states of emergency is Oren Gross and Fionnula Ní Aoláin, *Law in Times of Crisis: Emergency Powers in Theory and Practice* (New York: Cambridge University Press, 2006).
2. For an especially sophisticated development of this approach, see Oren Gross, "Chaos and Rules: Should Responses to Violent Crises Always Be Constitutional," *Yale Law Journal* 112 (2003): 1011, 1099.
3. Bruce Ackerman, *Before the Next Attack: Preserving Civil Liberties in an Age of Terrorism* (New Haven, Conn.: Yale University Press, 2006), 19, 60. For an earlier version of Ackerman's proposal and the intense debate it triggered, see Bruce Ackerman, "The Emergency Constitution," *Yale Law Journal* 113 (2004): 1029; David Cole, "The Priority of Morality: The Emergency Constitution's Blind Spot," *Yale Law Journal* 113 (2004): 1753; Laurence H. Tribe and Patrick O. Gudridge, "The Anti-Emergency Constitution," *Yale Law Journal* 113 (2004): 1801; and Bruce Ackerman, "This Is Not a War," *Yale Law Journal* 113 (2004): 1871.
4. *Home Building and Loan Association v. Blaisdell*, 290 U.S. 398 (1934).
5. See Peter Irons, *Justice at War: The Story of the Japanese American Internment Cases* (New York: Oxford University Press, 1983).

CHAPTER 17: Residents Who Are Not Citizens Should Be Granted the Right to Vote

1. Jeff Manza and Christopher Uggen, *Locked Out: Felon Disenfranchisement and American Democracy* (New York: Oxford University Press, 2008), 291–292, note 6; Elizabeth A. Hull, *The Disenfranchisement of Ex-Felons* (Philadelphia: Temple University Press, 2006), 5.

PRO

1. This essay was adapted from *Democracy for All: Restoring Immigrant Voting Rights in the United States* (New York: Routledge, 2006).
2. The terms *immigrants, foreign born, aliens, émigrés, refugees, asylees, green card holders, newcomers,* and *noncitizens* refer to the same persons—persons who are not citizens by birth right or naturalization—and the terms are used interchangeably. Similarly, *noncitizen voting, alien suffrage, immigrant voting, resident voting,* and *local citizenship* refer to the same practice—voting by individuals who are not U.S. citizens.
3. Nancy Foner, Ruben Rumbaut, and Steven Gold, *Immigration Research for a New Century* (New York: Russell Sage Foundation, 2001).
4. National Research Council of the National Academy of Sciences, *The New Americans: Economic, Demographic, and Fiscal Effects of Immigration,* ed. James P. Smith and Barry Edmonston (Washington, D.C.: National Academy Press, 1997); and National Research Council of the National Academy of Sciences, *The Immigration Debate: Studies on the Economic, Demographic, and Fiscal Effects of Immigration,* ed. James P. Smith and Barry Edmonston (Washington, D.C.: National Academy Press, 1998).
5. Joaquin Avila, "Political Apartheid in California: Consequences of Excluding a Growing Noncitizen Population," *Latino Policy and Issues Brief,* no. 9 (Los Angeles: Chicano Studies Research Center, University of California, Los Angeles, 2003).
6. Jamin Raskin, "Legal Aliens, Local Citizens: The Historical, Constitutional, and Theoretical Meanings of Alien Suffrage," *University of Pennsylvania Law Review* 141 (1993): 1407 (emphasis in the original).
7. Joseph A. Ranney, "Aliens and 'Real Americans': Law and Ethnic Assimilation in Wisconsin, 1846–1920" *Wisconsin Lawyer,* www.wisbar.org.

CON

1. This essay is adapted from Stanley A. Renshon, "Allowing Non-Citizens to Vote in the United States? Why Not," Center for Immigration Studies, September 2008, www.cis.org/articles/2008/renshon_08.pdf; and Stanley A. Renshon, *Noncitizen Voting and American Democracy* (Lanham, Md.: Rowman and Littlefield, 2009).
2. "A Citizen's Right," *New York Times,* April 19, 2004.
3. Daniel Munro, "City Citizenship and Democratic Multiculturalism," paper presented at the Annual Meeting of the Canadian Political Science Association, June 1–4, 2006, 2–3 (emphasis added); Lisa García Bedolla, "Rethinking Citizenship: Noncitizen Voting and Immigrant Political Engagement in the United States," in *Transforming Politics, Transforming America: The Political and Civic Incorporation of Immigrants in the United States,* ed. Taeku Lee, Karthick Ramakrishnan, and Ricardo Ramirez (Charlottesville: University of Virginia Press, 2006), 17 (emphasis added).
4. These requirements are from the Immigration and Nationality Act 312 (1, 2), 8 U.S.C. 1423.

5. Andre Blais, Louis Massicotte, and Antonie Yoshinaka, "Deciding Who Has the Right to Vote: A Comparative Analysis of Election Laws," *Electoral Studies* (March 2001): 41–62.

6. Reynolds Holding, "Voting Block," *Time,* April 12, 2007.

CHAPTER 18: The Government Should Require National Service for All Youth

PRO

1. Some parts of this essay are adapted from "The Obligations of September 11, 2001: The Case for Universal Service," in *United We Serve: National Service and the Future of Citizenship,* ed. E. J. Dionne Jr., Kayla Meltzer Drogosz, and Robert E. Litan (Washington, D.C.: Brookings, 2003).

2. "A National Service Debate," *Wall Street Journal,* May 29, 1981.

3. Robert D. Putnam, *Bowling Alone: The Collapse and Revival of American Community* (New York: Simon and Schuster, 2001).

4. Congressional Budget Office, "An Analysis of the President's Budgetary Proposals for the Fiscal Year 2010" (Washington, D.C.: U.S. Congress, 2009).

CON

1. Some parts of this essay are adapted from "Service and the State: Should We Politicize Social Bonds?" in *United We Serve: National Service and the Future of Citizenship,* ed. E. J. Dionne Jr., Kayla Meltzer Drogosz, and Robert E. Litan (Washington, D.C.: Brookings, 2003).

2. Arthur C. Brooks, "A Nation of Givers," *The American* (March/April 2008), www .american.com/archive/2008/march-april-magazine-contents/a-nation-of-givers.

3. Remarks by the president and first lady at a "United We Serve" service event, June 25, 2009, www.whitehouse.gov/the_press_office/Remarks-by-the-President-and-First-Lady-at-a-United-We-Serve-Service-Event/.

4. Everett Carl Ladd, *The Ladd Report,* 2d ed. (New York: The Free Press, 1999).

CHAPTER 19: The Federal Government Should Ensure That No Firm Is Too Big to Fail

1. See "Greenspan Calls to Break Up Banks 'Too Big to Fail,'" *New York Times,* October 15, 2009 (quoting Greenspan saying "If they're too big to fail, they're too big. . . . In 1911 we broke up Standard Oil—so what happened? The individual parts became more valuable than the whole. Maybe that's what we need to do."); Louis Uchitelle, "Volcker Fails to Sell a Bank Strategy," *New York Times,* October 20, 2009 ("The only viable solution, in the Volcker view, is to

break up the giants."); and Ben Bernanke's testimony before the Senate Banking, Housing, and Urban Affairs Committee on December 3, 2009, in which he described the "too big to fail" problem as "perhaps the central issue in financial reform." According to Bernanke, "The only way to [solve the 'too big to fail' problem] is to find a way to let those firms fail" (http://features.csmonitor.com/politics/2009/12/03/senators-grill-fed%E2%80%99s-ben-bernanke-over-bank-bailouts./).

PRO

1. Margin commentary to E. F. Schumacher, *Small is Beautiful: Economics as if People Mattered—25 Years Later . . . With Commentaries* (Point Roberts, Wash.: Hartley and Marks, 1999), 47.
2. Jerry W. Markham, *A Financial History of the United States,* vol. 3 (Armonk, N.Y.: M. E. Sharpe, 2002), 131.
3. Frederic L. Pryor, "New Trends in U.S. Industrial Concentration," *Review of Industrial Organization* 18, No. 3 (May 2001), 301.
4. CNNMoney.com, http://money.cnn.com/magazines/fortune/rankings/.
5. Cliff Mason, "Breaking up the Banks?" May 14, 2009, www.cnbc.com/id/30747571/site/14081545?__source=yahoo%7Cheadline%7Cquote%7Ctext%7C&par=yahoo. Ironically, even prominent central bankers in the United States and United Kingdom have begun to suggest that such large organizations will have to be dismantled or reduced in size. See Colin F. Cooley, "Fiddling over Reform," www.forbes.com/2009/10/27/volcker-mervyn-king-glass-steagall-opinions-columnists-thomas-f-cooley.html. For a review of the legislative proposals that have been introduced in Congress as a result of this change in sentiment and in support of the views expressed in this part of the debate, see, for example, Peter Boone and Simon Johnson, "How Big is Too Big," *New York Times,* Nov. 26, 2009, http://economix.blogs.nytimes.com/2009/11/26/how-big-is-too-big/. For a review of the legislative proposals that have been introduced in Congress as a result of this change in sentiment and in support of the views expressed in this part of the debate, see, for example, Peter Boone and Simon Johnson, "How Big is Too Big," *New York Times,* Nov. 26, 2009, http://economix.blogs.nytimes.com/2009/11/26/how-big-is-too-big/.
6. See John Gapper, "Too Long in the Spaceship, Hank," *Financial Times,* March 4, 2009, reporting that Hank Greenberg, former CEO of AIG, had suggested that a successor, Edward Liddy, was inadequate to the task: "I keep hearing that it's too complicated for someone to run. . . . It is too complicated if you take someone who has been driving a horse and buggy type of company and put him into a spaceship." In 2005 Greenberg was forced out as CEO amidst an accounting scandal, and in August 2009 he paid a large sum to the Securities and Exchange Commission in settlement of charges that he had made material misstatements in order to inflate the apparent earnings of AIG.
7. Schumacher, *Small Is Beautiful,* chap. 5; Joseph Pearce, *Small Is Still Beautiful* (Wilmington, Del.: ISI Books, 2006), chap. 7.

8. Verifying the efficiency record of very large banks (assets over about $500 billion) is difficult because there are so many factors to take into consideration, including the structure of the bank portfolio, its equity and asset leverage, and the ultimate return to shareholders. However, my extensive review of bank profitability, efficiency ratios, return on average assets, and return on average equity indicates that very large banks have not performed as well as their smaller counterparts, including "large" banks with assets of between $10 billion and $500 billion.

9. Gary H. Stern and Ron J. Feldman, *Too Big to Fail: The Hazards of Bank Bailouts* (Washington, D.C.: Brookings, 2004), 65 (citing statistics from reports of the Comptroller of the Currency).

10. Ibid., 39.

11. Charles E. Lindblom, *Politics and Markets: The World's Political-Economic Systems* (New York: Basic Books, 1977), chap. 13.

12. See the "Heavy Hitter" charts made available by OpenSecrets.org online, www .opensecrets.org/orgs/list.php?order=A.

13. See, for example, the report by CNBC, "Bailed-Out Banks Spending Big—on Lobbyists," July 21, 2009, www.cnbc.com/id/32035486.

14. Josef Ackermann, "Smaller Banks Will Not Make Us Safer," *Financial Times,* July 29, 2009, www.ft.com/cms/s/0/9aef3d00-7c6d-11de-a7bf-00144feabdc0.html. Ackermann is the CEO of Deutsche Bank.

CON

1. The opinions expressed in this essay are those of the author, and are not intended to represent the views of Sidley Austin LLP or its clients.

2. Eric Dash, "If It's Too Big to Fail, Is It Too Big to Exist?" *New York Times,* June 21, 2009, www.newyorktimes.com/2009/06/21/weekinreview/21dash.html; Theo Francis, David Henry, and Matthew Goldstein, "Too Big to Fail: Still an Issue," *Business Week,* May 6, 2009, www.businessweek.com/magazine/content/09_20/ b4131000086928.htm.

3. For a detailed discussion of the "too big to fail" issue, see Gary H. Stern and Ron J. Feldman, *Too Big to Fail: The Hazards of Bank Bailouts* (Washington, D.C.: Brookings, 2004).

4. Ben S. Bernanke, "Regulatory Restructuring," testimony before the Committee on Financial Services, U.S. House of Representatives (Washington, D.C.: U.S. House of Representatives, July 24, 2009), 3 (emphasis added).

5. *Financial Regulatory Reform: A New Foundation* (Washington, D.C.: U.S. Department of the Treasury, June 2009), 5, 19.

6. Dash, "If It's Too Big to Fail, Is It Too Big to Exist?" The phrase *too big to fail* is said to have been coined by Rep. Stewart McKinney of Connecticut following the Continental Illinois bailout that, McKinney argued, created a new class of banks, "those deemed too big to fail."

7. Josef Ackermann, "Smaller Banks Will Not Make Us Safer," *Financial Times,* July 29, 2009, www.ft.com/cms/s/0/9aef3d00-7c6d-11de-a7bf-00144feabdc0.html. Ackermann, chief executive officer of Deutsche Bank (which weathered the credit

crisis of 2008–2009 without government assistance), likewise argues that breaking global financial firms into smaller banks confined by national boundaries "would enhance rather than reduce risks to financial stability" because "it is not size as such that is the problem but the interconnectedness of banks."

8. *Financial Regulatory Reform*, 3–31.
9. Bernanke, "Regulatory Restructuring," 4.
10. Henry J. Pulizzi and Damian Paletta, "Obama Sets Tone for Financial Regulation Reforms," *Wall Street Journal*, June 17, 2009, http://online.wsj.com/article/SB124524649229423271.html.
11. The bailout of General Motors appears to have been motivated as much by a desire on the part of the Obama administration to avoid additional "bad news" regarding job losses at a time of rising unemployment (and, perhaps, to mollify labor interests that were instrumental in helping Obama capture crucial electoral votes in Michigan) as by any legitimate concern that requiring GM to reorganize through the normal bankruptcy process would devastate the nation's economy. Ironically, one of the first cost-saving measures announced by the restructured GM was the closing of more than one thousand dealerships nationwide, which will result in the elimination of tens of thousands of jobs.
12. Sherman Antitrust Act of 1890, 26 Stat. 209, codified at 5 U.S.C. §§ 1 *et seq.* (July 2, 1890); Clayton Antitrust Act of 1914, 38 Stat. 730, codified at 5 U.S.C. §§ 12–27, 29 U.S.C. §§ 52–53 (October 15, 1914).
13. Riegle-Neal Interstate Banking and Branch Efficiency Act of 1994, P.L. 103–328, codified at 12 U.S.C. § 1842(d)(2)(A).

CHAPTER 20: Congress Should Pass the War Powers Consultation Act

PRO

1. National War Powers Commission Report, http://millercenter.org/policy/commissions/warpowers/report.
2. "The Role for Congress and the President in War: The Recommendations of the National War Powers Commission," Hearing before the Committee on Foreign Affairs, House of Representatives, 111th Cong., 1st Sess., March 5, 2009; "War Powers in the 21st Century," Hearing before the Committee on Foreign Relations, U.S. Senate, 111th Cong., 1st Sess., April 28, 2009.
3. James A. Baker III and Warren Christopher, "Put War Powers Back Where They Belong," *New York Times*, July 8, 2008, www.nytimes.com/2008/07/08/opinion/08baker.html; James A. Baker III and Warren Christopher, "War Act Would Ensure That President, Congress Consult," http://blogs.usatoday.com/oped/2009/03/war-act-would-e.html.
4. See, for example, Larry Berman, *Planning a Tragedy: The Americanization of the War in Vietnam* (New York: W. W. Norton, 1982), 33.

5. *Youngstown Sheet and Tube Company v. Sawyer,* 343 U.S. 579 (1952) (Jackson, concurring).

6. See, for example, James L. Sundquist, *The Decline and Resurgence of Congress* (Washington, D.C.: Brookings, 1981).

7. P.L. 93–148, 87 Stat. 555 (1973), 50 U.S.C. Sec 1541–48 (2000).

8. Max Farrand, ed., *The Records of the Federal Convention of 1787*, rev. ed., vol. 2 (New Haven, Conn.: Yale University Press, 1937), 318–319.

9. For a detailed look at past efforts to revise the War Powers Resolution, see Appendix 1 of the commission's report, "An Overview of Proposals to Reform the War Powers Resolution of 1973," http://millercenter.org/policy/commissions/warpowers/appone.

10. Former secretary of state Baker noted in congressional testimony that the only times that authorizations to use military force were *not* used were in the interventions in Grenada, Panama, and Bosnia. See "The Role for Congress and the President in War: The Recommendations of the National War Powers Commission," Hearing before the Committee on Foreign Affairs, House of Representatives, 111th Cong., 1st Sess., March 5, 2009. Also see Appendix 3 of the commission's report, "An Overview of Facts Relevant to War Powers Issues in Selected Conflicts since World War II," http://millercenter.org/policy/commissions/warpowers/appthree, for a more detailed history of authorizations to use military force.

11. See Appendix 1 of the commission's report, "An Overview of Proposals to Reform the War Powers Resolution of 1973"; and Constitution Project "Deciding to Use Force Abroad: War Powers in a System of Checks and Balances" (Washington, D.C.: Constitution Project, 2005), www.constitutionproject.org/pdf/War_Powers_Deciding_To_Use_Force_Abroad.pdf.

12. National War Powers Commission Report, 8, 12–13. Also see "The Role for Congress and the President in War: The Recommendations of the National War Powers Commission," Hearing before the Committee on Foreign Affairs, House of Representatives, 111th Cong., 1st Sess., March 5, 2009, 40.

13. National War Powers Commission Report, 44–48. The full text of the proposed statute appears on these pages. All quotes hereafter from the text are from these pages.

14. *Immigration and Naturalization Service v. Chadha*, 462 U.S. 919 (1983).

15. Ibid.

16. National War Powers Commission Report, 30.

17. See "The Role for Congress and the President in War: The Recommendations of the National War Powers Commission," Hearing before the Committee on Foreign Affairs, House of Representatives, 111th Cong., 1st Sess., March 5, 2009; "War Powers in the 21st Century," Hearing before the Committee on Foreign Relations, U.S. Senate, 111th Cong., 1st Sess., April 28, 2009.

18. "The Role for Congress and the President in War: The Recommendations of the National War Powers Commission," Hearing before the Committee on Foreign Affairs, House of Representatives, 111th Cong., 1st Sess., March 5, 2009, 32.

19. See, for example, the prepared statement of Sen. Thomas F. Eagleton, July 13, 1988, in "The War Power after 200 Years: Congress and the President at a Constitutional Impasse," Hearings before the Special Subcommittee on War Powers of the Committee on Foreign Relations, U.S. Senate, 100th Cong., 2d Sess., July 13, 1988, 364–370; and Constitution Project, "Deciding to Use Force Abroad," 31–32, commenting that the current War Powers Resolution "defines the president's defensive war powers too narrowly" (31), and is therefore "underinclusive by failing to acknowledge well-accepted defensive presidential war powers within the scope of the President's authority to 'repel sudden attacks' and affirmed by historical practice" (32).

20. "The Role for Congress and the President in War: The Recommendations of the National War Powers Commission," Hearing before the Committee on Foreign Affairs, House of Representatives, 111th Cong., 1st Sess., March 5, 2009, 34.

21. Constitution Project, "Deciding to Use Force Abroad," 40.

CON

1. This essay is adapted from William G. Howell, "A Restoration of Balance? A Critical Examination of the Proposed War Powers Consultation Act," paper presented at the "Future of the American Presidency" conference, Robertson School of Government, Regent University, February 6, 2009.

2. But see "War Powers Patch," *Wall Street Journal,* July 25, 2008, A14.

3. On one side see Louis Fisher, "To War or Not to War," *Legal Times,* March 10, 2008; and Dahlia Lithwick, "Wrestling over War Powers: Congress Is Always Too Deferential, Too Credulous and Too Timid to Check a Strong President in Wartime," *Newsweek,* July 21, 2008, 18. On the other, see "The War Powers Gambit," *New York Sun,* July 10, 2008, 6.

4. But see David Keene, "What Should Be Done with the War Powers Act?" *Washington Times,* July 13, 2008, M12.

5. David R. Mayhew, *Congress: The Electoral Connection* (New Haven, Conn.: Yale University Press, 1974).

6. For a historical overview of the unitary presidency, see Stephen G. Calabresi and Christopher S. Yoo, *The Unitary Executive: Presidential Power from Washington to Bush* (New Haven, Conn.: Yale University Press, 2008). And for a critique of the unitary theory itself, see Gene Healy, *The Cult of the Presidency: America's Dangerous Devotion to Executive Power* (Washington, D.C.: Cato Institute, 2008).

7. William G. Howell, *Power without Persuasion: The Politics of Direct Presidential Action* (Princeton, N.J.: Princeton University Press, 2003).

8. Andrew Rudalevige, *Managing the President's Program: Presidential Leadership and Legislative Policy Formation* (Princeton, N.J.: Princeton University Press, 2002).

9. David E. Lewis, *The Politics of Presidential Appointments: Political Control and Bureaucratic Appointments* (Princeton, N.J.: Princeton University Press, 2008).

10. Brandice Canes-Wrone, *Who's Leading Whom?* (Chicago: University of Chicago Press, 2006); George C. Edwards III, *On Deaf Ears: The Limits of the Bully Pulpit* (New Haven, Conn.: Yale University Press, 2003).

11. Stephen Skowronek, *The Politics Presidents Make: Leadership from John Adams to Bill Clinton* (Cambridge: Harvard Univeristy Press, 1993); George C. Edwards III, *The Strategic President: Persuasion and Opportunity in Presidential Leadership* (Princeton, N.J.: Princeton University Press, 2008).

12. As Neustadt notes, "Everybody now expects the man inside the White House to do something about everything. Laws and customs now reflect acceptance of him as the Great Initiator, an acceptance quite as widespread at the Capitol as at his end of Pennsylvania Avenue. But such acceptance does not signify that all the rest of government is at his feet. . . . A president, these days, is an invaluable clerk. His services are in demand all over Washington. His influence, however, is a very different matter." Richard E. Neustadt, *Presidential Power and the Modern Presidents* (New York: Free Press, 1990), 7.

13. William G. Howell and Jon C. Pevehouse, *While Dangers Gather: Congressional Checks on Presidential War Powers* (Princeton, N.J.: Princeton University Press, 2007).

14. See, for example, Edward S. Corwin, *The President, Office and Powers, 1787–1948: History and Analysis of Practice and Opinion* (New York: New York University Press, 1957); Robert J. Spitzer, *President and Congress: Executive Hegemony at the Crossroads of American Government* (New York: McGraw-Hill, 1993); Neustadt, *Presidential Power and the Modern Presidents*; Michael A. Genovese, *The Power of the American Presidency: 1789–2000* (New York: Oxford University Press, 2001); Thomas E. Cronin and Michael A. Genovese, *The Paradoxes of the American Presidency* (New York: Oxford University Press, 1998).

15. See *Chevron U.S.A., Inc. v. Natural Resources Defense Council, Inc.,* 467 U.S. 837 (1984).

16. Paul Findley and Don Fraser, "The Battle over War Powers: Limits Imposed by Congress on the President in 1973 Should Not Be Eased," *Los Angeles Times,* September 22, 2008, A17.

17. As Kenneth Shepsle put it, Congress is best thought of as a "they" rather than an "it." Kenneth Shepsle, "Congress Is a 'They,' Not an 'It': Legislative Intent as Oxymoron," *International Review of Law and Economics* 12 (1992): 239–257.

18. Eugene Wittkopf and Mark Dehaven, "Soviet Behavior, Presidential Popularity, and the Penetration of Open Political Systems," in *New Directions in the Study of Foreign Policy,* ed. Charles Hermann, Charles Kegley, and James Rosenau (Boston: Unwin Hyman, 1987); William D. Baker and John R. Oneal, "Patriotism or Opinion Leadership? The Nature and Orgins of The 'Rally'Round the Flag Effect,'" *Journal of Conflict Resolution* 45 (2001): 661–687.

19. James Campbell and Joe Sumners, "Presidential Coattails in Senate Elections," *American Political Science Review* 84, no. 2 (1990): 513–524.

20. William G. Howell and Jon C. Pevehouse, "Presidents, Congress, and the Use of Force," *International Organization* 59, no. 1 (2005): 209–232; Howell and Pevehouse, *While Dangers Gather.* Also see David H. Clark, "Agreeing to Disagree:

Domestic Institutional Congruence and U.S. Dispute Behavior," *Political Research Quarterly* 53, no. 2 (2000): 375–400; Douglas L. Kriner, "Hollow Rhetoric or Hidden Influence: Domestic Political Constraints on the Presidential Use of Force." Paper presented at the Annual Meeting of the American Political Science Association, Washington, D.C., September 1, 2005.

21. Linda Fowler, *Dangerous Currents: Party Conflict at the Water's Edge* (book manuscript).
22. Kriner, "Hollow Rhetoric or Hidden Influence."